THE PROFFERED CROWN

THE JOHNS HOPKINS UNIVERSITY
STUDIES IN HISTORICAL AND POLITICAL SCIENCE
105TH SERIES (1987)

1. *Nobles in Nineteenth-Century France:*
The Practice of Inegalitarianism
by David Higgs

2. *Liberty and Property: Political Economy*
and Policy-making in the New
Nation, 1789–1812
by John R. Nelson, Jr.

3. *The Proffered Crown: Saint-Simonianism*
and the Doctrine of Hope
by Robert B. Carlisle

The Proffered Crown

SAINT-SIMONIANISM
AND THE DOCTRINE
OF HOPE

ROBERT B. CARLISLE

THE JOHNS HOPKINS UNIVERSITY PRESS

BALTIMORE AND LONDON

This book has been brought to publication with the
generous assistance of St. Lawrence University.

The Johns Hopkins University Press,
701 West 40th Street, Baltimore, Maryland 21211
The Johns Hopkins Press Ltd., London

The paper used in this publication meets the minimum
requirements of American National Standard for
Information Sciences—Permanence of Paper for Printed
Library Materials, ANSI Z39.48-1984.

Library of Congress Cataloging-in-Publication-Data

Carlisle, Robert B., 1928–
The proffered crown.

(The Johns Hopkins University studies in historical
and political science; 105th ser., 3)
Bibliography: p.
Includes index.
1. Saint-Simonianism—History. I. Title. II. Series.
HX632.C39 1987 335'.22'09 87-45481
ISBN 0-8018-3512-7 (alk. paper)

For
Susan,
both Julias,
Bruce, and Chris

Steamboats, Viaducts, and Railways

Motions and Means, on land and sea at war
With old poetic feeling, not for this
Shall ye, by Poets even, be judged amiss!
Nor shall your presence, howsoe'er it mar
The loveliness of Nature, prove a bar
To the Mind's gaining that prophetic sense
Of future change, that point of vision, whence
May be discovered what in soul ye are.
In spite of all that beauty may disown
In your harsh features, Nature doth embrace
Her lawful offspring in Man's art; and Time,

Pleased with your triumphs o'er his brother Space
Accepts from your bold hands the proffered crown
Of hope, and smiles on you with cheer sublime.
                    —Wordsworth, 1833

[Humanity] reserves to the pupils of Saint-Simon,
If they give it hope, a crown more beautiful
than that of the first Christians.
                    —Saint-Amand Bazard

CONTENTS

ACKNOWLEDGMENTS

THE PRESENT WORK is, in part at least, the product of my major and steadily increasing irritation at the divergence of published accounts of Saint-Simonianism from what I know to be true. I must thank Edward Whiting Fox of Cornell University for long ago first directing my attention to the Saint-Simonians. During the intervening years the debts of Saint-Simonian investigation have piled up. In France, René Rémond and Louis Girard opened many doors, and Professor Girard for years has been a courteous listener and an encourager of this project. St. Lawrence University Presidents Foster Brown and Frank P. Piskor, Deans D. Kenneth Baker, George Gibson, and Andrew Rembert, and Librarian Mahlon Peterson have all devoted energy and resources to the encouragement of research in a small college setting. I am indebted to them all. My first Saint-Simonian researches were undertaken during the tenure of a Cornell University–Glasgow University exchange fellowship and continued with Fulbright, Lilly Foundation, and St. Lawrence University–Ford Foundation grants. Professor Friedrich von Hayek kindly accepted sponsorship of the Lilly Foundation Grant in 1968–69.

Those around me have probably thought my Saint-Simonian obsessions exaggerated, but I owe much to the persistent encouragement of my former students and now friends, Professor Peter Rutkoff of Kenyon College and David Emblidge. Through the years I have enjoyed jousting with Barrie M. Ratcliffe of Université Laval. We invariably disagree, but he always makes me think. To my St. Lawrence colleague George McFarland I owe the Wordsworth poem from which the book's title is drawn. Barbara and Bob Wheaton and Joan and Dick Kepes have offered food, shelter, and friendship throughout.

Some libraries have become second homes in the course of this study. Major thanks must go to that particularly atmospheric enclave, the Bibliothèque de l'Arsenal in Paris, and its collection of more than 40,000 Saint-Simonian manuscripts. And particular thanks must be given to *mesdames et messieurs, les magasiniers,* who have walked many a heavily burdened mile on my behalf. The Bibliothèque Nationale has mellowed over the years, or perhaps I have, and its resources when obtainable are unequaled. The Goldsmiths' Library of the University of London at Senate House holds some rare Saint-Simonian pamphlets that I have been able to use. The Harvard College Libraries have been a steady and necessary support in the United States. The Bibliothèque Thiers, attached to the Institut de France, was opened for me under special circumstances, and I am grateful for that.

A major collaborator in this work has been Jean Deese. In the process of typing the manuscript she has perhaps become a Saint-Simonian convert, and she has certainly embraced the word processor with a technocratic zeal the Saint-Simonians would have cheered. William Waller has done much to improve the original version of the book.

It is customary at this point to conjure up guilty visions of self-sacrificing wives and neglected children. But on the whole I suspect that the advantages of a Saint-Simonian existence have been for Susan Carlisle and our children greater than the disadvantages: enamored of France as she is, and able, with justice, to jeer at their father's lamentable accent as they are, all have found the game worth the candle. I do, nonetheless, dedicate the book to them all and to Julia N. Goodman with love.

THE PROFFERED CROWN

INTRODUCTION

I N THE LATE summer of 1832 three young Frenchmen were found guilty
of outraging public morality and violating the laws on public association. Two were jailed, and one went to a rest home. With their banish-
ment, Authority assumed that the danger from the Saint-Simonian school,
religion, and program had come to an end. Authority was wrong. These
young men and others like them who had been students of the ideas of
Henri Saint-Simon would reemerge as the builders of railroads, editors of
newspapers, founders of banks, administrators of colonies—themselves
embodiments of Authority. By the 1850s one of them could with some
justice describe even the Emperor Napoleon III as "a Saint-Simonian on
horseback."[1]

The categorical imperative of Saint-Simonian thought was the call to
apply the scientific knowledge of competent experts to society's problems.
The Saint-Simonians were pacifists, feminists, and antiracist economic
expansionists: they believed in the exploitation of the globe but not of the
men or women on it. They were planners and engineers, scientists and
romantics, nationalists and cosmopolitans, at the same time. They would
replace gerontocracy with technocracy, liberty with order, one kind of
individualism with another. They have been accused of fathering fascism
and communism but would have repudiated both. Their impact lay in the
fact that they were not totally reasonable men; had they been, no one
would have paid them any attention. This romanticism was the essential
condition of their success, but the foundations of their thought were
systematic, rational, pragmatic, inclusive, and inextricably mortised.

Saint-Simonianism invented and exemplified the technocrat in whom
the abstract idea and the particular act marched hand in hand. This
achievement alone gives the Saint-Simonians historical importance. But
the school also offers a microscope slide on which one can examine *de
près* an age that was obsessed by the relationships between science and
society.

The school, like a microorganism under study, moves, changes shape,
reveals new forms, is elusive. Thus, the essential oneness of Saint-Simonianism is not always recognized. Saint-Simon himself predicted that
scholars would pose the most problems for the movement. Economic historians tend to denigrate the intellectual bases of Saint-Simonian material

achievements. When the Saint-Simonians became businessmen, intellectual historians tended to lose interest in them. One is puzzled by the oceans of ink devoted to proving that the Saint-Simonians were *unimportant*. The quantity is itself a refutation of that thesis.[2] One is equally puzzled by assertions that the Saint-Simonians were important in ways that, on examination, have little to do with what they thought or did. Although scholars for over 150 years have tried to render it less, Saint-Simonianism is greater than the sum of its parts. The piranhas of specialized and particular interest have attacked the corpse of Saint-Simonianism and left its bones bare. But the skeletal structure persists all the more visibly.

The Saint-Simonian story has never been fully told in English, and when told at all it has been used to fortify the biases of the authors involved, liberal or conservative. The classic French version by Sébastien Charléty, written in the 1890s, has seen three editions, but, excellent as it is, it suffers from the myopia of its time and the perspective of a solid French Third Republican academic.[3] Saint-Simonian notions on family, property, marriage, and women are seen as scandalous or comic. Assertions of Saint-Simonian influence in the years after the formal dispersion of the school are viewed as pathetic. Saint-Simonian notions of intellectual authority and technical competence did not square with Republican notions of equality. Much of the color and much of the anguish of the Saint-Simonian experience could not in 1894 be examined in detail. When Charléty began his work, the president of the Republic[4] was the son of a Saint-Simonian, and Pierre Curie, grandson of the Saint-Simonian Dr. Paul Curie, was in a sense a colleague of Charléty himself.

The Saint-Simonian story would be worth retelling in contemporary terms for its own sake and as a chapter in the history of the romantic agony. But the concerns of the Saint-Simonians and of their founder are so much ours that there is a point not only in telling their story but also in coming to terms with their ideas. In an earlier study I established to my own satisfaction that there was a real connection between the ideas of Saint-Simonian youth and their mature achievement. But in the process of investigating that achievement I found that almost no published account gave a clear and accurate portrait of Saint-Simonian thought. Most accounts assume that the Saint-Simonians "stole" Saint-Simon and perverted him to their ends. He was, says Frank Manuel, "certainly not a Saint-Simonian."[5] The point is arguable and will be argued.

But there are certain persistent issues and themes in the history of the history of Saint-Simonianism that by their very nature indicate the importance of the school, the passions it can arouse, and the perversities of interpretation it can encourage. Saint-Simonianism has seldom been studied for its own sake. As a doctrine it was eclectic and provided threats and opportunities for other doctrinaires. It also provided fertile grounds for conflict and schism among its own adherents. Since Saint-Simon's death in 1825 the significance of the movement has been assessed differently in every generation — almost in every decade — in terms of current historical situations. In all this time few have undertaken the admittedly burdensome task of finding out what the Saint-Simonians *said,* far less tried to understand what they *meant,* and still less related what they did to what they thought.

One persistent theme that is sensibly discussed in a number of places by Saint-Simon's best biographer, Manuel, is the question of Saint-Simon's originality in relation to Auguste Comte, who was for a time his secretary.[6] Another is the question of Saint-Simonianism's relationship to Charles Fourier, which was clear and close. What most literate people to this day know of Saint-Simon they will have learned in the paragraph of a history textbook devoted to the "utopian socialists" of the early nineteenth century, Saint-Simon, Fourier, Blanc, and Owen. They were first so described by Marx and Engels in the *Communist Manifesto,* at a moment when Saint-Simon's ideas were having a much greater impact on events than Marx's own. The label has stuck ever since, even though Saint-Simonianism was neither utopian nor, in the Marxist sense, socialist. But the frequent references to Saint-Simon and the Saint-Simonians in the *Collected Works* indicate how annoying and troublesome Saint-Simonianism continued to be. Eventually Engels's estimate of Saint-Simon was considerably higher than that of Marx. Marx reveals himself (it is not rare among Saint-Simonian critics) as ignorant of fundamental Saint-Simonian principles.[7] But from this first encounter of early socialist doctrinaires comes one of the major impediments to an understanding of Saint-Simonianism. The Marxists may have been to some extent Saint-Simonians. The Saint-Simonians, to paraphrase Manuel, are certainly not Marxists.

A parallel theme emerging out of contemporary political experience is that of Saint-Simonian totalitarianism. The Saint-Simonians, as we shall see, preached the authority of what was known to be true. They were, at least on the surface, much more "socialist" than "individualist." They preached a religion of humanity, and they proposed a priesthood to administer it, designated a supreme pontiff to direct it, and sought a female messiah to complement him. To the liberals of the 1820s and 1830s all this constituted a threat and a scandal, an outrage to public morality that occasioned the downfall of the formally organized Saint-Simonian religion. The accusations of proto-fascism and right- and left-wing totalitarianism that emerge in the works of a Friedrich von Hayek or a Georg Iggers a century and a quarter later begin with that attack.[8] But the presentists of the 1950s were not totally to blame. Some of the Saint-Simonians, embarrassed by the sexual connotations of Prosper Enfantin's priesthood, wrote and spoke their own versions of events and doctrine. Their dominant

3

theme was that they had been attracted by economic and social doctrine, by technocracy, but that the religion and the feminism were aberrations of Enfantin, who had perverted Saint-Simon's revealed truth.[9] The consequence of this "disengagement" was two-edged. It propagated the erroneous notion of a discontinuity between Saint-Simon and the Saint-Simonians, and it simultaneously suggested that mature achieving men of the 1840s and 1850s had abandoned the follies of their youth.

On the other hand many mature and achieving men, in the 1850s and after, proclaimed their Saint-Simonianism and created what sceptical critics described as a Saint-Simonian "myth" attributing *all* the considerable achievements of Napoleon III's Second Empire—railroads, shipping, urban planning, manufacture, Suez—to Saint Simonian imagination and enterprise.[10]

Here enter the economic historians temperamentally incapable of admitting a connection between what is thought and what is done. Rondo Cameron, for example, wrote that the Saint-Simonians by their example and influence converted a generation of Europeans to a belief in the possibilities of economic progress more effectively than a shelf of philosophical treatises would have done. This statement, of course, simply underlines the point that the Saint-Simonians began with and added to a large shelf of philosophical treatises.[11] In a study of public-works policy under the Second Empire, Louis Girard[12] gave the Saint-Simonians their due in detail, but others have raised quizzical eyebrows at the claims made.[13] The Industrial Revolution and the railroads, they say, would have come in any event. Many industrialists were not Saint-Simonian. And was the *Crédit Mobilier* either original with the Saint-Simonians or the maker of modern French banking? The perversities of this quarrel go even further.

The myth of Saint-Simonian omnipotence during the Second Empire was propagated in part by the Saint-Simonians and in part by their enemies, who identified Saint-Simonianism as Jewish by virtue of its links with the Pereire brothers and theirs with the French Rothschilds. There is the hint of a suggestion that to believe that the Saint-Simonians had great importance in Second Empire France is to be anti-Semitic. This is an argument that clarifies nothing but that is symptomatic of the very complicated reactions Saint-Simonianism can arouse.[14]

Why? Perhaps because if one accepts the proposition that there is a coherence and a continuity, if not an identity, between Saint-Simon's thought and that of his followers; if one accepts the proposition that what young men and women thought, older men and women might continue to be moved by; if one accepts the proposition that the achievements of these older men and women made a difference to the economic, social, and political development of their nation, their century, and subsequent generations—then a good many received explanations might have to be abandoned. Certainly they would have to be examined and modified.

One example, among many such explanations, is that offered in the years following the Second World War of France's failure to modernize and industrialize, duplicating the "German miracle" then taking place.[15] It was the character of the French businessman that was at fault: unimaginative, fearful, unwilling to take risks or to release personal control, self-satisfied, dominated by a sense of "enough-ness." This character explained France's failure in the nineteenth century and her unwillingness or inability to move in the twentieth. The only trouble with the explanation was that during the Second Empire French businessmen manifestly had not been like that and many of the most prominent of them had been Saint-Simonian. Saint-Simonians either had to be ignored or relegated to the role of primitive, amusing, irrelevant precursors. The first approach proved impossible; the second imposed and — sadly — continues to impose itself.

The saraband danced by historians of France to the Saint-Simonian tune is dizzying in its complexity and stunning in the noise produced to drown out the essential interest of the Saint-Simonian theme.

Perhaps the best example to cite from the large number available is that of Theodore Zeldin's *France, 1848–1945,* constituting two volumes in the Oxford History of Modern Europe. Zeldin has manifestly read everything there is to be read on modern France; the book is a brilliant effort to see and understand France in new ways; it is beautifully and often wittily written; and its account of Saint-Simonianism is enough to make anybody knowledgeable about the school weep at its repetition and rearrangement of indefensible assertions.

A rather close look at the Zeldin account is probably worthwhile, because its caricature can suggest the reality of the subject while attempting to disguise it. The eight pages Zeldin assigns to Saint-Simon and the Saint-Simonians might be regarded as a masterpiece of compression if they were not equally a masterpiece of distortion.[16] We are told that Saint-Simon was a genius and a madman and that his philosophy was "first of all a philosophy for orphans." What that judgment means is not at all clear. It is said that Saint-Simon enjoyed passionate relationships and sought love, attributes that would seem merely to enroll him in the ranks of humanity. "He might have been the founder of modern sociology or even a precursor of *planification* but that is no excuse for assuming that his thinking was predominantly rational." Neither is that a reason for supposing that his thinking was *not* rational. Zeldin accurately identifies Saint-Simon's concern for individuality, which has usually been denied, but he asserts that the "problem of conflict within the new order was never analyzed by Saint-Simon and this might be justification for calling him Utopian." The last statement is quite simply untrue. The whole point of Saint-Simon's last work, *Le Nouveau Christianisme,* is precisely such an analysis.

When Zeldin turns to the Saint-Simonians, he puzzlingly, even astonishingly, seems to rely on the most worthless general work, Georges Weill's *L'École Saint-Simonienne.*[17] He tacitly admits that Saint-Simonianism was alive and well in "the mid-19th century and that it laid stress on religion, financial investment and the emancipation of both the proletariat and that class of whom so little had hitherto been heard in the writings of political theorists, women." But the program "failed to win a mass following." It remained the creed of an elite, "a remarkable and influential élite" whose members, however, "had emotional problems."[18] The *sous entendus* dropped in half a paragraph are stunning. A movement is a failure if it does not attract a mass audience but does attract an elite. A "remarkable" elite is without historic significance, particularly if, like the rest of humanity, it has emotional problems. The surface statements are true; their assumed implications are highly questionable.

When Zeldin moves on to Enfantin, the leader of the Saint-Simonian religion, we are told that "highly intelligent men worshipped him and listened respectfully while he talked absolute nonsense," which is true, but the same intelligent men listened while Enfantin talked great good sense.[19] The account of the movement continues without any attention to chronology, development of doctrine, or historical context, and again the failure of the movement is seen in its incapacity to attract workers, an assertion that is only partially true. But one who does not know what people believe cannot know whether their views have prevailed.

Zeldin's only discussion of Saint-Simonianism is in the context of the Revolution of 1848, but "the importance of Saint-Simonianism in the future was to lie in the way of thinking it had imprinted in their youth on many subsequently important individuals. Its direct influence, however, has generally been exaggerated."[20] One wonders what he means by "direct" influence.

These "subsequently important" individuals, according to Zeldin, "never ran the new industry of the Second Empire as is too often believed." But in another place we are told that the Pereires, "Jews from Bordeaux, cousins of Olinde Rodrigues who had been Saint-Simon's secretary, . . . handled the finances of sixteen firms with a combined capital of one billion francs, equal to one-fifth of the value of all stocks quoted on the Paris Bourse."[21] The Pereires (who were cheerfully and openly Saint-Simonians, not merely the "cousins of Saint-Simon's secretary") may not have "run" French industry, but they certainly had leverage in it. They were not by any means the only Saint-Simonians involved in that industry.

The persistent "yes, but" approach to Saint-Simonianism, the almost instinctive resistance to admitting that admitted ideologues might in fact have practiced—successfully—what they preached is clearly illustrated in Zeldin. He is heir and fortifier of a long and, to put it mildly, exasperatingly obscurantist tradition that is the product, at best, of ignorance and laziness of mind and, at worst, of a willful refusal to take account of fact.[22]

There are other examples in Zeldin. The discussion of Napoleon III is sound on the emperor but bad on the Saint-Simonian doctrine. The discussion of Edouard Charton's career guide, to which Zeldin apparently attaches much importance, nowhere mentions that the work is a clear by-product of the Saint-Simonian concern with "classification according to capacities."[23]

One is finally left open-mouthed by the summary statement. Having dismissed financial, colonial, and imperial achievements, Zeldin suggests that the Saint-Simonians were skilled publicists and that their greatest triumph was that "some of their doctrines ceased to bear the specific imprint of Saint-Simonianism because everybody came to believe in them."[24] In other words, everybody to some extent became a Saint-Simonian! Despite the denigratory rhetoric the Saint-Simonians appear to have accomplished a good deal, and their influence seems to have been startlingly direct.

It is not the purpose of this book, although it may be of another, to establish the variety and solidity of Saint-Simonian achievement. Rather, the quarrel about the nature of that achievement suggests the need to know what the Saint-Simonians thought and how they came to think it. Before one can decide whether a given act, a given creation, a given person was Saint-Simonian, one needs to know what a Saint-Simonian was. And I would submit that no one, including the virtuous Charléty, has in over a hundred years bothered to find out. He, in particular, was little able to evaluate the importance of Saint-Simonian feminism, and it is this aspect of the doctrine that has received the most sympathetic audience in the last ten or fifteen years.[25]

Like Charles Kindleberger,[26] I see Saint-Simonianism as embodying a French tradition of technical virtuosity and as sharing in a heritage that "calls for planning, technical decision, order imposed from above and rapid change." But more than that, I think it important to understand the movement's originating role, if any, in the history of modern communism, fascism, liberalism, nationalism, imperialism, feminism, cosmopolitanism, economic planning, and social organization. The elements of the list seem mutually contradictory, but the Saint-Simonians have at various times and in various circumstances been blamed for or credited with a share in each of them. The first and obvious step in such an understanding is to establish the Saint-Simonian "text," and the second is to examine what it meant to Saint-Simonians and how it came to be theirs.

These are the two objectives pursued in this book, and they are relatively modest. Why bother? For a generation, at least, narrative history and the history of ideas have both been rather out of fashion. The "event" is passing, not permanent. It is the "conjuncture" of circumstances that accounts for change. In brief, and perhaps unfairly, history is what happens to humans and not what humans make happen. It is my own conviction that the Saint-Simonians were a group of people whose shared ideas had consequences; consequently, it becomes important to know what those ideas were. A William Sewell, whose *Work and Revolution in France: The Language of Labor from the Old Regime to 1848* is an excellent example of the "new" history, might doubt the importance of this history of ideas.

Nor are the methods employed by most intellectual historians very useful. Here the main problem is the analytical primacy of the author in intellectual history. Intellectual historians are trained to see thought as emanating from the minds of authors and thus to continually refer ideas back to the authors and their biographies. This method . . . breaks down when confronted with collective movements of thought of the sort that characterize transformations in workers' consciousness.[27]

Granted that Sewell's problem is not the same as mine, there is nonetheless in this paragraph just a hint of disbelief in the procedures of historians of ideas, a disbelief that in the case of the Saint-Simonians might be dispelled. The present work is the study in effect, of group authorship arising out of group discussion that is extraordinarily well-documented. The group, obviously, is more restricted in size than "the working class," but the process of formation of the "ideological discourse" of Saint-Simonianism and its relation to the lives of its members may be instructive beyond the history of Saint-Simonianism itself. The close examination of Saint-Simonian lives cannot fail to tell us something about all lives lived in postrevolutionary France. The book must rest finally on the conviction that there is a point in examining "consciousness," interesting as the "unconscious" may be. Indeed, the only way of getting at the second is with the key that the first represents.

CHAPTER I

PARIS, FRANCE, 1825

A T THE CROSSING with the rue des Petits-Champs, the sun at noon might bathe the rue de Richelieu in warmth and brilliance. But, in 1825 as now, the height of the buildings, the narrowness of the roadway, and the vagaries of climate dictated the indirect light swallowed up by passages like the one at number 34. There, on the first floor above the passage Hulot, lived Comte Henri de Saint-Simon, at the physical and moral center of his life but swiftly approaching his end.

A brisk five minutes' walk to the east were the offices of the Messageries Royales, crossroads for Parisian arrivals and departures.[1] Five minutes to the south was La Régence, a café where "interesting parties . . . pass hours in profound silence over a game of chess" and where "the Emperor" had been a regular. Five minutes or so to the north were the splendors of the many-pillared, about-to-be-opened home of the Bourse, construction of which had been started by that same emperor. Down the spiral stone steps of the arched and flagged passage Hulot and across the rue de Montpensier was an entrance to the gardens of the Palais Royal, center of Paris's pleasures, follies, and vices since before the Revolution.

Looking up and along the relatively straight vista of the rue de Richelieu, one could see a line of double-windowed, chimney-potted facades rising to five, six, or seven stories. The height depended on the ingenuity of builders in tucking hidden living space under the seventeenth- and eighteenth-century garrets. Along the street, crowded with people, carts, and carriages, one passed houses in which Molière and Diderot had died and ones in which Comte and Stendhal would live and write. The King's Library, keeping the civilized hours of ten to two, was a few steps away. Facing it was the site of the Opéra, leveled after the assassination there in 1820 of the duc de Berri, heir to the throne, and now being prepared as a memorial to the dead prince.

The neighborhood could be seen as both physical and moral center of Saint-Simon's life because, although he had traveled widely—Spain, the Americas, England, Germany, Switzerland—he had always returned not just to Paris but often to this part of it. And this *quartier* had special meaning for the course of his bizarre and quixotic career. He was supposed during the Directory (he denied it) to have been involved in a "Saint-Simon Coach Company";[2] he had certainly been a speculator and gambler when the Bourse occupied a portion of the Palais Royal and, later, was situated on the nearby place des Victoires. He had frequented and continued to frequent La Régence. He could often be seen walking uncertainly, aided by a stick, in the gardens of the palace, where, as a younger man, he had frequently used the restaurants, the cafés, and — in all likelihood, given his reputation — the prostitutes of that elegantly disordered garden. Saint-Simon had flirted on more than one occasion with the rigors of the law. The assassination of the duc de Berri had followed within days the publication of what was taken as Saint-Simon's inflammatory attack on the Crown and the royal family.

During his great days Saint-Simon had inhabited the Hôtel Chabanais not far from his present lodging. During most of his life the Palais Royal, the rue de Richelieu, and the rue Vivienne, with their fashionable shops, elegant apartments, theaters, and cafés, had constituted the heart of Paris, and he had always quickened its beat by his presence, his projects, his eccentricities, and his scandals.[3] It was in this vivid quarter of Paris that he felt most at home, and his disciples would be like him in this respect.

In 1825 Saint-Simon was sixty-five years old. He was a familiar figure in Paris, described by memorialists and contemporary historians as volatile but frail, sallying forth to the receptions and salons of his acquaintances (Lafayette, the hero of two worlds; Laffitte, the banker and politician) in search of disciples. Exciting mirth, embarrassment, and irritation, he was to be avoided because his friendship might be socially compromising — or financially demanding.[4] He was somebody to be pitied, because he had fallen so far, but not ignored, because he had scaled great heights. He was able to call forth serious attention from the same persons who avoided him.[5]

For a time Saint-Simon had deserted the Right Bank of the Seine for the Left, in pursuit of the wisdom of the Ecole Polytechnique and the Ecole de Médecine. There, at Le Procope, the restaurant of Voltaire and Rousseau, a youthful admirer described him as handsome, athletically built, charming, and a brilliant conversationalist.[6] He had been and remained casually chic and aristocratic, that is, high-nosed, high-browed, fine-boned. (For a long time Saint-Simon's skull was on display with that of Descartes at the Musée de l'Homme in Paris — that fact, but not the association, would have pleased him.) His portraits show an aquiline nose, brilliant eyes under heavy, arched brows and lids, and an upturned mouth whose smile bears an altogether Parisian hint of malice. His was very much the bearing of a great lord of the Old Regime, which, in fact, he was.

Nature frequently imitates art, and had Saint-Simon not existed, Balzac would have invented him. Balzac might also have rejected him as too extreme an example of the human comedy to be believed. Count Henri de Saint-Simon was a distant connection of the duke whose memoirs give life to the courts of Louis XIV and the Regency. The family claimed descent from Charlemagne and would come to believe in its descent from a late Roman emperor of the West. Saint-Simon himself had been a rebellious son jailed by an angry father for his refusal to take his first communion. In his teens he had fought briefly in the American Revolution, and he had publicly welcomed the French Revolution. The guillotine had cast its shadow over him but failed to fall. A partnership with the Prussian ambassador to England in speculating on the national lands of revolutionary France resulted in a great fortune.

Saint-Simon lived grandly under the Directory, earned a reputation as a great libertine, spent millions, broke with his partner, lost his fortune, and engaged in blackmail and in endless fruitless legal efforts to regain it. He was for a time supported by his former valet, whose function had been—so the Saint-Simonian legend says, and it is not hard to believe—to rouse the count each day with the words, "Get up, my lord, you have great things to do today!" He had been a clerk in the National Pawn Shop. During Napoleon's Hundred Days he was given a post as librarian at the Bibliothèque de l'Arsenal, which was destined to be the chief guardian of his memory. He had despaired and attempted suicide, and he was subsequently cared for by his old and prosperous friends. During this complicated life he had married for a year, fathered a daughter, and gathered to himself a following of loyal and fascinated young friends who found something behind the disordered facade that spoke convincingly to their needs and aspirations.[7]

Saint-Simon's life was marked by intrigues, quarrels, miraculous escapes, lawsuits, mysterious comings and goings, ecstasies, sloughs of despond. Had this been all, Saint-Simon might have survived in memory as a colorful and strange footnote to the history of early modern France, an interesting exemplar of those who somehow bridged two ages across the torrents of Revolution and Reaction.

There was, however, more. Threatened by business troubles at the end of the Directory, approaching his fortieth year, Saint-Simon simply abdicated from the life he had been living and turned his attention to the achievements of science and medicine in an effort to understand his chaotic world. For a time he took up residence near the Ecole Polytechnique, then housed in the Palais Bourbon on the Left Bank. He cultivated the professors of that newly founded and elite school as well as the doctors situated not far from Le Procope, a bit farther to the east. He was to comment that the wise men who came to his table ate much and talked little. For a year, in 1801 and 1802, Saint-Simon, married, held forth on the rue Vivienne in his old quarter as patron of the arts and sciences. As early as 1798 he had gone to Belgium to undertake a "reforming noviatiate" and had tried to persuade his business friends to take part in a great

11

real estate speculation that would dominate first the Bourse and then the world. He traveled to Switzerland, possibly to propose marriage to Mme. de Staël, and to England and Germany during the Peace of Amiens, saying later that he had found no few fact of importance. His writings continually belie that assertion.[8]

It is Saint-Simon's written work that makes the difference. From 1802 until his death in 1825 there poured forth from his pen or those of his instructed, devoted, sometimes complaining secretaries a mass of disordered, irritating, ill-written inconsecutive pages. They embodied a vision of the world as it was and as it would have to be if men were to escape the Armageddon that he thought imminent. The essays, pamphlets, letters, journals, and books have no order and no system. They often bear the unattractive mark of the toady and the opportunist looking to the main chance. Yet from beginning to end there are recognizable themes. These found echo in the minds of the eager generation of listeners who came to maturity in the 1820s and who hoped in the postrevolutionary chaos to find or make some harmony, to bring to some triumphant finale the disappointments of Waterloo and the Restoration.

It was the coming together of Saint-Simon's vision with the young men who surrounded him in his last years that gave both their historical importance. Without Saint-Simon there would have been no Saint-Simonians, and without the Saint-Simonians the vision would in all probability have faded from view without consequence. Again, it would have constituted a footnote to the history of socialism, of positivism, possibly of fascism, an early anticipation of the direction of industrial society—that is all.

Saint-Simon's definitive biographer has commented, as we have seen, that he was not a Saint-Simonian.[9] It is a point to be argued. And it is a point that has to be argued on the basis of what a Saint-Simonian was. A Saint-Simonian, at least at the beginning of the movement in 1825, was an admirer of Saint-Simon who found in his writings, from the *Lettre d'un Habitant à Genève* of 1802 to *Le Nouveau Christianism* of 1825, a call to apply the scientific knowledge of competent experts to the solution of social problems.

The call was heard at a crucial moment. That society was in crisis was announced everywhere in 1825, and nowhere more loudly than in Paris and among the young. A generation was arriving at maturity, born in the last days of the Revolution, remembering vividly the glories of Napoleonic France, seeking a place and direction for its talents and energies. It was a generation acutely aware that ten years earlier opportunity had been unlimited, that the legendary marshal's baton or its equivalent could have been found in every knapsack. It was a generation equally, and bitterly, aware of the consequences of military defeat and diplomatic subjection,

of political reaction and narrowing horizons.[10] Every man of this generation was a Julien Sorel and a Rastignac. The feeling of despair was particularly acute among those whose families had profited from the Revolution
and suffered in one fashion or another from Napoleon's defeat: those
whose training would once have guaranteed a brilliant career but now
offered a minor provincial post, and, for example, Jews, whose educational avenues were blocked by the religious policies of the Restoration.
The despair was perhaps most acute of all among the *polytechniciens,*
products of the elite scientific school, which had attracted Saint-Simon's
interest, which was to be "the canal" through which his ideas would flow,
and which had as its ideal the wedding of scientific theory with engineering practice.

What theory would justify what practice? That was the question facing
the young of 1825. Amid all the theoretical abundance of nascent romanticism, Saint-Simon's theory appealed to the young Augustin Thierry,
Auguste Comte, Prosper Enfantin, Isaac and Emile Pereire, and Olinde
Rodrigues; to the not-so-young Saint-Amand Bazard; and to the scores of
other men and women who eventually—at varying depths of understanding and commitment, for varying periods of time, and in combination
with varying alternatives—constituted the Saint-Simonian movement. In
responding to Saint-Simon's theory and in constituting a movement these
same people created a continuing Saint-Simonian tradition with important and visible consequences for France and for the world beyond.

By the winter of 1825 Léon Halévy had replaced Comte and Thierry in
the chain of secretaries who had done so much to get the master in print.
Thierry had been described as *"fils adoptif"* on the frontispiece of *L'industrie,* and Comte had worked with Saint-Simon from 1817 to 1824.[11]
They, with two older friends, Dr. Burdin and Dr. Bailly the phrenologist,
and, shortly after the suicide attempt of 1823, Olinde Rodrigues, were
most likely to frequent the rooms above the passage Hulot. The rooms
were disorderly, with books and papers strewn on the chairs and tables.
Saint-Simon might be seated on the floor in a corner engaged in his favorite reading, romantic novels, "the worse, the better." Saint-Simon was
tended by his faithful servant, Julie. On the occasion of the introduction
of Prosper Enfantin, the rooms were filled with the yapping of the poodle
Presto. They were also the site of conversations on the nature of society
and the programs that could make it sane.[12]

The members of the circle that gathered in these rooms were making
plans in the spring of 1825 to start yet another journal when Saint-Simon
fell ill. His friends assembled, removed him to new chambers in the rue du
Faubourg Montmartre, and settled down for one of those edifying deathbed scenes so dear to the nineteenth century and, in this case, resonant
with Socratic echoes. Saint-Simon refused to discuss his illness or his

pain and adjured his followers to greet the star of the nineteenth century at its rising, to be filled with passion, and to encourage the development of human potential. His last words were "Our business is well in hand."[13]

With Saint-Simon's death on May 19, 1825, Saint-Simonianism was born. Its first faint cries of life were to be heard in the journal *Le Producteur,* vying for attention with all the concerns and all the alternatives open to Restoration Paris. Before one can appreciate the relevance of Saint-Simon's ideas to his society in his time or the luxuriant growth to be produced by the Saint-Simonian fertilization of those ideas, one needs a sense of the Parisian soil in which they grew. Perhaps more than ever before, the Paris of 1825 was the capital of Europe.[14] It provided the backdrop and the reference point not only of Saint-Simon but also of the work of his followers. It was the stage on which the Saint-Simonian dramas would be played out for all Europe to witness, to remark on, and to absorb.

The search for the Paris of Saint-Simon and the Saint-Simonians has to be conducted simultaneously in space and time. The point of view of a traveler may be the best way to move back and forth from Paris known to Paris discovered. Descending in 1825 at the offices of the Messageries Royale on the rue Notre-Dame-des-Victoires or arriving at one of the "ports" along the banks of the Seine, those broad, cobbled ramps descending directly into the river from the quais, our travelers would share with all visitors to Paris the unpreparedness, the readiness to be astonished and to be struck by the ordinary, and the need to establish fixed points of navigation. They would find a Paris in many ways different from that of today and yet remarkably the same. Ironically they might find a Paris more like today's than it was to be for the next hundred years. No great European city has been more insistently itself, as continuous and as changing as the Seine that flows through it.[15]

Travelers would be armed, probably, with a *New Conductor of the Stranger in Paris,* starting with a lesson on "the manner of pursuing one's business and living comfortably according to one's fortune."[16] They would be expected to see the Tuileries Palace (now gone) and its gardens and terraces (much the same); the Louvre (now restored to its initial proportions); the Palais Royal; the church of the Madeleine, still being constructed; the place Vendôme; the King's Library; the Bourse; Notre Dame; the Panthéon, recently restored to the church; Saint-Germain-des-Prés; the Hôtel des Invalides; and Saint Eustache. Travelers would not find Sacré Coeur, the Eiffel Tower, the present day Opéra, or the completed Arc de Triomphe. Beyond the present place de la Concorde one was almost in forested country. The boulevard des Italiens was not yet paved, but it was lined with trees along the route it still follows. Saint Eustache was, as it had been since the Middle Ages, in a market area not yet endowed with those lofty iron and glass pavilions, les Halles, that are now only a memory replaced by a regret.

Paris was already in the eyes of its inhabitants an "immense" city, but it was also, as it remains, a manageable one. Its population was over 750,000. The perimeter was smaller than it is today, and even within it there was much open land and a number of low-density areas. But the living city offered the visitor bustle, crowds, noise, the smells of midstreet gutters, and, above all, a diversity of peoples and occupations.[17]

One would explore the complexity of this 1825 Paris from a center. One might stay at the Meurice on the rue Saint-Honoré, close to the Tuileries, where "apartments" might be had by the day, where guests might dine in public or private, and where the linen was washed "three miles from Paris with soap" and "not beaten or brushed." It had an office for changing money, confidential couriers, and interpreters. Return carriages for Calais, Boulogne, and all parts of the continent might be obtained. The charge for a room was perhaps five francs.[18]

Sallying forth from their hotel to explore the city, travelers would plan their day in terms of the changes in Parisian customs over the previous thirty years. They would breakfast between ten and noon and dine at six or seven. But in their easy day of exploration there would be points of rest and refreshment among the city's 2000 cafés, without counting those of "the inferior order." It would be "impossible to conceive of their elegance without having seen them. Among a more domestic or less gay populace a tenth of them would not find support, but in Paris many cafés are crowded to excess and almost all are well-frequented."[19] In this Paris all classes mixed, strangers conversed with one another (although it was wise to avoid political topics), newspapers were read, dominoes were played, and coffee, sugar and water, and liqueurs were drunk. The rooms were "open and magnificently ornamented." There were, however, subterranean haunts near the Palais Royal where one should "guard against the designs of courtesans and pickpockets." Among the important cafés were Le Procope and La Régence, haunts of Saint-Simon, and the Tortoni, famous for its ices and frequented by stock market speculators and ladies of the opera.

For dinner there were *traiteurs,* who catered meals, and *tables d'hôte,* to be treated with caution because they were frequently used by apparently well-bred and agreeable people "all too willing to entice the unwary into games of chance for high stakes."[20] In any event the diner would fare well at the best restaurants from a menu of three hundred dishes for about two francs. At lesser places twenty-two sous would procure soup, three main dishes, a dessert, bread, and wine.

Little wonder that the travelers' guidebook would tell them that "this lively metropolis is the most attractive emporium of pleasure and literature in the world and at the same time the cheapest for the advantages it presents; circumstances which render it the general rendez-vous for all nations of the globe." Paris was also "salubrious." Unlike London, where "every building is blackened by smoke, where the eye looks down upon suffocating steam and mists, Paris seen from the towers of Notre Dame, the Panthéon, or the heights of Montmartre is complete; there is no indistinctness or confusion. . . . Every palace, church and public edifice stands directly before the eye, and interspersed with the foliage of the gardens and the boulevards the whole forms a prospect at once grand and beautiful."[21] The more things change, the more they remain the same.

As one moved about the Paris of 1825 the deviations from the guide-book's picture of pleasure would be striking. The networks of streets behind the leafy, unpaved boulevards were dirty and stinking. The runnels between the sloping surfaces emptied sewage into the river, from which came bottled drinking water; cholera would persist in Paris until the 1850s. A common sight was a renter of planks to fastidious street-crossers. In a city that used horses as the most common means of transport, that contained fifteen hundred market gardens within its boundaries, that was heated by wood, and that had a limited number of public baths, the smells, although familiar, were formidable. Paris was also a city of dark. Here and there lanterns swung over the middle of streets, and carriage drivers were required to suspend two lanterns to warn pedestrians. But after the closing of the cafés at 11 P.M. the city was as dark as it had been in the Dark Ages. Gaslight would come in 1829.[22]

These drawbacks would be particularly evident in the more crowded parts of Paris, which had an overall population density estimated at 22,000 per square kilometer (57,000 per square mile). The density in the Fourth Arrondissement in 1817, for example, has been estimated at 216,000 per square mile.[23] Paris had grown by 50 percent in twenty-five years, but its growth in some quarters on the Right Bank over fifty years had been on the order of 150 percent.[24]

The average residents of Paris, we are assured, were above average in height, blue-eyed, and blond.[25] Perhaps half of these residents in the rapidly changing and growing city were internal migrants from the east. They were the victims of overcrowding and periodic unemployment. Cut off from the systems of social control of their places of origin, the newcomers were viewed with suspicion, fear, and hostility by "real" and "respectable" Parisians. Provisioning Paris's enormous and rapidly growing population required fifteen hundred sacks of flour a day, weighing 325 pounds each. In the course of a year 24 million gallons of wine, 1.3 million of brandy, and 790,000 of beer were brought into the city. Parisians consumed 76,000 cows, 74,000 calves, 363,000 sheep, 89,000 pigs, 1.3 million pounds of organ meats, and 3 million pounds of cheese. They spent 8 million francs on butter and 4 million francs on eggs. Milk, salt, tobacco, and water accounted for another 30 million francs. The sums do not speak for themselves. The proportions and the totals do, as measured against the two-franc cost of an elegant dinner in an elegant restaurant.[26] They also convey a sense of the work and the workers in what Zola would call the womb of Paris, as well as the dreadful disparity between lavish supply and chronic working-class misery.

Where did the money come from? What did Parisians do? Obviously the business of feeding themselves was important. There were five public slaughterhouses, thirty-five breweries, five hundred bakeries, six hundred butchers, and twenty sugar refiners.[27] A million and a half tons of merchandise arrived by water, and transshipment was an important element in Paris's economy. The rivers and the recently completed canals of Saint-Martin, Saint-Denis, and l'Ourcq carried from the east 11,000 boatloads a year of fruit, grain, wood, stone, firewood, flour, tiles, brick, iron, and wine. From Rouen to the west came colonial goods, glassware, salt, cider, and foreign grain.

Paris sent forth in a thousand boats its own goods. Preeminently these included the "articles of Paris," small, highly finished, and expensive. The two hundred and fifty establishments producing these employed three thousand people. Three-fifths of the jewelry and gold-work of France came from Paris.[28] Another three thousand workers were to be found in fifty printshops. There were four thousand building contractors. Four thousand men made wallpapers. There were six hundred cotton workers in the Richard-Lenoir firm. There were watchmakers and clockmakers, makers of fans, ten thousand woodworkers, tailors, hatmakers, specialists in gloves and breeches, umbrella makers, and cobblers. There were perhaps forty thousand domestic servants.[29]

Within Paris were fifteen hundred market gardens, whose produce would continue to be widely sought until the transportation revolution made the produce of the south available.[30] Porters, shoeblacks, and chimney sweeps abounded. On another level of labor there were perhaps twenty-five thousand bureaucrats and a company of lawyers whose center was the Palais de Justice on the Ile de la Cité. Primary schools housed eighteen thousand pupils, and more thousands were at the lycées, the Ecole de Médecine, and the Ecole de Droit. Ten thousand officers and troops defended Paris and the Crown. Bankers and stockbrokers, limited in number but living grandly and in the public eye, inhabited the new quarter of the Chausée d'Antin. The Marais contained discreet bodies of *rentiers,* and along the Left Bank, west of the schools, were the *hôtels particuliers* and attached gardens of the old nobility. Meeting the needs of these grander classes were hairdressers, coach makers, booksellers, and printmakers.[31]

Under the Restoration five seminaries and twenty-one convents flourished. Several of the former were devoted to the training of clergy from abroad. Nine hospitals, including one for treating children, and a dozen shelters for the incurable, the aged, and orphans were spread about the city.[32] Although the Paris population was young, children were a disproportionately small part of it. It seems to have been standard practice to place the very young in households outside the city until they reached an age to help their families or at least fend for themselves in urban conditions.[33] The city also had a hospital specializing in venereal diseases. The only serious account of nineteenth-century prostitution in Paris, running through several editions before 1900, reported the presence of 60,000 by 1832.[34]

The police were charged with health, workers' inscriptions, weights and measures, and keeping of the peace. Six companies of horse and foot soldiers of the Gendarmerie Royale were stationed at the rue Mouffetard, the place Royale, the Faubourg Saint-Martin, and at the customs barriers of Hell, the Throne, the Etoile, and the Villette. There were 636 firemen, seventy-three pumps, and two fireboats to defend a city that, although much of it was stone and brick, was highly combustible.

By 1825 Paris had many of the characteristics of a modern city, including most of its problems. Crowding would shortly stimulate the first stages of a real estate and building boom whose ultimate expression would be the remodeling, thirty years later, of the capital of the Second Empire. It was a city picturesque in detail but practical and organic, its parts interrelated. There were twelve *arrondissements,* each divided into four "quarters," assuring centrality and individuality at once. Eight of the *arrondissements* were on the Right Bank, three on the Left; the Ninth Arrondissment comprised the Ile de la Cité and the Ile Saint-Louis.

Given the variety and density of the population, particularly at the center, it is not surprising that many Parisians lived almost entirely in their own neighborhood and, unless driven by administrative or business need, felt little urge to move about the greater city.[35] Each of the quarters, as is still largely the case, had its own life. There were around twenty-nine thousand dwelling houses in Paris. Most of these provided a variety of apartments and rooms. Myth has taught that the arrangements stimulated a democratization of the Parisian populace: the rich lived on the lower floors, the less rich higher up, the poor at the top. A more suspicious analysis modifies the myth. In the populous quarters, to be sure, there were shops at the ground level, the shopkeeper living behind or above the business. And rents did decrease as stairways rose. But it appears that in a given neighborhood the same sorts of people tended to live within the same walls. The established doctor might occupy the first floor, the young lawyer or the middle-level civil servant would be above, and the ministerial clerk could be found under the roof. There was less egalitarianism than legend has supposed as tenants met on the landings. And, as anyone who has encountered fellow tenants in a Paris apartment house can attest, jolly camaraderie is not the rule.

There were, in any case, areas historically defined as working class—the Faubourg Saint-Antoine near the site of the Bastille, for example—or devoted to special functions. The same quarter was a center for furniture and woodworking and remains so to this day. The Left Bank was, as it had been for centuries and as it continues to be, the center of academic life and the home of the old aristocracy, the ministries, the churches, and the hospitals, whose lands stretched to and beyond the customs barrier at Hell—today the place D'enfert-Rochereau. The wine trade centered on the eastern quais of the Right Bank at Bercy and on the new Halle aux Vins on the Left Bank. The Champs-Elysées were still largely parkland. Fingers of urbanism pointed toward Montmartre. There was a beginning of industry at Chaillot, then a country village. Beyond the site of the Bastille one found market gardens. At the center, the Ile de la Cité, occupied by Notre Dame, the Hôtel-Dieu, the law courts, the Conciergerie, and the place Dauphine, was populous, characterized by networks of streets and alleys around the great public monuments. It was the scene of Eugène Sue's "Mysteries of Paris."

There was in this Paris a rhythm to the day and the season. While the worker was still resting from "the fatigues of a painful day," six thousand peasants arrived at Les Halles bent under mountains of soup vegetables. They were followed by wagons of butter and eggs for the wholesale market, which transformed itself into a retail market at 9:00 A.M. At dawn milkmen, arriving before the heavy transport wagons, tangled with diligences bringing travelers to town. The workers were up at 6:00, and soon after the shops were filled with the sounds of the anvil, hammer, and saw; work went on until 6:00 P.M. in the building trades and 8:00 in the factories. Merchants were up at 6:00 in summer, 7:00 in winter. Hospital rounds took place at 5:00 A.M.; the lycées opened at 8:00; and "libraries and museums fill at 10:00." Lawyers were in their offices at 9:00 A.M. Around Saint-Simon's Palais Royal and the Chausée d'Antin everything was quiet until 10:00, when the "stockbrokers and bankers begin to ready themselves for the 2 o'clock trading at the Bourse." The ministries filled with supplicants until 4:00, when all great affairs ceased. "Then one abandons one's self to repose, or delivers one's self without reserve to pleasure." The bourgeois dined gaily, the rich taking their carriages to private dinners. Foreigners and single people crowded the restaurants; cafés were crowded until 11:00. The quieter citizens returned home, abandoning the city to the noisy carriages of the fashionable on their way to "balls, ruinous gaming and futile pleasures," never finding "the happiness and the real joy reserved to a moderate labor, the love of learning and the exercise of virtue."[36]

19

The moralizing of the guidebook authors is less hypocritical than one might suppose. As Emile Barrault, eventually an ardent Saint-Simonian, was to write about this period:

Now, after this vast radiance extinguished with Napoleon, France which had seemed capable of living only in the dust, the smoke, the noise of battle and in the blaze of victory, this France sheathed its sword and took up again the great book of study at the place marked when it ran to the club and the bivouac. What energy after the frightful and showy materialism under which words, thoughts even, were sedition! What movement in all minds, what questions reviewed, what puzzles attacked in all the sciences![37]

More soberly, Barrault's fellow Saint-Simonian Isaac Pereire wrote, "The truths in which we will have to believe are not yet formulated; those that were believed for centuries are overthrown with the institutions that were their social expression."[38]

In 1825 the permeation of literary romanticism into all areas of human intellectual life—even economics—was well under way, and the Saint-Simonians themselves were to formulate an economics of romanticism in the years immediately ahead. But at this moment France was viewed as primarily a center of scientific culture. La Place, Gay-Lussac, Arago, Fresnel, Ampère, and Carnot were stars of the physical sciences; Lamarck, Cuvier, and Geoffroy Saint-Hilaire shone in biology. Many years before, Champollion had broken the code of the Rosetta Stone, and Bougainville had embarked on his travels. The fascination with the remote in time and space found examples in students of Near-Eastern and Oriental languages. Quinet, Michelet, and the same Augustin Thierry who had served as Saint-Simon's secretary were discovering the history of the Middle Ages. Thierry's *Histoire de la conquête de l'Angleterre par les Normands* was delivered into Saint-Simon's hands shortly before his death. Mignet and Thiers were defending the French Revolution and Guizot was working on his history of the English Revolution. The lines dividing social France were being drawn by historians who were also politicians.[39]

Political theory offered the young of 1825 three alternatives: that of the Catholic Royalist Revival, that of the "ideologues," and that of the "doctrinaires." For those who found the atheism and materialism of the Enlightenment, the disorder of the Revolution, and the disillusion of the Napoleonic experience distasteful and degrading, the message of Joseph de Maistre and the Catholic Revival—that "in society there are no rights, there are only duties"—might be appealing. But it was not a message that appealed to the young of 1825 any more than it appeals to the young of the 1980s. The ideologues had built a temple to the power of enlightened reason and individual liberty derived from the evidence of the senses. But again the young might question the results of the application of reason they saw about them and the substitution in this political alternative of sensual delight for passion (this was the year of the publication of Brillat-Savarin's *Physiologie du goût*).[40] Finally, doctrinaires and eclectics, by their very nature, are suspect to the young. They are smoothers out of differences, makers of middle ways, supporters, in this case, of the Charter, advocates of constitutional and bourgeois supremacy, defenders of "religion and the social order."

The authoritarianism and devotion to a dead past of a Louis de Bonald, the extreme rationalist individualism of a Benjamin Constant, and the stuffy status quoism of the doctrinaires were, each in its own way, unsatisfactory. Here one touches on the central problem of those who were young in 1825. They were in a trap, and they sought to gnaw their way out of it. The trap had been set by old men and, in consequence, old men's doctrines had to be rejected.

What was the nature of the trap? France was becoming young.[41] A record number of births occurred in 1826. Those under forty years old constituted 67 percent of the population. The death rate was decreasing. A quarter of those who had lived under the Empire had already died. To be a member of the Chamber of Deputies one had to be at least forty. Revolution and Empire brought into important administrative positions a generation of relatively young men. In 1818, 15 percent of the prefects were over fifty, and by 1830, 55 percent were over fifty. There had been retrenchment in the army. Education emphasized the literary and theoretical studies that produced lawyers, administrators, teachers, and doctors. Business was scorned.

"The youth was, therefore, bulging with lawyers without cases, doctors without patients, sons of workers and peasants whose studies had incapacitated them for manual labor [and] . . . young bourgeois furious at having to mark time in waiting rooms or seeing themselves hopelessly relegated to subordinate administrative positions."[42]

It was young men such as these who had come to Saint-Simon in his last days, drawn by their needs and his insights. Although Saint-Simon had attracted the interest and support of the ideologues, the economic and political liberals, the medievalists and royalists, and the compromisers, he promised something more, something different, a unique amalgam for those who were scorned, condemned, or disregarded by the Establishment of Restoration society. Saint-Simon's attraction was to those—businessmen, engineers, Jews suspect in a revitalized Catholic world—who were finding it difficult to make a place for themselves in the Paris and France of 1825 and whose own hidden injuries of class and occupation would sensitize them to the injuries, injustices, and potentialities of that most numerous and poorest class that had filled the Paris stage to overflowing during Saint-Simon's lifetime.[43]

21

June 1, 1825, saw the signature of an act of forming the Saint-Simonian Society. With it there stepped forward to the apron of the Parisian stage a group that for seven years would never be completely out of the public eye and that would, at its most active point, form the dominant intellectual movement of Paris and, consequently, of all Europe. The announced purpose of the society was the publication of a journal, *Le Producteur*. Among the initial subscribers one finds the distinguished banking names of Ardoin and Laffitte, but the leadership went to the young disciples Olinde Rodrigues, Saint-Amand Bazard, Philippe Buchez, Charles Laurent, and Prosper Enfantin. Three of these, Rodrigues, Bazard, and Enfantin, emerged as leaders of Saint-Simonianism during the period of the *Le Producteur*. Rodrigues was a brilliant mathematician whose academic career had been blocked by his religious origins. The son of a banker, a former mathematics tutor of Enfantin, and a friend of Auguste Comte, he spanned the worlds of banking, the Polytechnique, and a group of young Jews whose Jewishness was to be significant for Saint-Simonianism.[44] Bazard had been a founder of the Carbonari in France and a friend of Lafayette. He was an illegitimate child and sensitive on that point. He has been described as an overzealous father and an unhappy husband.[45]

Enfantin, who had met Saint-Simon only once, was the son of a strong-minded mother and a father who, through no fault of his own, had gone bankrupt. The father was still being pursued by creditors fifteen years after the event. His son, as a result, was viewed as unsuitable for an army commission and as husband for the woman he loved and wished to marry. He did, however, gain entrance to the Ecole Polytechnique, where Comte taught him mathematics and where Enfantin himself boasted that he was the best ball and billiards player and a leader of his peers.[46]

Enfantin dropped out of the Polytechnique following the Hundred Days, worked in the wine business in France and Germany, and held a partnership in a new French bank in Saint Petersburg. While there he joined with several *polytechniciens, en mission,* in the study of political and economic theory. Returning to Paris in 1824 to continue his economic studies, he renewed an acquaintance with Rodrigues, who took him to Saint-Simon.

The common traits of these three are obvious. All were young in 1825 (Bazard, at 34, the oldest), were outsiders in French Restoration society, were to some degree frustrated in making careers suitable to their talents, and had both personal and general criticisms to make of the regime. They all sought to impose themselves on their time and their place—Paris. They had all been seeking an intellectually satisfactory base from which to launch themselves. That base they formed in the ideas of Saint-Simon and in the Paris where already Lamartine's *Méditations poétiques,* Hugo's *Nouvelle odes,* and Stendhal's *Racine et Shakespeare* were signs of a romantic revolt that, as Bertier de Sauvigny shows, "had deserted the royalist camp in favor of the liberal opposition."[47] The founders of *Le Producteur* were romantic young men and were about to announce an economics of romanticism. The identity between them and the literary romantics was obscured by the nature of their study, the dismal science, and by the fact that, as the young romantics moved left towards liberalism, Saint-Simon and the Saint-Simonians had moved yet further left to what was to be called socialism.

In time Hugo, Lamartine, and George Sand would all recognize a sympathy for and even a debt to Saint-Simonian economic and social theory. Stendhal would write a pamphlet against them. But in 1825 these seemingly unromantic young romantics were about to embark on a campaign for the conquest of their Paris and their France whose strategy had been laid out in the ideas of Henri de Saint-Simon.

CHAPTER II

"IF . . ."

SAINT-SIMON was always acutely conscious of context, and his vision was always shaped by it. His experiences and the times—and place—in which he lived were the raw materials of the program he designed. He saw his society much more clearly than most of his contemporaries or their subsequent historians.

When he was moved in 1798 to "reflect on his experiences" and to establish "general principles" drawn from them, the fundamental fact of Saint-Simon's life had been conflict.[1] The key to his thought was to be the idea of cooperation or association. The dust of Revolutionary and Napoleonic battle once settled, Saint-Simon saw what scholars have only relatively recently begun to appreciate. The Revolution had been won by a conservative, land-owning, and, to a surprising degree, aristocratic group that had to be persuaded to use its wealth, power, and influence for the benefit of the poorest and most numerous class.[2] Persuasion failing, Armageddon would ensue; conflict would continue to the detriment of all.

Ultimately despairing of this group of *oisifs*—sluggards—the philosopher turned his ever-hopeful eye to the sort of men with whom he had worked during the Directory and who continued to support him: bankers and industrialists searching for investment and for profit, who were more open, more amenable to change, and more willing to believe in an expanding and evolving economic universe.[3] But they, too, must submit themselves to the governance of idea, plan, direction, association. The new world would be the product of hard work, hard knowledge, competence, and universally accepted goals. It is to the experts in the sciences, the arts, technology, and industry that we must look for precise knowledge of what is possible and for the capacity to make the possible real.[4] In his last year Saint-Simon concluded that to bring the diverse elements of society together in harmonious functioning and to achieve that universal acceptance of goals, there must be born a new Christianity, a religion that would create the Heavenly City on earth. Certainly one of Saint-Simon's crucial ideas, and one of the most interesting, is that any given religion is the expression of the scientific understanding of the epoch in which it flourishes. As science itself becomes more certain, inclusive, and demonstrably accurate, it must inevitably transform religion. We must believe what is true, and belief will provide the incentives to make the transformations that truth requires of society.[5]

This world view, whose parts must be examined more closely, raised and continues to raise questions of more than ordinary concern. Saint-Simon is, first, a "socialist," in the sense in which that word is properly used before Marx; that is, the object of his attention is society. He seeks universal and underlying principles that hold society together against the historical or accidental tendencies that pull it apart. We must find the laws so that we can obey them and, in obeying them, fulfill human potentiality. The emphasis of Saint-Simonian thought is certainly social. It is also, in a certain limited sense, authoritarian. It supposes the existence of law and the discoverability and expressibility of that law. It further supposes that discovery, expression, and administration are the products of special, rare, and highly trained talent that demands obedience in recognition of capacity.

These characteristics of Saint-Simon's thought have always disturbed individualists and liberals of whatever persuasion or generation, and in particular they have disturbed those who consciously view themselves as heirs of the French Revolution or as defenders of freedom against tyranny.[6] Saint-Simon has been seen as an ancestor of both communism and fascism, although, as has already been said, he would have repudiated both. He is undoubtedly an intellectual ancestor of the technocracy that is feared as putting the problem before the person. He is discounted intellectually as the grandfather of a superficial positivism fathered by his sometime disciple, Auguste Comte. He is dismissed as utopian by Marx because of his insistence on the associative, while at the same time Marx borrows Saint-Simon's notions of class.

But against these shocked reactions, which push Saint-Simon out of the mainstream of Western liberal history to the Left or to the Right, one must place the shocked reactions of Saint-Simon himself to the liberalism and individualism of his own time. Saint-Simon's objection was not merely authoritarian, it was also humane. He reminded a generation that had apparently forgotten the fact that humans are social animals with social needs. The equality of people's abilities did not exist, but the validity of their needs did.

What Saint-Simon saw in Restoration liberalism was unchecked egoism, head-to-head competition, duplication of effort, waste, inefficiency, and incompetence in the administration of both things and people. He had a clear notion that in a laissez-faire world of uncontrolled competition somebody wins and somebody loses. He had an almost Marxian intuition that there are more losers than winners. He had a personal friendship with misery and had himself been a "loser." Consequently, he hoped that association could replace competition, that peace might replace war. He believed that cosmopolitanism was better than nationalism, that production for social purposes was good, that there should be areas open to talent, and that the individual should enjoy self-expression. Everyone had capacities, but the social order must be organized to extract from these capacities their fullest and most appropriate expression.

For Saint-Simon freedom was the result of civilization, not its object. He was not alone in the effort to square the circle of freedom and authority. Like his great predecessor Rousseau and his great successor Mill, he had much to say on both topics. The reaction of economic and political liberalism—that Saint-Simon's road led to serfdom—must be balanced against the fact that liberal theory and liberal practice, with the best will in the world, have not in two hundred years succeeded in building a detour around that same road to serfdom. Saint-Simon's voice continues to be heard, and he may indeed have more to contribute to the debate on freedom and authority than his opponents have ever been willing to recognize.[7]

For Saint-Simon authority's claims must always be judged against the authority of expanding knowledge. Authority does not exist for its own sake. The unique theme in Saint-Simon, what differentiates him from most of the other major thinkers of his age, is that he emphasizes one side of the intellectual coin that was struck in the nineteenth century, whereas most of his great rivals gaze on the other side. For Darwin, Marx, and Freud, for socialism, liberalism, and nationalism, conflict is the key to understanding and to change. Each embodies notions of solidarity, of synthesis, of resolution of conflict as the means to victory in the universal struggle; but struggle is uppermost. One sometimes senses that the *Origin of Species* or *Das Kapital* could as easily have been written from the point of view of cooperation as from that of conflict, but they were not. Saint-Simon's views are also marked by conflict, particularly when he deals with the ambiguities of Franco-British relations, but cooperation remains always in the foreground.

The Saint-Simonian emphasis on cooperation may have contributed to the doctrines of solidarity that formed the underpinning of radical leftist and radical rightist ideology in his century and ours. It may have contributed to the widespread notions of the nation, of the class, of sex, and of the generation that are everywhere the sources of differentiation and conflict. Saint-Simon's ideas certainly provided the intellectual basis for the creation of a new order of beings, the technocrats, and thus for a new industrial order in France and elsewhere.

Proponents of those doctrines and ideologies based on the struggle for survival castigated Saint-Simon as utopian. But the Saint-Simonian world view was illuminated by the obvious fact of the interrelationships existing in the social order and by the probable increase in the interdependence of all things and all people in a world increasingly marked by a specialization of functions. The point at which Saint-Simon differs from his socialist contemporaries and the other ideologues of his age is that he seeks to exclude destructive social conflict by including all elements of society — from the richest to the poorest, from the most to the least able — in the functioning of the body politic.

The image of the body politic is exact, since one of the two pillars supporting the pediment of Saint-Simonian thought is the idea, derived from the medical practitioners of the Directory and the Empire, of society as obedient to the same general laws as is the individual human organism. (The other pillar is Saint-Simon's historicism.) Saint-Simon's science of society was to be biological, that is, evolutionary, historical, developmental, experiential, pragmatic, and materialist.

Every commentator on Saint-Simon has had to say, at some point, that his work never succeeded in elaborating the system whose arrival it incessantly trumpeted. The totality of Saint-Simon's work is more Wagnerian than Mozartian, and themes have to be caught where they are clearest. The present discussion is less concerned with an examination of the intellectual sources and the process of construction of Saint-Simon's thought than with the totality of the work as perceived at the end of his life by those who would guarantee a hearing for it.

The best and clearest expression of the organic character of Saint-Simon's thought is in a work bearing his name but in fact written by a collaborator, E. M. Bailly. "Physiology Applied to the Amelioration of Social Institutions" expresses in their most coherent and succinct form the principle elements of Saint-Simon's organicism and, by implication, the principle elements of his historicism.[8] At this stage of Saint-Simon's life one senses an urgency to expose what is in him. It is less important to him to compose personally the epistles of his doctrine than to have clear and systematic expression given to the ideas that had been simmering for the better part of twenty-five years. Much earlier than "Physiology" Saint-Simon had written in "The Science of Man":

It is by frequent mulling over of one's thoughts that one succeeds in analyzing them completely, that one becomes familiar with them and gives them a solid foundation. I know that this mode of composition renders the reading of a work painful . . . that it must displease a majority of readers; this doesn't matter to me. . . . Literary glory is not the object of my ambition.[9]

and later:

I am pushed to this plan of my work more by conviction that society needs it than by the sentiment I have of my capacity to meet the demands of such a long and difficult course. I declare in undertaking it that I am ready to quit the direction of the enterprise, that my greatest desire is to see a person more capable than myself take charge of it, and I shall become from that moment a collaborator to be used as needed.[10]

From Saint-Simon's own pen, therefore, we have justification for taking the Bailly essay as an appropriate and clear expression of what Saint-Simon thought. Bailly by no means took over Saint-Simon's enterprise, but he did explain it more sequentially than the Master was able to do.

Bailly tells us that the domain of physiology is all the data having to do with organized beings. Physiology examines the influence of exterior agents on organization, in relation to human functions. It makes known those whose action is deleterious and those whose effect strengthens our resistance and procures for us a greater sum of pleasures and enjoyments.

Physiology is not merely a science that with the aid of chemistry and anatomy seeks to better understand the workings of our tissues. Nor is it merely a science of experimenting with the workings of particular organisms. It is not just a comparative study of the functions of parts shared by a variety of organisms. And it is not limited to a study of monstrosities and sicknesses.

Physiology rises to higher social considerations. Individuals are, for it, only the organs of the body, "because society is not a simple agglomeration of living beings whose actions, independent of all final ends, have no other cause than the arbitrariness of individual will nor other result than ephemeral accidents; society, on the contrary, is an organized machine all of whose parts contribute in a different manner to the working of the whole." The union of humanity constitutes "a veritable Being" whose existence is more or less vigorous or feeble according to whether its organs regularly acquit themselves of the functions confided to them. The social body displays different characteristics at different periods in its development. The physiology of the child is not that of the adult."[11]

The history of civilization, Bailly writes, is the history of the life cycle of the human species, of the physiology of its different ages and institutions, and of the "hygienic knowledge" that has been used for the conservation and betterment of the general health. Politics, morality, legislation, and all that constitutes the general administration of society are merely a collection of hygienic rules, whose nature varies according to the state of civilization. General physiology is the science that can determine what that state is and has the capacity to describe it.

Physiology, then, is not only the science of individual life but also of all life, of which individual lives are only the parts. In any machine the perfection of results depends on the maintenance of the primitive harmony established among all the springs that compose it; each of them must necessarily furnish its action and reaction. Disorder ensues promptly when perturbation augments the activity of one at the expense of the others.

European society has successively known periods of sickness and critically disruptive movements. Like individuals, it has had ages of illusion and superstition, terrible convulsions, and frightful revolutions, resulting in the overturning of social organization; it has also experienced periods of organic dominance. Society now having arrived at a period of its growth where the errors of childhood can no longer blind it, where it can profit from the knowledge acquired by so many years of trouble and revolution, has reentered the domain of physiology.[12]

Saint-Simon himself added certain important amplifications to this outline by Bailly of his thought. The first was that the greatest social evil is lack of useful work. Social organization must stimulate all classes to undertake work useful to society. The second amplification was that the feudal and religious society had justification in its beginnings. Nobles were continuously occupied in war, and priests were the sole body of knowledgeable men. By implication neither of these justifications remains. The feudal and the religious must be replaced by the industrial and the scientific.

The third amplification, an important one, eventually, for Saint-Simonian theories of sexuality, was that societies, like individuals, were regulated by two moral forces of equal intensity and acting alternatively: the force of habit and the need for novelty. At the end of a certain time habits become bad, since they derive from conditions that no longer correspond to the real needs of society. The need for the new, which constitutes the real revolutionary state, has been expressed since the fifteenth century and will continue until a social system radically different from the feudal-religious system is established. In that new system people whose occupations and habits are pacific must exercise the primary influence, and among the peaceful, the most capable must direct national interests. The most capable are the artists, the scholars, and the industrialists.[13]

"Physiology" embodies most of the themes of Saint-Simon's thought, although it exhausts none of them. What certainly becomes clear from it is that "society" is reified into an organic being, whose "health" is dependent on proper "hygiene" and the proper functioning of its organs in harmony. Interestingly enough the imagery employed in "Physiology" is as often mechanical as organic—illustrating the transitional nature of the movement—but the message nevertheless remains clear. Society can be scientifically understood, and physiology is the science most appropriate for its understanding. The fundamental physiological law is cooperation.

There is amid all the divagations and apparent inconsistencies in Saint-Simon's thought an iron consistency. Physiology is on the verge of becoming a "positive" science, and, as Frank Manuel has so clearly shown, the roots of Saint-Simon's social understanding are to be found in his understanding of the history of scientific development.[14] As science is the basis

29

for his attack on social problems, so the possessors of scientific knowledge are to be the heroes of the social revolution he proclaimed. One of the leitmotifs running through his thought is the notion of the "alternativity" of approaches to a scientific understanding of historical epochs, of "critical" and "organic" dominance, of conflict and its resolution. But the fundamental laws of organic survival apply to individuals, to societies, to nations, to historical periods, and to the human species.

The body politic has had its history. Historical periods correspond to stages of development in the growth of the organism to maturity. The process of historical growth proceeds from crises to ever higher stages of organization, which themselves experience crises and breakdowns. Individuals and societies are perfectible and progressive. Each experience of crisis casts off that which is no longer appropriate to society's proper functioning and takes on that which is conducive to social health, efficient social organization, and the perpetuation of society.

The individual's relationship to this historical process lies in a duty to understand where history might be at a given moment and to hasten the historical process through work. Individuals, like societies, are creatures of habit and seekers after change. Work as the instrument of change becomes the embodiment of moral behavior. Moral behavior is that which moves history more swiftly between the banks that positive knowledge and reflection on experience have defined for it.[15]

The infinity of details in Saint-Simon's taxonomy of history and the infinite meanings attached to specific and ill-understood historical wholes do not, in themselves, merit much attention. What is important is that Saint-Simon, like many of his contemporaries—sometimes for similar reasons and sometimes for quite different ones—viewed the Middle Ages as a prime example of an organic epoch:

We affect a superb scorn for the centuries that are called the Middle Ages. We see there only a time of stupid barbarism and ignorance, of disgusting superstition, and we do not understand that it is the only time when the political system of Europe had been founded on a true base, on a general organization.[16]

The true base was faith, and the general organization was for conquest. The two, in Saint-Simon's opinion, complemented each other; they were, as he would put it, "homogeneous." In his medievalism Saint-Simon resembled some of his romantic contemporaries, who, casting back to the idealized model of the Middle Ages, hoped to find there the healthy roots of a new theocracy, a new monarchy. The Bonalds and Maistres were more royalist than the king, more papal than the pope, perhaps as a revolutionary in their delineation of a new social order based on the medieval past as Saint-Simon himself. The difference was that although Saint-Simon drew from them his admiration of that past and his conception of the organic society as something that was not only possible but had also, in fact existed, he also, somewhat more practically than they, viewed the light of that society as having been extinguished.

A new flame giving even more light must be lit. The Reformation had been the fatal fever of feudalism. Since the sixteenth century Europe had tended toward disorganization. The eighteenth century had erased feudal functions and, with them, their justifying principles embodied in religion.[17] In the nineteenth century science had outstripped the religion that had once unified society. The central problem of the nineteenth century was to replace the unifying power of the medieval church with an intellectual system and an institutional organization that would make society once more one.[18]

The ways by which this was to be done perhaps constitute Saint-Simon's most original, most appealing, and far-reaching insights. Peace should replace war, and cooperation, conflict through the agency of the *industriel*. The word had a double meaning, consciously played on by Saint-Simon, denoting all those who worked but, in particular, all those whose work was the providing of work.[19] The *industriel* came to dominate Saint-Simon's thought in the 1820s. He finally despaired of persuading the moneyed landowning class and the traditional-minded professionals and *rentiers* of the middle classes to invest their resources in a development and organization of labor materially transforming the productive capacities of the French nation.

Saint-Simon called the *industriel* to a revolution involving the undertaking of great works for public benefit, such as canals, roads and the drainage and forestation of wastelands. Increased agricultural production would be the first result of his program; expanded markets by means of improved communications, the second; interdependence of country and town, region and region, the third; and increased purchasing power and increased stimulus to production, the fourth.[20] What Saint-Simon foresaw was an ever-expanding economy spilling over from the backward village to the region, the nation, and the world in an endless and delirious process of productivity. It was his genuinely original, and not in the least utopian, vision that was to be realized in the century to come. Economic liberalism had preached the benefits of free trade, as would the Saint-Simonians, but it had hardly articulated the notion of an ever-growing economy providing sufficiency for all and thus eliminating the need for competition.

To be realized the vision required its acceptance as an achievable goal by those who possessed capital, and the mobilization of capital itself. The vision thus depended on those who knew how to accumulate capital to the best advantage — bankers — and on those who knew how to deploy it best — engineers. Ultimately, it depended on those who could invent a program—Saint-Simon himself, for example—and other "savants." And it depended on those who could dramatize and render "attractive" the results proposed—artists.

At various times in his career Saint-Simon appealed to the rich to support a subscription at the Tomb of Newton (women would be allowed to participate), to Louis XVIII to call a central budget committee, and to the rulers of France and England to take steps to unite the major material and spiritual powers of Europe. These appeals showed that he recognized the need for a central sanctioning authority behind his new system.[21]

Authoritarianism and the accompanying "stateism," which have been so much held against him were in fact functions of Saint-Simon's practicality. What needed to be done and what it was possible to do were perfectly clear. How one was to begin presented a problem. And it must be said that aware as Saint-Simon was of context, he could not help knowing that the possessors of French capital were unlikely to embark on economic adventures without state guarantees. The projects themselves were not viewed entirely by those whom he approached as expressions of madness. For extensive periods his publications were supported by some of the most eminent names in the French business community, among which one could even find a duc de la Rochefoucauld.

There was, however, a break with the past when Saint-Simon began to build his arguments for economic and social reorganization on the need for a "terrestrial morality," an attack on the Restoration church and on "feudal" society. The famous "Parabola," whose timing was unfortunate and whose argument was devastating, marked the opening of the final phase of Saint-Simon's work. In it the "industrialist" freed from his liberal chains becomes the hero of a new technological age dedicated to "the only reasonable and positive end that political societies can propose—the production of useful things."[22] Why? Because we must terminate the task of the first Christians. The code of Christian morality has linked all humanity by sentiment but not by interest. All people must in the future feel the reality of a common interest.[23] This view is quite different from that of the doctrine of the invisible hand arranging matters so that all individual enlightened self-interests add up to the common good. In Saint-Simon's view there is a common good prior to and often contrary to liberal egoism.

Nevertheless, Saint-Simon turned to those who had been most identified with the liberal creed of progress in elaborating the doctrine of the industrial society. He began by asking them to suppose what would happen "if" France were to lose "Monsieur, the brother of the king, Monseigneur the Duke of Angoulême, Monseigneur the Duke of Orléans, Monseigneur the Duke of Bourbon, Mademoiselle de Condé, . . . the great officers of the crown, the Cardinals, Bishop, Prefects, judges and the

10,000 richest proprietors of France who live nobly." Such an accident, wrote Saint-Simon, would afflict the French because they "are good-hearted and could not look with indifference on the simultaneous loss of so many of their compatriots." But the loss of those who in theory capped France's social pyramid would cause sorrow for purely sentimental reasons, "because no political harm would result from the loss."[24]

On the other hand, if France were to lose its three thousand most notable scientists, engineers, merchants, and bankers, "the real flower of French society, the nation would become a body without a soul." To be French is to be industrious. The day of the sluggard, the coupon clipper, the lawyer, and the feudal lord is at an end.[25] New principles of society demand new principles of authority and a new social hierarchy to wield that authority. *Industrial* as an adjective describes the society in which the new hierarchy administers all things in the interests of all men.

In the "Parabola," for once, Saint-Simon was thoroughly concrete and completely clear. He devotes the first two pages of the first issue of his series of essays, *L'Organisateur,* to listing those Frenchmen whom he sees as the "most essentially productive," and "the most useful to their country, those who bring it most glory, who contribute most to its civilization as well as its prosperity." The list includes bankers, merchants, iron manufacturers, tanners, printers, masons, locksmiths — all those most capable in the sciences, fine arts, crafts, and trades, adding up to the three thousand most able scholars, artists, and artisans of France.[26]

To the list is added an illuminating footnote, in which Saint-Simon acknowledges that *artisan* usually refers to a simple worker but that he means all those concerned with material production *and all those whom they employ.* Productive function is the real definer of social position. There is, for the moment at least, an identity of manager and employee with the common end they serve.

This first issue of the *Organisateur* probably received more immediate and widespread notice than anything else Saint-Simon wrote. Its appearance was followed shortly by the assassination of the heir to the throne, and it was viewed by the authorities as an incitement to that event. Saint-Simon successfully disengaged himself from these accusations, but they tended to disguise both the genuinely revolutionary character of the appeal and the kind of revolution that he prophesied.

Saint-Simon's socialism, it has already been argued, is best understood as sociology — the science of society. It never looked to the working classes for leadership, although it assumed that they would be participants in, and beneficiaries of, the new social order. Failure to bring about the new social order would mean class conflict and social disintegration. Saint-Simon's primary appeal was to the nascent group of middle-class business-men, entrepreneurs, and technicians as against the intransigent propertied classes, who would not see the social danger they were perpetuating or take steps to correct what they could not see. Like Marx a little later, Saint-Simon saw the industrial and commercial bourgeoisie as the most revolutionary class. His socialism was, in the most literal sense, bourgeois. It was to this class that he looked for the administration of men and things. Its members were to constitute a board of directors for society, whose shareholders would reap the benefits of wise administration. It is not without significance that in French *société* can mean "company" or "society" and that *sociétaires* can mean "shareholders" as well as members of society.[27] The play on words reflects exactly the Saint-Simonian understanding. But there is no suggestion that the shareholders might vote out the directors. Competence is manifest; incompetence is self-destructive.

The *industriels* did, however, pose some problems. Like Saint-Simon in his earlier days, they tended to subscribe to the principles of economic and political liberalism. They were much under the influence of the economist J. B. Say, with whom Saint-Simon himself had enjoyed cordial relations.[28] The difficulty, which Saint-Simon began to recognize in his last years, was that economic liberalism was essentially competitive and political liberalism was essentially egoist. The *industriels* could be neither. Their social object was well defined: the necessary conditions for their success were peace, order, and cooperation. The *industriels* had permitted themselves to become the tool of groups that were interested in power, conflict, and disorderly revolution. It would not do.

Society must be administered by those who know how to do it rather than governed by those who have simply seized power. "Administration," in the Saint-Simonian vocabulary, had implications beyond its ordinary meanings. Administration is the carrying out of what everybody agrees to. Government is the mediation among conflicting interests.[29] The point of the "Parabola" had been to flatter the French *industriel* to rise above the liberal vision, while profiting from its results, and to create a new hierarchical authority. In short, the *industriel* is to translate economic and intellectual power into political power.

Liberalism is revolutionary sickness. The search for individual gratification is symptomatic of a dangerously high social fever. The body politic must be cleansed of these ills, and the health of the organism must be encouraged in all its parts. But the parts of the body politic are ordered in hierarchical importance. Artists, scholars, and industrialists make up the brain, and the worker represents the cell. The old feudal order, to strain the comparison to the breaking point, can be seen as bodily waste.

There is also a problem for the bourgeois industrialist implicit in the role assigned to him. In a society where work is the passport to admission, function the determinant of class, and capacity the determinant of function, the roles of property and inheritance become questionable.

Saint-Simon clearly intended that people should be rewarded in accordance with the value and importance of their contribution—no more, no less. The Restoration bourgeois industrialist can be forgiven if this threat to his accumulation of fortune made him wary of the Saint-Simonian future. Balancing the Saint-Simonian attack on inherited position, however, was the assurance of Saint-Simonian economics that in the new society there would be enough for everybody and that all careers would be open to talented people. Once again the thrust of Saint-Simon's argument was not that the bourgeoisie should be eliminated. Rather, he insisted that the bourgeoisie should be an ever-renewing class—defined by function, open to everybody, perpetuated by competence, and indifferent to anterior fortune or circumstances of birth.

The benefits that Saint-Simon offered to both the directing class and the mass of society were work, assurance of the fulfillment of material needs, and appropriate opportunity. The object of industrial activity was a humane one: to alleviate material suffering and provide psychological security, peace, and the exercise of feeling and passion in the service of universally acknowledged and accepted human objectives. Body, soul, and mind were to exist in delicate and reciprocal balance. Each was of equal importance. Creating consciousness of the common interest of individuals and groups and of their capacity to associate was the most urgent task of the 1820s. Saint-Simon was the first to recognize that he might be called utopian in his belief in the ability of seemingly conflicting social and economic groups to join forces in the search for social peace.[30] Returning to one of his crucial ideas, that religion is the expression of the state of scientific knowledge at a given period, and now furnished with the principles of a science of society, he proposed the creation of a new Christianity.

Le Nouveau Christianisme takes the form of a dialogue between a "conservative" and an "innovator." The innovator professes a belief in God and in the perfection of His creation but distinguishes between God's message and what theologians have done with it. "The theory of Theology needs to be renewed at certain epochs as much as that of physics, or chemistry, or physiology."[31] That part of a religion that is divine is expressed in the dictum "men should act as brothers one to another." It is the most general principle humankind has ever employed, Saint-Simon tells us, the most elevated produced in the course of eighteen hundred years. The new Christianity, in applying this principle, will direct humanity toward the great end of the rapid betterment of the condition of the poorest and most numerous class. It will have its morality, its worship, its dogma; it will have its clergy, and the clergy will have its leaders.[32]

The leaders will be chosen from among those most capable of directing the works that will increase the well-being of the most numerous class.

The job of the clergy is to teach the faithful what their conduct ought to be in order to accelerate the arrival of the most numerous class at its destination.

Catholicism and Protestantism have both failed in their missions. They have lost sight of the spirit of Christianity, which comprises sweetness, goodness, charity, and, above all, loyalty and whose arms are persuasion and demonstration.

The program of the new Christianity would be to find a great number of works to accomplish, demanding the highest possible development of human intelligence. There should be a general plan to render the earth as productive and agreeable as possible. This program would accomplish more than charity possibly could, and by its means *the rich would enrich themselves while enriching the lives of the poor.*[33]

Saint-Simon is quite clear about his approach. "I have had first to address myself to the rich and powerful. . . . I have had to make artists, scholars, and industrial leaders feel that their interests were essentially the same as those of the mass of the people." While assuring the princes of Europe that the revolution he proposes will be a peaceful one, he nonetheless concludes that the new Christianity recognizes royal legitimacy only when kings employ their power in the interests of universal human betterment.[34]

Le Nouveau Christianisme contains other observations, on the means of making people *feel* as well think the new gospel, that were to be important to Saint-Simon's followers. There is an insistence on morality as the center of Christian belief and on the scientific and positive character of moral behavior. There is a fixing of particular means—great public works, built according to plan and executed by experts—by which this moral goal could be accomplished.

Saint-Simon had begun his philosophical career with a search for general principles. He sought always for a first principle. In science it had been Newton's laws of universal gravitation; in morality and religion it became "All men are brothers." One can suspect that Saint-Simon saw the force of gravity as a metaphor for the irresistible and universal spirit of association of which he dreamed. But in his mind science and society are one.

With *Le Nouveau Christianisme,* Saint-Simon reached a point of rest. Incorporating everything that had gone before, pointing to an imminent future, licensing a new religion and a new priesthood with broad powers, the essay—it is hardly more—validated Saint-Simon's dying assertion that his work was well in hand. But if all men are brothers, the Saint-Simon who was acutely conscious of context could not ignore two of the major forces of his time. The doctrine he had elaborated emphasized cooperation over competition, labor over laziness, peace over war, and universality over particularity. But in dealing with these concerns Saint-Simon had to face the very real presence of nations, in particular, England and France.

Saint-Simon's nationalism has not been given the attention it deserves. Much has traditionally been made of the French Revolution's impact on the national sentiment of those who were toppled. Saint-Simon's outlook suggests that France's defeat by England had a similar impact on at least one Frenchman. Did not France's defeat encourage Saint-Simon's search for and claim to some unique French genius that would outweigh in the scales of history Britain's indubitable military and economic superiority? His conception of the role of science and industry had to be derived from the most striking example of their success in his time: perfidious Albion, enemy of France and victor in the wars that had climaxed the eighteenth century.

Early in his career Saint-Simon had written:

A nation has to unite two sorts of superiority over all others to be decisively classed as first by impartial historians. These two sorts . . . are military and scientific. The English and the French are now rivals for first place. I hope that we have military superiority, but I can't hide that from the scientific point of view we are inferior, since it is the Englishman Bacon who is the patron of our philosophical school, since in physics it is Newton who serves as guide, and since the few words we babble on the science of man have been taught us by Locke. Newton, Bacon, and Locke are English, and our most distinguished scholars have been no more than commentators on them.[35]

It may well be that Saint-Simon's visit to England during the Peace of Amiens and his discovery that meat formed part of the daily diet of the ordinary family there had much to do with his views on the necessity of industrial organization and with the dual role that England was to play in his thought and the thought of his followers.[36] For if England was to be admired, she was also to be envied and despised. The English political system "has been produced by an insular people for its own use."[37] Such a people could not hope to achieve the elevated point of view necessary to embrace continental and island interests simultaneously. The English constitution had to be seen as intermediary between the feudal regime, which had been undermined in the preceding critical epoch, and the industrial regime, which would characterize the epoch presently gestating.

Since the English were admittedly superior in their grasp of practical politics, they would rush to recognize French superiority in "organic conception" and to accept a system in which "wise administration will be superimposed on existing political structure." The result would be a union "frank and indissoluble between the two most industrial peoples of the globe." The union of France and England in pursuit of the common objective of industrial and organic society would constitute the most considerable social force in the civilized world.[38]

A resolution of the conflict between nationalism and cosmopolitanism is implicit in the passages cited. Nations are organs of the body politic associated in support and perpetuation of social life and all human existence. Nations must not, however, conflict. They must cooperate to achieve a human good greater than the good of any of humanity's subdivisions. This resolution reveals the persistent pattern of Saint-Simonian thinking about nationalism, as well as underlining its obsessive concern with the organic model. Nationalism is recognized, but it is transformed from a warlike, divisive force into a cooperative, pacific, and constructive force. France is seen as the possessor of a particular and essential genius without which the new age cannot be built. But France's ability to achieve its goal rests necessarily, uncomfortably on English foundations. The activity of neither country has point without the other.

If France is to rank high among industrial societies, her industrialists must overcome their vision of affairs across the channel. English industrial success had been equated by French businessmen with political liberalism. Once again the English model serves as a source of both hope and frustration for Saint-Simon. He must simultaneously encourage the industrializing tendencies of French businessmen and discourage emulation of the political behavior that renders England "intermediary" between feudal and "administrative" society.[39]

Saint-Simon's view of the relationship of England and France was complex, compounded of envy, admiration, disgruntlement, pride, and puzzlement. But his nationalism was not merely a function of his Anglophobia. Love of country, legitimate national pride, and a sense of brotherhood also contributed to its formation. An appeal to the king is made. He is to found a council of two hundred civil engineers, fifty poets, and fifty artists. They will make a plan. Canals, roads, and reclamation of wastelands will provide work, lessen misery, and bind men together as brothers. These projects are to be not only useful but also beautiful. All France, Saint-Simon says, is to be turned into a superb *"parc a l'anglaise."* What only the rich had enjoyed now everybody will enjoy—and doubly, in that all have shared in its building and its rewards.[40]

Saint-Simon's disciples were to take up this hope for a national plan of work for the public good, and it was to inform their ambitions for fifty years after his death. Like him the Saint-Simonians were deeply immersed theoretically and practically in the advancement of the French nation.

Given this overwhelming concern for the national idea that emerges from Saint-Simon's own writings, what is left of his cosmopolitanism? One object of his program was to make France and England pilot experiments in the organization of humanity. These experiments were to be duplicated, in time, by other nations. One of his earliest appeals had been for the organization of a European parliament.[41] Eventually all people, European and American, Eastern and Western, would arrive at fundamental agreement. French glory would not derive from political domination but from general recognition of her role in the conception of a universally pacific and prosperous organization of the globe. British glory, an idea that would be developed in detail by the Saint-Simonians, would derive from providing the French with the material means to express this moral leadership and to make it real.[42]

The tensions between the national and the cosmopolitan do not disappear in Saint-Simonian theory. But the characteristic tendency of Saint-Simonianism was to seize on those ideas that fortified the central theme of the universality of the doctrine. One of the chief among those was the integration of the force of nations into the fabric of a new worldwide social and economic order. The organic analogy persisted. Nations had functions and occupied places in a hierarchy, but they were, like all other forms of life, interdependent. Conflict killed; cooperation created.

From the individual to the universal Saint-Simon sought and found general principles on which to build a new and, as he saw it, desperately needed social order. The difficulties he experienced in enunciating the principles have been noted. The circularity of his thought is evident. The problems with the system have been suggested. But when one looks at the totality of his views, one is struck by the internal solidity and consistency, the originality, and the power of intellect displayed. One comprehends something of the riches he left his disciples. His "utopianism," his "authoritarianism," are much less clearly established than his critics over the past century and a half would have us believe. His insights into his own society and into the probable nature of the future have in many ways been confirmed. His understanding of the role of the technocrat and the industrialist, his understanding of the weight of science and the search for belief, and his understanding of class and function have had vast consequences. His insistence on humans' social nature and the expansive powers of industrial activity have become all-pervasive.

Saint-Simon's hatred of war, his search for peace, and his appeal for international organization hardly need be defended in the last quarter of the twentieth century. Above all, the essentially human objective of his social philosophy, the betterment of the poorest and most numerous class, is not, as we have since his day discovered, totally divorced from considerations of personal freedom and personal fulfillment.

The weaknesses of Saint-Simonian theory in the eyes of those who opposed him during his lifetime or have done so since his death are real. We have quite properly learned to fear class selfishness, whatever the class involved, unbridled authority, and manipulated mass opinion. But the tendency to see in Saint-Simon the source of these evils should not blind us to those evils he fought. There were real and rational circumstances, at least before 1848, that might have led one to believe in the "utopian" association of classes so execrated by Marx. The label *utopian* has to be shared with the liberalism that Saint-Simon detested and that so distrusted him. No more than he have traditional liberals proved that certain political arrangements will faithfully guarantee the personal freedom of everyone. No more than he have they proved that a certain set of economic arrangements will provide a sufficiency for everyone. And unlike the traditional liberals Saint-Simon would never have written off a given percentage of the population as necessarily expendable in the economic struggle.

One aspect of Saint-Simon's thought that has never been given sufficient weight is that a corollary of function and competence is diversity. The organic society, by definition, not only had room for individual difference, but also had a demand for it. The unique characteristics of each human personality and the special contribution to the perpetuation of the whole of society were what Saint-Simon sought. This, in effect, was what he meant by the notion that freedom is not society's object but its consequence.

The solidarity Saint-Simon hoped for and preached found its source in a more complex and realistic understanding of both individuals and societies than that of his more "scientific" successors. Their scientism, class consciousness, and faith in working-class solidarity owed much to utopianism. His "socialism," discounted because it was not the exclusive possession of the workers, was, by that, more human. His authoritarianism belongs as much to his socialist successors as his utopianism belongs to his liberal rivals. The sins of Saint-Simon are not his exclusively.

Saint-Simon's virtues—his recognition of the enormous crisis facing the nineteenth century, of the enormous possibilities inherent in that century, and of means and methods for dissolving one and realizing the other— constituted his legacy to his disciples. On his deathbed he adjured them to greet the star of the nineteenth century at its rising. It would be the disciples who, in time, would become the high priests of the new Christianity, although their initial effort was to spread the message: "The meaning of the labors of my whole life is the giving to all members of society the greatest latitude for the development of their abilities."[43]

CHAPTER III

THE YOUNG TECHNOCRATS

THAT A NEW RELIGION was to be one of the brightest stars of the nineteenth century was not a fact immediately visible to the earliest Saint-Simonians. *Le Nouveau Christianisme* appeared early in 1825, and by November Prosper Enfantin was writing from Paris to a possible convert at Lausanne: "You have made some objections relative to *Le Nouveau Christianisme.* I have to say to you that it is a subject on which I feel little disposition to follow Saint-Simon. . . . I have to avow that, not understanding popular religious feeling, I haven't yet discovered a way of thinking about it."[1]

These doubts seem to have been shared, for the moment at least, by the other men who on June 1 had formed the Saint-Simonian Society and whose intention it was to publish a weekly journal. The title of the journal, *Le Producteur,* made it clear that Saint-Simon's ideas on production and its organization were to occupy center stage. While convinced of the virtues of the Master, the followers were equally aware of his shortcomings. The "bizarre"[2] fashion in which Saint-Simon had expressed himself and the fear of being seen as utopians[3] led the group to color all its articles "so that the public can interest itself in the form without completely understanding the foundation."[4] The Saint-Simonians hoped to find a nucleus of reasonable men "who read to learn, not to amuse themselves."[5] It was also Enfantin's idea that the Ecole Polytechnique "must be the canal through which our ideas flow into society; it is the milk imbibed at our dear school that must nourish the generations to come. There we learned precise language and methods of research and demonstration that today must be the motive force of political science."[6]

There is irony in these expressions of doubt and affirmation. Subsequent generations of writers have chosen to believe that the Saint-Simonians, in forming a religion, betrayed and falsified the intent and purpose of Saint-Simon. The reverse is true. The betrayal, if there was any, lay in the resistance to the adoption of religious themes during the initial period of the movement, when emphasis was placed on the instrumental and technocratic aspects of Saint-Simon's teaching.

The bent of these founding Saint-Simonians was far from religious. Certain of the subscribers, Dr. Bailly, for example, probably regarded their support as an expression of loyalty to Saint-Simon and the journal as a kind of memorial to him. Others, such as the bankers Jacques Laffitte, Jacques Ardoin, and Guillaume-Louis Ternaux, long familiars of Saint-Simon and intrigued by Rodrigues's or Enfantin's intelligence, may well have been moved, in this first year of the reign of Charles X, by the political ambitions that would bear fruit in the Revolution of 1830. To subsidize a press venture friendly to businessmen and bankers made good sense. The younger men who were to carry on the real work of the journal were at this point more moved by the notions of economic transformation and social regeneration than by the religious needs that many of them, in time, would feel deeply.

The lives of three of these young men would henceforth be confounded with the history of Saint-Simonianism. These were Olinde Rodrigues, Saint-Amand Bazard, and Prosper Enfantin. Each brought with him to the movement a world and a point of view markedly different from the others'. Their similarities have already been touched on. They were young, ambitious, outside the society of Restoration France, in one fashion or another, thwarted, critical, but finding echoes of themselves and their respective talents in the teachings of Saint-Simon. The three men had remarkably vigorous and vivid personalities, intelligence (though not of the very highest order), and good looks. The movement came to prize all three qualities.

The living link with Saint-Simon and the older circle that had surrounded him in his last days was Rodrigues. A photograph by Nadar of Rodrigues in middle life reveals a Lincolnesque face that conveys a sense of the tragic. There is coarse, thick, dark hair; a beard framing the line of the jaw; thick, dark, down-turning eyebrows above deep-set eyes; an aquiline nose with widely flaring nostrils; and a wide, thin-lipped mouth. The lines around the eyes and those defining the sharply planed cheeks suggest both weariness and humor.

Rodrigues was the scion of a family of Sephardic Jews who had settled in Bordeaux. His father, Isaac, had become an accountant, written books on the subject, and eventually moved to Paris. There he had worked for the Fould banking house, had become a stockbroker, and had, incidentally, taught bookkeeping to the young Gustave d'Eichthal and to his nephews Emile and Isaac Pereire. These last three were to play essential roles in the development of Saint-Simonianism and in the perpetuation of its ideas. By 1825 Olinde Rodrigues and his brother Eugène had begun to follow their father's career in banking.

But Olinde had had other ambitions. He had been sent to the Lycée Napoléon, an unusual event for a Jew in his time, and had been a tutor for the Ecole Polytechnique. He had earned a doctorate in mathematics (suitably enough, for a future Saint-Simonian, on the subject of the "attraction" of spheroids) but had also been discouraged from entering the Ecole Normale and had thus been denied the university career he sought.

At the Lycée Napoléon Rodrigues had introduced d'Eichthal to Auguste Comte, who in turn presented d'Eichthal to Saint-Simon. Rodrigues had succeeded Comte as Saint-Simon's chief disciple and had first known Saint-Simon about the time of the suicide attempt in 1823.[7] Rodrigues's world was first that of a Jewry in the earliest stages of assimilation into French society, then that of a financial and business society whose rules were beginning, but only beginning, to change, and finally that of a technically trained intellectual elite.

Among the founders of Saint-Simonianism, Rodrigues was the most disposed to follow the religious inclination of the Master. He had been closely associated with the writing of *Le Nouveau Christianisme,* his family had already moved away from Orthodox Jewish practice, and traditional Christianity was suspect. Where should one go? What should one believe? The religion of humanity provided an answer to these questions, but whether out of calculation or conviction it was the businessman, the mathematician, and the engineer who presided over the beginnings of *Le Producteur.*

The best known in 1825 of the three leaders, although he was not of the founding group and had not himself known Saint-Simon, was Bazard. Almost no one, d'Eichthal was to comment, came to Saint-Simon who had not known some painful personal or family crises. In Bazard's case it was his adulterine birth, which caused the separation of his parents, that was the source of pain. Bazard never knew his actual father until the time of his own marriage, and the success of that marriage was compromised by an "ill-engaged wedding night." Mme Bazard had been "raised on the knees of Volney and the Abbé Morellet," and was the daughter of a "Revolutionary" bishop, Joubert. Claire Bazard, like her husband, would have a central role to play in Saint-Simonian discussions of marriage, family, the role of women, and sexuality.[8]

But in 1825 Bazard was best known to the public as a friend and protégé of the marquis de Lafayette and as a political conspirator. He had been in 1819 an employee of the internal customs administration, a Freemason, and with Philippe-Joseph-Benjamin Buchez a founder of the Lodge of the Friends of Truth, whose "solemn puerilities" served as a mask for political action on the part of the young.[9] The lodge was most active in the schools of Law, Medicine, and Pharmacy, but on Bazard's suggestion it also began to recruit from the ranks of young commercial apprentices. The lodge was thus in a position to take part in popular agitation. The assassination of the duc de Berri in 1820 (which had caused trouble for Saint-Simon) and the Belfort conspiracy of the same period ushered in a policy of severe government repression of political dissidence.

In 1821, forced underground, Bazard, J. T. Flotard, and Buchez founded the French Carbonari, whose object was "to return to the French nation the free exercise of its right to choose the government that suits it best." The striking feature of the Carbonari was organization. It had a center, the Haut Vente, and subsidiary Ventes Centrales and Ventes Particulieres. Each of these outlets had no more than twenty members, thus avoiding the prohibitions of the law on associations. The groups could multiply to infinity unknown to one another, and they pledged to obey blindly the orders of unknown chiefs. Lafayette was apparently involved in the central organization, but its plans for general insurrection did not succeed.[10]

By 1825 Bazard was interested in more peaceful means of social regeneration and entered the Saint-Simonian group by way of Auguste Cerclet, who later would edit *Le National* and the *Journal des Débats*. What Bazard brought to Saint-Simonianism, then, was an essentially political outlook. Louis Blanc described his soul as "male,"[11] admitting only clear ideas, holding on to revolutionary instincts, having a taste for easily applicable theories, and hating vigorously. But with all this Bazard was slow, methodical, heavy of intellect, and anxious in manner. His tenderness was not "calming"; he spent hours correcting the notebooks of his children and sermonizing on the results. He was the oldest of the founding group and physically of a type the French describe as *"beau garçon."* He was conventionally handsome, with regular features, flashing eyes, and curling hair. His age, his method, and his apparent gravity would mark him out as a logical spokesman for the school when it moved from the printing press to the public stage. What Bazard offered at the beginning was his intense hatred of official Restoration society, experience in administration and organization, important liberal political connections, and a group of like-minded adherents who would follow him into the doctrine. Among these were Buchez, a fellow Carbonari who in time was to become a noted Social Catholic; Mme Bazard's niece Cécile Fournel and her husband, Henri, who would approach the movement from different directions; the economist Adolphe Blanqui; and the journalist and publicist Armand Carrel.

Like Bazard, Enfantin had from birth to cope with irregularities in his personal life. Born illegitimate in 1796 (the *mœurs* of the Directory seem to have been a sore trial for its progeny) and subsequently legitimized, Enfantin was further marked by the failure of his father's bank, the uneasy *ménage* maintained by his parents, and his mother's formidable temper.[12] Balancing these sources of insecurity, however, was his father's connection with the Nugues family, which was landed, important in the Napoleonic armies, and engaged in wine bottling and distribution in the Dauphiné region at Romans. Among these relatives Enfantin was always an object of concern, love, understanding—and influence. It was their influence that found him a place at the Lycée Napoléon in 1810. Three years later, with the help of Olinde Rodrigues, who was then a tutor at the lycée, Enfantin was received at the Ecole Polytechnique.[13]

The Ecole Polytechnique was of capital importance for the history of the Saint-Simonian movement. It had been created to provide engineers, military and civil, to the French state at a moment of great need. It had been the home, under the Directory, the Consulate, and the Empire, of some of the major mathematical and scientific minds of the age. Saint-Simon himself had looked to it for inspiration and had sought among its students for disciples (Comte had been the most notable success). The programs of the school were technical, pragmatic, and, in the eyes of at least one commentator, antihumanistic. Hayek has argued that we owe our notions of social engineering, planning, and all that the contemporary world equates with technocracy to the founding of the Ecole Polytechnique. He sees technocracy as the creation of the engineer and equates Saint-Simonianism with the engineers who contributed so much to the doctrine.[14]

For Hayek the engineering mentality is related to the "ideal of conscious control of social phenomena."[15] He tells us that "most of the schemes for a complete remodeling of society bear . . . the distinct mark . . . of the engineering point of view."[16] The salient feature of the engineer, determining his outlook, is that "his characteristic tasks are usually in themselves complete; he will be concerned with a single end, control the efforts directed towards this end, and dispose for this purpose of a definitely given supply of resources."[17] The application of engineering techniques to society requires that the director possess the same complete knowledge of the whole society that the engineer possesses of his limited world. Central economic planning is nothing but such an application of engineering principles to the whole of society, based on the assumption that such a concentration of all relevant knowledge is possible.

It is from this basis that Hayek attacks the "counterrevolution of science" and links engineers, *polytechniciens,* and eventual Saint-Simonians. Saint-Simon had declared that in the past "if one wanted to know whether somebody had received a distinguished education one asked, 'Does he know Greek and Latin authors well?' Today one asks, 'Is he good at mathematics? Is he familiar with the achievements of physics, of chemistry, of natural history; in short, of the positive sciences and those of observation?'"[18]

Hayek maintains that those questions of Saint-Simon are the starting point for "a whole generation . . . to whom the great storehouses of social wisdom, . . . the great literature of all the ages, was a closed book. For the first time in history that new type appeared who was regarded as educated because he had passed through difficult schools but who had little or no knowledge of society, its life, growth, problems and its values which only the study of history and literature can give."[19]

The Hayek argument is worth attention, because it does establish a takeoff point, perhaps arguably, for the origins of technocracy. It further links technocracy to the Ecole Polytechnique, the Polytechnique to the engineers, and the engineers to the Saint-Simonian school. These links make good sense, but the inner content of the argument needs closer examination.

We can perhaps accept the model of the ideal engineer, and we know that many engineers who passed through the Ecole Polytechnique would become Saint-Simonians. What is less clear is that these Saint-Simonians were the ideal engineers of Hayek's model or the builders of the road to serfdom. Enfantin is a case in point. The Polytechnique was the major formative experience of his life. There he was "loved by all." Comte may have thought him mediocre, but his reference to "our dear school" and the lessons he learned there indicates that he did indeed partake of the "engineer's mentality." On the other hand, there was always in Enfantin "the merchant in search of an honest fortune."[20] The Polytechnique was, before 1815, one of the best available avenues for attaining that goal. It has been said that in 1810 there were only two hundred trained engineers in all France. Obviously, careers could be made in the field. The school, drawing on, and creating, a highly self-conscious elite, also created an esprit de corps in its students that would be valuable whatever path a graduate might follow. To have been an "X," the nickname given to students of the school, was in the last days of the Empire, and would continue to be, a social and financial passport.[21]

Enfantin, like many other *polytechniciens,* was clever, engaging, and careerist. It is not surprising that he and his contemporaries were drawn to an economic and social program that was so clearly directed to their training and talents. But if these young men came to Saint-Simonianism, it was precisely because they felt a void in their lives that could be filled only by social action and the alleviation of human needs. Technocrats they were. If, however, the engineers as a consequence of their training lacked humanistic purpose, they were well aware of the fact and eventually saw Saint-Simonianism as a means of repairing the lack and of making technocracy humane.

The search for humanity and the keen sense of social injustice that Enfantin shared with the other founding Saint-Simonians had, by his own account, its beginning in his personal experiences during that crucial turning point for a generation, the defeat of the Napoleonic Empire. Enfantin had been in process of moving with the école to Fontainebleau at the moment of the arrival of the coalition armies at Paris. He had participated with his classmates, bravely, in the defense of the city. So, incidentally, had Bazard, who received the cross of the Legion of Honor for his courage. Enfantin's outraged parents had condemned the school for exposing their nineteen-year-old son to such dangers. On returning from the battle Enfantin was greeted by a flung book and a three-day maternal silence.[22]

More importantly, the end of the Empire meant the end of Enfantin's career at school. The Restoration was not going to be favorably disposed to the relatives of Napoleonic generals. What the future held was made clear to Enfantin when he was presented, with the hope of a commission, to M. d'Hautepoul, lieutenant of the Royal Bodyguards. The reception was initially favorable. Enfantin's technical training would be useful in forming an artillery division. But what did his father do? Where was his business? Had the bankruptcy been liquidated? From this experience Enfantin drew conclusions about the effect that his family background would have on his entire life. Upset, he refused to pursue the commission, and the Royal Guards did not pursue him.[23]

Taken as a secretary, during the Hundred Days, to the Italian campaign, Enfantin finally returned to Romans and there fell in love for the first time. "I still recall the minor details of my virginal love. . . . I lay at her feet in fields of clover, I kissed her hands. . . . The father refused me for the same motives as M. d'Hautepoul. This second rebuff was decisive for me."[24]

The links of property and love, property and influence, and property and family were in these experiences made clear to Enfantin. They would indeed touch all his life, but in ways that as a youth he could hardly foresee. His definition as the son of a bankrupt, the denial of love in favor of property, were wounds from which he did not recover. The personal injustice that Enfantin suffered was the well from which he drew his scorn for his society. The themes of property, inheritance, and sexuality interwoven were to sustain his thought and his actions for nearly fifty years.

Eventually escaping from "bottle washing" and "vat filling" at Romans, the disillusioned Enfantin traveled in 1821 as a wine merchant in France and Germany. On his travels he encountered the closest and dearest friend of his life, François Arlès-Dufour. Then, on his father's advice and with his aid, he took a partnership in a newly formed bank at Saint Petersburg. He lived in Russia for nearly three years, and the experience was important in two ways. It involved a complicated, stormy, and highly romantic affair with the wife of a colleague. More important in the long run, however, was Enfantin's encounter with a group of *polytechniciens, en mission* in Saint Petersburg. With them he engaged in a course of reading and discussion. It was there that he made his first acquaintance with political economy. He was particularly drawn by one Storch, who attempted to translate economic classifications into moral categories. After three years Enfantin left his mistress fainting in the arms of his schoolmates Lamé and Clapeyron. After a brief stay at the Nugues home, Curson, where he contracted yet another liaison that was also to be a constant in his future life (see the next chapter), he returned to Paris.[25]

There, in 1824, he found Olinde Rodrigues again. The two men reviewed Enfantin's economic studies. Rodrigues brusquely declared that they had had no value, refused to examine Enfantin's moral-economic charts, and demanded that he pay attention to him. "When he made me hear *Le Nouveau Christianisme* in Saint-Simon's presence, I was so shocked by the form that the foundation escaped me—it is the lot of all those books that appear at a moment when mass society can't understand them." This reading of *Le Nouveau Christianisme* by Rodrigues was the only time Enfantin was to have any meaningful contact with Saint-Simon. It was also the occasion on which Saint-Simon's dog tried to bite him. Significantly, Rodrigues never told Enfantin what Saint-Simon had said of the encounter—and Enfantin never asked.[26] One report, not wholly to be trusted, asserted that Saint-Simon had described Enfantin as a "nothing."[27] If so, Saint-Simon was wrong.

Enfantin later described himself as "one of those lovable beings who is followed."[28] It was an accurate description, and his attributes, lying somewhere between intellectual distinction and athletic prowess, were those that the admissions offices of American universities like to see as related to "leadership." By 1825 Enfantin had certainly had a wide experience of the world, had traveled much, and was enthusiastically admired by many of his former peers at the Polytechnique. His contemporaries were united in their estimation of his extraordinary good looks. The portrait available from this period is, consequently, puzzling. It depicts a dandy wearing a widely padded and puffed coat, broad stock, and cravat. He is carefully barbered and pleasant looking but with something of a softness or lack of definition in the face. Enfantin's appearance was to change radically in the next years, but one has to assume that in the flesh he was more striking than the portrait suggests.

At a later date Laffitte's English partner Blount would sum up Enfantin "as that rare combination difficult to find outside France, of the mad visionary, the polished man of society, and the shrewd man of affairs."[29] It was, perhaps, the last Enfantin who led *Le Producteur* to concentrate on the categorical imperative of Saint-Simonian thought: the call to apply the scientific knowledge of competent experts to the solution of the problems of society. It was this call that could unite, up to a point, liberal bankers and businessmen, radical political revolutionaries, and state-trained engineers in search of careers and fortunes. Their common enemy was a political Restoration that threatened the advances of a new class of adventurous entrepreneurs born in the Revolution, that stifled free speech and broadly representative government, and that blocked the expectations of a generation born in glory and matured in defeat.

Of all this *Le Producteur* only hinted. It was not a declared organ of Saint-Simonian propaganda, and it brought together many people who were only marginally interested in the movement. Capitalized at 50,000 francs with Rodrigues and Cerclet as secretary-general and editor, *Le Producteur* called on Adolphe Blanqui, Comte, and others who stood in an uneasy relationship to the doctrine of the faithful. The *Producteur* circle quickly became visible as such in Parisian society. Its members were to be seen at Lafayette's Tuesday salons and at weekly dinners in the fashionable Prévôt restaurant in the Palais Royal. The editors met in the rooms of Rodrigues, Enfantin, Cerclet, and, eventually, Bazard. That process of imperceptible diffusion of Saint-Simonian ideas, characteristic of the movement for the next years, had begun. Cerclet brought Bazard, and P.-M. Laurent was introduced by Carrel. Michel Chevalier, Abel Transon, and Euryale Cazeaux, students living in the same house as Enfantin's friend Lambert, asked to be included. Rodrigues brought his younger brother Eugène and his Pereire cousins to the circle. And all these brought back from their encounters to their banks, offices, and schools word of a new dispensation seemingly issued precisely for men like themselves.[30]

The first issue of *Le Producteur* appeared in October 1825. Its prospectus announced that economists had been concerned with material production but had not felt the importance of moral and intellectual production. The editors of *Le Producteur* wished to develop the notion of productivity in its largest sense. They hoped to unify scholars, industrialists, and artists in drawing society out of its evident crisis. They wished to bring about the definitive triumph of work over idleness, of positive capacities over vague knowledge. A new social system was needed, and a positive character must be given to the moral sciences. The exclusive reign of imagination was over. Industrialists and particularly bankers must achieve an understanding of their own importance. "Our journal has for its end the development and expansion of the principles of a new philosophy based on a new conception of human nature. The end of the species . . . is to exploit and modify external nature to its—the species'—greatest advantage."[31]

The means to be used in reaching this goal were physical, intellectual, and moral. The methods of the doctrine would be recognized as progressive, because they were based on a scientific understanding of history. Each generation added its riches to those of the past, with knowledge becoming constantly more extensive, certain, and positive. The increased knowledge of natural law would permit additions and rectifications of the acts of the doctrinaire. The new philosophy would become increasingly certain of its destiny and its capacity to develop the principle of association. "The battle is over, we must fight no more, liberty is won, we must now profit from it."[32]

This first Saint-Simonian salvo merits examination. To repeat, the foundations of Saint-Simonian thought were systematic, rational, pragmatic, and inclusive; its parts were mortised inextricably together. What was to follow was implicit in *Le Producteur*'s manifesto. First, there is nothing in it that does not find its origin in the thought of Saint-Simon himself. Notably, the program is not announced as his, nor does it include a concern for the new Christianity. It does deal with moral as well as intellectual and physical regeneration. Emphasis is on production, work, and precise knowledge brought to bear, through the association of the competent, on the exploitation and modification of external nature. There is nothing utopian in the enunciation of the principles, nothing at all romantic in the goal; nothing in any way conflicts with Saint-Simon's vision. For a hundred and fifty years the founders of *Le Producteur* have been accused of these shortcomings with no justification whatsoever.

Equally important, given the developments to come, was the proper Saint-Simonian emphasis placed on history as an open system. Change was seen as a constant; knowledge accumulated; rectification of error was automatic. This conception of progress was closely tied to the Saint-Simonian understanding of liberty. A generation later Leo Tolstoy in the second epilogue to *War and Peace*[33] would state what the Saint-Simonians had already sensed: the accumulation of natural law defined the areas of human freedom. The more law we know, the less free we are. The Saint-Simonians had committed themselves in *Le Producteur* to the battle of organization versus freedom. They would say, however, that without organization there could be no freedom.

Certainly much in *Le Producteur*'s manifesto was disingenuous. Enfantin's family had worried about the political implications of the journal. He hastened to reassure them that on its appearance they would understand how it proposed to spread an understanding of the relationship between political economy and social organization: "'political economy' becomes 'industrial philosophy,' politics is 'social physiology.'" The terminology would give a "positive," "scientific" tone to political discussions and would abandon the "liberal metaphysics" of the "rights of man," a metaphysics that made power tremble because of its destructive eighteenth-century role. These were the only subterfuges to which the editors would resort.[34]

The manifesto did squarely meet the question of contemporary liberalism in two ways: (1) in its insistence on industrial association rather than industrial competition and (2) in its final declaration that the liberal metaphysic was passé and irrelevant:

We tend toward an epoch when those things of most interest to social well-being will be directed by the men most capable of appreciating their productive power. Thus you will see in the first issue an article on the joint stock company, which facilitates the most productive use of the capital of the idle, and articles on the new means of communication adopted in England (railroads), which tend, in bringing distances together, to conform the interests of the provinces and states through the common link of production. All these articles will include some general considerations of the social future that will not be totally foreign to politics but that will not deal directly with the subject.[35]

The articles during the first half of *Le Producteur*'s fourteen-month life were overwhelmingly specific and technical in character. They embodied the belief of the liberal economist J. B. Say, cited in one of them, that "under all forms of government a State can prosper if it is well administered."[36] The irrelevance of partisan politics in the face of overwhelming and evident social need provided the basis for the glorification of the administrator, for the assertion that the person who knew how to do a thing ought to do it and that the person who knew what ought to be done should be obeyed. When positive knowledge existed, argument was futile. "We do not talk of freedom of conscience in physics or chemistry" wrote Bazard, and he and his fellows were asserting a like precision of knowledge and a like irrelevancy in the "sciences" of economics and society.[37]

Irrelevancy was an important concept, because in some sense the Saint-Simonians were playing a double game. They did not wish to arouse the fears of Restoration authority. Nor did they wish to arouse the ire of the liberal theoreticians and businessmen from whom they could expect a certain amount of support and whom they hoped to convert to the wiser ways of politically neutral, technocratic administration. To preach the irrelevancy of creeds in the face of the necessity for acts was also to preach Saint-Simonian authoritarianism, the division of society by capacities, and the slogan "from each according to his capacities; to each according to his works."

For the Saint-Simonian, freedom was the result of the right people fulfilling their individual nature in the right place. Obedience to the laws of one's own nature was liberty. Such liberty could exist only if economic and social life were organized to achieve it. Resources as well as people needed to be associated; credit should be widely available; business organization should be more flexible so that great communications might be undertaken, not by and for individuals but on a social scale. The consequence would be the expansion of opportunity for the expression of each talent.

It is easy, as it always has been, for critics of Saint-Simonianism to point out fallacies of reasoning in the argument of *Le Producteur*. The fallacies are, nonetheless, fewer than has been generally supposed. The chief naiveté of the group, however, was to suppose that their views would not arouse alarm and condemnation among all those whom they wished for the time being to placate. The high priest of French political liberalism, Benjamin Constant, condemned the new doctrines in a public lecture at the Athenée, thus giving them wide publicity.

Bazard and Constant met on one famous occasion at one of Lafayette's "Tuesdays." Constant launched into a performance of a kind familiar on the French stage, railing against all philosophic doctrines and all social direction emanating from above to those below. He illustrated his point with a crushing enumeration of all the evils that came from on high: hail, snow, thunder, deluges. At the conclusion of this tirade Bazard remarked sweetly, "Ah! Monsieur Constant, you forgot to mention only one thing—the light!" Constant turned away, leaving Bazard master of the battlefield.[38]

The story is quite perfect and apparently not apocryphal. It sums up the overwhelming conviction pervading all Saint-Simonian thought. In later years the Saint-Simonians would insist to their critics, enemies, and one another on certain points: their sincerity, their right to their own understanding of freedom, and the "provisional" and "progressive" character of the doctrine at any of its stages. The force of authority would always be subjected to the light of experience. Doctrine and dogma were not synonymous.

This last characteristic was very clear in the work of *Le Producteur*. In effect the contributors were invited to provide material for a never-ending seminar on questions of key importance to the Saint-Simonian outlook. Every view was possible and provided the occasion for useful discussion. Every industrial innovation might offer an opportunity.

Enfantin wrote on the limited-liability company, advocated the progressive lowering of rents, and reviewed Léon Halévy's *Résumé of the History of the Ancient Jews*. Comte, Rodrigues, Bazard, and the journalist Michel Rouen contributed articles on such subjects as "Philosophic Considerations on the Sciences and Men of Learning," "Considerations on the Present State of Industry and Commerce in Egypt," and "General Thoughts on Industry." From January to March, 1826, there were articles on discount banking, on cosmopolitan bankers, on the respective usefulness of railways and canals, on "the facts that tend to prove the tendency of society to organize," on "competition in industrial enterprise," on "The Influence of Public Holidays on the Well-Being of Society," and "On the Partisans of the Past and Those of Liberty of Conscience."[39]

What is striking about the list is that it not only represented the current interests of the group but also introduced those questions and activities that were to make the Saint-Simonians famous less as journalists than as men of action. The articles on Egypt and the Jews foreshadowed Saint-Simonian orientalism and plans for Suez; those on banks and banking

carried in them the seeds of the Credit Mobilier; that on railways anticipated all the activities of the Saint-Simonian engineers and financiers
during the July Monarchy and the Second Empire.

Comte recapitulated the themes of Saint-Simon. Enfantin wrote that
"modern societies must organize for peace as the ancient Romans organized for war. Public occasions should call the attention of the multitudes
to their common interests." Throughout *Le Producteur* there are references to the "spirit of association," a catch phrase that was to become
universal in the political, social, and economic discussions of the 1830s
and 1840s. Capital and capitalists, nations and peoples, workers of every
description must unite: "It is no more a question of being independent,
but of being happy; no more a question of separating one's self by civil,
political, national, or other liberty, but of finding the links that ought to
unite men."[40]

In France the spirit of association was developing slowly and in limited
fashion; its industry was inferior to that of England. Certainly lack of
intelligence was not to blame. It was not even true that French capital was
insufficient; it simply needed wider distribution. "Our speculators place
the totality of their fortunes in one enterprise directed by themselves.
When unforeseen circumstances arise, they are totally ruined."[41]

The strategy of the first two semesters of *Le Producteur*'s publication is
clear. The journal was indeed designed to attract support from wherever
it might come and was hiding under the neutral cover of the need for
economic, industrial, and technical organization. It flattered those already working in industry, who possessed technical skills and talents. It
preached, by a variety of examples, the virtues of association and cooperation. Where these directions fitted into the larger theory was obvious to
the Saint-Simonians, although not yet insisted upon. The virtues of
knowledge and capacity and the authority they conferred began to emerge
as central and troublesome to any doctrine of technocracy. There was little, as yet, to be read about the betterment of the poorest and most numerous class, nothing about religion, and nothing directly and explicitly
dangerous to the regime in power. To be sure, Stendhal accused the Saint-
Simonians of a *complot contre les industriels,* but the fact is of more
interest to literary history than to Saint-Simonianism.[42]

There *had* begun during these first months of publication a process that
would be characteristic of Saint-Simonianism for the next seven years.
While publication of theory proceeded at one level, discussion of the
meaning and direction of the doctrine was proceeding at a deeper and
more intense level. *Le Producteur* made some noise in intellectual circles.
The reactions of Constant and Stendhal had helped. But the sad truth was
that the technical discourse of the journal, the rather heavy style, were
thought dull. In a romantic decade the dismal science seemed more dismal

than ever. Readers were few; even the *polytechniciens* voted against sub-
scribing to the journal, which they thought *"ennuyeux."*[43]

In April 1826 *Le Producteur* announced its transformation from a weekly to a monthly and the withdrawal of Cerclet and some others from its
board. This defection signaled the first of many schisms which were to
mark Saint-Simonian history.

Behind the announced changes was the shared conviction of Enfantin,
Bazard, and Rodrigues that the veil should be lifted and the visage of
Saint-Simon revealed in all the pages of the journal. Polemic and the
proclamation of the new vision of humanity would draw more attention
than the deceptively general and neutral tone of the first phase of publication. Attached to this decision were difficulties in the administration of
the magazine. Cerclet was, in effect, discharged, less because of editorial
disagreements than because of his role in the life of Comte. Comte's first
wife was a former prostitute whom he had first known as such. Subsequently she had been set up by Cerclet in a bookstore in the Palais Royal.
There Comte met her once again in 1822 and married her. *Le Producteur*
brought this triumvirate together again. The Saint-Simonians believed
that Cerclet's intervention in the Comtes' domestic life precipitated
Comte's first psychological collapse in 1826.[44]

Although he had not participated in the editorial meetings, Comte was
a figure of importance in the eyes of Saint-Simon's followers. He had been
Saint-Simon's secretary for seven years, he was the author of the third
book of the *Catéchisme des industriels, système de politique positive.*
Despite having quarreled with the Master, Comte was the most authoritative representative of his thought. He had contributed to *Le Producteur*
and was in this same winter of 1825–26 attracting attention with a series
of public lectures that would eventually appear as *Cours de philosophie
positive.* The father of positivism's relationship with Saint-Simon and the
Saint-Simonians had always been uneasy. They would from this time forward be frankly inimical. Frank Manuel has sensibly examined the question of primacy and plagiarism in the work of Comte and Saint-Simon,
and such questions certainly loomed large in Comte's mind.[45] Comte's
break with Saint-Simonianism was not simply a matter of the "anecdotal
and picturesque," present though these elements were, but it raised, perhaps for the first time, a question that has never ceased to plague any
understanding of Saint-Simonianism: what *was* a Saint-Simonian?

Insofar as Comte had been encouraged by Saint-Simon, insofar as he
had contributed to Saint-Simon's doctrine, and insofar as he had collab-
orated with the group, he must be considered up to 1826 as among the
faithful. He was not *only* a Saint-Simonian in the course of his life, but he
was so for some good and important part of it. And Comte's positivism
was certainly shaped by his earlier experiences. What is true of him is true

of a number of other schismatics who will be found in these pages. The notion that Saint-Simonianism was a bloc and that its believers were either subscribers to the total doctrine or to none of it is based on naive psychological principles and is contrary to fact.

The interesting question is not how much intellectual baggage those who parted with the doctrine left behind them. Such questions cannot be answered with quantitative precision. But in the case of a Buchez, for example, it makes more sense to suppose that his social Catholicism was an outgrowth of Saint-Simonian experience than to suppose that it was written on a tabula rasa. "What would a Buchez have been without Saint-Simonianism?" is a proper question. A like question could be asked of the lives of many of the group. Hippolyte Carnot, who did not follow Enfantin to the end of the doctrine, sums up this aspect of the movement very well: "Serious minds . . . will remember that the thought of individual and social perfectibility and the sentiment of human solidarity have nowhere been professed and practiced with more sincere ardor than in the Saint-Simonian school."[46]

Carnot was not alone in his assessment and is a good example of those who drank of the Saint-Simonian spring without drowning in it.

Halévy, Carrel, de Caen, and Bodin followed Cerclet out of *Le Producteur* (some would return to the movement), leaving the work of the next period largely in the hands of Enfantin. Between April and the last issue of the monthly in December 1826, out of one hundred articles forty-nine were by Enfantin himself and fifty-one came from the pens of Rodrigues, Bazard, Buchez, P.-J. Rouen, and Laurent. The burden was heavy, since Enfantin had simultaneously acquired an appointment as liquidator of a commercial house, which paid him six thousand francs yearly.[47] It also fell to him to write the prospectus for the new monthly magazine. It was, in Enfantin's words, "our FIRST CREDO."

Le Producteur would continue to seek "to unify ARTISTS, SCHOLARS, and industrialists through a philosophical doctrine favoring the future progress of humanity in SCIENTIFIC, MORAL and INDUSTRIAL areas."

Le Producteur would continue to examine "SCIENCES in their philosophical and political aspects from the point of view of SOCIAL EDUCATION confided to SCHOLARS and ARTISTS and would continue to examine the exploitation of EXTERNAL NATURE in terms of SCIENTIFIC projects executed by INDUSTRIALISTS."

The principal questions (and this was new) of political economy, and particularly that of "CREDIT," an element of union between workers, were to be treated from the point of view of their influence on the successive liberation of all productive classes and on the development of "the spirit of INDUSTRIAL ASSOCIATION."

"The FINE ARTS," which ought to be the expression of moral sentiments and which could contribute to the forging of social links, "are today beyond the masses." *Le Producteur* would summon artists to their noble mission. Everything with which it would deal would be considered from the point of view of is effect on the physical, intellectual, and moral betterment of all those who worked.[48]

The contents of *Le Producteur* for the next seven months reflected the shift in emphasis announced by the "credo." Moral regeneration was constantly present, and the masses became a matter of concern. Four long articles recounted the life of Saint-Simon. Buchez, a doctor, wrote extensively on physiology and its lessons for society. Rouen wrote on the working class and on agricultural exploitation. Laurent asserted that *inequality* was the source of the progress of mankind; thus he mounted an attack on those who feared the Saint-Simonian categorizing of groups and the possible authoritarian result of it. The veil was, indeed, lifted. The editors made it clear that under the leadership of artists, scholars, and businessmen they proposed to modify the political and social structure in the interests of all workers and against the interests of all idlers.

But the changes had little effect. The readership did not increase. The businessmen were unwilling to pay the continuing bills and were, perhaps, temperamentally closer to Constant than to Saint-Simon. The moment was approaching when the Saint-Simonians, not content with material support, would ask for their moral conversion as well. Artists did not rush to fulfill their "noble mission." In December 1826 the last issue of *Le Producteur* appeared. As the dramas of the schism of the preceding April were to be replayed many times, so was the eager enunciation, always premature, of the death of Saint-Simonianism.

The journal could not go on, but the idea of a journal did. The leaders who were forced to sign the death warrant of *Le Producteur*—Bazard, Buchez, Enfantin, Laurent, Rodrigues, and Rouen—continued to meet and to discuss doctrine. By the spring of 1827 the editors knew that they had in one Resseguier (who turned out to be "frightfully ugly"), at Castelnaudary in the south of France, a convert and an apostle.[49] At about the same time the former *polytechnicien* Margerin was writing to Henri Fournel that "A new school arises. . . . Founded by H. Saint-Simon some years ago, modified by Auguste Comte, limited to a small number of adepts, the new school pursues its work silently; it is to the future that it addresses itself; the present doesn't know it or understands it not."[50]

This year of 1827 was one in which the doctrine might appear to be sleeping, but in fact it was the gestation period for the startling and dramatic success it was to know from 1828 to 1832. Out of the exhaustion of failure and a series of crises in his own life Enfantin would bring his fellows to the proclamation of a Saint-Simonian religion and a doctrine of the rehabilitation of the flesh. Bazard would expose the thought of the school without disguises and in all its fullness. The men of *Le Producteur* had accomplished their object: public exposure, recognition, the diffusion in a tentative way of the least frightening of Saint-Simonian ideas, and the acquisition of "that circle of serious men who read to learn rather than to amuse themselves." They were henceforth never to be out of the public eye, and their ideas would from now on play a dominant role in the intellectual life of Paris and, consequently, of Europe.

The Saint-Simonians were men with a spiritual mission. They were, like Enfantin, "merchants," or engineers, or bankers, or doctors in search of an "honest fortune." They had publicized not only their ideas but also themselves. It has sometimes been suggested that self-interest rather than ideological committment best explains their adoption of the Saint-Simonian creed. But the suggestion that an ideology is valid only if it runs counter to the interest of those who adopt it is surely a curious one.

What is most important about the young technocrats who made *Le Producteur* is that they suggested an avenue to follow, a means to arrive at the end of the road, a new social class and a new social program for meeting the problems that Saint-Simon had defined as crucial for the century to come. The vision of the future was astonishingly accurate; the means were in many ways remarkably sensible. The question yet unanswered was how the vision and the means could be made persuasive.

CHAPTER IV

"THE OLD FAMILY"

N O PUBLIC PROCLAMATION, no public teachings, no public stir followed *Le Producteur*'s demise. But to describe the period from January 1827 to December 1828 as one of "silent expansion"[1] is neither entirely accurate nor helpful in understanding the growth of Saint-Simonianism. At the end of 1828 the doctrine, first delivered orally and then committed to print, was to emerge stunningly as the most striking social movement of the day. It demanded European attention, attracting the fashionable, the chic, and the brilliant as well as masses of the poor and uninstructed. Between the death of *Le Producteur* and the *Exposition* of Saint-Simonian doctrine something had obviously taken place.

What took place has to be pieced together, with less certainty than any other aspect of Saint-Simonianism, from reminiscences, hints, contemporary descriptions, and later mutual recriminations. In any event, what certainly did take place was conversation: a return to the sources, a posing of questions, a discussion of moral and intellectual leadership. Precisely because the expansion was *not* silent, we can know less of it than we can of those periods when conversation, lecture, and debate were augmented by correspondence and publication.

Each of the leaders of the Saint-Simonian movement would later assert that to him alone belonged the credit for keeping it alive during these two years. Each certainly contributed something to its liveliness. In all likelihood it was Olinde Rodrigues who during this period reasserted the claims of *Le Nouveau Christianisme* to serious consideration. He had been a collaborator in its writing, had brought Enfantin to its first reading, and had perhaps been most moved among the earlier followers of Saint-Simon by the need for a spiritual anchor for the doctrine.[2]

Certainly it was in this period that Enfantin's copy of Saint-Simon's last work became well-thumbed and dog-eared.[3] Consideration of a religion of humanity inevitably raised questions of leadership. Bazard, the former conspirator and inventor of the system of *ventes*, was powerfully attracted by the ideas of Bonald and Maistre on spiritual authority. It was an attraction consistent with the Saint-Simonian distaste for doctrinaire liberalism and was the source of that flirtation with authoritarian Catholicism in which the Saint-Simonians engaged for a number of years. This same attraction to authority was also the source of the Saint-Simonian concern

58

with the nature of priesthood and, indeed, the nature of God.[4] These last two concerns were to become obsessive with Enfantin, who was ultimately persuaded by Buchez and Fourier that God, if existent, was androgynous.[5] From that doctrine would emanate Saint-Simonian feminism and all the crises that would divide the movement and, incidentally, its historians.

One begins to see, in this period, the pattern of development of Saint-Simonianism as distinct from, although an extension of, the teachings of Saint-Simon. The leaders were busy propagating the doctrine that was already clear and were equally busy, within a more restrained circle, in extending its reach. Later, the revelation of the inner circle's discussions would shock. A pattern emerged in which at the moment of impact of a new revelation, even more startling investigations would already be under way. So it was during 1827 and 1828.

The members of the *Producteur* circle continued to meet with those, particularly the young, who had been drawn by the relatively pure explanation of the economic and social teachings of Saint-Simon. They also began to work among themselves toward some more inclusive statement of their principles. To accomplish this work they had to take stock of their efforts to date, assess the weakness of their previous strategies for attracting public attention, and reexamine the writings of the Master for clues to future success. There was thought of a revived *Producteur* and of a philosophical dictionary for the nineteenth century. But there was also, it would seem, the thought of an organization, a hierarchy, a church, a religion.[6]

The setting of a new course for the movement faced impediments. Enfantin described the months following the end of *Le Producteur* as offering everybody who had been involved in it time in which to be ill. Enfantin, himself, suffered from an excruciating "burning of the entrails."[7] His collaborators apparently experienced a range of comparable disabilities. In ways that both drew him away from active participation in the doctrine and back to it, 1827 was traumatic and decisive for Enfantin.

At his family's country house, near Curson in the Drôme, Enfantin had met on his return from Russia in 1824 one Adèle Morlane, née Riffi. She was a widow with a daughter, had been befriended by Mme Enfantin, and was thought of as a suitable match for Enfantin's bachelor cousin, General St.-Cyr Nugues. Enfantin and Morlane fell passionately in love. When Enfantin returned to Paris, she followed him, established herself at Saint-Mandé, and began a liaison that lasted stormily, unsatisfactorily, and painfully for the better part of thirty years. The central difficulty was Morlane's desire for respectability—that is, marriage. This desire became more intense when in August 1827 she gave birth to a son, Arthur, delivered by Enfantin himself. Arthur was eventually legitimized. The relationship of Enfantin and Morlane never was. It caused pain to Enfantin (who, nonetheless, remained convinced that marriage would have been an "unforgivable *bêtise*"), to Enfantin's family and friends, and, needless to say, to Morlane herself. The pain was increased by her inability to comprehend or accept the directions in which Enfantin would shortly move.[8]

The "anecdotal and picturesque" aspects of Saint-Simonianism can never be separated from what is fundamentally serious in it. The relationships of lover-mistress, father-mother, and father-son assumed dramatic coloring in 1827 for Enfantin. They forced him to face questions of sexuality, male-female relationships, paternity, and the bourgeois imperatives associated with these relationships. It should not be forgotten that the circumstances of Arthur's birth paralleled those of Enfantin's own and that his manifest sensitivity to social slight must have made him aware of the probable consequences for his own son.

The personal confrontations undoubtedly colored Enfantin's picture of the doctrine's future. Gustave d'Eichthal noted that he had only twice seen Enfantin blush (although the implication is that there were many occasions when he *ought* to have done so), and one of these occasions was when Enfantin revealed that he had fathered a son.[9] There are hints in 1827 that exhaustion, ill health, and the new turn of events in his life produced a *crise de nerfs* of a sort that was to recur at other critical periods of his life. Tears, nervousness, a tremor evidenced in his handwriting, and a paralysis of will described in his letters were its characteristics.[10]

At this juncture Enfantin spoke in his letters to his cousins of joining them at Curson. Interestingly enough this appears to be the only time in his life when he was not enthusiastically welcomed among them. His cousin, Thérèse, spoke of how dull it would be for him, how he would miss the attractions of Paris. Was he quite sure that this sort of repose was what was most useful for him? The possibilities of a thunderous atmosphere in the country were abundantly evident. Usually Enfantin could count on the support of his female cousins (indeed, the same d'Eichthal would record the *potin* that they had both and simultaneously been Enfantin's mistresses),[11] but the men of the family were readying themselves to disapprove of Enfantin's life, lack of career, Saint-Simonian associations, and conduct towards a woman who had been of their world.

By early September the skies at Curson had sufficiently cleared so that Enfantin could plan to spend the winter there. But the year had not yet exhausted its capacity for shock and pain. In early November word came from Italy of the illness and death of Auguste, his older brother. Added to the forced confrontation with the ethical bases of his life was now added another confrontation with the most fundamental questions of life, death and time. One senses in Enfantin's correspondence during the weeks and months following his brother's death a dialectic tension between the exploration of the religious themes of the Saint-Simonian doctrine and the traumatic experiences current in his daily life, between the questions already raised by Bazard and Buchez about the nature of God and the role of women in society and his own sense of confusion and guilt in relation to his mistress and newborn son. In all this the death of the much loved older brother took on the significance of a punishment.[12]

Before Auguste's death various Paris friends had urged that Enfantin return. Michel Rouen wrote, "As for the Saint-Simonian church, it sleeps . . . and for all but us it resembles a bad joke." Buchez added: "The school is as if dissolved since your departure; you are the chain that linked the parts. We miss you, my dear Enfantin."[13] Auguste's death brought Enfantin back to Paris in mid-November to be with his parents, and the return launched him again on Saint-Simonian seas.

By February 1828 Enfantin was writing to his lifelong and most intimate friend, Arlès-Dufour at Lyons, that *Le Producteur*'s failure had lain in the intrinsic aridity of economic doctrine, the narrow materialism, of which the Saint-Simonians had been accused: "We touch a more delicate chord. It is in morality, in theology, in poetry that we wish to be Doctors."[14] The passage was not metaphorical. It summed up what Rodrigues, Bazard, and Enfantin had achieved in the preceding year and where they would go in the months to come.

What had the achievements been? Where would Saint-Simonianism go? The questions have to be answered on at least two levels, that of organization and that of theory. The hope for the movement's future lay in its capacity to persuade the young and the able of its relevance to their needs. Saint-Simon himself and his most important followers were always on the lookout for significant conversions among the famous proponents of rival or related ideas. They would at various times have high hopes for such diverse characters as Prince Metternich, John Stuart Mill, Thomas Carlyle, and the marquis de Lafayette. The grand prize would eventually become, in their eyes, Louis-Philippe or his heir. They were not uninterested in the mother of the future Napoleon III.[15] But it was Enfantin who had declared that the canal through which their ideas must flow was the Ecole Polytechnique, and it was Bazard who had as leader of the Carbonari emphasized the importance of attracting young commercial and business apprentices to his movement.[16] The Rodrigues family and its connections provided just such young people, and it was largely from the ranks of the *polytechniciens,* the Carbonari who continued to follow Bazard, and the Rodrigues connection that the most promising recruits were initially drawn.

The situation of such young people has been outlined in Chapter 1. By and large they were suffering from a *mal du siècle,* were seeking new faiths, and were the romantic standard bearers of a much romanticized generation. The engineers, in particular, had practical uses. They were already in place. They provided, once converted, a cheap and convenient missionary corps. On leaving the Polytechnique they became civil servants, the nature of whose profession scattered them across France and placed them on the ladder to central administration. The *polytechniciens* were, for example, desirable as husbands. Wherever they went they enjoyed an entrée to locally significant people. The esprit de corps of the school guaranteed an effective and widespread hearing for the ideas that might engage any of them.[17]

Young businessmen, bankers, and stockbrokers, although less secure than the engineers, were even more promising. Working in the worlds of finance, promotion, and persuasion they had the technical skills to bring about, and could be trained to envisage, economic and social transformation. Between these two groups was a body, perhaps the most interesting of all—young, possessing wealth or social position, shoppers for ideas, *hommes d'élite,* as they would one day be called—who by their connections demanded attention. Among these were P.-M. Laurent, Hippolyte Carnot, and others, who, while interested in Saint-Simonianism, had also been tied to the Order of Templars, which supposedly taught a doctrine holding the key to social reform. It was in the course of 1827 that these young men broke noisily with the Templars and for some time devoted themselves to Saint-Simonianism.[18] The first achievement, then, of the not-so-silent expansion was the acquisition of a central group of convinced Saint-Simonians.

The names of some of that group have already surfaced. The earliest disciples were often to be the most persistent, the most faithful to the doctrine, and, in the long run, the most significant to the world outside it. The separate worlds from which they were drawn often overlapped. One has to keep in mind that Restoration society was to a high degree conspiratorial and paranoid; one has the evidence of *The Red and the Black* and the oeuvre of Balzac to testify to that fact. The police were assumed to be everywhere, and the law prohibiting meetings of more than twenty people was enforceable and often enforced. The secret society, the club, the underground, the "mysteries of Paris," and the police spy were in everybody's consciousness. There had been Carbonari influence at the Polytechnique; the "Congregation," a supposed Catholic conspiracy, was everywhere feared; and Freemasonry was seen as a counterweight to it. Saint-Simonianism itself would have to meet the accusation of having incited insurrection, and it might, rather unconsciously and despite itself, have done so.

But even granting the infinitude of possible sources for new Saint-Simonians, there were certain networks of acquaintance that gave first and most to the movement. The most visible is that of the Rodrigues family, which through Olinde had drawn Enfantin himself to the school and which, in the person of Olinde's younger brother, Eugène, would provide the catalyst for transforming Saint-Simonianism from discussion group to religion.[19]

Eugène, who died young and a virgin at twenty-four, remained alive in Saint-Simonian memories for his ardor, his beauty, and his spirituality. George Sand described him as the "tenderest of hearts, most naive of intellects."[20] He greeted each new stage of the doctrine with enthusiasm and showed himself zealous in accomplishing the betterment of the poorest and most numerous class. His Saint-Simonianism was unconditional, and he was, perhaps, fortunate in not living long enough to be torn by doctrinal schism.

Quite other were the Rodrigueses' cousins Jacques-Emile and Isaac Pereire. They are usually referred to as "the Pereires," although time and reflection would make clear that there were considerable differences between the two. They were, however, associates in Saint-Simonianism as they were to be in some of the major banking and industrial enterprises of the nineteenth century. Emile was born in 1800, and Isaac in 1806 — the year of his father's death. Grandsons of a distinguished scholar who had invented a method of teaching the deaf and dumb and who had been a representative of the Bordeaux Jews in Paris, the brothers had joined their uncle Isaac Rodrigues in Paris in 1822 and 1823, respectively. Both lived in the Rodrigues household. Emile married his cousin Hermine; Isaac, eventually, his niece Fanny.[21] They were close to their cousins Olinde and Eugène, who brought them to Saint-Simonianism along with the Rodrigues brothers-in-law Sarchi and Baud.

Even the Rodrigues parents, at a certain point in the development of the school and despite some reservations, seemed to form part of the doctrinal group. The Pereire and Rodrigues brothers were certainly at the heart of the discussions of doctrine and objectives that took place throughout 1827 and 1828.

The Rodrigues-Pereire involvement is inevitably related to the ambivalent and ambiguous discussions of Saint-Simonianism and Jewishness that plagued, and to some degree continue to plague, efforts to understand Saint-Simonian doctrine. What is clear is that Jewishness was not irrelevant to either the doctrine or its organization. One can suspect anti-Semitism in some of the efforts to discredit Saint-Simonianism. One can see their Saint-Simonian past used on many occasions to ridicule or discredit prominent Jews. The Pereires during long and vigorous lives would be both prominent and well hated. They were vulnerable to attacks from anti-Semites and from the enemies of Saint-Simonianism. They refused to regard either identification as a badge of shame and, on the whole, persisted in taking pride in what they were and what they had been. Emile would remain at least nominally Jewish and was generous to both Saint-Simonian and Jewish causes. Isaac, more completely and emotionally committed to Saint-Simonianism, would perpetuate the cult and would transmit to his descendants a veneration for Saint-Simonian ideas. In Isaac's library, in a velvet-lined case, was the skull of Saint-Simon himself.[22]

Aside from the question of anti-Semitism being directed toward some Saint-Simonians, Jewishness was important for the doctrine and was tied to the Rodrigues-Pereire circle. Their business was business: stock-jobbing, accounting, banking. They were a significant group in a relatively small and close circle of people like themselves: first Sephardic Jews, then Jews, then Jews in Paris, and finally Jews involved in Parisian finance. Their acquaintances and their family ties put them in touch with persons in the larger world of business and finance susceptible to the influence of the Saint-Simonian economic program. And the program as it eventually emerged always showed signs of a concern for Judaism in Saint-Simon's historical stages, in its relation to Christianity, its "Oriental" origins, and its possible role in bringing about a meeting of East and West.

The search for the "female Messiah" was informed by the notion that she would be found in the East and that she would be a Jew. On a somewhat less exaggerated level the objective of building a canal at Suez and Saint-Simonian involvement in Egyptian politics during the 1830s and 1840s gave rise to a remarkable conception of Enfantin's that by uniting the international Jewish community in the exploitation of Palestine one could bring to the Middle East the benefits of Saint-Simonian technocracy. With it one could create a social model for export to the undeveloped Far East. Some such vision appears to have informed later conversation and correspondence between d'Eichthal and Metternich. Like so many Saint-Simonian projects it was bizarre, if not baroque, in detail while at the same time clearly anticipating some possibilities that would be realized in the future.[23]

Saint-Simonianism was not, however, a Jewish sect. Cynics have suggested that some Jews, notably, the Pereires, unable to live with their traditional faith, incapable of embracing conventional Christianity wholeheartedly, and nonetheless needing faith, solved the problem by inventing a new faith, neither Jewish nor Christian. If so, they were neither the first nor the last to resort to such a solution. But the fact remains that the new Christianity was the work of Saint-Simon; and if the Rodrigues-Pereire connection was attracted by it, its members did not invent it. Nor was it a faith whose most devoted members were necessarily Jews.

This qualitatively, if not quantitatively, important group did give to Saint-Simonianism yet one more perspective on social existence characterized, on the whole, by open-mindedness and generosity of spirit. As with women and workers, so with Jews, the Saint-Simonians saw not merely an injustice to correct but an opportunity to set free energies and talents frustrated by their social system. In later years Enfantin and some of his associates would be capable of uttering conventional anti-Semitic slurs, but these were usually the reflex response of irritation (very often at the Pereires) and not the expressions of deeply felt and systematic prejudice.

Saint-Simonianism, then, owed much to this constellation: Olinde Rodrigues, "dry and brusque"; Eugène, his brother, zealous and "inflamed" for the doctrine; Emile Pereire, generally thought to be the more "serious," the more "interior" of the brothers; Isaac, who in the eyes of one unfriendly commentator was "cleverer" and more the "intriguer" as well as the more enthusiastic Saint-Simonian; and the brother-in-law Sarchi, who had much influence on Eugène, clever, cynical, and a "very good elaborator" of doctrine in company with Eugène, Olinde, and Enfantin.[24]

Outside the immediate family circle there were others linked to the doctrine through it. Olinde was an organizer of the Caisse Hypothécaire; early in 1828 Enfantin became cashier of the bank, and on its governing board was Baron Duveyrier, whose son Charles was to become an enthusiastic apostle. Constantly around the circle of the Rodrigueses, although not deeply immersed in Saint-Simonianism until 1829, was d'Eichthal, who became one of the movement's most passionate, troubled, and faithful members.[25] Both like and different from the Rodrigues family, d'Eichthal was the son of a banker, born Seeligman, who was created Baron d'Eichthal by the king of Bavaria. The baron had recently moved to Paris and had founded a bank in the place des Victoires.

D'Eichthal's awareness of Saint-Simon had, perhaps, preceded Rodrigues's own. He had gone to Comte for tutoring and at Comte's had been presented to Saint-Simon during the last period of their close relationship. He commented that in those days (1822) it was an acquaintanceship he did not wish to pursue. He saw Saint-Simon "as a kind of madman" with whom contact would be "compromising."[26] Tortured through a long life by questions of Jewish identity and sexuality, d'Eichthal, when he had decided that Comte wished to make of him a "cold machine," was ready for the attractions of the doctrine already familiar to him. German Jews, and the d'Eichthals in particular, more recently and less completely emancipated than the Sephardim of Bordeaux, and more frankly assimilationist in outlook, might be expected to display self-doubt and anguish. The attraction was all the greater in that Rodrigues père had been his instructor in bookkeeping and the Rodrigues children were already his friends.

A word should be said about members of the older generation that had given birth to these young deviants from bourgeois ideals. Far from looking upon their progeny as a nest of vipers, they seem to have had a remarkable degree not only of love but also of tolerance, charity, and sympathy for their troubled and searching young. They seemed to have shared in that affective individualism that Lawrence Stone identifies as one of the most important phenomena of early modern history. In many cases, although troubled by the involvement of their children in what came to be seen as a scandalous and dangerous movement, these parents often displayed a largeness of mind that offers some insights into the nature of post-Napoleonic family life itself. For the d'Eichthals, Gustave's devotion to Saint-Simonianism was a grave embarrassment, but his father sent money to ensure a decent burial for Enfantin's mother.[27] Without the Rodrigues family there might well have been no movement. And Enfantin throughout the most excessive and bizarre moments of the movement's history could count on the moral sustenance of his own family of nonbelievers and skeptics.

Enfantin had had high hopes, for a time, of bringing into the Saint-Simonian fold the father of Olinde and Eugène Rodrigues and had written him about developments taking place in the doctrine. Isaac Rodrigues replied on November 5, 1828:

The School of Saint-Simon, which interests me in more ways than one, includes men of high intelligence and proven rectitude. The doctrine it professes with rare candor appears to the greatest number of persons who know it and believe they comprehend it to be a tissue of dreams and chimeras. The end of the doctrine is the noblest, but the means of execution that could assure its success appears impossible to find. Human intelligence is limited in its action; beyond a certain point it must revolve in imaginary spaces. To believe that it may ever be possible to govern mathematically a great society, to watch over all its members, to place each individual in the class where his aptitudes, his tastes, and his penchants will render him most useful to his brothers, to SUBSTITUTE social direction for natural direction, to REPLACE paternal solicitude by the solicitude of bankers, to change the constitution of property in such a way that one's own can no longer be transmitted by inheritance, to ENFEEBLE family feelings by absorbing them in social sentiment, is it not to misunderstand human nature and to consider men as solely rational beings?[28]

The objections are clear, but the language is up to a point friendly, even complimentary. A similar letter was written at a later time by the father of the Talabots, expressing irritation and sadness at his son's Saint-Simonian involvement but expressing as well an openness to new social ideas that was apparently not rare in this older generation.

Whereas family ties and connections characterized the group initially associated with Rodrigues, the whiff of revolutionary conspiracy and adventure appears to have been the source of attraction for those who clustered around Bazard. His circle included Hippolyte Carnot, P.-M. Laurent, Auguste Cerclet, Buchez, and Armand Carrel. Carnot, of these, was in the post-*Producteur* period the most prized recruit. Son of the great revolutionary general who had known and admired Saint-Simon, he had been involved with the Society for Christian Morality and with the Templars. Both organizations appeared in 1827 and 1828 to be flirting with ideas of social renewal and revolution. During this same period Bazard was complaining that Enfantin and Rodrigues were concentrating their energies on business matters. He, on the other hand, hoped to take up the political mission of the school and to refloat *Le Producteur*. The project of a new journal attracted Carnot, who was already an editor of *Le Gymnase;* he soon occupied a central position in the discussions at Bazard's apartment. Most importantly when formal public expositions of the doctrine were undertaken, it was Carnot who became responsible for the task of writing down and editing Bazard's words for publication. Carnot's contribution to Saint-Simonianism, then, was of major importance. The *Exposition* of 1828–29 was to become the best known source for the understanding—and the misunderstanding—of the movement. Until then a sweet manner and his father's name, "so useful for knotting relationships," were his only titles to consideration. He was otherwise judged of quite ordinary intelligence and *"très lymphatique."* But he sometimes rewrote the Bazard sermons six times.[29]

Those others tied to Bazard came from the Carbonari past and, with the exception of P.-M. Laurent, would go on to other careers. Buchez would persuade Enfantin of the importance of women and invite him to blend the ideas of Fourier with those of Saint-Simon. By 1827 Buchez was already looking more to Enfantin than to Bazard for leadership, and while Bazard continued to think in political, if pacific, terms, the "new doctrine" was being elaborated by Enfantin, Sarchi, Olinde, Rodrigues, and the elder Pereire. There was one exception, or one pair of exceptions, in the Bazard connection, the Fournels. Henri and Cécile were drawn in a number of ways to Saint-Simonianism. She was the niece of Mme Bazard. He was an engineer and *polytechnicien* who was for a time director of one of France's major industrial enterprises, the Creusot Iron Works. To him in 1826 Margerin, another engineer associated with *Le Producteur,* had written:

It is time for some good mind to discover that technology ought to be a deduction from chemistry, mechanics, and economics; founded on this idea our government would be worthy of the name, that is to say, capable of introducing into the diverse processes of technology the uniformity and perfection to which they are susceptible. Surely such a work would be neither without glory nor without profit.[30]

Henri Fournel was always vulnerable to the technocratic appeal but would be equally vulnerable to the personal appeal of Enfantin. Among the lives tortured and exalted by Saint-Simonian experience none would be more so than those of the Fournels. They perhaps typified many Saint-Simonians, drawn into a dynamic movement from one source or another but, once immersed, finding a fluid and ever-changing situation that required choices and decisions, the forming of alliances and rivalries, and the following of one or another of the leaders.

Underneath the seeming uniformity of the movement and the purpose of its leaders there was a ceaseless rise and fall of the tide of ego, a constant seeking for primacy, a constant confrontation of men and ideas. The motive force in this restless sea of Saint-Simonianism was undoubtedly Enfantin. He was able not only to gather to himself a body of followers from outside the movement but also, as time passed, to woo to his side many of those who had first come to the movement by way of Bazard and Rodrigues. The base of Enfantin's support was largely among the *polytechniciens* and engineers. His attachment to the Polytechnique; his air of a friendly older brother, experienced, worldly, and traveled; his much-discussed charm and looks; and his great "calm" account for the initial attraction. He was "another incarnation of the *'heros fatal'* whose great prototype had died a few years earlier on Saint Helena. . . . A man not without vision and not without ideals, but with a strange lack of moral good taste, a strange childishness, and absurd pretensions."[31]

During 1827 and 1828 Enfantin's methods were, one suspects, largely conversational, one on one. Bazard, meantime, gave formal instruction to groups and because of his age, political and social visibility, and connections seemed to be assuming public leadership of the group. Rodrigues, embodying as he did the "living tradition" of Saint-Simon, had always appeared to lack some essential quality of leadership; he was too quick, too brusque perhaps. To Bazard's "methodical slowness" Enfantin opposed an "impatient, inexhaustible initiative: confessions and redoubtable confidences were made to him. . . . He possessed the art of justifying by the most rigorous dialectic the most surprising paradoxes." By a combination of charm, logic, and moral blackmail, by a capacity to link his followers to one another through himself, Enfantin, at first quietly and then more persistently and openly, moved to the forefront of the school.[32]

Among those initially identified with Enfantin were the Talabots (Paulin, Léon, Edmond, and Jules), Rancourt, Lamé, Clapeyron, Jean Reynaud, Félix Tourneux, Lamoricière, the Chevalier brothers Michel and Auguste, Abel Transon, Jules Lechevalier, Euryale Cazeaux, Ressegiuer, Edouard Charton, Emile Barrault, Cappella, Bigot, Lambert, Lemonnier, Jean Terson, and the Petit family. Most members of this considerable list would in the generation to come build notable, even brilliant, careers. At one point Enfantin drew up a list of eighty-eight engineers strewn across France whom he viewed as Saint-Simonian.[33] Whether the allegiance to the movement and to Enfantin was passing or permanent is a question to be discussed elsewhere. But in the course of 1827 and 1828 there was a continuous flow of interested young men to the apartments of Bazard and of Hippolyte Carnot on the now nonexistent rue Taranne.

Although many of the young engineers at the Ecole Polytechnique were drawn to the Saint-Simonians, not all the Saint-Simonians associated with Enfantin were engineers, nor were all of Enfantin's group situated in Paris. A notable supporter of the movement for many years, one who never shared the life of the school but who was always ready to advance its cause and to subscribe to its central ideas, was the remarkable Lyonnais textile broker, banker, and entrepreneur François Arlès-Dufour. At the funeral of Enfantin, shaken by emotion, Arlès would declare, *"Je suis saint-simonien,"*[34] but the declaration was hardly surprising to those who knew the man, nor would it have been to anyone permitted to follow the lifelong Arlès-Enfantin correspondence.[35]

One account, impossible to confirm, asserts that the Enfantin-Arlès friendship began at the defense of Paris in 1815 when the weeping adolescent, Arlès, threw himself into the arms of the heroic and defeated defender, Enfantin.[36] It is more likely that the two encountered and knew each other well during their travels in the Germanies in the early 1820s. The relationship was complex, unlikely, and equal. Arlès occupied a peculiar and difficult position in his city of adoption. He was a convinced anticlerical in the most Catholic of French cities and a convinced socialist in the midst of the Lyonnais silk-manufacturing oligarchy. He presents an attractive picture of honesty, independence, and occasional despair in the face of the world around him. The Lyonnais atmosphere had led him to believe that revolution was better than evolution, "especially when I have seen many men and have found them all gangrenous."[37] But it is clear that he had early seen Enfantin as destined to great achievement and as spokesman for views with which he heartily, consistently, and totally sympathized.

At one level Arlès was the practical man of affairs, the success, a notable of the July Monarchy and the Second Empire. At the same time the support and encouragement Enfantin would count on from him was not the product of patron-client relationship. It was clear that Arlès looked upon his constant support of Enfantin as both duty and privilege. He saw in his friend the capacities for bringing about social transformations whose necessity he accepted even when they seemed most inimical to the sort of society in which he himself successfully maneuvered.

Enfantin was, throughout, accepting of the admiration given by Arlès. He was probably never happier than during the period in the 1840s when his business career seemed destined to equal that of Arlès, and he still carried about him the aura of prophet, to which Arlès had not been the last or least important contributor.

Arlès-Dufour was only one of many connected to Saint-Simonianism who, if they could not give the movement respectability, gave it by their interest and presence guarantees against the consequences of a lack of respectability. Baron Duveyrier, Baron d'Eichthal, Talabot père (a judge), and General St.-Cyr Nugues were always in the background ready to spring to the defence of their relatives or their relatives' friends. The time would come when society would exact a punishment of the Saint-Simonians, but it was not, in material terms, severe. The reintegration into society of the punished (notably in the case of Michel Chevalier) was by and large made easy, until having been a Saint-Simonian was seen not as a disqualification but as positive recommendation for high office.

The ambivalence or, perhaps, the dialectic tension of Saint-Simonianism was as evident in its leading personnel as in its ideas. Much has been made here of the Saint-Simonians as outsiders in Restoration society. Outsiders they were, in many ways, but when they went outside the canons of that society, they never shut behind them the doors leading to the inside. They talked of the betterment of the poorest and most numerous class, but they talked *to* such of the directing classes as they could reach. They were indeed willing to knock on any door, to whisper into any ear, to enlighten any despot about how best to attain Saint-Simonian ends.

This trait, which was as characteristic of Saint-Simon as of his followers (and whose manifestations were not always very attractive), needs discussion and understanding, because it subtly deforms the meanings of the movement. The deformation depends on the point of view or, more likely, the *parti pris* of the critic. But in the process the question of the validity of the program is confused with the question of its sincerity. Could such trimmers, such power seekers, such lackeys of the possessing classes have anything useful to say to the masses? Was the vision of the technocratic society exploiting the universe for the benefit of the poorest and most numerous class simply an application for political and social license to be exercised by a new kind of totalitarian? Did the Saint-Simonians care either for the bourgeoisie whom they begged to see the light of the dawning century, *or* for the working classes, whose misery they would regulate? Were they not simply *arriviste* careerists seeking to pull the wool over the eyes both of potential patrons and potential followers for their own private and, on the whole, reprehensible purposes? And if the answer to the last question is yes, then are not the theory, the movement, and the men discredited?

These questions remain to be answered. The raising of such questions, whether from purely moral and rational grounds or more narrowly ideological grounds, is possible only by disregarding the historical context within which the Saint-Simonian movement grew. It grew in the France of the "notables." Naturally and rationally the Saint-Simonians turned to the conversion of notables as a means to an end. As far as the Saint-Simonians could see, that was how society worked. Yes, indeed, they wanted power. But the power they sought was always for a purpose—the preservation of social life through the elimination of those miseries that threatened its existence. In this they resembled their master.

Saint-Simonians, individually and collectively, were acutely aware of their talents, training, and competence. They may, indeed, have patronized workers. But who did not do so in the 1820s and 1830s? The Saint-Simonians were often originals, but their originality was defined by their time and their society. They were also individuals, each deeply involved in the working out of ways to reach the shared goal. As individuals the Saint-Simonians did not react uniformly to all opportunities or act with perfect consistency. There was, however, a remarkable consistency in the eclecticism of their approach to the desired end.

As individuals the Saint-Simonians were also deeply involved in working out the ways in which the doctrine applied to themselves, and here, obviously, the responses differed from person to person. Some cut themselves off from established society totally; others sought to use it. They did not, however, cease to be sons and daughters, brothers and sisters, husbands and wives, workers, professionals, or *rentiers* when they became Saint-Simonian. That there were social and psychological dimensions to the Saint-Simonians as well as the purely ideological is obvious.

Condemnation of the Saint-Simonians and their ideas might legitimately rest on the degree to which they had not freed themselves from the faults of their times and the limitations of their experience. It should not rest on the degree to which they *had* freed themselves. The faults, after all, lay in the times and the limitations, not in men and women beating their frontal bones against the ribs of a calcified social universe. The doctrine is not discredited because its preachers were human; it is, rather, justified by the all-too-evident humanity of its earliest propagators.

The formation of that tightly grouped band of propagators, a "new" family built on the foundations of the "old," possessing all the strengths and weaknesses described here, constituted half of the major preparatory work of 1827 and 1828. The other half lay in the development of theory— how to bring about a reign of reason in a garden of love.

CHAPTER V

THE REIGN OF REASON IN THE
GARDEN OF LOVE

BY NOVEMBER 1828 the intense discussions of the preceding eighteen months had begun to produce firm conclusions and programs. The objections raised by the senior Rodrigues in his letter to Enfantin of November 1828, Enfantin's voluminous correspondence with his cousin Thérèse Nugues from midsummer through the autumn of the same year, and the letters by various Saint-Simonian notables welcoming and instructing the southern convert Resseguier all offer clues to the map the Saint-Simonians had perfected for the future. But the clearest projection of the Saint-Simonian vision is to be found in Enfantin's "Mémoires d'un industriel de l'an 2240."[1] In the collected Œuvres of Enfantin and Saint-Simon a misprint assigns it to 1838, but it was in fact a product of this crucial year of 1828. The writings are, in part, explanations and justifications and, in part, testings for reaction to developments in the organization of the movement. By December a "hierarchy" of members had been established, a Saint-Simonian "religion" founded, and a public hall hired in which the doctrine was to be announced to the world.

It was in all probability the determination to "go public" that had elicited from Isaac Rodrigues the letter, previously cited, that expresses his understanding of the doctrine and, incidentally, provides an unconscious index of what was "old" and what was "new" in it. Rodrigues, it will be remembered, finds the ends "noble." Intelligence has limits: to govern "mathematically," to watch over all the members of society, to "place each individual in the class where his aptitudes, his tastes, and his penchants will render him most useful to his brothers, to SUBSTITUTE social direction for natural direction, to REPLACE paternal solicitude by the solicitude of bankers, to change the constitution of property in such a way that one's own can no longer be transmitted by inheritance," and to "ENFEEBLE family feelings by absorbing them in social sentiment" was to "misunderstand human nature and to consider men as solely rational beings."[2]

It should quickly be noted that Rodrigues accepts the notion that the program *is* suitable for solely rational beings. His criticisms are essentially those made more than a hundred years later by Hayek, who also rejects the mathematical arrogance of the school and sees it as neither human nor humane. The Rodrigues criticism also expresses the outrage of the good bourgeois who sees property and family attacked and love undermined.

But there is more. Certain key words were for the Saint-Simonians resonant with as yet publicly unspoken meanings. *Penchants* was almost exclusively used by Enfantin with a sexual reference. "*Enfeeblement*" of family feelings not only touched on inheritance but also implied a wider sense of "family" with more complex systems of familial relationships. What a good bourgeois of the Restoration thought "natural" the Saint-Simonian would soon denounce as unnatural. *Paternity* and *paternal solicitude* were terms that would soon provide explosive issues for debate.

In judging the doctrine professed by the Saint-Simonians a "tissue of dreams and chimeras," Rodrigues betrays a greater knowledge of what the movement was seeking than appears on the surface of his letter. The anxiety he expresses is greater than would be justified even by the prospect of the reconstitution of property and the absorption of family feelings in "social sentiment."

Rodrigues had quite accurately perceived that the Saint-Simonianism of 1828 entailed a radical attack on bourgeois values and society. It can be argued and will be shown, however, that the society sought by the Saint-Simonians was very respectable, very bourgeois. Their attack on the bourgeoisie was not directed at destruction but at reconstruction. Nevertheless, they were indeed radical in their hope of creating an essentially middle-class world, in mounting the triumph of the bourgeoisie.

Once again the Saint-Simonians must be seen in historical context. Liberal and bourgeois critics insist on viewing them as precursors of what socialism became or what fascism is. Such a reading misses the point of the Saint-Simonians. They saw their doctrine as the cement holding the bricks of a new society together. But the new society was neither working-class society nor society composed only of gifted technocrats like themselves. Society embraced everybody with the arms of middle-class work, talent, training, and energy. To coin an ugly but useful neologism, the Saint-Simonians sought to "bourgeoisify" a world still essentially rural, agricultural, and caste-, rather than class-, conscious. This "bourgeoisification" could take place only through a radical transformation in middle-class structures that would be attractive and have meaning to those both above and below in the existing social hierarchy.

To maintain the thesis that the Saint-Simonians were bourgeois radicals devoted not only to the preservation but also to the extension of the sway of the middle classes, notwithstanding their unquestioned desire to modify the institutions of property, family, marriage, and religion, may be taken as both courageous and perverse. But if one follows the path to the foundations of Saint-Simonian religion and examines the effulgent fantasy of Enfantin, the incongruities in the thesis are found to be less sharp than one might suppose.

By 1828 the institution of property, its role in society and the stumbling block it presented to the "golden age that lies before us," had moved to the center of Saint-Simonian discussion. Saint-Simon himself had seen private property as inadequate to the tasks of the future. He had assigned to the agencies of the state (which in time would replace it) the mobilization of capital for the making of the new world. His philosophy of history had implied progress, change, and the perfection of institutions, including the institution of property. The direction the doctrine was taking in 1828 represented no break with the Master's thought. It was rather a perfectly logical attempt to resolve the dilemma he had posed.

The dilemma was made clear in Rodrigues's fear of changing the institution of property "in such a way that one's own can no longer be transmitted by inheritance." The question of inheritance was crucial. The bourgeoisie subscribed not only to the values of hard work, punctuality, and regularity but also to the accumulation of rewards for these virtues. These rewards had point and validity, however, only if they were substantial enough to escape the erosion of life and time. The obvious avenue of escape was the family. The obvious strategy for survival was marriage. An attack on the institution of property was obviously an attack on marriage and family. Such an attack would be resisted all the more fiercely because it appeared to invade not only the world of material things but also the world of sentiment and the fortress of the family erected against a hostile universe. The point of the discussion on property, then, was that it made imperative a different view of the family, of marriage, of sex, and of the relations of men and women if the conversion of property to the service of humanity was to be brought about.

Conversion was the operative word. Nothing short of a transvaluation of all values would suffice. As Saint-Simon had insisted, it was only by an appeal to a new Christianity, the "familyhood" of all men (and women), that the necessary material transformations could be realized. So, again, what has usually been described as aberration of, translation of, or break with the word of Saint-Simon has to be understood as a series of rigorously logical deductions from the premises that had become central to Saint-Simonian thinking by the time of *Le Producteur*.

In announcing the formation of a Saint-Simonian religion Eugène Rodrigues would assert, "We do not love one another enough."[3] This was the clue leading to the revelation not of a mystery but of a profound insight into the nature of Restoration society.

Insight it might provide, but was the slogan any less revolutionary and destructive for being true? Yes. The Saint-Simonians were not opposed to rewards or accumulations of property. Least of all was this true of Enfantin,

that "merchant in search of an honest fortune." They believed in and ultimately would proclaim the slogan "From each according to his capacity,
to each according to his works." What could be more bourgeois than that
sentiment?

The meanings of Saint-Simonian slogans are sometimes revealed in
much later Saint-Simonian acts. Arlès-Dufour took to heart, as literally as
the law allowed him to do, the Saint-Simonian adjurations and left only
a quarter of his fortune to his family. The residue went to a variety of
good and, above all, useful works.[4] But where the Saint-Simonians differed from their liberal contemporaries and their later liberal critics was in
their rigorous and universal application of essentially liberal ideals, ideals
that were certainly not foreign to the roots of liberalism but that liberal
successes tended to undermine. It was the Saint-Simonian conviction that
property should not become a barrier to ability or give an advantage in a
race where all runners started even in each generation.

It has often been said (sometimes by the Saint-Simonians themselves) —
but it is not true — that Saint-Simonianism was not egalitarian. In one
strict sense the doctrine was completely egalitarian and totally democratic. Its insistence that the life chances of any individual should be as
great as those of any other, given like competencies, abilities, and desires,
and that whatever the abilities and competencies of any individual there
should be opportunity for their full realization was evidence of its subscription to the rationalist, libertarian, and egalitarian creeds of the
French bourgeoisie. The chief sin of the Saint-Simonians was that they
were more rigorously egalitarian than successful liberals were willing to
be once they had acquired fortunes and families. For the Saint-Simonians
the shiftless son of the fortuned manufacturer would and ought to get
from society that which he deserved by his own works. The fortune of the
manufacturer might help fertilize the talents of gifted and industrious
sons of the poor, and it might even help fertilize the talent of a gifted and
industrious son of his own, but the touchstone for the reception of aid
must be merit.

The Saint-Simonians were quite frank in their understanding of different levels of merit and capacity. They foresaw a society managed by
those best qualified for the job. They did not suppose all people equal in
their talents, but they absolutely ruled out the exercise of power by incompetence. They absolutely held that society was not for sale.

THE "Mémoires d'un industriel de l'an 2240" is Enfantin's attempt to
imagine what life would be like under the new dispensation. The "industriel," who is Enfantin in fantasy, could have sat comfortably for a portrait by Ingres. In the picture of unending toil, the mobilization of capital
and men, the flowering of deserts, and the leveling of mountains one

senses the apotheosis of the businessman and the engineer. It is a picture from the same school as Goethe's *Faust, II* and apparently not unrelated to it.[5]

The "Mémoires" represents the culmination of the specifically technocratic ambitions first apparent in Saint-Simon and in *Le Producteur,* and at the same time it hints at what is to come and what has been under discussion in the inner circle. Completed in the spring of 1828 the "Mémoires" were described by Enfantin as a slightly more animated version of the ideas of Emile Pereire on property; they represent an effort to answer the question "What in the new society would be the relationship of the directors of great works with the workers themselves?" The immediate answer seems to be that the salons of the future business leaders will be the habitual meeting place of the workers.

How will that happy result come about? Enfantin launches into a fictional description of his "life and circumstances." Born at Lyons, his father was a master weaver working in "the corporation of the Silk Masters, the oldest of such corporations." The "doctors" of the corporation sent the boy to school for eight years. The system and its objectives would best be described by the specialists in education central to this society. Briefly, however, students were to be brought to comprehension and appreciation of the different sorts of work in which their parents were engaged. They were to be led to understand their membership in a great family of work, were to be exposed to the interrelationship of work within the country, and were to see the role played by the *industriels,* "who nourished the nation with their sweat." Throughout, the students were encouraged to find new things to love.[6]

Under this system it took some years to determine the aptitudes that would determine our *industriel's* "ultimate social position." This position was a *definition* of aptitudes and tastes, *not* a determination of degree. Beyond the primary level were four general schools: industry, science, fine arts, and industrial propaganda. Each year these schools introduced more and more special classifications. Our hero finds himself placed among the "most general," who were to be programmed to facilitate combinations of efforts and ideas. These candidates were further trained in one of seven more special schools of "application" or "public administration" confided to the direction of the banks of each of the great corporations. These banks were the motive centers of social productivity and, not so incidentally, supported the students and the schools.

The curriculum of the schools provided a résumé of knowledge about "the acquired wealth of humanity," the work relationships of the masses, and the characteristics of special aptitudes. But there were also courses provided by engineers on scientific knowledge, "the intimate relationships of science and industry, public hygiene, and great public works" and on "how the usefulness of these last should be judged."[7]

Having passed through these schools the hero is "classed" on the social register as "active generalizer." He is assigned to a "general bank," where his duties deal with agricultural banks at the departmental level (France's geographic administration has apparently *not* been reorganized). He assesses current needs, future projections, and the appropriations of the councils of engineers. He is also charged with relating the banking needs of agriculture to those of commerce and manufacturing. Finally he is expected to work out with the "spiritual college" the ways and means of improving the lot of the workers and the distribution of the cost of education and pensions. Essentially, the banking network has replaced the political state, and government is carried on by committees of experts raised with care from childhood and seasoned by experience. It is a very French picture; it is also a very Saint-Simonian one.[8]

As the narrator's career progresses and "as our armies imposed our civilization on the Orient," he is charged with the control of military costs. Here he is involved with a military-industrial complex of bankers, jurists, generals, and engineers whose combined function is to follow conquest with roads, canals, the transformation of the means of production, and the improvement of "social" property.

Having performed well and having received "bright" evaluations, he becomes chief of the agricultural section of Lyons and at the same time (having "arrived"?) falls in love with a woman of "mobile" nature. "The vivacity of her sensations frightened me; my slowness, her." But the story ends happily with a mutuality, each "giving as much happiness as the other."[9]

At this juncture the *industriel* undertakes an impact study on a technical innovation: What industries can best use it? Who should produce it and in what quantity? What population displacement will be required? How will it be deployed? With these questions a few philosophical observations are permitted. Society ought always to seek what is new. The division of labor need not be degrading. The tendency of the *industriel*'s recommendations should be less toward the *division* of labor and more toward the best *combination* of labors to produce desired ends.

Finally, the *industriel* has done so well as generalizer and combiner that he is entrusted with a colonizing enterprise and given an immense amount of matériel. He creates industry, agriculture, and a new community where he is loved and venerated. He has become an industrial arbiter and spends his last years bathed in "the ease and consideration my works have secured me."[10]

In the society that Enfantin fantasizes, the *oisif* is made to work, the widows and orphans are supported by the "corporations," the banking system guarantees against financial catastrophe, and the army is industrial and pacific. Its mission in "imposing" itself on other civilizations is to wipe out slavery. The artistic and human sensitivities are incorporated in social organization and in great public works. Public censure and hard work deal with those who do not voluntarily contribute or who are unsatisfactorily socialized—who do not love enough.

Enfantin's "Mémoires" is far from being the most brilliant or insightful of the Saint-Simonian writings, but it is nonetheless of the first importance in understanding the movement and Enfantin's eventual leadership of it. First, it tries to make sense of Saint-Simon's conception of government as administration. What appears is a network of banks whose function is the determination of social needs and the allocation of social capital by competent experts in agreement with one another. A chimera? The relations of present-day Western banks with Third World economies, or even with their own, do not seem too different from the Saint-Simonian prospectus.

In creating the "social" individual, contrary to Hayek and Rodrigues, an educational system assigns a place, and an important one, to the human and the sentimental, one that emphasizes the importance of the "generalizer" as well as of the technical expert. Here there is certainly a bow to Enfantin's understanding of himself, incompletely trained as engineer but nonetheless "a lovable being who is followed." There are certainly imaginative devices for attaining the announced ends of education. Enfantin would appear to have predicted the business school, the school of public administration, the "case" method, internships, psychological testing, public works—and Peace Corps–like armies—and social security.

The proposed educational system tries to meet the problems of transition from the limited loyalties of the nuclear family to a love of one's fellow man. Enfantin touches, if only timidly as yet, on the nature of love and marriage. He ennobles work. Though there is classification, there is no degradation of work at any level. Throughout the system *combination* is emphasized over *division,* and cooperation over competition.

The education proposed by Enfantin is manipulative, but one might reasonably ask what educational system is not. The deviant, the *oisif,* the outsider is subjected to public censure and forced to labor for social good. On these grounds Hannah Arendt has compared Enfantin to Goebbels,[11] and Georg Iggers has seen the dawn of the concentration camp.[12] But is Enfantin's solution any more grim than Foucault's understanding of liberal society's prisons as a paradigm of the way all social life ought to be? In Enfantin's case, at least, the social criminal was defined as one deficient in love.

"Classification" and "social position" are likely to send shudders, somewhat unrealistically, down the spine of the contemporary reader, but one must keep in mind the Saint-Simonian assumption that all is known.

Science constantly perfecting itself and its applications clarifies the needs and wants of individuals; it does not determine them. Such an assumption may be naive, but it is not inconsistent nor necessarily antilibertarian. The Saint-Simonian notion that obedience to the laws of one's own nature constitutes liberty is nowhere more clearly expressed than in the "Mémoires." And nowhere in Saint-Simonian writings is it clearer that the object of the new society is to make obedience to those laws of individuality possible within the social framework.

The special school of propagandists can also make one shudder in anticipation of what was to come in the twentieth century. But here the Saint-Simonians, seeking always to create "new" human beings, tried realistically to meet their fundamental problem. Knowing "truth," they must find some means of implanting that truth in a society whose history and every impulse was to deny and reject emotionally what could be demonstrated rationally. People must be taught to love and to express their love practically. Saint-Simonian propaganda was directed to fostering the "spirit of association," the "religion of humanity," the new Christianity, which would unite the material and spiritual worlds.

Here, of course, is the central difficulty for the critics of school and doctrine. "Humanity" bound in a "spirit of association" to further the reign of a single "truth" adds up to totalitarianism, implies dictatorship, and threatens to block alternative and equally or more valid paths to self-expression. Such patterns of thought, history has taught us, are dangerous and destructive.

But it must be said that this danger is not exclusively or even especially Saint-Simonian. It is a difficulty present in all forms of Christianity, in Rousseau and in Marx, in Mill and in Tocqueville. It is not Saint-Simonian, this problem of individual and society, authority and freedom; it is Occidental. The Saint-Simonians came perhaps closer to squaring this circle than do their critics. They accept the opposites and try to synthesize them. Authoritarian and totalitarian as they may appear to be at one level, they are pluralist and individualist at others.

One of the most exciting, romantic, and, as it happens, realistic characteristics of the Saint-Simonians is their "possibilism." Their notion that there are an infinity of talents and social relationships, an infinity of needs and satisfactions, and an infinity of knowledge is fully as important in their thought as notions of capacity, function, hierarchy, and priesthood. These last were means to ends. Like Christianity Saint-Simonianism offers hope, but unlike Christianity it offers hope for here and now.

The burden of Saint-Simonianism is that "we must love one another." It is not the most evil message history has left us. To denigrate that message because its means were inventive, novel, suggestive, and sometimes dubious is to miss the point. Means do modify the ends, and Saint-Simonian means have often been adapted to the service of other ends—but not by the Saint-Simonians. Their concern for freedom was real. Ironically Rousseau, who occupies a position as high priest of democracy and revolution, was in *The Social Contract* mainly concerned with the legitimacy of "chains." The Saint-Simonians, interested in the freeing of human possibilities by pacific means, have been cast in the role of prophets of totalitarianism.

In the "Mémoires," to be sure, Enfantin's armies do "impose our civilization on the East." We may be dealing here with an early example of cultural imperialism, but a complex rather than a simple one. What is the justification? To eliminate slavery. Again, this is not an evil or antilibertarian motive.

But the pacific armies of the "Mémoires" anticipate problems that would emerge later as divisive, complicated, and, on the surface, insoluble. Two years after the "Mémoires" was written the movement would be shaken by the generous impulses that urged France once again to advance the cause of liberty by intervening militarily against the tyranny of czarist Russia in Poland. One of the classic liberal attacks on Saint-Simonian theory is built on the militarism and expansionism of some Saint-Simonian writers during this period.[13] But one cannot have it both ways. Pacifism meant acceptance of tyranny; military intervention would be justified by the extension of liberty. In 1830 the movement, for better or worse but at least consistently, came down on the side of pacifism.

The dilemma touched on in the "Mémoires" was not a Saint-Simonian problem; it was, and is, a problem of liberal bourgeois society. An associated topic hinted at in the "Mémoires" as well as in *Le Producteur,* was the question of the "East." The *industriel* goes to the East to "impose" his civilization. For Saint-Simonian historicism, assimilating Eastern experience into Saint-Simon's cyclical theory was a problem. To the Saint-Simonians Eastern experience seemed not to have changed or moved at all. It would require the energizing impulse of the West to set the Eastern motor going again. It would be, in some vague way, the removal of what was "sluggish" in the East, as in the West, that would bring about a new organicism. The prelude to the new organicism would be a "critical" epoch introduced by confrontation with the West.

The questions of the East and of the pacific army are only hinted at in Enfantin's early work, but they are persistent and recurrent themes tied to the themes of an ever-expanding economy and universal association that are central to the doctrine. The Saint-Simonians were too perceptive to believe that humans could be forced to be free. They must believe, they must have faith in the new Christianity before its goals can be realized. And while Enfantin was at work on the "Mémoires" he was also dealing with the question of faith, the character of religion, the nature of priesthood. But before leaving the "Mémoires" we must examine again the thesis of its essentially bourgeois character. There is in Saint-Simon him-self a startling statement that there are growing numbers of *industriels* in society and that eventually all people will form a part of that class.[14] *Industriel* as used by Saint-Simon in this context means "all those who work" as well as all those who work at providing work. Certainly the work ethic dominates the world of 2240. Merit rigorously applied is the standard for movement in this society. The narrator, son of a weaver, becomes an arbiter by dint of hard work, good reports, and successful realization of his assignments. Success is productivity, and productivity satisfies material wants.

Our arbiter enjoys ease and consideration. He marries but need not worry about the future. Widows and orphans do not inherit property but are cared for by the administrators of society. Social position, work, and rewards in new generations are determined by capacity and individual character. There are no bank failures, no industrial crises, no unemploy-ment. The government of men has been replaced by the administration of things—but men have not become things. The ideal seems almost Peri-clean: good men make good societies, and good societies make good men. What is perhaps missing, save for a passing but important reference to the passions of women, is what makes good women and what good women will make and do in this society.

The object of the good society—the betterment of the lot of the poorest and most numerous class by all possible means—rests on hard work, intelligence, and productivity. The society provides rewards, the opportu-nity for the expression of individual needs, the security of families, con-sideration, and ease; it stimulates learning and classifies by individual capacity and merit. There is little here to offend middle-class mores. There is every reason to suppose that all will be formed in a middle-class mold. The culture heroes will be the Laffittes of the new era, in whose houses and gardens the workers will meet to dine at tables with fifty places, to dance in great ballrooms, and to restore themselves in beautiful parks.

Such is the world of the year 2240. One would like a few more details about the reign of reason in the garden of love, but even the most severe critics can hardly deny that the *industriel* of the year 2240 was consider-ably more attractive than the *industriel* of the year 1828.

Enfantin's essay is somewhat revelatory of himself and of his historical experience. He casts himself in a very attractive role. He is a "generalist"; not for him the tedium of bookkeeping or drafting. He is loved by those whose destinies he guides. He is the leader of a *"mission civilisatrice"* and of an industrial army. He rises by merit. Interestingly enough he is the "stable" personality and his wife the "mobile" personality in their mar-riage. We hear nothing of parenthood at this stage of his career. But we do get a picture of the "new man," the technocrat who was so central to Saint-Simonian thought.

The *industriel* has banking experience, is an allocator of resources, and is involved in "impact" studies requiring engineering and manufacturing expertise. He is a determiner of needs, moves populations, builds cities, and reclaims wastelands. He is judged in terms of his capacity to get done what demands to be done. He is always changing, seeking the new. His is an ideal society precisely because it is not a stagnant one. Possibility and progress are built into it as axiomatically good.

Here in the figure of the technocrat and in the projection of the new society are perhaps the chief defenses against the accusations of totalitarianism. Betterment is an ongoing process, not a dead end. The "perfecting" of society does not stop, nor does that of individuals. There is no fixity, and thus there is no tyranny. Enfantin described the "Mémoires" as an imagining of how things might be, one among a possible many. As such it conveys the efforts he and others were making during 1827 and 1828 to move from ideas to action. The Saint-Simonians were fully as aware as their critics of the pitfalls to which their ideas might lead them. They were, however, satisfied that their view of developing history would permit escape from such pitfalls. They did not resort to polite disclaimers in defense of unattractive ideas; rather, their appeal was to a central doctrinal conviction that everything might change.

IF THE "Mémoires" was in part designed to comfort disturbed bourgeois like Rodrigues *père,* another important question discussed during the same period was equally disturbing to Enfantin's family. Religion, and particularly the notion of a Saint-Simonian priesthood, seemed as fraught with dangerous possibilities for freedom as did technocratic arrogance and the universal family discussed in the "Mémoires."

As with all its other theoretical debates the Saint-Simonian group began with the position of the Master himself. Saint-Simon on his death bed had said: "Our last work, *Le Nouveau Christianisme,* will be the last to be understood. *All the doctrine is there.*"[15] It will be remembered that Saint-Simon had also defined religion as the institutional embodiment of the scientific knowledge of a given age. It followed, then, that the creation of a religion conforming to the state of human knowledge at their epoch was not only a consistent but also an imperative step for the Saint-Simonians to take. It was also imperative that this religion carry within it the seeds of its own destruction, in that contemporary knowledge incorporated the notion of necessary change. A bit later Olinde Rodrigues would comment that "our religion commands us to resign our place when another shows himself worthier than we."[16] So much for the totalitarian, authoritarian, dictatorial character of that Saint-Simonian "aberration," the Saint-Simonian religion.

The religious discussion had been pushed—Enfantin confirms this—by Rodrigues, "then me, then Bazard, always the rebel."[17] It was as early as July 1827 (and precisely amid his personal crisis) that Enfantin had written to Dr. Bailly posing the question "Do psychological givens or observations permit one to recognize the existence of religious sentiment as being a disposition independent of reason?"[18]

Enfantin asks if we can accept as true that humans have the faculty of perceiving intuitively matters about which they do not reason and formulating that perception as a social institution, having the characteristic of common belief, called religion—a religion submitted in its refinement to the simultaneous development of the sciences and industry.

Humans, he goes on in the letter, are one, and they are double—moral and physical. Their morality is further divided into rational and intuitive activity. The universe is also one and double, consisting of simple and organized bodies (this was an idea of Saint-Simon's). He quotes Rodrigues to underline the distinction: "Where the reasoner sees life, he studies movement; where the artist sees movement, he senses life."

The language and the questions are cumbersome, but Enfantin is, in effect, reporting on the Saint-Simonian difficulties of the moment. "We are reasoners whereas so many industrialists are only machines, or instruments, and think only of their physical upkeep. The absence of religious sentiment among ourselves gives us nothing to conclude for the future." Bazard, for example, is said to recognize the existence of a mystic disposition but sees it as only one among many equivalent social attitudes, such as the love of parents for children or of a man for a woman. Enfantin argues that if one sentiment suggests all the others, it is because they are all linked, all susceptible to systematization. Simple philanthropy will not be sufficient for Saint-Simonian needs, because they must be linked not only to each other but also to the universe itself. They need the motor of religion.[19]

In another place Enfantin adjures: "Recall what Saint-Simon said about simple bodies and organized bodies. Analysis and synthesis . . . must ride astride the two branches of the universal trunk. One must trace both rivers to their common source. One must give to the pump's piston a double motion to be a true child of our master."[20] Pursuing the same theme a year later Enfantin commented that precisely because the love of men of learning for their science and that of *industriels* for their works could lead the ones to build observatories and the others to transform themselves into machines, the men who loved society above all must recall to both their social duty.[21]

The search, then, for a religious vehicle to carry the technocratic doctrine into the hearts of human beings was, in part at least, motivated by the desire to avoid the dehumanizing of learning without purpose and technique without social understanding. The search also had roots in the teachings of the Master. Enfantin's letter to Dr. Bailly was viewed by 1832 as one of the most important Saint-Simonian documents, "explaining our state of mind at the end of *Le Producteur,* and THAT explains in advance the later schisms."[22]

One question remains. Was the religion a manufactured object made to suit the specifications of the doctrine? Was it simply a technique, or was it, as the Saint-Simonians would so often say, "felt"?

The letter to Bailly was written in July of 1827, and in August, Enfantin wrote a note to Resseguier that can perhaps stand as a declaration of religious intent:

At our epoch we must strike on all doors, attack each specialty, present to artists a sentimental end for humanity, to *industriels* another, to scholars yet another in such a manner that these ends confound themselves in one, at which time an image enclosing them all could be presented to the masses without producing confusion and obscurity.[23]

Is one dealing in all this with a public relations campaign to sell soft social soap, or is one dealing with religion? The answer is "both." The problem was how to sell truth. But truth itself involved a religion of humanity. Saint-Simon had argued that one must convert the Christian world after eighteen centuries of Christianity to the social application of *aimez-vous, les uns les autres.* But it was not simply philanthropy that was in question. Philanthropy was goodness without purpose: mysticism enunciated purpose without goodness.

Religion, Enfantin would come to say, is the motor that drives from passivity to activity, from the center—the self—to the circumference—society—from individuality to universality, from the "I" to the "non-I."[24] And it was this motor that was sought and that was less built by the Saint-Simonians than believed to exist, as yet, in hiding. The search had been the subject of the "intimate" meetings of the group. It fed the correspondence with Resseguier that had begun early in 1827 and that culminated in his leadership of a Saint-Simonian "church" in the Midi. Eugène Rodrigues published that correspondence in 1829, and it has been viewed as the turning point of Saint-Simonian doctrine. But it is more likely that the correspondence reports the turning point, rather than constitutes it. It is, in any event, clear that Rodrigues's writings were subject to the inspiration and correction of Enfantin.[25]

By midsummer of 1828 the discussions had reached a point at which Enfantin wished to prepare those near him for the future direction of the school. The anticipated transformation is mapped in the correspondence with his cousin Thérèse Nugues in 1828 and 1829. As with every stage of the developing doctrine much is revealed, but there is always more to come. In the letters to Nugues there are hints of the priesthood, the doctrine of the liberation of the flesh, and Caesarism, but there are also a wealth of conviction and an absence of duplicity that give the letters a particular value.

The first of these letters is probably the most complete and most important. "I want to show you that the doctrine leads straight to heaven and is an obligatory accomplishment of the God who has wanted the human species to constantly better its physical and moral existence in order that He might receive the worship worthy of Him."[26] Humans are to be blamed if God does not receive this worship, because contemporary humans are richer and better instructed than were the Christians of the Middle Ages. Misery, ignorance, and vice invite commiseration and blame. "How impious an idea of God to suppose that He would wish to be worshipped in the present as He had been worshipped when the peoples of the Earth were perennially at war; when one part of humanity was exploited by another; when one worshipped the God of Armies, the God of Blood."

The peaceful God of labor, the God who willed that humankind pass through a long initiation of suffering to accomplish his law one day in all its philosophical purity, is indeed "the vengeful God, the terrible God invoked by our ancestors." He is always the same God, "but is He not better understood by us than He could be by men who lived in barbarism? Can WE not more worthily sing His praises who have reached the era when His reign is going to come? . . . We know what He wishes, what are the laws His wisdom imposes on us to assure our happiness."[27]

Past visions had seen God as king and dictated the rendering unto Caesar that which was Caesar's. But Caesar is no more and certainly ought not to be a crowned sword. The new Caesar will be the chief director of peaceful works; he will be the man who will employ all his power to constantly better the condition of the poorest class. Caesar will be the man most capable of presiding over the execution of the plan traced by God for the betterment of his privileged creation. The poor, the feeble are the chosen creation of God. It will be by "our devotion to this class that He will judge our merits, that He will chastise or reward us."[28]

Enfantin asks his cousin if the language of priests should remain always the same. He notes that she is wounded by attacks on priests but thinks that they ought not to mingle in politics. "If the reign of God is going to come," he responds, "is it not the function of the ministers of the Lord to make His laws felt? . . . When the God of Peace breaks the idols made by Caesar . . . must not the priests talk politics?" He points out that the

Romans presided at the butchery of slaves, soiled themselves with all the vices, played in the filthiest debauchery, and knew no God but gold but were, after all, converted to Christianity. Why should one despair of the present age? The Saint-Simonians believe that God still presides over human destinies. They believe, especially, that He has given the means of knowing what must be done so that humanity presents to His view what He expects of it: "that is to say, a pacific society, organized for great works, directing in common all its efforts to better the Earth He has created, to make better the men to whom He has given the power of ceaselessly drawing nearer to him; to elevate their sentiments by developing their intelligence."[29]

These means of organizing as God desires constitute the science of politics, according to Enfantin. It is the function of God's ministers to teach the elements of this science, to make its grandeur admired, to make its utility cherished. "There is the theology of our days, the knowledge of God. And how are we to know God if not by His works, and what work is more sublime than humanity?"

Enfantin turns to a personal and revealing note. "Don't look for traps," he tells his cousin. "I have changed much, rejected military glory and constitutional divinities. . . . My God is not immutable in His expressed will, because man changes at each epoch. . . . Why would He reveal all in advance that could not be FELT (think about this word). . . . It is precisely because His plan is drawn for all eternity that His language varies with each floor humanity constructs."[30]

The first religious letter to Thérèse Nugues concludes with a passionate attack on materialism uninformed by sentiment. Enfantin had loved his recently dead brother. Is it Auguste's "*organization* that I loved and love? There is more, and it is to the understanding of the 'more' that religion devotes itself and by its understanding converts not only the intellect but the life of the emotions as well."[31] It is the point of the letter, as of so much else written in this period, that before the possibilities of the material universe can be realized through the agency of technology, technocracy, and planning, people must *want* and *feel* the attraction of that new world. The religious sense of universality and of applied Christianity must precede the material transformation. It is to the cultivation of that wanting and feeling that the Saint-Simonian religion of love would be directed.

There is no doubt that by the fall of 1828 the Saint-Simonian faith was seeking a form. In subsequent letters to Nugues responding to her objections, Enfantin rejects the accusation that he sees himself as Luther, or Mathew, Mark, Luke, and John. "We have taken the apostles as our models." It must be understood that the "doctrine of Saint-Simon can also penetrate to the HEART of humanity, that it recognizes the passions, that it demands of its disciples the sacrifice of their present well-being, and that we do not put this passing well-being before everything else."[32] Later Enfantin says: "I know what there is of the extraordinary in my language and my ideas for you. Saint Paul speaking to the Jews and to Roman skeptics must have astonished them in the same way."[33]

The astonishment was to grow. Already the nuclear group of Saint-Simonians had begun to refer to themselves as the "College." During the time Enfantin had been cashier of the Caisse Hypothécaire he had met on Wednesday evenings at his apartment at the bank with all those interested in refloating *Le Producteur*. Notable in this group were Isaac Pereire, Eugène Rodrigues, Sarchi, Margerin, Fournel, and Carnot. Usually Bazard set the theme for discussion. By the end of 1828 the major question had become what practical steps to take to expand knowledge of the doctrine. A new *Producteur? A Philosophical Dictionary?* There were financial difficulties. What else? Regularizing and formalizing the group and giving it more public identity were essential. The leaders decided to form a "second degree" of initiates, who were installed at a ceremony on December 7, 1828.

Eugène Rodrigues addressed that meeting in words, guided by Enfantin, that were "ill-understood and which displeased": "We are called by the first disciples of Saint-Simon to the glorious work of mediating between them and all those who aspire to enter the doctrine. Our first duty is the propagation of the doctrine orally and in writing."[34]

Enfantin had told the new apostles that the strongest among them would be those who had formed the largest circle of believers. "Yes, my friends, it is a question of conversion," said Rodrigues. "Our fathers have versed torrents of light into our souls. Let us be fathers in turn, let us seek out the children that God has certainly given us!"[35]

Each of the disciples must cast out the "old" man, assure in himself the harmony of thoughts and feelings.

Children of the century, let us become children of eternity. . . . We shall be links in the eternal chain. . . . We are on the boundaries of two worlds: the Christian world and the world of the future. . . . Happier than the pupils of Plato and Aristotle, because we have their experience before our eyes, we see clearly on the one hand the doctrine of Saint-Simon, which corresponds to the philosophy of Socrates, and on the other we perceive, confusedly as yet, the religion corresponding to that of Christ in which the doctrine will be resolved.[36]

Enfantin later noted that this "revelation" of the younger Rodrigues marked the beginning of the Saint-Simonian usage of the titles "father," "son," and "brother" and, more importantly, the transformation from philosophical credo to religion. "It was the first time that the thought of eternal life had occupied so large a place in our thought and that the expectation of a religious revelation had been so clearly expressed."[37]

These last considerations perhaps explain the "displeasure" that would grow and be a source of schism. But hard on the heels of the initiation, Henri Fournel, who was there, wrote that at the regular Wednesday gathering of December 10, 1828, the decision was made to begin a regular *exposition* of the doctrine to which the new apostles would bring friends. A week later, on the seventeenth, Enfantin's rooms proved insufficient to hold the crowd, and an invitation was given for a meeting at a public hall in the rue Taranne. In the meantime, on the twenty-fourth the minutes of the seventeenth were read by Hippolyte Carnot. Edmund Talabot and Eugène Rodrigues read papers by themselves and by Fournel. This meeting of December 24, 1828, was the first session reported in *Doctrine Saint-Simonienne: Exposition, Première Année* and constituted the official founding of the Saint-Simonian religion.[38]

The "silent" expansion was over. For the next four years the Saint-Simonians would become increasingly vocal, visible, and eventually scandalous to their contemporaries. Much had been accomplished, and much had been clarified, but much was still hidden, doctrinally, from all but those at the center of the movement. An increasing number of young men and some women were being drawn by a technocratic vision appealing to emotion as well as reason.

From early 1827 Resseguier was spreading interest in Saint-Simonianism outside of Paris and in the south of France. Arlès-Dufour at Lyons was also propagating the new ideas. The *polytechniciens* formed a special group within the circle of the faithful. Bazard's expository talent was about to be displayed before a large audience, and the Rodrigues brothers had moved consideration of the new Christianity to the foreground of Saint-Simonian thought. Obviously Enfantin's extraordinary charm and energy were at work on both the old and new members of the group as they marched out into Paris to preach "the good news."

CHAPTER VI

THE GOOD NEWS

W HAT THE SAINT-SIMONIANS produced in the *Exposition* of their doctrine was their most striking intellectual monument — one of the central texts of romantic socialism. The one writing of theirs that is known, it is frequently disliked from left to right on the political spectrum and seldom praised. Without exegesis it does the school a certain injustice and masks important conflicts among its authors. It has usually, and mistakenly, been taken to be the final and authoritative statement of Saint-Simonian doctrine. Context is all important to its understanding; a recognition of its didactic and polemical nature is required. But with all these caveats it made a noise in its time that was heard across Europe.

The *Exposition* may be unique in that it was the statement of a movement rather than of a single person, genuinely collaborative in nature. In this respect it was unlike the writings of Owen, Fourier, Blanc, or Saint-Simon himself. The sermons, as they must now be named, were delivered on alternate Wednesdays by Bazard. Carnot edited the published texts. The content and form of each sermon came out of the discussions of the central group: Enfantin, Bazard, Buchez, Olinde and Eugène Rodrigues, Laurent, and Margerin. These met on Mondays and Fridays, usually at Enfantin's apartment in the Caisse Hypothécaire. The public sessions took place at 12 rue Taranne, now gone, but in 1829 occupying the area of the boulevard Saint-Germain between the rue de Rennes and the rue des Saints-Pères.

Later it would be found easy to condemn Enfantin as the corruptor of Saint-Simon's doctrine and of Saint-Simon's followers, but the condemnation would not be just. The religious bent of Saint-Simonianism was attributable to, above all others, Olinde and Eugène Rodrigues. Bazard's lectures were informed by discussion and criticism of the entire group. Carnot reports having revised the texts for publication five or six times. Enfantin, to be sure, was present, important, and, since the death of his brother, ready and eager for some view of a future life and a religious present. But he was by no means alone. The Saint-Simonian religion was a Saint-Simonian, not an Enfantinian, product. The insistence of the Rodrigues brothers on religious themes derived, in turn, from Olinde Rodrigues's presence at Saint-Simon's own death bed and from Saint-Simon's last work, *Le Nouveau Christianisme.* Eugène had translated a work of Lessing on education as accompaniment to his *Letter on Religion* because of the equation Lessing makes between religion and scientific knowledge, a link also found in Saint-Simon.

The point of the *Exposition* was to provide a kind of *Summa Contra Gentiles,* a rational form of persuasion for the unconvinced that the Saint-Simonians had indeed found a chain to link the visible and the invisible worlds. At the first meeting, when challenged by a listener as to Saint-Simonian purposes and intentions, Olinde Rodrigues replied: "We are both the heirs of Catholicism and the continuers of the Revolution. We want to achieve the destruction of what remains of throne and altar and on the debris reconstruct society and authority."[1] In that summation most of the complicated themes of the *Exposition* were revealed.

Of that first meeting we have Edouard Charton's eyewitness account.[2] A provincial just come to Paris, hearing loud noises on his landing, he investigated and saw

a large crowd. The atmosphere was stifling. Seated at a table in the middle of a row of young men, two middle-aged men commanded everybody's attention. Their bearing and looks evidenced great will power; their stature bore witness to remarkable physical strength. One of them spoke; words emerged slowly from his lips; he turned a wooden pillbox between his fingers, and his head, nearly motionless, swayed almost imperceptibly backwards. He raised his eyes only when he wished one of his sentences to be felt more vividly than the rest. "What's his name" I asked my neighbor.

"Bazard."

"And the other?" I asked, indicating the second personage, who with a singularly majestic air cast a caressing glance over the assembly.

"Enfantin."

Charton, drawn especially to Enfantin, would become an ardent Saint-Simonian.

From this first meeting the group was engaged, in a sense, in the composition of a New Testament. There was nothing whose sources could not be found in Saint-Simon, but there was an efflorescence in the *Exposition,* a definition and development of ideas that the Master had lacked. There were also hidden recesses. As with *Le Producteur,* so with the *Exposition,* what was discussed in public was a formulation of the conclusions of discussions already past. Private discussions did, however, continue, and at the time of the *Exposition's* delivery additional conclusions that the Saint-Simonians collectively judged too daring yet to expose to the public view had already been reached. "It is not," Paulin Talabot was to comment a bit later, "necessary to say everything everywhere."[3]

The usual view, which depicts later developments of the doctrine as an Enfantinian revolution, a Saint-Simonian heresy, is simply astigmatic.

The questions of sex, marriage, and paternity were already under exploration by 1830. The questions of hierarchy, authority, and priesthood had already been answered by 1830 and would be broached publicly in the second year of the *Exposition*. Enfantin would indeed emerge as the single "father" of the Saint-Simonian religion seeking a female Messiah. But this role was not attributable to new doctrine but to acceptance of Enfantin's interpretation of a doctrine long ago agreed upon by all the central members of the school.

Misunderstanding of this process accounts for the fundamental failure of so many critics to understand the school and its doctrine. The *Exposition* was a faithful reproduction of some, but only some, of the central ideas of Saint-Simonianism. It was designed to interest, to attract, to fascinate but not, precisely because of the more sensitive questions already raised, *not* to reveal all.

What then is revealed? What transformation has been achieved since the death of Saint-Simon and the death of *Le Producteur*? The doctrine emerges as more muscular, more nervous, more synergistic. Connections have been made, the relationships of parts to the whole have been worked out, and the possibilities of extensions of the doctrine begin to become clear. The reader may find the result intellectually repellent or intellectually compelling, but there is a rigor, a clarity of design that had been lacking heretofore and that accounts for the impact of, and reactions to, the *Exposition*.

Given the previous manifestoes of the group, two themes in the *Exposition* have some degree of novelty: that of religion and that of what is disingenuously referred to as the "*beaux-arts*." These two intertwined themes are essential to each other, and they rest on Saint-Simon's understanding of history and of physiology.

The *Exposition* begins with a picture of the present moment in history. "Everywhere there is disorder." Clearly the world since Luther and up to the announcement of Saint-Simon's message has been suffering under the destructiveness of a critical epoch. But there is no cause for fear. To those who understand the way in which history moves, who can see the comparable events in each epoch, who can sense the "homogeneity" of history and the place of any given event in the "series" of necessary events, the imminent birth of a new organic epoch is clear.[4]

Luther and Socrates proclaimed critical epochs, and Moses and Christ, organic ones. Saint-Simon is the most recent organicist. The common characteristic of all three is that they are givers of law; they announce the truth as it is known in their time. History does not move in circles, it progresses. The age of Christ knew more than the age of Moses; the age of Saint-Simon knows more than the age of Christ. Religion is the expression of what is known and lays down the law of what must be done in accordance with what it knows. God reveals what people are capable of "using" at any given time. Since knowledge is cumulative, the laws must change. God does not expect the nineteenth century to worship Him as the ages of Moses or Christ did. Hence the need for a new religion. What was wrong with the old? The separation of the temporal and the spiritual, of matter and mind, of the now and the hereafter, of reason and emotion. The new religion must bridge these chasms and must make human social organization whole.[5]

Here is the role of the fine arts and of the artist. Art and artists represent the affective side of humankind. *Their* existence proves *its.* They possess a truth that is not reasoned but *felt,* intuited; it is not less true for that. Religion and the capacity to recognize its truth depend on this human capacity for feeling and its encouragement.[6]

The Saint-Simonians were arguing that the historical moment was ripe for a renewed religion; the religion would bring feeling, an intuitive acceptance of what was rationally required to resolve the crisis of intellect and the crisis of a society divided by greed and egoism. "We must love one another" had been the message of Christ and of Saint-Simon. The Saint-Simonians would add, "We must love one another here and now."

Society requires organization, direction in thought and action, to exploit the globe for the moral, intellectual, and material betterment of humanity. The new religion could destroy, root and branch, the dichotomy between spirit and matter. It will rehabilitate the material world. It will, from its moral and loving foundations, dictate the goals to which intellect should bend itself so that everyone will know sufficiency and material satisfaction, including the satisfaction of "the most secret joys of private life." This religion will be the expression of the organic epoch whose coming is inevitable and imminent.[7]

Saint-Simonian talk of the "fine arts" is initially an irritant and a mystification. The words have a special meaning, applying "to all expressions of sympathy and antipathy"; they equal the passionate life of humanity. The fine arts can be scientifically observed, conclusions can be drawn from the observations, and moral imperatives can be based on them. These observations are best carried out by the most loving, most sensitive, and most intuitive of humans—the artists.

In turn, artists are not simply the possessors of certain skills. Painters, pianists, and poets, they are the possessors of the insights that call these skills into being. It is the particular kind of intelligence, the flash point of feeling and understanding, that characterizes artists and authorizes their priesthood in the new religion, their role as givers of law.[8]

Yes, there will be a priest and a law, but these in the early stages of the *Exposition* lurk behind the fine arts and their affective nature. Fundamental in the earliest preaching is the view that the disorder ruling the life of intellect and the life of society will persist until these are given purpose and direction by the pronouncements of Saint-Simon.

The objections that could be raised against the proposed reliance on intuition were as clear to the Saint-Simonians as to their opponents. Science builds upon reason, having nothing to do with superstition. Freedom of thought and of the person were legacies of the recent Revolution. Submission of intellect and emotion to a higher authority had become anathema; the mobilization and planning of society can lead to tyranny. But it is the conviction of the Saint-Simonians that their religion, their priesthood, their mission need not end in this way. Even if they were to do so, such a future might be more desirable than the present, from which Saint-Simonians are seeking liberation. "Society presents the image of two armed camps," that of the religious or political defenders of the Middle Ages and that of the partisans of new ideas, all those who applauded the overthrow of the Old Regime. "It is between these two armies that we come to bring peace. The doctrine preaches not only a horror of bloodshed but also the horror of battle—of antagonism, opposition, and competition. We recognize in human beings no natural right to disembowel one another."[9]

The Saint-Simonians are aware of the widespread fear of despotism and of the view that common beliefs and actions are an affront to individual pride and are only a new yoke. But the *Exposition* attempts to persuade its audience that a common view, a common purpose, a common direction will bring about liberation from social disorder, not oppression. How successful the school might be was to some degree a function of how convincing its picture of disorder really was.

The school sees disorder as the only organizing principle of society at the time. Starting with scientific inquiry, it points out the randomness of inquiry, the variety of conclusions, the gap between scientific theory and social practice, and the inability to translate insights about the nature of the physical universe into operational concepts for the social universe. Science, the Saint-Simonians believe, is an activity divided between the perfection and the application of theory. They fault science for its absence of the hierarchical organization of ideas, its lack of general direction. There is no inventory of achievements, no overall grasp of work under way. Isolated scholars are doomed to duplicate one another's work and are besieged by competition.[10]

To expand the realm of the purely theoretical a combination of luck and ability is required—a rare combination. Discoveries once made are not easily translated into the educational process and, consequently, have little effect. The sciences present a spectacle of complete anarchy deriving from the absence of agreement on the place of science in society. If one can discover such a common view, one will find the remedy for the anarchy.

There is in this rapid overview of science one of those original aperçus that give Saint-Simonianism much of its permanent interest. Whatever the exaggeration and whatever the shortcomings of the Saint-Simonians' portrait of the sciences, there is in their critique, more than implied, a vision of science as an institutional activity carried on collectively and efficiently. It is an activity that will move faster in its efforts to map the universe by eliminating waste motion, reducing destructive competition, making known its results, and addressing itself rapidly to the social implications of these results. A science whose social relevance is made clear through education will be the recipient of the social capital required for its maintenance, its continuity, and the accumulation of truths upon which society must build.

Just as Saint-Simon foresaw the character of the industrial world that was coming, so his disciples foresee the character and structure of science as it might and will be. Whatever the baroque decorations of their theories, the sight of the Saint-Simonians is keen. But it must also be said that in the description of science the problem that pervades the whole doctrine is present. The response of the pure scientist to the Saint-Simonian critique would be that it is the object of the scientist to know, not to be socially programmed for social purposes. The objectives are antithetical. The Saint-Simonians respond that an organized science will know more faster, that the objectives are not at all antithetical. What science wants, organization and direction can give it. Without denigrating the achievements of science, and while admitting that those achievements have already had an impact on technology and industry, the *Exposition* asks, "Couldn't social improvements have been more rapid?"[11]

Industry is as subject to disorder as is science. It is as marked as science by the expense of isolated efforts. The only sentiment dominating all industrial thought is egoism. The industrialist cares little for society. His family is for him a means of production and of increasing his personal fortune. "*Voila* his humanity, his universe, his God!"[12] Industry is managed by stupid people who have not recognized their self-interest in knowing what they need to know, in seeing that industry should be organized. Industry must see itself as a deduction drawn from science, as applying the scientific givens to material production. Industry ought not to be a simple collection of routine procedures more or less confirmed by experience.

Yet in the organization of work everything is left to the chance of individual understanding and judgment. It is essential that those interrelated components of industrial organization be understood: (1) its technology, (2) the division of labor leading to production and its relationship to distribution, and (3) the human relations of workers with the owners of the instruments of labor. In short, the social implications of industry (like those of science) demand planning, organization, and purposiveness.[13]

Against this view the proponents of laissez-faire press the claims of individualism, egotism, and free competition. But the Saint-Simonians point out that in a competition somebody wins, and somebody loses. It is their ambition to make everybody a winner. This is the thrust of their attack on their society. It is an ambition, they maintain, that can be fulfilled by knowledge, by foresight, by organization, and by universal acceptance of the announced goal. This is the hope they offer their audience, their century, and the future.

Laissez-faire supposes that the general interest is always in harmony with particular interest. Everything balances out. But "are the miserable to be patient, because statistics prove that in a number of years they will have bread?" The conquests of industry should not be like those of war; "funeral chants should not be mingled with shouts of victory."[14] The belief that everybody can be a winner, that there is enough to go around, can be verified, but only when the means of production, land, workshops, and capital are confided to the cleverest hands, to those who really understand the nature of industry, who are themselves possessed of productive industrial capacities. As things stand in 1829, capacity is a very feeble claim to credit. To get credit you have to have it already. This last observation reflects the frustration of young Saint-Simonians full of ideas, unable to get them financed, and consequently determined to modify the banking system.

To bring about such modifications the doctrine will condemn inheritance and elevate the role of individual liberty and intelligence. Before embarking on these stormy seas, however, Bazard and his colleagues felt it necessary to further examine the state of anarchy in the fine arts.

The arts are languishing. Why? They consist of a poetry, a spirit, and the forms and techniques that express them. Poetry, or the animating force, disappears, and techniques survive. Artists become antisocial; their preferred forms in literature are satire and elegy. But the real reason for the languishing of the arts is that when society has no love, the arts have no voice. For artists to reveal themselves there has to be an echo for their song, an echo to receive and return their soul. The love does not exist; the echo is not heard.[15]

The "critical" character of Restoration society demands, in industry as in science and the arts, a rejection of the currently received notions of individualism and libertarianism. The notions are not bad in themselves, but under the Restoration they are masks presenting benevolent faces that hide a hideously pockmarked and deformed social reality. Under laissez-faire each person sees all others as enemies. A few fortunate people triumph but at the price of the complete ruin of innumerable victims. Honest and laborious people are destroyed, and morality is mortally wounded. Trickiness, corner-cutting, and calculation replace honest work, and once this path is followed, all is lost. In this cold, calculating, hypocritical, essentially unreasonable, destructive, and suicidal universe there is no room for philanthropy. Philanthropy will return by way of an artistic explosion displaying, exciting, arousing, and exemplifying the love of humanity that must be the motive force in bringing about change.[16]

All the great themes of Saint-Simonian doctrine are outlined, if ambiguously, in the first lecture. They are sufficiently unambiguous, however, to permit an understanding of what has aroused the suspicion and distaste of subsequent generations of libertarians and individualists. One cannot reiterate too often that the Saint-Simonians' attack is directed to conditions as they saw them in the 1820s. The conditions were there.

The Saint-Simonians were acute observers; they were intensely sensitive. They themselves felt the lacks they described. They did not feel free; did not find scope for their own individualism in their own society. They were filled with an immense, if sometimes patronizing, compassion for all those much less fortunate than themselves. They even displayed compassion for those who saw themselves as fortunate but who inevitably suffered from the human poverties of the existing social system: "In sketching a painful picture we only wish to be truthful. We spared you all the pain one has to feel in penetrating the intimacy of these families without faith, without belief, turned in on themselves, attached to society only by taxes."[17]

Saint-Simonians in their first *Exposition* of doctrine had a sense of what science might be, of what industry and work might be, and of what people might be. They had a clear vision of what freedom was not and of what unbridled individualism might become. In subsequent sessions Bazard would explore details, fill in gaps, and chart a course for the future, but in this first session Saint-Simonianism declared war on the world of the Restoration. It proffered to all humans a crown of hope as a reward for their labors.

How ARE humans to realize their hope? First, they have to grasp the significance of the present crisis against the background of history. In the face of this crisis the Saint-Simonians announce themselves as "calm" (a word that before the movement reached its flood tide would be rich with particular resonances for members of the school), because the present crisis is like, though not identical with, crises of the past. Saint-Simon supposed a history obeying laws of physiological and progressive development. These laws required humans to "gravitate" toward universal association, toward the formation of a collective being all of whose organs, performing separate functions, would contribute to perpetuating the life of the whole.

The word *gravitate* is not metaphorical but assumes "gravity" as a principle explaining not only heavenly motion but also the motions of people in relation to one another. Universal association is inevitable as an expression of the laws of nature. The twentieth-century parallel to Saint-Simonian thought might be found in the widespread use of the term *relativity* to describe moral relationships as well as those of the physical universe. It will be remembered that one of Saint-Simon's earliest proposals was that scholars, industrialists, and workers gather at the tomb of Newton to open a subscription for the revitalization of society. Gravity may indeed be one of the more baroque ornamentations of Saint-Simonian theory, but it is an ornament central to the design of the entire edifice.[18]

Gravity explains historical motion, and thus history can be analyzed scientifically. In the first year of the *Exposition* the discussion of history, like the discussion of fine arts, is elliptical, sometimes opaque, and irritating in what it does not say. Perhaps out of a desire not to be overly metaphysical, perhaps because the audience is thought to be unready, Bazard speaks of Saint-Simonian revelations without displaying some of their interconnections. To understand fully this first sketch, one has to keep in mind what Saint-Simon suggested and remember that he largely confined himself to Western history.

History is seen as obeying physiological laws based on the fundamental law of gravitation discussed earlier. The "collective being" in formation is a social "person" subject to the physiological laws governing the life of any human being. The social person experiences an organic growth and decay like that of the individual. The social being goes through "organic" and "critical" stages—is born, matures, dies, and is reborn. Every period is subject to the same stages—the era of cooperation (organic) and the era of competition (decay and death). In these characteristics every period resembles every other; in a sense history repeats itself. There is a prescribed *series* of events in the life of every society, and to understand one's own society and one's own history, one needs to know the relationship of specific events in one's own time to the prescribed series in the life of all societies. One needs (it is an anachronistic comparison) to be able to take the temperature and the blood pressure of one's own society and measure it against the "normality" of organicism and the "pathology" of the "critical" age. With time, experience, and accumulated history, the ability to take the accurate measure increases and, with it, the ability to control and correct social health. History is cyclical but also progressive, and its progress is in the direction of universal and harmonious association.[19]

In these views, then, is a haunting suggestion of Darwin's "tangled bank," imagined in the *Origin of Species* thirty years later, where bushes, birds, earthworms, and a multitude of other forms live out their individual history on one time scale and the common history on another.[20] There is also an intuition of what the Annales school would later describe as *conjoncture,* the coming together at a given moment of a totality of experience producing or accounting for change. "The present," Bazard says, "is only a point in space, a moment in time. It is the unseizable link between past and future; it encloses a résumé of one and the germ of the other."[21]

History, then, can be analyzed scientifically. The conceptions of Saint-Simon can best be verified by Western history. It is the best known and most "progressive" history; it has arrived faster and moved further than that of the "Orient." Saint-Simon had not been troubled by questions of cultural relativity; his followers were. The Orient was anywhere east of Athens and south of Marseilles. The Saint-Simonian concern for the East was less with China or India than with the world of Islam and Judaism. It represented the soul searchings of such assimilated Jews as Gustave d'Eichthal and at the same time the need to assimilate into their thought the Algiers that in the next year, 1830, became French. But at this juncture the Eastern question was handily taken care of by the assertion that Western history was best known and richest in examples of the "series" of events that would be the raw materials of a predictive historical science.[22]

Saint-Simon's views can be verified by history. It is the mission of his followers to develop those views. The most all-inclusive of them is the idea that history displays a moral progress that will lead humankind to recognize its social destiny. Political institutions are the instruments of bringing about this recognition, of applying the concept to given social circumstances. The process itself must depend on emotion, intelligence, and action as agents of historical inevitability.

Those qualities must be developed in sympathetic people who know how to communicate to the masses. A constant progress of the intellect is already visible. Industry, having profited from the advance of intellect, must devote itself to organizing the harmonic action of humanity on nature.

History is composed of a series of events marching on, and removing barriers from, the path of perfectibility. The law of perfectibility is so absolute that whenever a people become stationary, the germs of progress compressed by it are immediately transferred elsewhere, to a soil where they can develop. The decadence or fall of empires can be explained by this emigration of civilization. Present civilization will flourish and spread as a consequence of ending warfare, personal, social, and national.[23]

If the law of progress is so clear, its results so inevitable, why does it need explanation or examination? Because there is a link to specific events. To understand where you are is an essential step in arriving at your necessary destination; it is, in itself at this moment, an element of the law of progress. Historians in the past concentrated on individual actions and thought of individuals as totally developed at the moment of action. They supposed that history repeats itself and concluded that the past could teach or guide the present in given situations. But from the point of view of a law of progress that sees a necessary series of events as contributing to social fulfillment, such lessons are illusory. The same circumstances do not have the same meanings if they do not reproduce themselves at the same point in the series. They are not, in fact, the same for the collective being any more than like events would be the same at different stages in the life of the individual. There is the undifferentiated time in which all events take place, and there is the clock that marks the time of a particular evolution of a particular civilization. The two are not identical, and the meanings of historical events within the two temporal frameworks are no more identical.

Conventional history has made people out to be abstract reasoning beings, and historians have reconstructed individual lives. But none has studied the life of humanity. Some historians speak of infancy, youth, and virility in order to explain decadence or to demand that Europe model itself on young America. Others announce a progress or a perfectibility in a void. The greatest events are explained as the product of contingency, chance, unforeseen genius, fortuitous discovery. In this kind of analysis one does not see the state of society as the consequence that rendered these events necessary; one does not see each evolution as the indispensable result of an anterior revolution.

History studied from the Saint-Simonian point of view becomes quite other than a collection of experiments or dramatic facts good for enlivening the imagination. It presents successive tableaux of the physiological states of humankind considered in its collective existence. It constitutes a science that assumes the rigor of the exact sciences. "If we insist on history so much as verification, it is because we are future-minded but wish to start from a scientific base. Our foresight has the same bases as those that appear in scientific discoveries. The genius of Saint-Simon is of the same nature as that of Kepler and Galileo."[24]

If there is in the connection of facts such rigor as the *Exposition* describes, is the result fatalism? The answer to the question is yes. If people could make a complete abstraction of their desires and hopes and coldly and rationally deduce the future from the past, they would have to regard themselves as subject to fatality. But no such people exist in nature.

People intuit their destiny; they imagine, *feel* their destiny. When they have examined their intuitions and have assured themselves of their legitimacy, they advance with ardor and confidence toward the known future. Sure of their destiny, they direct their will and their energy toward it; they know before acting what the general result of their action will be. In some such fashion they become free and intelligent agents of their destiny. If they cannot change it, they can at least hasten it. The more people are conscious of their destiny, the more they work in concert with God to realize it.[25]

The lengthy excursus on history in the second session of the *Exposition* is of central importance. The authors are laboring with language to describe that which does not yet exist. On one level the discussion pleads for a history that is social, that deals with collectivities, total experience, and *conjoncture,* that deals not with isolated events but with the meanings of events and with the patterns they form.

The Saint-Simonians were certainly not alone in seeking to make history scientific. They were not alone in resorting to biological metaphor, and not alone in believing that obedience to law is liberty. But they would not agree with Tolstoy's perception that the more law we have, the less free we are. They were perhaps unique in their understanding of historical process as both subject to law and open-ended.

Saint-Simonianism supposes that humanity tends toward universal association. What the character of that association may be, what its forms and expressions may be, how it will move toward its ends are reflections of a never-ending process. There is always the possibility that more science, more history will open more possibility, more movement. Time does not stop; consequently, neither do institutions, beliefs, experiences. There is no danger of submission to persons or to creeds, because persons and creeds are themselves subject to historical processes and are constantly under judgment by them.

History has already told us some truths, and more will be revealed. With revelation social transformation becomes automatic. There is in this vision a fatality of futurity that constitutes freedom. One can perhaps become shrill in defending the Saint-Simonians as libertarians, but it is undeniable that they were such, that they cared for liberty in their fashion and as they understood it. Their audiences at least understood their description of un-freedom and, it was hoped, would see history as liberator.

The fourth, fifth, and sixth sessions of the *Exposition* enter into an analysis of Western history and what the doctrine takes it to mean. History moves "antagonistically" toward its end. The alternating character of historical epochs is only a regular "series" of efforts made to attain a defined end. The end is universal association, but association is, in turn, a means. What is *its* end? Means and end are confounded by a historical flow toward peace.

There are only two human conditions, present antagonism and future association. In the state of association the classification of the human family presents itself as a division of labor, as a systematizing of efforts to attain a common end: each class or group sees its own prosperity and growth in the prosperity and growth of all the others.[26]

The Saint-Simonians in this analysis appear to be trembling on the brink of Hegel and Marx. Progress is always progressing, but hate and antagonism are always present. Within each of the series of social states there are always battles of present and future and conflict in the present itself, in the family, the city, the nation, and the church. "The battle is waged in the family between the sexes, between generations and brothers, between soul and intellect. The seeds of division within each association are perpetuated after its fusion in a greater association but with always decreasing intensity in the measure that the circle of association extends itself."[27]

There is evidence to suggest that this view of historical process was derived from Kant in a form publicized by Comte, to whom, however, it had been introduced by the now ardent Saint-Simonian d'Eichthal.[28] The conceptions of internal contradiction and classification do seem to beg for the wording that such a social epoch bears within it the seeds of its own destruction. There is no doubt that when the Saint-Simonians speak of "classification," they mean classification by economic function and economic reward. There is equally no doubt that the young Marx read the *Exposition*.[29]

Concluding this part of the argument is the proposition that antagonism in preparing the way for a larger association would devour itself and disappear. All the past has been a vast state of systematized warfare between the classes of masters, plebeians, and slaves. The entire contemporary working class is only a prolongation of the slave class. In the past the place of individual progress was ill-defined, and the social combinations favoring moral, intellectual, and physical development were not capable of improvement.

There must be an *organization* of progress. Again it is necessary to insist on the literal application the Saint-Simonians gave the biological term. Each organ in its specific way contributes to the life of the body politic. The past has been marked with the exploitation of man by man. The future will be marked by the exploitation of nature by man associated to man, by class and function associated with class and function.

Europe, "metropolis of the world," exemplifies and verifies these general propositions. Since the birth of Christianity the Orient has ceased to enlighten the West. The Hebrew nation received from Moses an organization stronger than that of its companions in emigration and exile. Its mission was not to conquer in warlike fashion but to spread its conception of unity against the division of temporal and spiritual power, of the peaceful and warrior society. The Christian church was founded on the brotherhood of man, but the French Revolution overturned the throne of Caesar and delivered the last blow to the chair of Saint Peter. From now on humanity must work to transform education, legislation, and the organization of property. Humanity is afflicted by war over commercial

101

privilege, by the empire of physical force in governmental forms, in legislation, and in the relations of the sexes. It is doubtful that the transactions
of masters and workers are really free.[30]

No one ought to be paralyzed by the circumstances of birth. There
ought to be exchanges between families and individuals of different
classes. Then, at least, exploitation would be moved from place to place
in society. But such exchanges have not taken place, and one aspect of the
social scene is clear—the inheritance of misery by a class of proletarians.
The entire mass of workers is exploited by those whose property it uses.
The worker, a direct descendant of the slave, can exist only under conditions imposed by a small class that legislation, the daughter of the right
of conquest, invests with the monopoly of wealth, with the right to dispose, without any labor on its part, of the instruments of labor. How can
workers develop their abilities? There must be a durable, legitimate revolution to better the condition of the poorest and most numerous class.[31]

Looking at the prospect of universal association from an industrial
point of view, one finds that the source of exploitation is heredity. Property must be seen as an institution with variable meanings. It is the base of
social order. But like all other social factors the institution of property is
subject to the law of progress. It can be defined, understood, and regulated in a variety of ways.

The exploitation of man by man must disappear; the constitution of
property by which this exploitation is perpetuated must also disappear. It
is sometimes argued that what the worker gives is a just return for use.
But who ought to determine use? Who should own the tools, and how
should they be transmitted? To justify the existing state of affairs, an appeal is often made to natural law, divine law, or utility. But laws are always progressive (that is, relative), and utility varies with the stages of
progress.

Today a major change is necessary. It is the duty of the moralist to prepare for the change and, later, for the legislator to prescribe it. The law
of progress is moving to establish an order of things in which the state and
not the family will inherit wealth, because that wealth is the financial
spring of industrial productivity.[32]

The authors of the *Exposition* hasten to add that they are not advocating a community of goods—not what was then understood as communism. Everyone in society will be classified according to capacity and will
be rewarded according to work. Without an inequality of rewards the attractive power of emulation would be lost, and equal contributions would
be expected from unequal capacities—an injustice.

What, then, would be a just constitution of property? In the moral order
there is a perpetual state of antagonism between that which is good and
right and that which is useful and bad. Humanity must choose between

these alternatives rather than, in vain, trying to reconcile them. In a "critical" epoch the most reputable and wisest people choose utility over virtue. The consequence is that people are constantly torn between duty and interest, devotion and egotism, perpetual sacrifice and immorality. But the oppositions are false. Human conscience has always been able to be in harmony with the different conceptions of property, whether they entail the right of the eldest or of all equally.

Transferring the right of property to the state would, in effect, create the association of all workers. The sole right to wealth in that association is capacity. Work is the title to property. The sole human right to property arises from directing its use, using it, or deriving benefit from it. The right is justified, since in divine law everyone is of the same family. People are called to liberty in the use of property, not to the cruelest slavery in being used by it.[33]

As things now stand, property is composed of wealth not destined to be immediately consumed and giving right to a revenue—these are the "funds of production," the instruments of labor. Proprietors and capitalists are depositories of these instruments. They certainly do not deliver their services cheaply. They create crises and catastrophes, and they do not bring much intelligence to the job.

Good productive practice demands that the means of production be distributed where and how they are needed by those most capable of managing production to avoid shortage or surplus. None of these conditions is presently being met. There is no overview. Industry is managed by the ignorant and the isolated, who do not know the needs of industry and of people or how to bring them together. A new social institution is needed, vested with the functions so badly performed now. It will be the depository of all instruments of production, preside over all material exploitation, and perceive all parts of the industrial whole.[34]

In this new world everything has been changed. Intellectual and moral qualities coexist peacefully. Work is done as well as the state of society permits. The circle of people who can aspire to be its princes and chief embraces all humanity. The chances of making right choices increase; the means of decision making are perfected. The disorder resulting from lack of understanding and the blind partition of the agents and instruments of production disappear. And with these disorders also disappear the reverses of fortune, the failures from which no peaceful workers can presently believe themselves sheltered. Industry is *organized,* all is connected, all is foreseen, the division of labor is perfect, and the combination of efforts becomes each day more powerful.[35]

POLITICS makes no sense without industry, and at the center of industry are banks and bankers. To transform politics and industry one must change banking. On the one hand, there must be centralization embodied in a directing and unifying bank. On the other, there must be banking specialties, organized vertically and hierarchically, feeding information to the apex so that there can be an intelligent distribution of credits and a higher degree of productivity.

This reorganization of banking must rest on the reconstitution of property. The central bank becomes the depository of all wealth. To it and its immediate subsidiaries flow all the demands, and from it flows all that is necessary to the project. Central banks could grant credit, after having balanced general needs and assets, to individuals through the local and specialized banks. These credits would produce a tax to support "intelligence and sentiment." Always sensitive to accusations of fantasy, the authors of the *Exposition* point out that what they propose for banking is no more chimerical than the organization of an army.

"The colonel does not own troops or guns"; they are assigned to him. "He who produces can love glory, can have as much a sense of honor as he who destroys." What is described is, indeed, an industrial army of producers. And in this sketch one can perceive something of how "government" is to be replaced by "administration."[36] The big problem is production. Successful productivity rests (as the critical Hayek correctly notes) on an assumption of total and self-revelatory information dictating courses of action.[37] One operates from what is known to what is needed. The question of force or repression does not arise.

The industrial army performs its acknowledged and accepted tasks. One has moved from the government of men to the administration of things. Eyebrows may rise at the oversimplification of social issues, but the outline of economic organization anticipates in a curious way the hint of intellectual and industrial organization characteristic of Western societies. The philanthropic foundation or the state performs the functions of a central bank, and the universities and research institutes perform those of the subsidiary banks, feeding demands, distributing rewards, and determining the direction of intellectual productivity. In both processes there may be ample room for frustration, but there is nothing inherently undemocratic or oppressive in the procedure.

The parallel is no accident. In another stage of his life Enfantin would elaborate the notion of a Crédit Intellectuel (like the Pereires' Crédit Mobilier), which would be viewed with as much astonishment in that realm as the notion of a central controlling and inciting banking system for industry and a reorganization of property was viewed in the 1830s.[38]

In any event the *Exposition*'s audience was assured that the passage from the old to the new system would not be brusque and violent. It would be prepared for by the simultaneous action of imagination and demonstration. A consciousness of that property, as presently constituted, is not a given is reiterated along with Rousseau's dictum: *"Celui qui mange dans l'oisiveté ce qu'il n'a pas gagné lui-même, le vole."* In the end the unquestioned title to property is work.[39]

One of the more fascinating sidelights of Saint-Simonian views on property is the history of the ways in which the idea of the regulatory banking system and the industrial and pacific army became central, a century later, to the creed of the liberal politicians and economists who most distrusted Saint-Simonian authoritarianism. But that is a story for another time and place.

From the ninth to the seventeenth sessions of the 1829–30 meetings the *Exposition* concentrates on the education essential for the acceptance of the ideas already offered as a model for the new society. Education comprises all the means employed to appropriate each new generation to the social order to which it is called by the march of humanity. Again one winces at the definition so baldly directed to indoctrination. But one must ask, in all fairness, when has education been anything else? One may indoctrinate the young with the values of an open society, self-exploration, disinterested learning, and general freedom, but one is nonetheless indoctrinating. The Saint-Simonians' chief sin was to say what everybody knew to be true but what nobody else was prepared to deal with.

Education would be devoted to developing the three faculties recognized by Saint-Simonianism, the emotional-intuitive, the rational, and the industrial. The methods of development would be:

1. The initiation of the individual into the nature of social life, inculcating a feeling of the love of all. The unifying of all wills in a single will moving toward a common end.
2. The transmitting to individuals of the knowledge necessary to them and to society.[40]

This last would involve special or professional education.

In this realm, as in others, the Saint-Simonians know quite well what reactions their educational program will invite. All systems suppose that the end of society is known, clearly defined, and loved. But "today this end is a mystery." There is a widespread belief that those who have directed the masses have generally abused them. Suspicion of authority is understandable. But do not people, after all, have some duties to their fellows, their society? The answer is yes, but how is the sense of these duties acquired? Only by legislation and by force. Enlightened self-interest, the creed of the liberals, is the negation of all social morality. The object of education is to put the feelings, calculations, and acts of each individual in harmony with the needs of society.[41]

In any age there will be those whose personalities revolt against the generally adopted order, but the solution to that problem is moral education.

Education should follow citizens throughout their existence. No one should ever lack the possibility of instruction. If the division of labor has limited the contemplative capacities of some people, it has permitted others to give themselves totally to the contemplation of the general. Continuous and constant education is a possibility.

What should education be? Rational faculties should not be perfected at the expense of emotional faculties. Each should be equally developed. If the first, reason, seems to dominate in the early nineteenth century, it is because there is so little association among humanity. It is by emotion that we live, that we become "sociable"; it is emotion that attaches us to the world, that ties us together. "If one removes the sympathies uniting a man to his fellows, which make him suffer their sufferings, enjoy their joys, live their lives, it is impossible to see in societies other than an aggregation of individuals without ties or relationships and having as a motive for living only egoism."[42]

It is emotion that brings us to question our destiny, and it is emotion that reveals that destiny to us. Science verifies inspiration and revelation, but emotion alone gives the will and force necessary to attain the desired intellectual end.

All the moral existence of humans is not enclosed in their rational faculty; there are other means of knowing than the positive method, other roads to faith and conviction than a scientific demonstration. The results of social science have to be presented dogmatically. The *industriel* must not only know what his ends are but also love and desire them. Scholars can indicate directions but cannot convince. Emotions belong to another class, to those whom nature has made particularly sympathetic. In all places and in all times the direction of society belongs to those who speak to the heart.[43]

THE transformation from head to heart, from social to religious or, more accurately, cultist themes, is revealed in the tenth session of the *Exposition*. The man of sympathy is what another age would call the charismatic leader. The transformation of humanity, the creation of the "new" man, would be brought about by the Saint-Simonian "priest." His instrument of transformation would be "confession." "Confession has been condemned as a means of seduction and of espionage"; if one is repelled by Catholicism, one will also be repelled by the idea of the confessional. But confession is useful as long as the doctrine remains in harmony with the needs of humanity. Confession is the means of applying the general doctrine to each individual.[44]

This subject, like so many other aspects of the doctrine, is revealed, sketched, and passed beyond. It will recur, but here the conclusion is that humanity's religious future depends on the questions of the priesthood

106

and the confessional. Can there be a religion with a ritual or a cult? The answer is evidently no.

The priest envisaged here is a kind of technician who from the confessional derives the material to direct the life of the confessee. He is more psychologist than priest. His technique, as will be seen, more closely resembles the famous "talking cure," which would revolutionize psychotherapy two generations later, than it does the confession and forgiveness of sins. There is, in places other than the *Exposition,* evidence of the importance attached to dreams as keys to what could not yet be called an Unconscious, and the importance of sexuality and fantasy had already been hinted at in Bazard's preaching.

In addition to the function of confessor as *revealer* of the disciples' nature to themselves, one must keep in mind the essentially psychometric functions of the religious leader. The priest is to match, as in Enfantin's essay on the industrialist, temperaments and talents to patterns of life and work. These essentially scientific or technocratic skills are wedded to the priestly function because of that central notion of Saint-Simon and his followers that science and religion are always one.

In this early discussion of the priesthood there is an admission that Saint-Simonianism implies theocracy. People live by their feelings, by them and through them becoming "sociable." It is feeling that attaches us to the world. Science can tell us how to attain an end, but emotion must tell us what end to attain. The scientist cannot do it, but another class endowed with sympathetic capacities can. "The direction of men has always belonged to men of HEART,"[45] of practitioners of a CULT, or of the FINE ARTS.

The education proposed by the priesthood will be accessible to all in accordance with the intelligence, capacities, and vocations of each individual, and, importantly, it will be an education available throughout life.

The Regulation we announce for the future offers a new, a very great guarantee of moral order; feeling and reason combine to show us missed careers, forced feelings, imposed professions, and the disgust and hateful passions arriving from them. The source of these will be dried up by our rule. Assuredly we don't pretend to say that error, accidents, even partiality will never have a place in this new distribution of education and social advantages. We recognize a large role for human imperfection. It is perhaps not given to societies to attain the LIMIT they conceive as the determined end of their progress. But by this alone—that they march toward this limit in making use of all the enlightenment, of all the strength, of which they can dispose—by this alone let them realize their progress, let the accidents of injustice become exceptions.[46]

Realization will be the result of an education by "the paternal care of the directors of humanity seeking a society that is loving, ordered, and

STRONG. Legislation and the laying down of rules are the complements of education. In an organic society the political chief is legislator and judge. . . . 'He is the living law'— a bishop, a paterfamilias, a medieval seigneur." But once again the Saint-Simonians are quick to meet obvious criticism: "For us there is no chief by conquest or birth but only by capacity. In society as we conceive it, any man who judges his inferior has, also, superiors who judge him, especially in his relations of authority over others."[47] One harks back again to Enfantin's earlier work and is reminded of the collegial character of the *Exposition* itself. The two last passages cited from it are not deceitful disclaimers but constitute an honest recognition of the doctrine's difficulties and limitations.

The arguments about law, education, and the priest as educator and lawgiver nonetheless move in a circle around the central question. Can religion make sense in a post-Revolutionary, post-Enlightenment age? The argument is two-pronged. People need some foundation on which to build an affective life. The Saint-Simonian religion will not only answer the need but also demonstrate the truth of its answer. Secondly, Saint-Simonianism needs religious force and conviction to translate its science into action. Part of its science is, however, the inevitability of religious authority.

There is the rub: authority versus freedom. The Saint-Simonian proclamation of authority, intellectual and religious, would be the stumbling block for those for whom freedom was individual, recently acquired, and absolute, for whom religion was the lie agreed upon to make possible the moral and material exploitation of humanity. How the authoritarian "priest" of the Saint-Simonian "cult" would differ from priests and cults of the past, how with the best will in the world the Saint-Simonians would avoid tyranny over the faithful, was not easy to see.

THE LAST sessions of the *Exposition* were given over to the religious question and an effort, once again, to demonstrate the possibility of the squaring of the circle. The demonstration lies in the nature of the task to be accomplished. All that has come before has sought to establish the nature of the moral and material crisis in which the nineteenth century finds itself. To move out of that crisis, to resolve it and rise above its despair, a collective conviction and a collective hope must be born — a definition of the good and proper ends of society. Individual conviction, individual interest, and ego will not suffice. They all create conflict, competition, and the very social disarray that is exactly what must be overcome. Nothing short of religion's total conviction will do as a lever for moving the boulder of the present blocking the way to cooperation, order, and Saint-Simon's future golden age. It is the object of Saint-Simonianism to awake the need for religion, to encourage the feeling of brotherhood, and to provide a theater for its expression. But it is also the Saint-Simonian objective to offer exactly the religion that is needed, the dogma that is to be believed. Truth is one. Here, perhaps, is where the squaring of the circle takes place. "We have had particularly for our end to make you feel that society must be organized in accordance with a vision [*prévoyance*] and incessantly [*incessament*] brought in its whole and its parts into accordance with this vision."[48]

The key word is *incessament*. It suggests the character of the Saint-Simonian religion constantly, *ceaselessly* changing with what is known. It also separates Saint-Simonianism from conservative ideology in its concentration on the future and its joyous acceptance of change. The religion-science equation suggests that as investigation into the moral and material universe by rational and empirical methods pursues the ends of this life rather than another, more truth will be found. As more truth is found, as present truths are modified, so the content of the religion itself will be modified. And this *incessant*, collective search, fed by religious fervor for the betterment of humanity, is itself the best guarantee against the exercise of individual tyranny or the individual error. The notion of an *evolving* religion of humanity is the escape route from blind dogmatism to flexibility and to real freedom — the new Christianity.

"The Saint-Simonian religion will be a synthesis of all conceptions of humanity and all its manners of being. Not only will it dominate the political order, but the political order will be in its ensemble a religious institution."[49] With the suggestion that the political realm is religious, the liberal reflex will be to start away from it. But the Saint-Simonians seem to mean that the state is religious in the same sense as all other institutions, not that religion is the religion of the state. The safeguards that apply to the other institutions apply equally to the state, and all of them have as their imperatives love, brotherhood, perfectibility, progress, and peace.

If there is a naïveté in the Saint-Simonian position, it is in the idea that through reasonable investigation the truth will out and that religious passion will make it operative. If the first proposition is a naïve one, then it is one that the Saint-Simonians share with the high priest of nineteenth-century liberalism, John Stuart Mill — or perhaps he shared with them.

THE fifteenth and sixteenth "sermons" appear to digress from the central argument. The fifteenth attempts to cope with the ideas of Auguste Comte, which had been published, with some reluctance, by Saint-Simon himself as the third *Cahier* of the *Catéchisme des Industriels*. Bazard admits that many of the Saint-Simonians had come to Saint-Simon by way of Comte. Comte in the law of stages had seen theology as a precursor of positive knowledge. Bazard advances the view that Comte's argument was reflective of a period of transition from the critical to the organic epoch but that now "we" have gone beyond it.[50]

In the sixteenth session there is a return to the theme of disorder and of the difficulty any religion would have in being accepted in the current state of society. Byron and Goethe, *Don Juan* and *Faust,* are illustrative of the cultural crisis. They are pervaded by the "critical" demon. They plunge into hell, sing disorder, and paint vice and crime. Seeking, they never find. They demonstrate most dramatically the social crisis in terms of individual frustration, unrequited love, and unlimited ego. And in passing the question is raised of "acts of the flesh." What of women? "The most loving, the most passionate will be 'crowned.'" Faust, Don Juan, and later Othello become symbols of the fruitless passion of critical society, which, channeled into Saint-Simonian religion, will water the gardens of delight.[51]

The theme emerges here to underline the contemporary paucity and poverty of emotion, the romantic agony. There is an ambivalence in the discussion of Goethe, Byron, and Shakespeare. These artists have created symbols of a critical age; they cannot be seen as artists of the organic epoch. On the other hand, these creations, Faust, Don Juan, and Othello, heighten consciousness of the ills of the age and are thus useful. The artist of the future will create other symbols, but the artists of the present and past have their uses as well. The analysis of the sexual agony of romantic heroes once again lifts, but quickly drops, the curtain on the inner chamber of the place of women in Saint-Simonianism.

The seventeenth and final session summarizes what has gone before. It recognizes that there will be much resistance to a religious development for humanity. But the conception of God is the only way in which humanity can conceive universal order and harmony. Religion must not be the result of purely individual and interior contemplation. What good, after all, is that for the rest of us? Religion must be an expression of the collective thought of humanity, a synthesis of all its conceptions. To those who think morality and society are beyond the scope of the sciences it must be said that science is as hypothetical as any other area of thought. It has been moved faster, further, but what science has done, morals and society may do.

Religion itself has developed from fetishism to polytheism to monotheism. Religion in the West has followed the march of progress from a relatively "materialistic" Judaism to a relatively spiritual Christianity. But religion has not yet attained a living and absolute unity of being in the lives and acts of humanity.[52]

What that conclusion meant would be taken up in the second year of the *Exposition* by which time the Saint-Simonian religion had gone beyond definition to practice. While the themes of the second year's *Exposition* would be more dramatically developed in other forms and in a quite different context from those of the first year, they nonetheless do resolve the resounding chords of the first year and need to be quickly indicated here as an integral and continuing part of that first year's effort.

The approach to religion is somewhat more systematic. Saint-Simonian historicism proclaims previous religions "outworn." They are not wrong or bad, and they were appropriate for the times that bred them. The Saint-Simonians, indeed, had a good deal of respect for the contemporary Catholic thinkers Bonald, Maistre, and Lammenais. The archetype of the organic society was, for them as it had been for Saint-Simon, the medieval. The Middle Ages—marked by a single view of God and the Universe, organized with and by authority, hierarchical and providing a place and a significance for everybody—was what they hoped to recreate in forms appropriate to an industrial age.[53]

The main Saint-Simonian reproach of Christianity is directed to its "spirituality." The world and the flesh are of the Devil. Christianity rejected all three. Judaism, in the Saint-Simonian understanding, was exclusively "material," not other-worldly. Each religion failed to embrace the universality of humanity, and so was partial, incomplete.

The goal of the Saint-Simonian religion will be to establish a harmony between spirit and matter, to rehabilitate "matter," to rehabilitate the "flesh." With that note struck, the Saint-Simonians are on their way to an analysis of marriage, sexuality, and the place of women in society that is an outgrowth of the previous insistence on "passion," "emotion," and "sympathy." Where such sources of turbulence are to be examined, the need for "authority," "calm," and "order" imposes itself, and the priesthood of the most "loving" and most "SENSIBLE" is all the more imperative.[54]

What all these ideas would mean in practice, how they should develop, and whether the sense of individual limitation and the relative humility of the first year of the *Exposition* could be preserved became the questions that exercised the initiates as they began to make a visible mark on the world around them. The discussion, as one might by now guess, raged discreetly behind the public facade of Saint-Simonianism, whose construction will be described in the next chapter.

The first volume of the *Exposition* was a major achievement. It represented an effort to outline Saint-Simonian truth. And as the Saint-Simonians were fond of saying, "One does not discuss the truth, one teaches it." Whether or not they had the truth, the Saint-Simonians deserve the sympathetic reading they have seldom received. The dangers of their doctrine were obvious from its first utterance, and the Saint-Simonians were as conscious of these dangers as anybody who listened to them. But while they recognized that certain bad consequences could follow from some aspects of the doctrine, they also believed that these were not the inevitable. And that is where Saint-Simonianism differed from its critics whether in 1830 or 1980.

What does inform the *Exposition* throughout is a vision of harmony instead of discord, of cooperation instead of competition, of order instead of chaos, of love instead of hate, of charity instead of greed, of selflessness instead of selfishness, of passion instead of calculation, of joy instead of guilt, of fulfillment instead of frustration. The moral universe that Saint-Simon in *Le Nouveau Christianisme* had seen as the end of religion was about to be born.

Utopian? Perhaps. But the vision was accompanied by a program and a plan whole segments of which turned out to be quite the reverse of utopian. Saint-Simon practice deserves as sympathetic an examination as Saint-Simonian theory. The early stages of that practice were being worked out at the same time that the Saint-Simonians were proclaiming the arrival of the new Christianity.

CHAPTER VII

"FROM ON HIGH"

"**D**AYS OF ENTHUSIASM, happy days—days of illusion, days of sadness." So one of the Saint-Simonians mused more than thirty years later about the high point of the movement, between late 1829 and early 1832. For a little over two years, Louis Blanc tells us, "the stage was occupied entirely by the Saint-Simonian school."

It was given to this school to rehabilitate the principle of authority amid the triumph of liberalism, to proclaim the necessity of a social religion while the law itself had become atheist; to demand the organization of industry and association against the interest of the strongest and of the lying successes of competition. With an intrepidity without equal, with a vigor sustained by high talent and deep study, this school bared all the wounds of the century. It overthrew a thousand prejudices, it shook deep convictions, it opened to intelligence a new and vast career. The influence it exercised was great and lasts still![1]

Hippolyte Carnot, a good fifty years after, would say, "Serious minds . . . will remember that the thought of individual and social perfectibility and the feeling of human solidarity have been nowhere professed and practiced with an ardor more sincere than by the Saint-Simonian school."[2]

Ardor was certainly to be the hallmark of these years, and Enfantin was its personification. He began in 1829 to proclaim the authority to exercise a priesthood, which would eventually lead him to the role of supreme father of the Saint-Simonian religion. But he did not arrive there alone. A religion needs a theology. In 1829 discussion raged within the inner circle of the "college" over the content of that theology. A religion, Thomas Carlyle was to tell Gustave d'Eichthal, requires a symbol. He detected none in Saint-Simonianism.[3] The definition of the nature of God was derived indirectly from Fourier by way of Buchez. As early as 1828, in conversations with Buchez, Enfantin had decided that God must be androgynous. From this principle arose the need for that understanding of womankind that was one of the doctrine's major achievements. But it was also on the questions of the nature of woman and her role in the cult and in society that the Saint-Simonian bark would founder. Right up to the rocky coasts of schism, however, Bazard and Olinde Rodrigues shared fully in the piloting of that bark. These issues of religion, priesthood, and authority would be examined and exposed in great detail. But again,

Enfantin is neither the villain nor the hero. Ironically it was the first major victim of the doctrine of authority, Buchez, who first suggested that "some of us" would assume sovereignty over the school. Saint-Simon in *Le Nouveau Christianisme* had announced the religion of humanity and had further announced that this religion would have its cult, it would have its priests, "and its clergy will have its chiefs." It was the kind of statement of which Saint-Simon was fond when he had not been able to think through details. His disciples were justified after his death—even as Comte, Thierry, and Olinde Rodrigues had been forced to do during his life—in trying to work out logical conclusions from Saint-Simon's often sibylline utterances.[4]

In this effort Rodrigues played a primary role. The notion of *authority*, derived from the doctrine of competence based on the positive knowledge of what was true, was all-pervasive in Saint-Simon's work:

"'Why have you addressed yourself to savants, industrialists, artists instead of going straight to the people by way of religion?

"'I have had to make artists, scholars, *industriels* feel that their interests were essentially the same as those of the mass of the people, that they belong to a working class while they are at the same time its natural heads.'"[5]

There was nothing new in these teachings. What was new was the effort to give them some kind of visible substance so that they might be dramatized and might bring converts. It was in this effort that Enfantin, on his return from a trip to the north of France in the summer of 1829, was to distinguish himself. It was equally consistent with the teachings of Saint-Simon that the *structure* of the Catholic church should be seized upon as the suitable model for the new Christianity.

The *content* of conventional Christianity was viewed as outworn, as incomplete and inappropriate to the new organic epoch. Catholicism was the religion of unhappiness, Protestantism the agent of critical destruction. But Catholicism had provided the organic principle of the medieval world and had done so through the authority of a priesthood organized hierarchically. The *forms* were the mark of the organic society; the authority of the priest sprang from the possession of truth; and truth offered the means to salvation. What salvation was and how it was to be understood in the new world had yet to be determined. It was clear, however, that salvation would be achieved on this earth. The unity of spirit and matter required some other vision than the Catholic, some other description of God, and some other savior than Christ.

But at least until the autumn of 1829 Saint-Simonianism was firmly rooted in Saint-Simon himself. Enfantin was far from exercising a monopoly over the thought and practice of the school.

There is, however, an important question whose answer does rest with

Enfantin, largely because he left behind more evidence than his fellows. The question is one of sincerity and conviction. Was the Saint-Simonian religion simply a cynical and simultaneously naïve (C. P. Snow somewhere suggests that there is no more distasteful combination) effort to gather popular support for a group of ambitious opportunists seeking to displace the notables of Restoration France and to wield absolute power over obedient masses fed on the opiate of the people? Or was the Saint-Simonian religion the outgrowth of deep spiritual search, philosophical investigation, and ultimately profound faith in a new understanding of order in the universe?

The answer to the question is not simple. "There was perhaps not a single person in Saint-Simonianism who hadn't been pushed to it by some family anguish."[6] It is d'Eichthal who speaks, and he had reason to know. For Enfantin the death of his brother and the birth of his son had constituted a crisis—and a judgment. As late as 1827 he had said that he did not understand the new Christianity and that he did not know how to touch the heart of the masses. Two years later he was writing to his cousin Thérèse Nugues that the question of "woman, the future life, the material manifestations of God are not resolved in the teachings of the school," that everything was provisional, but that he hoped to be able to speak of them in the near future "ex cathedra."[7] Several months later: "We are everywhere eclectic. We take our advantage where we find it." He goes on, "You don't realize that young people who leave school today don't bring with them the irreligious hate or the spirit of revolt (which is the same thing) that we drank so deeply in our lycées. . . . Saint-Simon could not have conceived the new Christianity if he had not sensed the religious flame that runs in young souls."[8]

The question remains: Are we dealing with a shrewd analysis of what would "sell" or with a conviction? Are we dealing with a seeker after power or a seeker after the unknown? Enfantin certainly shared "the religious flame" of the "young souls." He certainly shared the family anguish of other Saint-Simonians, which had driven so many of them to seek security, certainty, faith. He gives evidence of all this in his correspondence with his cousin between 1827 and 1830. The conviction and the anguish were so strong that all those at the family headquarters at Curson felt the need to remonstrate, and Enfantin the need to respond.

These were people who loved Enfantin and whom he loved. It was important to him that they understand and approve of his work. There was little impulse to dissimulate and, indeed, with Thérès Nugues there was little possibility of doing so. She emerges from her letters as intelligent, perceptive, knowing, and loving her cousin well, but without blinders. What is said in these letters can be taken, for the most part, as honest expression of where Enfantin found himself. The horror, anxiety, or

115

irony of the family correspondents are evidence of how seriously and literally they took what they read from Enfantin's hands.

I busy myself with something for thee, my dear Thérèse; I hope to show you that our doctrine leads straight to heaven, that it is the obligatory accomplishment of the orders of God, who has willed that humanity certainly better its physical, moral, and intellectual existence in order to offer him a worship more and more worthy of him. . . . What is [the belief] leading us today? [It is] the life of the world, our love for the PLAN followed by humanity during all the length of its existence. . . . But this plan, who conceived it, who imposed it on the world? "A consequence of its mechanical, anatomical organization," Emile would say. Sad play on words; frozen imagination that chills all it approaches. Poor Auguste [Enfantin's brother], is it your organization that I loved? It is destroyed, and I love thee still. What does a well-made machine with perfectly meshing gears mean to me? I wouldn't lose a hair for it. Let the machine come alive, let it speak a human language to my heart, let it ask me to lend it the aid of my arms, my intelligence, let it implore me as does humanity to destroy all that is opposed to its free movement. [Then] I admire no more, I love, I give myself to it. And the world would be a machine without life? Impossible![9]

Enfantin's cousin Emile, through Thérèse Nugues, proposed a number of "yes and no" questions. She was imbued with a certain respect for Catholicism. Her male relatives were men of the eighteenth century, less shocked by Enfantin's critique of Catholicism than by the fact of his newfound religiosity. One of the questions was "Do you believe in Jesus Christ?" Enfantin subjected the question to all its possible analyses but concluded by saying:

He wishes to know if I believe that Christ, son of God, is seated on a well-stuffed cloud at the right of his father, who has a great beard, and if he chats with a pigeon named "Holy Spirit." . . . It is as usual Voltaire who questions, Voltaire robbing the sublime poetry of Christianity of its color. . . . The work of Creation has not been completed. God has not brought us to where we are in order to make us languish far from him at a distance never to be less great. His reign will arrive ON EARTH as in Heaven. . . . Has not Christ himself promised it?[10]

Enfantin had already admitted to Thérèse Nugues that he knew how extraordinary his conversion must seem. Referring to Saint Paul and Saint Augustine as predecessors, he recognized that to his cousins he must appear to have an unstable intelligence, "changing ideas with great facility and defending them with a ridiculous enthusiasm." The most whole-hearted and appalled response came from the great man of the family, General St.-Cyr Nugues. Having read the letters addressed to Curson, the general noted in distress that he was very far from all Enfantin's new opinions. He had not suspected that religious ideas had seized Enfantin's mind. He had known his nephew to be ill, but "you are consumed, devoured—you wallow in this new existence." Twice, the general notes, Enfantin has changed his life, and he is hardly past thirty years! "But my dear Prosper, how far from the past is the exaltation that possesses you today." Enfantin wishes to reform everything on earth. "In your ardor you have the pretension of remaking morality, you abjure all your old ideas, you scorn all ours. . . . You aspire to make the happiness of humankind through the centuries."[11]

From the general's distress and the skepticism of the cousin it would appear that Enfantin had persuaded those closest to him of his sincerity, his conviction, and, perhaps, of his folly. But one is left uneasy. Enfantin was a complex man, and his complexities like his religious and social ideas would reveal themselves over a long period of time. The English banker Blount would describe Enfantin as that rare combination, difficult to find outside France, of "the mad visionary, the polished man of society, and the shrewd man of affairs." As far as it went, it was a sound judgment. All three characteristics were undoubtedly present as Enfantin progressed toward leadership of the movement and the Saint-Simonian religion. E. M. Butler's comment that Enfantin's ideas were not invented to justify a disreputable practice but that he was nonetheless lacking moral good taste and possessed of "absurd" pretensions seems apropos at this point in his career.

In September and October of 1829, when Enfantin hoped he might soon speak *ex cathedra,* his religious ruminations did not yet enjoy the status of dogma, although his pretensions to authority and priesthood began to loom large. The time was ripe for action. The public *Exposition* of the doctrine had come to an end in the early summer. These lectures had attracted scores of more than casually interested listeners. Some of these had become converts. The conversion was often effected through the means of intimate conversation with one of the members of the "college" and, more particularly, with those of the "second degree," who had been instituted in December of 1828. These "sons" of the doctrine were guided by their "fathers" in the college.

It was in the development of these relationships that Enfantin had shown and was to continue to show particular strength as crisis and conflict began to develop behind the apparently united front of the doctrine. Some cracks had begun to show before summer set in. Enfantin had deplored to Bazard the impossibility of theoretical discussion devoid of displays of *amour propre.* An important and potentially dangerous development had been the acquisition of a journal open to Saint-Simonian influence.

L'Organisateur presented some embarrassments to the movement. Since 1828, without success, the college had tried to refloat *Le Producteur.* In August of 1829 P.-M. Laurent, a member of the college, was offered the direction of a journal devoted to new techniques of education. Laurent accepted the offer with the condition that space be made available for the propagation of Saint-Simonian ideas. But *amour propre* was very much aroused by this arrangement. Laurent, as editor, had no direct responsibility to the college, and the college had no direct control of the journal. The situation did not fit Saint-Simonian notions of hierarchy; it provided room for discord between two groups in the leadership, and it had been launched during Enfantin's absence in the south. *L'Organisateur,* nonetheless, served a useful purpose. Laurent, the editor, was an "old revolutionary, old atheist, old philosophe — one of those Lazaruses brought to life by Saint-Simon." But his editorship did give Saint-Simonianism a means of printed communication until it acquired its own *Globe* a year later.[12]

While the conflicts were beginning to fester, Enfantin was obliged to spend August and September in the south on business for his bank. He took the opportunity to cultivate the business of the school and, in effect, to found the Church of the Midi. Resseguier at Carcasonne had been an enthusiastic follower of the teachings of *Le Producteur,* had spread its message to Castelnaudary, Montpellier, and Sorrèze, and had gathered a group of eager discussants about him. In the course of his voyage Enfantin spent nine to ten hours of some days discussing doctrine, exercising his charm, and responding to an enthusiastic reception. He returned to Paris confirmed in his own powers as a proselytizer, convinced of the viability of the doctrine, and, not incidentally, accompanied by a sizable number of new converts.

During his absence the life of the Saint-Simonian family in Paris had been troubled by another incident that would be heavy with consequences for the future of the doctrine. At the moment the incident seemed trivial, but it appears to have offered Enfantin his first opportunity to be the "regulator" of the intimate lives of his followers. Eugène Rodrigues, young, ardent, brilliant, doomed, and still a virgin at twenty-two, had undertaken the conversion process of a young and beautiful woman. In the process he fell in love with her. Charles Duveyrier, young, ardent, brilliant, the son of one of the governors of the bank for which Enfantin worked, and considerably more *entreprenant* than his friend, urged Eugène to push his passion to its logical conclusion. When Enfantin heard the tale, he addressed a letter to Duveyrier scolding him for his influence on Eugène, making the point that Eugène rather than "abasing himself before the sacred tripod" ought to be looking into the intellect of his convert and assuring her conversion. Otherwise he would not merit the title of "priest."[13]

That Enfantin himself might merit the title is suggested not only by the loves of Eugène Rodrigues but by his correspondence with Eugène's brother Olinde. The older brother was trying to keep the group alive in

Paris while Enfantin and Bazard were absent. He reported that Wednesday meetings on doctrine were flagging and that "Buchez is an obstacle. . . . (He) still worries over the question of God, love, intelligence. He does not advance and pitilessly repeats the same objections."[14]

To this news Enfantin replied: "We must inevitably make some examples; there are already too many people in our midst who have acquired all they ever could of doctrine, dry formulas of social science. . . . We must make examples; there ought to remain twelve or fifteen only." Enfantin goes on to lay down a plan of work for the school, assigns topics of discussion for teams within the college, and insists on the necessity of eliminating some Catholic elements—creation, death, and angels—and developing a doctrine of future life. Finally, "If we want to get someplace, we have to recognize that only the doctrine concerns us and not unhappy personalities who embarrass us." Buchez, in particular, "ought to turn his tongue four times" when he supposes his person compromised. Enfantin himself admits he is "a little stubborn"; he will try to do better.[15]

Once he returned to Paris in mid-October, it became clear to Enfantin that the issue was indeed less that of articles of faith than of personality. Shortly he was urging Bazard to think of ways to improve the situation. "We, after all, are the doctrine." From this point, and under the direction of Bazard and Enfantin, the movement readied itself for an astonishing range of activity and achievement in a sufficiently astonishing year.

By July of 1830 a "credo" would have been worked out, some of the dissidents would have been purged, the authority of Bazard and Enfantin would have been publicly proclaimed, and the role of Olinde Rodrigues would have diminished. As before, the "woman question" stirred the private discussions while the public doctrine continued to draw audiences and converts in ever larger numbers. The question of "eternal life," which had preoccupied Enfantin for some time, would never during this period receive dogmatic definition, although its ramifications entered into other discussions as they had in Enfantin's letters to Thérèse Nugues.

Perhaps the most notable event of this period was Enfantin's occupancy in March of 1830 of an apartment on the rue Monsigny attached to a great house of the Palais Royal quarter. Progressively the entire building came into the hands of the school, became its headquarters, and housed the offices of the *L'Organisateur* and of *Le Globe*. It became the scene both of doctrinal meetings and of entertainments that drew all that was brilliant and curious in a Parisian society seeking revolutionary answers to the grave questions that were shaking Paris and Europe on the eve of the July Revolution itself.[16]

The rue Monsigny was a street recently pierced through the gardens of the great private mansions that had dominated the neighborhood between the present avenue de l'Opéra and the Bibliotheque Nationale. It was witness to a modernization of Paris that provided precedent and example for the better-known modernization of the Second Empire. A few minutes' walk away through the passage Choiseul was Saint-Simon's last residence and the Palais Royal. It was a quarter, as Louis Blanc said, dominated by "wealth and prostitution,"[17] a quarter appropriate, as it turned out, to the primary concerns of the Saint-Simonians. By mid-1830 many of the Saint-Simonians would be living in the mother house on the rue Monsigny. Many others would have lodgings in the neighborhood on the rue Sainte-Anne and the rue de Grammont. Most of the community would take meals together, and the doctrine would be lived day and night in an increasingly exalted atmosphere.[18]

These developments had become possible, in part, because the strains Enfantin found waiting for him on his return from the south quickly grew worse. By the beginning of December, Buchez, the brothers Alisse, and one Boulland formed a minority in opposition to the majority of the college founded the year before. The question dividing the group was the nature of God. The Buchez position seems to have been pantheistic: "God is IN everything." The Enfantian view was that "God IS everything." Connectedness, interrelationship, "unity," and associations constituted the godhead. Separating Creator and Creation was Catholic, competitive, and inorganic; thus it was inadmissible in terms of Saint-Simon.[19]

Heresy became a subject of discussion in the group of the "second degree" of the school, most of whose members sided with Enfantin and Bazard. Enfantin noted that for a long time when he and Bazard had spoken on any issue, their conclusions were accepted by the "family." Only Buchez persisted in views already ruled out. The reason for this authority was simple: "Bazard taught, and I wrote or caused to be written." One evening in early December, "leaving Bazard's with Olinde and Eugène after a heated discussion with Buchez, I said to [Olinde] Rodrigues that we could not continue in such anarchy, and I asked him and Eugène if they didn't think, like me, that we were making a Republic with its lies because, in fact, Bazard and I directed [the group]."[20] Olinde agreed that the matter of fact should become a matter of right.

Olinde then talked to Bazard, who, anxious about the impact on Buchez, asked for fifteen days of reflection. Finally he accepted the notion. Christmas day of 1829 was chosen to make the announcement of the elevation of Bazard and Enfantin as "supreme fathers" of the Saint-Simonian family. A consequence of the new and formal arrangement was the de facto demotion of Olinde Rodrigues. The meeting, which was put off because of Enfantin's illness, became the scene of the first Saint-Simonian schism. Buchez and some of his friends withdrew, proclaiming themselves the true Saint-Simonians. Olinde announced that he had never felt so completely Saint-Simonian as on this day when he had recognized those greater than he and raised them above himself, "sole pupil and embodiment of Saint-Simon." The meeting came to a close with Duveyrier and d'Eichthal demanding that everybody embrace everybody who was left—which was done.[21]

The first year of the Saint-Simonian era had been accomplished. A dual "papacy" was its major creation, and doctrine had become dogma. Heresy and heresiarchs had been cast out. The faith of the remainder remained intact. Buchez's reaction to the proposed changes, as reported by Bazard, cast light on the recent past and was prophetic of the future: "Ah! I am not astonished; now I understand why Enfantin corresponded so much, came and went with everybody, made so many converts. Bazard, I told you, Enfantin is *un ambitieux.*'"[22]

Enfantin would have been the last to deny the accusation. In response to his mother's protestations (she, like the rest of the family was vigorously anti-Saint-Simonian) he commented that if he was ambitious, it was because she was. But again one can wonder what was at work in the new developments and in Enfantin's mind as he engineered them. The preceding March he had praised the institution of the papacy as tending toward the unity that was the goal of the founder, of the doctrine, and of the school and that was the destiny of humanity. At the same time a dual papacy seemed to run counter to that principle of unity and almost inevitably meant future conflict.

At this moment, at the end of 1829, Enfantin and Bazard were certainly equals. They were seen and perhaps saw themselves as necessarily complementary. And there can be no doubt that on the religious questions that had divided the college Bazard and Enfantin were in agreement. In the new situation, however, there was a logic that encouraged conflict and competition by encouraging confrontation between two quite different personalities, bringing two quite different backgrounds to the Saint-Simonian experience.

Blanc, who appears to have been well-informed by eyewitnesses, describes the two men: Bazard represented reason, Enfantin, feeling. Bazard was deliberate, logical, heavy, slow; Enfantin was quick and endlessly inventive, nipping at Bazard to move on in his thought. The two locked in discussion for hours on end. There is significance in the choice of Bazard as spokesman for the *Exposition* of the doctrine. Oral presentation, as Jean Vidalenc has pointed out,[23] was of great importance in a society in which more than half the people were illiterate. Bazard's pace, clarity, and steadiness, even heaviness, were useful. But it was also true that within the college Bazard was less loved than was Enfantin.

Enfantin has been described as another incarnation of that fatal hero whose "great prototype had died a few years earlier on St. Helena."[24]

According to Henri Brisson, he had "the audacity of a Titan with all the material gifts: stature, looks, sweetness of speech and glance; he was easy, calm, graceful, dignified." In an obituary notice in *Le Temps* Brisson described Enfantin as having over men "superior in knowledge and character the superiority of those who do not hesitate over what they wish, who know where they're going." Naturally good and affectionate, "amiable and seductive . . . he distinguished himself especially by an unequaled perspicacity, which delivered up the entire soul of persons he was meeting for the first time. The most hidden recesses of the human heart had no secret from him." A single conversation was enough for him to plumb a person's mind and discover the key to its most discreet motives — motives that he then played upon with a marvelous dexterity. "Caressing, hard, familiar, mocking, always master of himself, he knew how to lead men, and he was not ignorant of how they can be broken."[25]

To all of which Bazard's now-aged widow reacted by asking, "Who, then, is this Monsieur Brisson who has so well understood Enfantin?"[26]

Against this overwhelming charm and capacity for empathy Bazard in the long run had little chance. Lambert, jotting down memories in Egypt, said of Bazard: "An old man with children on his back. That's ugly, a man in the prime of life — that's endearing."[27] This was the great difference between the two men. But aside from the differences in temperament there were also persistent differences in intellectual outlook. Although Bazard had firmly stated that he and Enfantin were in agreement on religious questions, Bazard's background had been that of political activist, libertarian, and revolutionary. Enfantin was essentially unpolitical. The forms of government did not interest him, and ideologies other than his own he thought irrelevant. For Bazard and Olinde Rodrigues the religion of humanity had been a means of social and economic regeneration; for Enfantin it had taken on far greater implications. Saint-Simon and Rodrigues had emphasized pacifism, harmony, the gravitational force of association, and conciliation. Bazard held on to a remnant of combativeness that emerged at moments of political crisis and that accounted for a strain of militancy in the writings of the school that was eventually rejected. More than a century later this uncharacteristic militancy would be interpreted as evidence of the totalitarian bent of the whole movement.

The differences between Bazard and Enfantin could usually be managed. Enfantin was willing to discuss an industrial, pacific *army* and to support specific measures of the July Monarchy extending political rights and personal freedom. Bazard had come to accept pacifism particularly as it extended to the relations of classes and to the notion of social harmony. But the intellectual history of the two as well as their temperamental differences had a role to play in the great confrontation that would take place between them nearly two years after their elevation to the Saint-Simonian papacy at the end of 1829.

THAT emotion-filled elevation took place in Duveyrier's apartment at the Caisse Hypothécaire, and the days following it were also filled with emotion. Eugène Rodrigues, after a short illness, died in January 1830. He had been a kind of golden boy of the movement much admired by, among others, George Sand. His loss reawakened the religious question and the question of eternal life. During this same month Enfantin's father fell ill and was watched over by a corps of Saint-Simonians, who apparently moved into the elder Enfantin's house at Ménilmontant and provided nursing, housekeeping, errand running, and moral support for him and his wife.[28]

As a consequence of these personal troubles Enfantin decided to lessen his work at the Caisse so that he might give more time to the organization of the school and its membership. The move to the rue Monsigny in March 1830 was the first step in the reorganization of his life. The offices of *L'Organisateur* were installed there. In July space became available on the principal floor and was absorbed by the Saint-Simonians, who initially used it for their public meetings. But when, after September, the crowds had become too great, a large public hall on the rue Taitbout was leased, and the rue Monsigny became the communal center of the school. Only on the third floor did a foreign element persist—the liberal journal *Le Globe*. Enfantin initiated discussions whose end was the absorption of *Le Globe*'s office space, of its editor, Pierre Leroux, and of the journal itself. By October 1830 the building at 6 rue Monsigny had become completely Saint-Simonian and served as a stage for the movement's most brilliant acts. The overture to these acts was the July Revolution, which briefly extended freedom, opened possibilities for the exploration of ideas, and made alternative courses of social action discussable. The liberals in power had, by conviction, to support a freer press and the right to assembly. In so doing they powerfully aided the Saint-Simonians in Paris and throughout France. Enfantin and Bazard, while reserved, as we will see, in their attitude to the new regime, were nonetheless willing to take advantage of it.[29]

Before the July days, however, Saint-Simonianism had begun to take on a structure and had absorbed many, if not all, of the striking personalities of the movement. Some of the names are already familiar. Rodrigues, the Pereires, d'Eichthal, Bazard, and, increasingly important, his wife, Claire. Mme Bazard's niece Cecile Fournel and her husband, Henri, were being drawn to the group. At this time Henri was director of France's major ironworks at le Creusot. Resseguier, organizer of the Church of the Midi, had been admitted to the college in February. To be sure, Buchez, the brothers Alisse, and Boulland had withdrawn. But there were additions. Enfantin shared his apartment at the rue Monsigny with Abel Transon, Jules Lechevalier, and Euryale Cazeaux. Transon in some ways replaced Eugène Rodrigues. Young, ardent, and handsome (good looks were to become increasingly important to Enfantin as time went on), Transon was an impassioned speaker and particularly persuasive with women.[30]

Transon and Cazeaux had emerged from the Ecole Polytechnique. Transon in this spring and summer of 1830 gave a special and successful course of lectures for his fellow *polytechniciens*. Lechevalier had been interested in *Le Producteur* but had more recently spent two years in Germany studying philosophy—particularly Hegel's—and had brought back to the movement his own interest in that country and its ideas. Edmond Talabot, one of four brothers, was the most intimately involved with the movement at this stage, but his brother Paulin, also an engineer, was in constant communication with it. By autumn yet another engineer, Michel Chevalier, would be called to Paris and editorship of *Le Globe*. Pierre Leroux's fellow editors of *Le Globe* in 1830, Eugène L'herminier and Charles-Augustin Sainte-Beuve, were also at this juncture passionately involved with the movement. Emile Barrault, a professor of literature, a remarkable lecturer, and a confirmed romantic, was to share in, indeed dominate, the "*prédications*" of the school. Duveyrier and Laurent continued to play a large role in publicity and conversion.[31]

For all these the doctrine was becoming or had already become the focus of their daily lives. It was Enfantin's intent to group as many as possible at the rue Monsigny in a common life. How was this to be done? There is a good deal of evidence, much of it conflicting, incongruent, or incomplete, on Saint-Simonian finances. But characteristically while Saint-Simonians admitted no limits to their imagination, they were scrupulous in their accounting. "We spend money as workmen spend theirs," they were to declare. The money they spent was apparently freely given and in large amounts. D'Eichthal estimated that the movement had cost him 190,000 francs; Enfantin may have given 70,000 and the price of the family house at Ménilmontant; the Fournels contributed 89,000 francs outright early in 1831 and signed over rights to the succession of another 150,000. Most of those who had thus far been active in the movement were obviously either frankly rich or well-off. Given the usual French discretion in such matters, it is difficult to determine even a century and a half later *how* well-off.[32]

The Enfantin family offers many puzzles. Enfantin's salary at the Caisse Hypothécaire was 6,000 francs. He had apparently, at some point, sold an interest in the family wine business at Romans. His father was officially bankrupt, but this fact did not affect the considerable possessions and property of his mother. Early in 1831 he felt free to give up his job. Whether d'Eichthal, scion of a rich banking family, or Duveyrier, similarly situated, enjoyed generous allowances or funds of their own is not clear. Edmond Talabot gave up his profession of lawyer "to live in the doctrine." Several young engineers compromised their careers by refusing, leaving, or failing to appear at assigned posts. What is fascinating in the personnel records is the indulgence with which these acts were greeted by superiors, who seem to have been as infected as their juniors by the movement.[33]

Another category of members, such as Rodrigues and the Pereires, professionals and businessmen, gave of their time and money while carrying on their daily work. It would later be argued that some of the financial titans of the Second Empire had never *really* been involved in the Saint-Simonian school and had held themselves apart from its "excesses." It was not that a Paulin Talabot or an Isaac Pereire was "apart" from the school emotionally or intellectually, but that they had lives to pursue and inevitable responsibilities. What is remarkable is the degree to which they gave of themselves and their purses while carrying on demanding careers.

It has been established that it was precisely such men who stayed with the movement in the wake of the "excesses," managed its finances punctiliously, and gave fulfillment to its ideas at a later date. Those like the Fournels and d'Eichthal who compromised the material existence of their entire lives are even more remarkable, and their actions provide an index of the degree of conviction that these young people brought to the movement. They practiced what they preached on questions of property and seem never to have regretted that aspect of their involvement.[34]

The physical concentration of the movement in and around the rue Monsigny would be most visible after October 1830. But in the early days of the year there had taken place an organization of the hierarchy. The eclecticism, not to say plagiarism, of the Saint-Simonians is self-evident. When it suited them, they borrowed the structure of the Catholic church. They talked of "priests" and "popes," of "confession" and "catechism." In organizing the faithful by "degrees" they probably had before them the Masonic model, with which Bazard, Carnot, and some others were familiar. They would devise ceremonies and costumes for the membership. Their theology is reminiscent of Universalism and Unitarianism. They never did, as Carlyle had so acutely pointed out, devise a characteristic symbol, a rite of communion, a personification of Saint-Simon's God. They did speak of themselves as the "family" that would incorporate all humanity; they addressed one another as "father," "mother," "son," "daughter," "brother," and "sister." The forms of address related to a defined position in the hierarchy, and increasingly the "fathers" were taken to be the "living law." At a particularly intense moment in the group's history one of the disciples, moved by a hallucinatory vision, begged Enfantin to "reveal" himself as the Messiah—which, somewhat regretfully, he refused to do. It was not an illogical development from all the rest.[35]

Membership in and placement in the hierarchy were constantly changing. And, although every advancement aroused enthusiasm and every demotion, as with that of Olinde Rodrigues, was accepted as a "placement" according to capacities, there is evidence of hurt pride, jealousy, anger, and triumph among the faithful. The "purge" in the fall of 1829 had left injuries that did not heal quickly. The elevation of Eugène Rodrigues and Margerin was thought (rightly in the latter case) suspiciously rapid. Regulating the advancement and proclaiming the merits of some while delaying and denying others created tension. With what one knows of Enfantin, one can suspect that these stages were manipulated with great skill for larger purposes. The pyramid or, more accurately, the ziggurat—of "fathers," a "college" that was in effect a cabinet, a second degree of initiates, and a third of aspirants and teachers—did give the school a structure, an identity, and a means of carrying on proselytizing.

One list, among many drawn up in 1831, includes the fathers Bazard and Enfantin; sixteen persons, including Claire Bazard, in the college; twenty in the second degree, including both Pereires, Charles Lambert, Adolphe Guéroult, and a number of women; and thirty more in the third. This list was far from inclusive. The degrees were degrees of priesthood; they did not exhaust those who were or thought themselves to be Saint-Simonian. In 1831 Enfantin would insist on the creation of a "privy council." This organ would be smaller than the college and would include Claire Bazard. Its function was to work out the most delicate questions of doctrinal development. The central table of organization was in place by the spring of 1830, however; the direction for the future was set.[36]

THE INTERNAL organization was designed to fortify the external and public work of Saint-Simonianism. The second series of lectures on the doctrine, devoted to religion, had been taking place at the hall on the rue Taranne. In April *L'Organisateur* adopted the subtitle of *Journal de la Doctrine Saint-Simonienne*. The Bazard lectures had been published and had sold eight hundred copies. On April 11, 1830, there began a series of "*Prédications,*" popularizations or sermons open to the public, which continued for nearly two years. These were different in kind from the *Exposition*, which was a systematic definition of Saint-Simonian dogma. The sermons were in effect homilies on aspects of the doctrine, and these were preached by those, unlike Bazard, who were encouraged in flights of rhetoric, romantic prose, and drama. In addition to Emile Barrault,

Laurent, and Transon, Jean Reynaud, an engineer summoned from Corsica, Edouard Charton, and Moîse Retouret were the speakers in the series. The sermons opened at the rue Monsigny but by October had to be moved to a public hall on the rue Taitbout (near the present Au Printemps and Galéries Lafayette department stores), where an audience of a thousand was not rare. Bazard's lectures had been considered fruitful if they attracted 150 to 200 people.

At the rue Monsigny itself on Tuesdays, Thursdays, and Saturdays the Saint-Simonians were "at home" in the evenings for conversation and private discussion. On Sundays the meetings of the "family," formerly at the Bazards', were now taking place at the rue Monsigny. There was music, singing, dancing (d'Eichthal and Duveyrier had first met at a dancing class where they were trying to learn the waltz), and talk. The rooms, although barely furnished and dimly lit, were elegant, and the company was lively. It became fashionable to be seen at the Saint-Simonian evenings. There were often a hundred guests in these early days. Eventually admission had to be restricted by formal invitation.[37]

Recruitment during 1830 and 1831 sought a larger and more varied audience. Back in the days of *Le Producteur* a few like-minded persons devoted to serious discussion had been the objective. Having gathered his few men of the elite, Enfantin, like Saint-Simon, had been interested in reaching the engineers, and this effort had been largely successful. Saint-Simon and the Saint-Simonians had been most concerned with those who had some leverage in their society. Bazard's appearances had been aimed at the instructed and philosophically sophisticated. Much effort had been expended to assure members of the bourgeoisie that their position was not threatened but enhanced by the new dispensation.

But now the targets of Saint-Simonianism were the artist, the worker, and the woman. The preachers had instructions not to lecture on history as historians or on science as savants, but to discuss these subjects in terms of their human applications, in terms of love, harmony, and association. The bourgeoisie received warnings about its lack of love and concern for the masses and was told that it must mend its ways to avoid destruction from below.[38] The workers who had begun to appear at Saint-Simonian meetings heard pleas to relinquish their hatred for their masters and to flock to a doctrine that had as its object raising them to the ranks and privileges of the bourgeoisie.[39]

This theme implicit in all Saint-Simonian social and economic doctrine is the most revealing and most important in defining the real character of the doctrine. It was socialist in the pre-Marxian meaning of that word. It sought to answer the question "How can society be held together?" The answer: by love, not hate; by association, not by competition; by sharing, not despoiling; by organization, not by anarchy. This governing idea embodied a hope that could be thought of as utopian and whose alternative was disaster and social disintegration.

The terms in which the Saint-Simonians proffered this hope of "bourgeoisification" to working-class audiences were patronizing to a degree difficult to comprehend in the late twentieth century. But to *"prolétaires"* hitherto offered nothing by the bourgeoisie and to a bourgeoisie enveloped in the war of each against each, the generosity of the offer seemed manifest. Equally patronizing, perhaps, at this point, was the interest in women and in artists. The Saint-Simonian priest had been described as an artist of souls, but the artist as more usually defined could play a role in dramatizing the Saint-Simonian message. Hannah Arendt's description of Enfantin as a kind of nineteenth-century Goebbels is absurd. But certainly painters, musicians, poets, playwrights, and novelists were all sought so that they might dramatize Saint-Simonian themes, so that they might devote themselves to social realism and social usefulness. This was no more original with the Saint-Simonians than any other aspect of the doctrine. Saint-Simon had given a good deal of thought to the environment of work and to the gratification of the senses of the workers. Saint-Simonian aesthetic theory was the element of doctrine most vulnerable to liberal attack in its subordination of individual expression to prescribed social themes. It was, however, an aesthetic not without influence. Heinrich Heine, Franz Liszt, George Sand, Sainte-Beuve, and Victor Hugo would all admit a serious, if passing, interest in Saint-Simonianism and were not unfriendly to it. Sand, however, in recording a visit to the rue Monsigny, commented, "There is one who is there only to display her pale blue dress and her feather boa, *toujour des farces.*"[40] Perhaps the most important acquisitions were Felicien David, a composer of merit who was doomed to live his artistic life in the shadow of Berlioz, and Raymond Bonheur, an amateur artist whose daughter Rosa would seem to have fulfilled some of the Saint-Simonian aspirations for both artists and women.

The relationship of the movement to women requires a chapter to itself. In 1830 and 1831 Claire Bazard had the responsibility of drawing women to the doctrine, discussing it with them, and instructing and leading them in Saint-Simonian ways. Obvious candidates for inclusion were the Rodrigues women—Olinde's wife and the sisters of him and Eugène, one of whom married Emile Pereire and another of whom married Sarchi, an early member of the group. Caroline Simon and Elisa Lemonnier, wives of recruits of 1829 and 1830, were early members. A somewhat enigmatic figure is Aglaë St. Hilaire, described as an intimate friend of the Enfantin family. She never assumed a place in the hierarchy, although she became in effect the manager of the communal household on the rue Monsigny. Enfantin depended on her for much and shared his views on doctrine with her. Her importance in the movement, from beginning to end, may have been greater and more consistent than that of many whose activities are better documented.[41]

By mid-1830, then, the public call to women could be heard. There was point and consistency in these new developments. There was a desire to act, to translate Saint-Simonian ideology into everyday reality; to make the politicians act on the need for economic reorganization; to create a body of support for such action; and to dramatize the wounds of society as they appeared in the workplace, the home, marriage, and the family. There was an effort to establish the connectedness, the unity, of all social questions. The Saint-Simonian internal organization appeared strong enough to carry out a program, and the external enthusiasm encouraged this hope. The time seemed ripe for change.

Blanc again is one of the best witnesses of France on the eve of Revolution. He issues an indictment in terms that are more than a little Saint-Simonian. "The moral interests of society appeared yet more compromised than its material interests. The Saint-Simonians undermined all the old bases of the social order." What one saw in 1830 was a battle of producers for the conquest of the market and a battle of the poor against the machines that were destined, in replacing them, to make them die of hunger. Big capital gained the victory in the industrial wars. Laissez-faire led to odious monopolies, and great farms ruined small ones. Usury taking over, modern feudalism became worse than ancient. Artisans who were their own men gave place to employers who were not. All interests were armed against one another; the proprietors of vineyards against the proprietors of forests, seaports against the interior, Bordeaux against Paris. Here markets overflowed—the despair of the capitalist; their shops closed—the despair of the laborer. All the discoveries of science were transformed into means of oppression. All the conquests of human genius over nature were transformed into arms of combat. Tyrannies multiplied through the agency of progress itself. The proletarian became the valet of a hand crank, in time of crisis seeking his bread between insurrection and charity. The father of the poor family died in the hospital at sixty; his daughter was forced into prostitution at sixteen; his son was reduced at the age of seven to breathing the pestilential air of the spinning mills. The bed of the day laborer, "without foresight in his misery," became horribly fecund, and the proletariat menaced the kingdom with beggars. That, according to Blanc, was society in 1830.[42]

But there was more: no common beliefs, no affirmations, and for religion, the love of gain. Marriage was a speculation, a piece of business, an industrial enterprise. And since marriage had been declared indissoluble by law, divorce was replaced nearly always by adultery. To disorders born in the family "by the fragility of the conjugal bond were added scandalous debates over inheritance."[43]

For the laboring classes the dissolution of the family had different origins but an even more deplorable character. In the register of prostitution, poverty figures as "the principle nourishment of debauchery." Marriage for the proletarian meant an increase of costs; libertinage, a softening of pain. "Poverty coupled with poverty, so that misery gave birth to concubinage and concubinage to infanticide." In a society where such oppression was possible, "charity was only a word, and religion only a memory."[44]

The moment of change was closer at hand in mid-1830 than the Saint-Simonians or almost anyone else had anticipated. They were not only psychologically but almost necessarily physically involved. The rue Monsigny was a few minutes' walk from the Restaurant Lointier, which served as Republican headquarters; a few minutes' walk from the Palais Royal, where insurrection would begin; and in sight of the rue de Richelieu, where the torchlight processions of the revolutionaries would shortly take place. The Polignac ministry of Charles X, in power for the last year, was reactionary and dangerous to the interests of the liberals. The Royal *ordonnances* of July 26, 1830, precipitated the uprising of July 27–29, and the Restoration monarchy came to an end. For a time, a short time, possibilities seemed infinite. Caught by surprise, the Saint-Simonians reacted to the July days in diverse and sometimes conflicting ways.

To the old liberal warhorse, Bazard, the smell of revolution suggested opportunity; to the younger, enthusiastic, Saint-Simonians some response seemed imperative. The *polytechniciens* invaded their Salle d'Armes, removed the buttons from the foils, sharpened their stolen blades, and took to the streets. Paulin Talabot, one of the great engineering figures of the July Monarchy and Second Empire, in his zeal charged his gun incorrectly and was unable to shoot at the barricades. Carnot and Laurent scouted political discussion groups and hoped for a republic.[45] There was some thought that the Saint-Simonians as a body would "go to the Louvre." They had, after all, been one of the groups most in the public eye and could be looked on as a political force. Bazard urged his friend Lafayette, who was a crucial figure in the July days, to assume a dictatorship. Lafayette was not disposed to do so, his main interest being in divesting himself of political responsibility.[46]

Despite the temptation to plunge into the action, despite the erratic deeds of many of the Saint-Simonians, and despite uncertainty in Enfantin himself, he and Bazard rather quickly developed a common "line" on the events through which they were passing. Essentially their position was to be above the parties. Neither Orleanist nor Republican programs would, in their view, resolve the social crisis described by Blanc, which they had been publicizing for five years:

"Alas! The holy revolt that has just taken place does not merit the name of Revolution, because it changes nothing in social organization." The moment had come to profit from the luck of the liberals. "What must be demanded ceaselessly and more loudly than ever is liberty of religion, liberty of the press, of commerce and of industry, liberty of teaching and association, and finally the abolition of hereditary peerage." This program was not designed solely in the interests of liberty but as the secret means of arriving at a truly social organization.

Remind the liberals what they must do as liberals, adjured Bazard. "We demand liberty for cults so that a unique cult can more easily be raised on the ruins of humanity's religious past. We wish a free press because it is the indispensable condition for a truly legitimate direction of thought, morality and science. We demand freedom of teaching so that our doctrine can propagate itself more easily . . . and may one day be the only one loved, known and practiced by all." The Saint-Simonians also called for the destruction of monopolies but only as a means to more rational industrial organization. Bazard's conclusion was that "society marches to complete dissolution," Enfantin's, that "the doctrine has spoken; [it must] speak more and more."[47]

The argument was taken up by Barrault at the *Prédication* of August 2 at the rue Monsigny. "We are the men of the future!" he announced, because the Saint-Simonians alone had studied the past to learn from it the rational justification for a new order. "We are the men of the future!" because the Saint-Simonians alone were above national prejudice and continued to preach universal association.

We are the men of the future because we lead all aspects of human activity toward unity, rehabilitated work, . . . sanctified scientific discovery, and industrial conquest to make them magnify the glory of God and the happiness of man; we alone have signaled the imminent reign of peaceful capacities, proclaimed classification and reward according to merit as the last stage of the emancipation of the most numerous classes, and have announced to our mothers, wives, sisters, daughters, so long our slaves and subjects, that they are to become what they ought to be — our equals, our associates.[48]

The July Revolution gave an impulsion to Saint-Simonianism that had been needed. In early July, despite all that had been accomplished over the preceding nine months, Enfantin sensed and complained of flagging energies. But in the wake of the July days the Saint-Simonians could not only describe themselves as men of the future but could benefit from the attention of those who were now disposed to believe them.

Barrault's *prédication* had summarized the social thrust of the doctrine and had given a new and special emphasis to the place of women in it. Enfantin had laid down a political line, which the group would pursue in the months to come: to advance the cause of liberalism and benefit from it,

131

but above all not to succumb to it. The rhetoric of revolution had certainly suggested a "totalitarian" viewpoint, which was neither new nor inconsistent with the past.

More importantly, if one takes Blanc's description of the society of 1830 seriously — a description couched in all its details in exact Saint-Simonian terms — one is reminded that the Saint-Simonian search for power was a means not an end. The ends described, every one of them, are liberating. It is possible to reward the frustration of the liberators with sarcasm as they seek to "force men to be free." But one can hardly argue that in 1830 most men or any women *were* free.

Bazard had in the days of *Le Producteur* declared that one does not discuss the truth, "one teaches it." Saint-Simon had offered a precedent for the dictatorship urged on Lafayette as a quick means for reaching Saint-Simonian ends. In speaking of the men of the future, Barrault had exposed a sensitive nerve: the force of nationality, the conflict of freedom-seekers and authoritarian regimes, the role of France in international politics, the question of armed intervention, and an ambivalence about the means of imposing a "French" doctrine on a waiting world were all implicit in his reference to universal association as opposed to conflict. These questions would provide problems in the months to come. The discussion would provide future critics of the doctrine with fodder for accusations of absolutism and despotism. But like so many other topics taken up by the school, these would provide provisional answers before arriving at a consistency difficult but not impossible to foresee.

L'Organisateur, soon *Le Globe,* a conscious missionary activity across France and beyond its borders, an effort to oragnize the lives of working-class adherents, and a seduction of the notable and influential in the rue Monsigny and in public halls across Paris would be the vehicles of this next effort.

There was disagreement over what the practical steps might be. As usual, behind the public scene there was to rage a battle over the next development in Saint-Simonian theory, whose results would be known only a year later. But by the fall of 1830 hopes were high, feelings intense, activity enhanced. The belief in an immediate consequence of all that had gone before was everywhere sensed by the Saint-Simonians. They were the men of the future, and the future was now.

CHAPTER VIII

THE MEN OF THE FUTURE

AROUND A VAST HALL on the rue Taitbout, under a glass roof, wound three tiers of boxes. In three rows at the front of the amphitheater, whose red plush benches were filled by an excited crowd every Sunday at noon, were seated a number of serious young men dressed in blue. Among them were a few women wearing white dresses and purple sashes. Soon Enfantin and Bazard appeared, leading the day's preacher. The disciples rose lovingly, there was a deep silence among the spectators, and the orator then began to speak. Many listened at first with "a smile on their lips and raillery in their eyes, but when he had spoken there was astonishment and admiration. The most skeptical could not defend themselves from a secret emotion."[1]

The family established at the rue Monsigny was like "a crackly hearth with the double virtue of attracting and radiating warmth."[2] From this center missionaries left to sow the Saint-Simonian word across all France and Europe. Everywhere, they left traces of their passage.

At the center, France's political situation in 1830 undoubtedly both smoothed the Saint-Simonian path in some ways and raised obstacles on it. The Saint-Simonian stance was to be above parties while supporting specific programs of the liberal regime headed by King Louis-Philippe and his minister Casimir Périer. This was, nevertheless, the "bourgeois" monarchy. Attacks on property and inheritance were likely to receive a cool reception; so were appeals to workers who had been useful in the July days but whose activities had given rise to fear in their masters. But there was hope, anticipation, curiosity, and the desire for discussion, and at the rue Monsigny all these needs could be met.

By the beginning of October 1830 forty members of the school, including the Bazard family, had settled in as residents. By the end of the year ninety-three would be taking their meals there regularly. Aglaë Saint-Hilaire was "governess" of the household. The neighborhood would house others of the school.[3] L'Organisateur's editorial offices were on the top floor. By the end of October the school had acquired Le Globe as its official organ. Le Globe had been a liberal journal in financial trouble by the time of the July Revolution. Enfantin had opened conversations with Pierre Leroux in the hope of bringing it, with Leroux himself, Sainte-Beuve, and L'herminier, the editors, to Saint-Simonianism. The last underwent an enthusiastic, if brief, conversion. Leroux, although fundamentally Republican and disliking the forms of Saint-Simonianism, was drawn by the social message and by Enfantin. Sainte-Beuve held his distance (he was, according to Michel Chevalier, "*un farceur*"), but cooperated. By November, Enfantin was able to summon Chevalier, an "old Voltairean" who had "learned his religion in the *Encyclopédie*" to come to take charge of *Le Globe* and all other Saint-Simonian publications.[4]

After a period of transition *Le Globe* revealed itself in December of 1830 as an organ of Saint-Simonianism. Enfantin, the man of affairs, had not wished to drive away the Republican subscribers. Chevalier, described as "gifted but with little initiative," was "marvelously clever at vulgarizing the ideas given him." He would become aide-de-camp to Enfantin and ultimately one of the great men of the Second Empire. Trained at the Ecole Polytechnique, like so many other Saint-Simonians, he had a literary, academic, and governmental career. At the point when he assumed editorship of the *Globe,* he announced that "we are new men" not compromised by the past.[5]

If one stands aside, for a moment, from all this activity and asks, "What did it add up to?" one can give two kinds of answers. Barrault would declare in the *prédications* that the Saint-Simonians were not interested in founding a commune but in refounding the universe. It would be easy to account for the stir made by the movement by simple curiosity, the invitation to mockery, the hieratic pose, the costumes ("henceforth the Saint-Simonian color is blue," Enfantin decreed in October),[6] free entertainment, and the possibility of personal advantage. One has to suppose that the police were not entirely absent from Saint-Simonian gatherings. Soon "a wealthy family of the Eighth Arrondissement," one of whose sons was attached to the movement, would be paying street toughs to break up meetings. The mayor was then able to prohibit meetings in the interest of public order.[7]

In time there would be accusations of embezzlements of members' funds and agitation over the young attracted to the cult. The Saint-Simonian image was not unlike that of those present-day religious cults accused of brainwashing and corruption of the young. Lamoricière, a general of the army at thirty-three and stationed in Algeria, had to reassure his mother that his devotion to the doctrine was not a matter of excess or eccentricity but of reason and conviction.[8]

But there must stand beside the skeptical approach to Saint-Simonian activity the ample evidence that Saint-Simonian ideas moved and persuaded in all classes and ranks of society. *Le Globe* was distributed, eventually, free of charge and of course to the influential as well as to ordinary folk. Metternich has been quoted already as saying that if the Saint-Simonians knew how much he read them, they would take him for a proselyte. John Stuart Mill met Enfantin in 1830. Carlyle, and thus Mill, had been aware of the movement by way of Gustave d'Eichthal since 1828. Both found much to sympathize with. Goethe was not pleased, and Mendelssohn asked that he not be sent *Le Globe*. Liszt appears to have been enthusiastic and to have overcome the reserve of George Sand.[9] The young Marx met Saint-Simonianism by way of his future father-in-law. There are clearly Saint-Simonian passages in the novels of Disraeli. One of "the most beautiful friendships ever seen" developed in the course of 1831 between Enfantin and Heinrich Heine.[10] The question of the long-range impact of Saint-Simonian "influence peddling" belongs in another place and to another time. But what is clear is that Saint-Simonianism stirred the curiosity of and demanded absorption in the world view of a large number of major political and intellectual figures, as did other similar movements. Saint-Simonianism stood out in 1830 and 1831 across Europe as the most interesting phenomenon in the intellectual life of a liberated Paris that was every European intellectual's second home.

Along with the distribution of *Le Globe* went the publication of broadsides, brochures, the "preachings," the "teachings," the *Exposition*. During the last months of 1831 fifty thousand copies of these were distributed. Given the high cost of newspaper subscriptions and the fact that *Le Globe* was free, one has to assume that every copy had many readers and that among the readers there were some converts. Indeed, one need not assume: it is known to be the case.[11]

By early 1831 Isaac Pereire would be charged with the correspondence of *Le Globe* and in a given month might have to deal with as many as twelve hundred letters. There were 240 regular correspondents in France's seventy departments. Much of this correspondence is extant and reveals loneliness, desperation, and the desire to be in touch with new ideas—the desire to receive letters. But the correspondence also reveals manufacturers who have instituted programs of worker education, apprenticeships, and improved working conditions and workers who confess that understanding has diminished the hate in their hearts. It reveals many who want to know more of Saint-Simonianism.[12]

Such people became targets for the missionary activity already in progress and about to be enlarged. One has the evidence of a Dr. Guépin at Nantes, who one day would appear in Pierre Sorlin's biography of Prime Minister Waldeck-Rousseau as a source of that minister's social conscience.[13] One has the evidence teased out by Maurice Agulhon confirming the persistent Saint-Simonian role in the politics of Toulon.[14] There is Ribes, professor of medicine at Montpellier, and all those others encouraged by Enfantin and Resseguier in the south. There was always at Lyons François-Barthélemy Arlès-Dufour, one of the most attractive figures in Saint-Simonianism. He wore no costumes and did not figure in the hierarchy, but his purse and his door were always open. His protection, as a leading figure in the Lyonnais business community, was important.[15] It was largely through Arlès that Lyons became a second capital of the movement. Elsewhere, by the end of 1831 crowds at Mulhouse would be standing patiently outside the house of Dr. Paul Curie to hear the Saint-Simonian good news.[16]

One has to imagine the process of diffusion in some such fashion as this—here and there in the provinces a single figure or a small group waiting for *Le Globe,* waiting to hear the living word from a passing Saint-Simonian, or easing the ennui of provincial life by discussion of Saint-Simonian ideas. Perhaps in the next season such people would pass to the next fashion, but perhaps not. At the end of 1831 the Saint-Simonians would be accused of responsibility for the workers' riots at Lyons. It was not the Saint-Simonian intention, but the message may well have had that result.

In Paris during 1830 and 1831 as many as eight "teachings" were taking place weekly near the Sorbonne, opposite the Palais de Justice on the Ile de la Cité, and on the boulevards. Thousands of auditors were present, scores were more than casually interested in the doctrine, and dozens became integrally involved with the movement.[17]

There is no way to quantify the influence and the appeal of Saint-Simonian ideas. One can see the movement as composed of pathetic and unimportant groupings persisting beyond the period of greatest publicity. One can liken Saint-Simonian activity to the Bible-thumping evangelism current elsewhere in the nineteenth and twentieth centuries, to a Salvation Army, or to the communalism attempted or proposed so widely both in that time and ours. But it does seem clear that if Saint-Simonianism caught the attention of an individual, it was likely to hold. There are evidences of this fact at all levels: social, economic, and intellectual. Hippolyte Carnot, fifty years after his involvement, declared that he had no regrets. The official biographer of Paulin Talabot, whose descendants were rather embarrassed by his Saint-Simonianism, testified that there was no doubt of his attachment to the principles of the doctrine. Alfred Pereire testified as to his grandfather's persistent attachment, as Adolphe d'Eichthal did to his father's. Aglaë Saint-Hilaire would after 1832 "try to do something for the working-class members of the family still in Paris." And Suzanne Voilquin, critical of Enfantin, would testify to the crucial importance of Saint-Simonianism in her life.[18]

Léon Halévy would mock the later stages of Saint-Simonianism, but the most serious early discussion of the economics of the school was the product of another Halévy, Elie, whose interest was an inherited one. The particular impact of Saint-Simonianism on the textile workers of Lyons, at least until 1848, is widely recognized. It may be because Saint-Simonianism was "the one blueprint for a new society already on the drawing board when the old world fell apart" that it had real impact. It may be that in the realm of thought, 1830 represented a *"conjoncture* Saint-Simonienne," which accounted for the persistence of the doctrine, in whole or in part, in the minds of the elite of an entire generation as well as its role in the actions of a despairing working class.[19]

The Saint-Simonians did constitute an elite; the eighty-eight engineers whom Enfantin counted as adherents were viewed by him as "the general staff of the industrial army."[20] They were, as has already been suggested, a powerful force automatically enjoying high status as products of the grandest of the *grands écoles.* They occupied provincial and overseas posts, where they were given immediate social consequence. Eventually they could be found from Turkey, Ethiopia, Egypt, and Algeria to Greece, Russia, and even America. Where they went, they took their ascribed status and their professional competence, a point of view, and a characteristic program.

Although the *polytechniciens* built a canal through which Saint-Simonian ideas might flow, it was not the only conduit. The importance of oral propaganda for the illiterate was important not only in Paris but also across France and into Belgium, Germany, and England. The missionary effort had begun to reveal a characteristic structure. It was not surprising that a number of Saint-Simonians, as a function of their practical careers, persistently raised the question of translating the doctrine into action, of utilizing the religious enthusiasm to attain visible ends. Henri and Cécile Fournel, along with Paulin Talabot, were driven by this need and in turn drove the "fathers" to consider concrete demonstrations of the workability of Saint-Simonian economics. Since 1827 Henri Fournel and Margerin, another engineer, had been interested in the possibilities of the railway. It was an interest that would have far-flung consequences, but at the end of 1830 Fournel was consumed by his perception of working-class misery.

As director of the works at Le Creusot, Fournel had been forced to close them down when there was no work. He recounts in a number of places the misery of three to four thousand who could not be paid. He enunciated the startling proposition that workers' wages should be as immediate a charge on a failing company as any other debt. His life itself had been threatened by a misery-maddened worker. Having already given up his fortune to the movement, Fournel left Le Creusot and in January of 1831 came with his wife to Paris. His mission was to direct with Claire Bazard the organization of working-class Saint-Simonians and to form an "industrial" degree. She at this time was also codirector with Fournel's friend Margerin of the mission to women.[21]

The point of the Fournel project was to provide dramatic illustration of the force of the "spirit of association." The phrase was to be heard everywhere in the 1830s and 1840s, largely as a result of Saint-Simonian propaganda. Its first manifestation was the creation of committees for each Paris *arrondissement*. The hope was that the poor would combine their resources, and undertake, as at the rue Monsigny but on a much less grand scale, a common life in a common dwelling, sharing the purchase and preparation of food, of child care, and of skills such as shoemaking and dressmaking. These units would be self-supporting, would display the virutes of "association" over "competition" and "socialism over egotism," and would consequently invite imitation and the expansion of the movement's ideas and memberships.[22]

Such a project had its dangers. The law on associations was still in force, forbidding meetings of more than twenty people; the new bourgeois monarchy was going to be suspicious of any organized working-class activity. It would assume that any such activity must have dangerous political implications either Republican or, strangely, in the case of the Saint-Simonians legitimist. With their new appeal to the workers the Saint-Simonians began to look dangerous. When the textile workers of Lyons rose in insurrection in the autumn of 1831, the school engaged the full attention of the government.[23]

Some months would pass between Fournel's arrival and the realization of the workers' associations, but he characteristically set up a system for their organization. Sundays from 4 to 6 P.M. had been set aside at the rue Taitbout for workers' instruction. Out of these meetings 220 formal adherents to the doctrine had been drawn. Attendance varied between four hundred and six hundred. It was a sizable pool of potential recruits. Each of the twelve Paris *arrondissements* had a director, a directress, and a Saint-Simonian doctor whose duty it was to instruct, encourage conversion, hear "professions of faith," and judge the worthiness of recruits for full membership and the benefits that might be derived from it.[24]

Here as elsewhere, amid religious ecstasy and social fervor the Saint-Simonians displayed a hard-headed practicality. They were fully aware that many might be drawn to the movement by some putative temporary advantage. They demanded and received information about the material and "moral" state of each candidate. They made it clear that "association" required the surrender to the group of all resources, in return for which the group undertook support and help for the weak based on the contributions of the strong.[25]

Practically and on the individual level this meant a multitude of small aids: providing layettes for expectant mothers, paying off pledges to pawn shops, and settling minor debts so that the candidates entered the association free of encumbrances, able to stand on their own feet and contribute to the welfare of the whole group. At times these contributions were so great a drain that the rent on the rue Monsigny itself could not be paid. Free medical care was obviously an attractive advantage, and at moments of epidemic the Saint-Simonian doctors became popular heroes. The doctors included Jallat and Lesbazeilles Fuster. The directors included Raymond Bonheur and his wife; Eugénie Niboyet; and Véturie Espagne.

The weekly reports of these officials give some indication of the hopes and disillusions in creating a degree of *industriels*. One report notes the presence of a police spy, who was a Republican and Freemason guided by considerations of self-interest. There is a clockmaker in the place Notre Dame "who employs six people, loves the doctrine, and accepts the idea of association." Borel thinks he can combine Catholicism and Saint-Simonianism; "he had better wait to enter the family." Biard reports from the Third Arrondissement the number of vaccinations given and the acquisition to the faith of a lady ninety-eight years old.[26]

At the end of December 1831 there were in the Second Arrondissement 109 interested people: a laundress, baker, box maker, shoemaker, *coiffeur,* carpenter, cabinet maker, seamstress, house painter, mason, and twenty-four tailors. There is a warm report on a Mlle Amélie Bourgeoise, "an interesting young person who had played children's roles at the theater of M. Comte" (next door to the rue Monsigny), who had exploited her. "She is not pretty, but has her springtime freshness" and "despite her somewhat scabrous profession perhaps, also, her purity."[27]

From the Tenth Arrondissement comes a report on Désirée Veret, twenty-one years old, a seamstress, "remarkable for her state of mind, facility in writing, and level of instruction." Lesbazeilles, director in the Seventh Arrondissement but doctor for the Sixth, Seventh, and Eighth, recommends that his directorate be taken over by "Voilquin and his wife." Suzanne Voilquin, like Niboyet and Veret, was to have a role to play in French feminism. There is in the Second Arrondissement a "Mme Rondet, holder of two patents, who has embraced her new faith with passion and propagates it with fire."[28]

In November from Parent in the Eleventh Arrondissement comes yet another report. Himself of working-class origins, he points up the difficulties, ambiguities, and weakness of the Saint-Simonians' relationship to the workers whom they profess to love but whom, above all, they wish to instruct. Parent describes four categories of workers: "(1) those who understand and adopt Saint-Simonianism by conviction, (2) those working for us who adopt the doctrine out of self-interest, (3) those hoping we will find work for them, and (4) those seeking alms." The first class is not the most numerous. There is a contradiction in trying to draw "the people" from ignorance through a doctrine that can be understood only by the most advanced minds of the time. "We can provide work . . . but it should be organized by trades rather than neighborhoods. . . . Many of the solid recruits refuse to associate with the lazy or incompetent." Many of the workers are suspicious about confiding their business to members of the privileged class. "They have so often been deceived."

The workers, Parent continues, cannot speak freely. They lose their spontaneity. "This is pretty much your fault. They know the details of work better than you do. They have, like womankind, revelations to make." The hand of the "fathers" should weigh less heavily. Saint-Simonian workers complain that "you don't give them enough attention," that they are treated as a society external to Saint-Simonianism. "I am not a rebel, but you must recognize that one can maintain all possible submission to the chiefs while speaking out freely."[29]

Parent's request was dated November 27, 1831, and came at the height of Saint-Simonianism's major internal crisis. Soon the workers' houses in the rue Popincourt and the rue de Helder, in existence for some months, would have to take a back seat while grave doctrinal issues were addressed. The houses became too expensive, the cooperative efforts of the workers were not adequate to the costs, and the funds of the school began to run out. This first effort to translate doctrine into action was, in short, a failure.

But again one cannot tell what the short- and long-range consequences may have been. The directors of the Paris districts report attendance at their meetings of "109," "220," and other comparable figures. In these months and at a neighborhood level there must have been two to three thousand workers who in one way or another were touched by the doctrine. At Lyons, a quite different situation, to be sure, from Paris, there is evidence of continuing Saint-Simonian loyalties and inspiration through the Revolution of 1848. Long after the dispersion of the school there remained a faithful group of followers in Paris. The attraction of the working-class experiment for a number of women — Niboyet, Voilquin, Veret, and Pauline Roland — was to have its impact on French feminism. One of the most impassioned reports is that of Niboyet, arguing that women could be placed in full charge of the association and begging for an opportunity to become a full-fledged *prédicateuse* of the doctrine.[30]

The long-range preoccupation of Henri Fournel had been the creation of the "industrial army" that would provide the muscle of Saint-Simonian ambition. By and large the Saint-Simonian directors were drawn to the artisanal, the virtuous, the hard-working — those capable, as Chevalier would say in *Le Globe,* of being raised to the rank of bourgeois. In addition to the neighborhood associations, for example, there existed a workshop of tailors and of seamstresses. Once the school had adopted a uniform for the fathers and the members of the various degrees, it apparently produced enough business to maintain these establishments in work. It then made of them Saint-Simonian "associations" rather than businesses providing service for a price. It was said of one of the tailors that he worked "slowly and badly" but had "effected thirty conversions."[31]

These were some of the faces in the Saint-Simonian crowd. The leadership suffered from a certain discomfort in the face of the *prolétaires*. They were filled with a sense of their own largeness of spirit in opening up possibilities to those whom they quite frankly saw as their social inferiors. The hope they offered suggested, "Look, you can be as wonderful as we, and isn't it wonderful of us to help you be that?" The reaction of Parent is understandable and just. But the reaction is evidence once again of the essentially bourgeois character of Saint-Simonian socialism. From the point of view of the history of working-class ideology this bourgeois character was a weakness. From the point of view of a modern industrial society the bourgeois appeal constituted a strength as yet unperceived by a majority of the French bourgeoisie.

Claire Bazard had early on noted how hard workers could be with one another and how the worker who had "arrived" at a superior economic or social rank was more rigid with and demanding of his former fellows than were the bourgeois themselves.[32] Duveyrier, the aristocratic charmer, "doesn't understand how to speak to workers," one report tells us. Niboyet warned that workers should not be "graduated" from degree to degree of the school, since such elevations created jealousies. Throughout the experiment with the workers there was a clear barrier of uneasiness and discomfort, a sense of two nations, a sense of "working classes, dangerous classes."[33]

What is remarkable, however, is that the effort to bridge the gap was made. It was, perhaps, the only such effort being made in the wake of 1830. As in every other aspect of Saint-Simonianism, so with the workers, one can patronize, one can find and accept a cynical interpretation for the school's deeds without much difficulty. But, here, as with the attack on liberalism, context is all important.

That the Saint-Simonian leadership was gauche, vain, and invincibly patronizing is less remarkable than that it tried to be something other. Who else was listening to workers' lives at that epoch? How many Fournels filled with horror and compassion at the workers' plight and determined to change it were there among France's industrial elite? How many Arlès-Dufours, filled with respect for workers and determined to advance their cause at considerable risk to himself? How many Enfantins, demanding an examination of workers' consciences and consciousness? Even this last aspect of the doctrine, while inviting suspicion of brainwashing and invasion of the worker's individuality, leaves us with a regret that the "professions of faith" were not recorded. As Parent said, "The workers have revelations to make."

With all their shortcomings, embarrassments, and prejudices, the Saint-Simonians were less inadequate than anyone else in their society at trying to arrive at an understanding of working-class alienation and at trying to construct an escape route from it. The workers complained of the emphasis

141

on working-class brutality and violence in the lessons they were given, but they were also much attracted by the hope of a place, a future, a security that society seemed to deny them. It is a decisive moment in the social history of France and of Europe. Saint-Simonianism can be dismissed as utopian, but there is ample evidence of workers' willingness to reach out to the helping hand it proffered — a willingness that would disappear definitively after 1848.

For such as Parent by December of 1831 it appeared that once again the people had been deceived. "Those two in whom the workers had put all their confidence," Claire Bazard and Henri Fournel, had "abandoned" them.[34] Schism threatened, the organization of the workers fell apart in its wake, but the notion of the "spirit of association" had spread in working-class ranks. Saint-Simonianism had earned a reputation for benevolence among the workers of Paris and a sympathetic audience for ideas of social reorganization. It had acquired for a time a number of striking personalities who would go beyond its teachings but were permanently marked by them.

WELL BEFORE Fournel's efforts to organize the Parisian workers Saint-Simonians had embarked on an effort to spread the doctrine and organize its followers outside Paris and outside France. The first notable effort had been Enfantin's in the south in 1829, but at the same moment Bazard was in Brittany and d'Eichthal in England. By and large the early missionaries profited from travels undertaken for other purposes and from connections formed in other ways to propagandize for the school. Thomas Carlyle's brother had been a guest of d'Eichthal's uncle in Germany, the d'Eichthal banking house opened exalted portals in Austria, and Enfantin had been traveling for his bank in the Midi. There were former subscribers to *Le Producteur* to be seen, and calls were made on the editors of local newspapers. Novelty and the presence of a new personality might set the society of Castelnaudary, Arles, Metz, or Rouen agog. As in Paris, and as during Saint-Simon's life, the search was for the influential, significant local person, like Resseguier, who, once attracted, might enthusiastically spread the good news. The close attention given the Ecole Polytechnique meant that almost everywhere in France by 1831 there was a state engineer already familiar with Saint-Simonianism, perhaps already wedded to it.

But the informal, if nonetheless considered, diffusion was only the beginning. The "Church" of the Midi had been formally organized in February 1830. Resseguier, its leader, had been admitted to the "college" at Paris in the same month, and the south was quickly rich in converts and activity. At Toulouse, Captain Léon Duprès; Ernest Albi; and Hoart; Roquelaine, eventual mayor of the city, welcomed the doctrine. Later, Hoart, an engineer, probably transferred because of his Saint-Simonianism, Charles and

Elisa Lemonnier, and Bouffard undertook a mission to Limoges. There they had audiences of twelve hundred and an open discussion three or four hours in length. "What applause! What jeers! What shocks! What pouring forth of thought of sentiment, of dreams, realities!"[35]

At Montauban, Bruneau, a captain of engineers, resigned his commission to join the group. In 1831 Hoart also resigned his, and on his death he left ten thousand francs to continue the propagation of Saint-Simonian ideas. Paris rejoiced in the acquisition of Jules Simon, brother-in-law of a prefect; Didion of the Ponts-et-chaussées, the government bridge and highway department; and Picard at Avignon. Montpellier was hostile to new ideas as was, closer to home, Versailles, where the Saint-Simonians were assumed to be Jesuits in disguise. There was, however, a favorable press at Rouen, Beauvais, LeMans, Liège and eventually Brussels. In Normandy, Adolphe Guéroult and Lambert—both destined for great careers, one as an editor and the other as an engineer and administrator in Egypt—came to Saint-Simonianism.

In the east of France, Jules Lechevalier, whose intellectual roots were in German philosophy, traveled to Dijon, Besançon, Mulhouse, Colmar, Strasbourg, Metz, and Nancy. In that region he found Capella, engineer and old friend of Enfantin, and Robinet, judge and notary. At Mulhouse he attracted Dr. Paul Curie, who was interested in Saint-Simonianism because he was a homeopath. Homeopathy operated, of course, by using like rather than opposing treatments for illness; it was, like Saint-Simonianism, "cooperative" rather than "competitive." Eventually crowds gathered around Curie's house to hear the Saint-Simonian message. There were audiences of 1,500 at Nancy and 2,000 at Metz.[36]

Officialdom was always unhappy at the appearance of missionaries. This milieu was the conspiratorial world of Balzac and Stendhal. It was always assumed that there were hidden agendas behind the public *expositions;* that any gathering of the size achieved by the Saint-Simonians was, in itself, dangerous; that there was a political objective; and that the artisan class was the most likely enemy of the regime.

Nowhere were these fears greater than at Lyons, and nowhere perhaps did a Saint-Simonian mission have a greater immediate impact or a more complex role to play. As we have seen, the central figure for the Saint-Simonians at Lyons was Arlès-Dufour. A convinced anticlerical in the most Catholic of French cities and a convinced socialist in the midst of the Lyonnais silk manufacturing oligarchy, he presents a picture of honesty, independence, humor, occasional despair, and, above all, "goodness." By virtue of his position of leadership in the Lyonnais business community, he could protect Pierre Leroux and Jean Reynaud, who arrived at Lyons in the spring of 1831. He could and did contribute largely to their material support. His sympathy could make it possible for respectable people like the Niboyets, his fellow businessman Drut, and De Caen, editor of Lyons's liberal journal, to come close to Saint-Simonianism.

Lyons seemed a ripe field for conversion. Leroux wrote to "My fathers" in May 1831:

It is in vain that nature has given this population two magnificent rivers, admirable lines of mountains, green hillsides in the bosom of the city. They are without poetry, without life, without love. . . . We were struck on arriving by the deformity of the Lyonnais complexion, yellow and sick, features confused and without harmony. In the calmest, most apathetic state their faces are a convulsion. . . . They live in such dwellings, in streets so narrow and so dark, bordered by houses so high that they have to lose their sight, they deprive themselves of it so voluntarily.[37]

The Saint-Simonian evangel quickly reached this population. A few days after Leroux's letter, he and Reynaud greeted 3,000 people at the Cirque des Brotteaux. All through the spring, summer, and autumn of 1831 the Saint-Simonian appeal grew. Part of its appeal lay in the always simmering hostility of the silk workers and their masters in a dying industry. By November insurrection had made the workers masters of the city between the Saône and the Rhone. The leaders of the Lyons Saint-Simonians, now François and Pfeiffer, attempted to preach pacification to workers and masters alike. The events of October and November ended with an appeal by the masters to the workers to talk things over.[38]

Le Globe, in Paris, used the events as an illustration of the truth of the doctrine. Without an increase in rates the workers would starve; with an increase in rates the masters would close down. The result: an impossible situation attributable to *oisiveté,* inherited wealth, and lack of economic organization. While expressing sympathy for the workers, the Saint-Simonians were equally clearly on the side of law and order.[39] But Saint-Simonianism was, for authority, baffling. The faith that was being preached everywhere, every day, at Lyons was believed to have contributed to the uprising.[40] It was difficult for the July Monarchy not to see in Saint-Simonianism a purely political movement whose object must be subversion of the regime. Casimir Périer, at least initially, subscribed to this thesis, and the beginnings of the Saint-Simonians' troubles with the law stem from the Lyons uprising. Saint-Simonianism was beginning to suffer from its success. Joined to other crucial events in November, Lyons contributed to the Saint-Simonian crisis, which would be resolved by the closing of the mother house in the rue Monsigny at the instigation of the government in 1832.

THE VOYAGES to England and the Germanys of various Saint-Simonians— d'Eichthal, Duveyrier, Arlès-Dufour—succeeded in arousing the interest of significant groups of people in the doctrine. The most ambitious hopes, however, centered on a Belgium in revolt against the Dutch monarchy imposed on it by the Congress of Vienna.

The Belgian experience underlined a division that had lurked in Saint-Simonian thought from its beginnings. The division was political. The Saint-Simonians declared themselves above parties, but the position in this year of revolution was difficult to maintain. The Saint-Simonians had always been cosmopolitan, but that, too, in a time of nascent nationalism was a difficult and olympian view to hold. Those difficulties were to some extent dramatized with the venture into Belgium. The mission there consisted initially of Carnot, Dugied, Laurent, and Margerin. All these had come to Saint-Simonianism by way of Republicanism and hoped that the refusal of Louis-Philippe to accept a Belgian crown for his son the duc de Nemours would make inevitable a Belgian republic.[41]

Margerin, attracted in the days of *Le Producteur* by Bazard, was chief of the mission. Increasingly attached to Enfantin, he played an important part in the development of ideology, shared with Claire Bazard responsibility for the mission to women, and was in January of 1831 on the brink of an emotional crisis that would end with his return to Catholicism. The other members of the mission distrusted and disliked him and were jealous of his special relations with Enfantin. On their arrival Margerin had ready a proclamation in support of a Belgian republic. His fellow missionaries refused to approve it. By September Paris would have taken the extraordinary step of excommunicating him publicly. Coupled with his political bad judgment was scandalous personal behavior embarrassing to the mission. And behind that scandal hovered a greater private scandal involving Mme Bazard.[42]

The issues present at the time of the Belgian mission had to do with the propriety of a French intrusion in the affairs of other states. The "fathers" deemed such intervention and its motives secondary to the overwhelming universal and cosmopolitan concerns of the doctrine. Carnot and Laurent would break with Saint-Simonianism, in part, because of its pacifism. At this juncture, however, they were good doctrinaires. Squaring the circle of national pride and interventionism, cosmopolitanism and pacifism, would be the work of Michel Chevalier. But the tension over intervention or nonintervention to aid revolutionary causes was one of many within the inner group soon to become public.

In Belgium the mission met a variety of responses. Catholic groups were publicly and violently anti–Saint-Simonian. Promised a disaffected church by the government at Brussels, the group failed to get it. At Liège the rector offered the main lecture hall, where Laurent and Barrault addressed audiences of 1,500. In April additional members arrived, headed by Duveyrier. They were refused space, not surprisingly, at Louvain, but between May and November Duveyrier published an *Organisateur Belge* devoted exclusively to Belgian Saint-Simonianism.[43]

The net results, again, cannot be quantified. In a fluid political situation any new doctrine might find an audience. By this time the Saint-Simonians were adept at creating one. They formed circles of adherents, they briefly became centers of public attention, and they made converts. One of them, Toussaint, was chef de bureau of the minister of justice. But events in Paris inevitably drew the members of the nuclear group back by November to deal with the impending schism. Only time could tell with what effect the Belgians had labored. The divisions in Paris would have the further effect of dividing Saint-Simonians everywhere in France and abroad.

The interest of Carlyle, Mill, Tooke, and Burns in England was flattering, but it was accompanied by reservations. The German jurist Warnkoenig wrote warmly of Saint-Simonian ideas, and early in 1832 the *Gazette* of Augsburg published an encouraging account by Heine.[44] Arlès-Dufour departed on German business trips laden with Saint-Simonian propaganda. The Young Germany Movement, thanks to Heine and Lorenz von Stein, would ultimately constitute a German audience, but not yet. Echoes of Saint-Simon would be heard soon in Italy by Mazzini and Garibaldi, in the Balkans, in the Middle East, and in East Africa.

What is clear is that wherever the Saint-Simonians traveled in 1830–31, they found those who wished to hear what they had to offer. Among those who listened as well as among those who spoke were an unusual number of people whose lives would mark their generation and their nations. One of the then interesting but seemingly minor occasions for Saint-Simonian propaganda occurred as early as 1829. Vieillard then had a conversation with the countess Saint-Leu and the duchess of Baden. Vieillard had been tutor to the countess's elder son; her younger would one day be Napoleon III, emperor of the French and, according to Adolphe Guéroult, another Saint-Simonian, "a Saint-Simonian on horseback."

To SENSE the exhilaration of the months between the Revolution of 1830 and the terrible and terrifying confrontations that broke Saint-Simonian unity in November of 1831 is not difficult. The house on the rue Monsigny was the command post in a battle to remake the world. Dispatches went out from Bazard, Laurent, and Chevalier by way of *L'Organisateur* and *Le Globe*. Isaac Pereire waged a war of correspondence. Leroux, Reynaud, Margerin, and Duveyrier carried on the work of the missions. Fournel organized and directed the workers' associations. Claire Bazard earnestly, but with limited success, directed the apostolate to women. The rue Monsigny witnessed a constant coming and going of the members of the degrees, of those who lodged and ate there or in the neighborhood on the rue de Louvois and the rue Sainte-Anne, of the guests, and of the curious. From early morning until after midnight the house bustled with activity, excitement, joy, music, conversation, and argument.[45]

Behind the obvious activity, as in the days of Le Producteur and throughout the history of the school, fiercer and more fateful debate between Rodrigues, Bazard, Enfantin, Claire Bazard, and some few others was taking place. And in the privacy of individual apartments those "confessions," "professions of faith," and estimates of "moral state" at which Enfantin was proficient were providing the material for the conflict that would soon come. For most Saint-Simonians, until October and November 1831, the sense of involvement, achievement, possibility, and fulfillment was overwhelming. The Saint-Simonian religion was on the march. In midsummer the religious character of the movement was underlined by Enfantin's and Bazard's refusal to serve in the National Guard on the ground that they were clergymen. Their pretension was rejected, but the point had been made.

THE PROBLEMS that had plagued Saint-Simon continued to plague his followers. Granted the reality of the religion, granted the justice of its social analysis, granted even the validity of its faith in science and in technical competence, what were Saint-Simonians supposed to do? They were emphatically above party, they were at least publicly apolitical, and their object was cooperation not conflict, association not fragmentation. What, practically speaking, did all this mean for the religious in their daily lives and in their collective actions?

At one point during the summer of 1831 Enfantin commented on a sermon of Barrault's, "Tears, kisses, everyone in an uproar, and what comes of all this—du vent."[46] It was an apt and embarrassing observation.

On one level the Saint-Simonians met this question of program by reacting to whatever political question might be under discussion in the larger world. Through the sermons, the pages of Le Globe and L'Organisateur a Saint-Simonian political position began to be worked out, but it was a position that had to confront first principles and that began to present problems for the purity and the orthodoxy of doctrine.

The Saint-Simonian response to these questions current in 1830 and 1831 has appeared to at least one commentator as the most complete statement of authoritarianism to be found in the nineteenth century. The Saint-Simonian picture of prison reform, in this view, was a precursor of the twentieth-century concentration camp; reason was a neutral and amoral tool for the achievement of dubious ends rather than a guide to truth. Saint-Simonianism was a politics of imperialism, racism, and militarism; rational goals were subordinate to the irrational ambitions and pretensions of the leadership.[47]

There is enough truth in the argument that it cannot be dismissed lightly; and enough perversity so that one sighs exasperatedly at the presence of certain twentieth-century blinders blocking out historical surroundings. What the Saint-Simonians meant, as opposed to the ways in which their ideas could be abused and distorted, has first to be understood. What was provisional and what was definitive have to be distinguished from each other. Much was entertained as possible and then dropped as irrelevant or inconsistent. It was certainly as much a problem for the Saint-Simonians to chart a course as it has been for their interpreters to determine what that course was.

What is most fascinating at this juncture is their odyssey, not their destination. The fundamental mistake in comprehension is to examine only that part of the iceberg that showed. There was in this phase of doctrinal exploration, as in all the others, a consistency of principle against which the ephemeral politics of the day were measured.

The Saint-Simonians understood themselves as pacifist, as on "the side of humanity," as against the old order of things, as against the privilege of inheritance, as for the amelioration of the poorest and most numerous class, and as in favor of the exploitation of the globe by means of "association" and competence. Given these principles, what then was their dilemma? In some matters the answer might be easy. Clearly they supported the suppression of hereditary peerage. Clearly they supported the freedom of workers to associate. They had recognized that in 1830 the workers were the instruments of change driven by bourgeois motors. When they looked at Europe and the world of 1830, however, there were cross-currents and schools through which it was difficult to navigate with ideological purity.

Saint-Simonianism was universal and cosmopolitan. The benefits of its message should come to everybody. But how? How other than by the intervention of a France that had arrived at a higher plateau of history than its neighbors? Ropes should be cast to Poles, Germans, Belgians — whoever sought a greater degree of the freedom that would ready them for the Saint-Simonian message. Intervention meant military action. But the Saint-Simonians were pacifists. How, then, to act without producing conflict among the nations? By association and by peaceful penetration.

Association, in effect, meant a kind of partitioning of the world among great powers. England possessed the greatest material power, France the greatest moral power — a Christ among the nations. Austria was "retrograde"; the destiny of the Germanies lay with Prussia. The "Orient" might be the sphere of Russia, which was at Warsaw an oppressor and at Istanbul a civilizer. Certainly the assumption was of the superiority of the West over all other civilizations. One has to keep in mind that at this date the Opium War had not yet taken place, Japan was still closed to the West, the East India company still ruled India, and Algiers had just fallen to the

French. The conventional view of the slumbering and mysterious East decorated by the romantic imagination was uninformed by any very accurate knowledge or any sympathetic comprehension. It was a given, not only for the Saint-Simonians, that the West was at a higher stage of development in every way than the rest of the world, that world salvation depended on the raising of world energies to Western levels.[48]

As doctrine it was all very misty. How "intervention" and "peaceful penetration," "association" of British technology and French "moral fervor" and the "industrial army" would bring their benefits without war and conquest was not clear.

Before the rue Monsigny closed its doors and *Le Globe* ceased to appear, an answer would be forthcoming. But in these months, responding to specific issues, there was a certain confusion about ends and means. Up until August of 1831 the Saint-Simonians advocated intervention on the side of Revolution, which they justified as part of France's *mission civilisatrice*. If the world forced war on France, let it take place. It would be the last war.

That militarism, authoritarianism, and racism are to be found in *Le Globe* is without question true. They are also present in the sermons of Barrault, Transon, and Laurent. But they are an aberration. Between August and February the ephemeral and antagonistic views underwent "rectification." The greater part of *Le Globe* during these months reiterated the permanent Saint-Simonian themes forcibly. It insisted on the eventual, but not immediate, abolition of property. It laughed at the notion that the abolition of property meant the abolition of the family—in that case only the propertied had families. It underlined the distinction between sluggards and workers of all classes. It pointed out that the abolition of hereditary peerage meant little if it was to be replaced by a hereditary bourgeoisie. *Le Globe*'s pages began to revive the banker as chief instrument of social transformation.[49]

Saint-Simonians asserted—it cannot be denied—the importance of authority and obedience, but they also mocked the notion of election by those who paid a given tax.

"From each according to his capacity, to each according to his works" thunders from every first page of *Le Globe*. The possibly destructive legacy of some Saint-Simonian ideas is evident, but it was also evident to the school. That the interventionist and culturally imperial themes went as far as they did was perhaps a function of the fact that the major Saint-Simonian energies were engaged in a quite different crisis in the latter half of 1831. The followers were given a freer hand in defining policies and attitudes judged by the leaders as transitory and marginal.

At a time when the doctrine seemed to have become most bizarre and most exaggerated, most difficult to understand, to follow, to act upon, it

149

was in fact returning to an orthodoxy. A program eminently practical and thoroughly consistent with the doctrine's intellectual foundations was in process of formation. Enfantin, far from being the corrupter and saboteur of Saint-Simonianism, was at the end of 1831 to rescue the doctrine from its somewhat confused liberal and legitimist rivals and to restore, for better or worse, its complex uniqueness.

In this effort Enfantin was not alone. It has often been maintained that "practical" men, embarrassed by the Enfantinian effort, left the school at this point and that only the *illuminés,* the bizarre, the sick, and the dangerous remained. Not true. In the months to come, despite many shocks, disagreements over tactics, and personal tragedies, it was the most practical men—Fournel, the brothers Pereire, Chevalier, Arlès-Dufour—who would sustain Enfantin and his understanding of the doctrine.

Paulin Talabot wrote in October 1831:

The future is certain. Like you, and by you, we understand it. We summon it with all our heart, we work with all our power to realize it. What is the SUREST and QUICKEST route? That is the question. We have given too much importance to preaching, teaching, and dogma, not enough to transitional measures. We ought to concentrate on material progress, exalt industry, praise industrialists, reinforce our pacifism and treat questions already ripe: banks, loans, tax base, and all this without a word of the future, of Saint-Simon; all this in holding rigorously to the national point of view. And would it not be for us all a great joy to see little by little, through our efforts, society moving WITHOUT SUSPECTING it toward the end we wish to attain? I say without suspecting it, and this is important. Not that I wish to hide the light under a bushel, but without hiding anything one is not obliged to say everything everywhere.[50]

Talabot's letter was a counsel of prudence from one of the men of the future, but it was also a testament of faith. Prudence was not to Enfantin's taste, and in the days to come Talabot's counsel was heeded at one level and ignored at another. Practical and important programs for action would be forthcoming; so, too, would revelation of the almost secret conversations that, as has been hinted many times in this chapter, would break the Saint-Simonian movement.

During all these months of 1831, while the Saint-Simonians announced themselves as the men of the future, the really serious question had been "And what of women?"

CHAPTER IX

THE NEW EVE

HAT OF WOMEN, indeed? At the moment when Saint-Simonians were congratulating themselves on their achievements and debating what their practical program might be, when consolidation of the evident gains of 1830 and 1831 appeared to be the next item on their agenda, the storm that had been brewing in the privy council of Enfantin, St. Amand Bazard, Claire Bazard, and Rodrigues finally broke. The results were schism, the "papacy" of Enfantin, public scandal, police intervention, imprisonments, and the dispersion of the faithful.

The quarrel, revealed to the faithful in November of 1831 but sensed from August 25, when Bazard suffered a stroke, was precisely over the place of woman in Saint-Simonian doctrine and organization. But the quarrel went beyond these issues. The question of the "call to woman," pushed most vigorously by Enfantin, was a question of the meaning of morality in its largest sense, of the family, of marriage, of sexuality, of human personality, and of how society could or should reflect reality rather than illusion. These questions were not aberrant to the main concerns of Saint-Simonianism but absolutely central to them. The impulsion to their discussion and the necessity of resolving them were derived quite clearly from Saint-Simon himself.

Saint-Simon, as has invariably been pointed out by Enfantin's critics, addressed not a single word to the question of women. In the *Lettre d'un habitant de Genève à ses concitoyens,* of 1802, Saint-Simon, urging a subscription at the tomb of Newton to forward the work of universal association, commented that "women may be admitted." In the edition of 1832 Olinde Rodrigues gave this almost parenthetical statement an increased importance by printing it in boldface capital letters and separating it from the text of which it was a part. The statement was without any doubt a slender reed upon which to rest the full weight of Saint-Simonian feminism.[1]

But what is equally true is that in *Le Nouveau Christianisme,* of 1825, Saint-Simon over and over again asserted that the central question of that religion was a morality based on love. What would differentiate the new Christianity from the old was the rehabilitation of the material universe, the gratification of human need here and now in the flesh, as well as in the spirit. Saint-Simon's criticism of Catholicism, his conviction of its contemporary irrelevance, lay precisely in its separation of spirit and matter, the symbols of which were a celibate clergy, hiding its "forms" in cassocks, and a sinful humanity. The economic and scientific programs of Saint-Simon leading to productivity and sufficiency were to be material expressions of the new morality informed by the Christian adjuration to love others as one's self. Material gratification was not sinful, it was of God. The disciples were justified in understanding love not merely as a spiritual sentiment but as an act.

The Christian universe of vice and virtue was the product of an incomplete science of humanity. It was a product marketed by those least capable of completing that science and most apt to benefit by its incompleteness. There was in Saint-Simon a rejection of original sin. It may be that without that concept Christianity has no meaning, but Saint-Simon and the Saint-Simonians would have denied it. Saint-Simon was no stranger to voluptuary delights, and in one of his visions of the future he saw all France as a sort of *jardin à l'anglais,* the site of workers' festivities and material joys.[2] His conception of matter was not limited to machines, canals, factories, banks. He saw it translated into a joy, love, and festivity if not as paradisiacal as Fourier's, fully as sensual. The inspiration of the Saint-Simonian discussion of woman was legitimately to be found in the Master, and his followers tell us that during it their copies of *Le Nouveau Christianisme* became dog-eared and tattered, with *"everything"* underlined.[3]

Equally to the point, equally connected to the question of woman, was the Saint-Simonian attack on the *oisif,* the do-nothing holder and inheritor of property. The attack on property was inevitably an attack on the family as it then existed. Saint-Simon did not intend to eliminate private property but to change the mode of its transmission, which was the family. In attacking inheritance, one attacked marriage, the relations of husbands and wives, and those of parents and children. What the Saint-Simonians were about to say of these relationships would shock their contemporaries and amuse their successors. The shock to come was as nothing, however, compared with the shock displayed by the Saint-Simonians as they looked at the family existing around them. Their amusement might have been even greater than that of those who jeered at them could they have looked at a twentieth-century world in which their "revelations" have been commonplaces.

The link "property-family" may have been the most chillingly solid in the chain of analysis forged by the school. The announced objective of Saint-Simon and of his followers had been the amelioration of the lot of the poorest and most numerous class. As the Saint-Simonians looked, really looked, at working-class life, they saw, as Louis Blanc later wrote, "The father of the poor, dead in the hospital at 60; the daughter forced to prostitution at 16; . . . marriage a kind of business, an industrial enterprise; . . . divorce replaced by adultery; among the poor misery gave birth to concubinage and concubinage to infanticide."[4]

The young Saint-Simonians (most in 1830 were not yet thirty years old, and most were not married) were particularly susceptible to the visible truths of Blanc's description of society. The neighborhood of which the rue Monsigny was a part, Saint-Simon's quarter, "the quarter of riches and prostitution" included the rue Sainte-Anne, which housed a number of Saint-Simonians and enjoyed one of the highest incidences of prostitutes on the Paris police registers.[5]

Sexuality was not for any of the Saint-Simonian men a philosophical abstraction. These were men, "loving women," virile, many of them relatively rich, many of them strikingly handsome. There was none, perhaps, who had not been drawn to Saint-Simonianism by some *chagrin de famille*. They had already become conscious of their guilt as bourgeois or aristocrats, and they were led by it to become aware of their guilt as men. They found themselves faced with daily and agonizing personal dilemmas.[6] The daughters of the poor swelled the ranks of prostitutes. The prostitute existed as an escape from the loveless, inhumane, and indissoluble marriage or as an alternative to the marriage that could not be made without sufficient property. He who used the prostitute was an exploiter of humanity; she who entered into the propertied bourgeois marriage became prostitute or adulteress. The high point of Saint-Simonianism was also the high point of French literary romanticism. The hope that love might be at once passionate, unrestrained, and pure spoke to the needs of the Saint-Simonians as to all in their generation.

The prostitute as symbol of social disintegration was linked to yet another concern: the omnipresence of venereal disease, the material manifestation of social and spiritual evil. The classic work of Parent-Duchatelet tells us that the dominant opinion of the day declared prostitution to be necessary, a contribution to the maintenance of order and tranquillity in society. There was general agreement that one must not encourage a cure for syphilis, because its success would encourage immoral conduct.[7]

Léon Simon, one of the Saint-Simonian doctors, revealed to Enfantin that it was his ambition to find such a cure and, in passing, that one of the Saint-Simonian brotherhood, who had died of cholera, had already been doomed to death as a syphilitic.[8] Lambert's reports of conversations with Enfantin in Egypt include the enigmatic remark that several of them who undertook the vow of celibacy at Ménilmontant had been "sheltered from all maladies of this kind."[9] The question of women, particularly of "fallen" women, touched all society and every Saint-Simonian.

There was, then, a readiness to deal with the question of womankind when the great controversy between "the fathers" became apparent within the school. But the consciousness of each member of the question's importance owed something to the "family sorrows" mentioned by d'Eichthal.

D'Eichthal himself said that it was in "witnessing the suffering of my mother during a union of thirty years with a man, good and estimable to be sure, that I felt pushed by an irresistible destiny to the defense of woman."[10] He himself suffered from some form of satyriasis and endlessly propagandized the advantages of the operation that ultimately relieved his problem. In the Saint-Simonian phase he seems to have been sexually obsessed.[11]

Bazard had apparently never come to terms with his own illegitimacy or the consequences of his "ill-engaged" wedding night. Sainte-Beuve, whose official passion in 1830 and 1831 was Mme Victor Hugo, was nonetheless reported to have been stalking a "young person" at a street corner.[12] Carnot was said to be involved with his maid. Léon Simon astonished observers by the coarseness of his language and behavior with women.[13] There was the case of Robinet, married, impotent, arranging lovers for his wife, who, however, died of "*chagrin.*"[14] Robinet, as it happened, himself died at the rue Monsigny, leaving his estate to the Saint-Simonian school. These circumstances gave rise to accusations of *captation* (undue influence) and to a legal case, won by the Saint-Simonians but contributing to their eventual discredit. Robinet's sister, Mme Petit, saw in the movement a solution for her son's problems — he was subject to torturing dreams and hallucinations. She was one of the major financial contributors to the movement and, like d'Eichthal, was tied up with Saint-Simonian finances long after the dispersion of the school. Like Enfantin, Adolphe Guéroult was the son of a ruined businessman embittered by the permanence of financial disgrace and suffering from a sense of incapacity for love. It was an incapacity that not even a Saint-Simonian "priestess," Pauline Roland, could dispel.[15]

The facts of Saint-Simonian sexual life can appear to be trivial, ancient gossip, but taken in the aggregate they assume a larger significance. The facts and their availability attest to that much-discussed power of Enfantin to see into the hearts of others.

Arlès-Dufour's biographer asserted that there had never been anybody so firm and energetic, with so much charm, sweetness, and goodness, as Enfantin. He was sincerely devoted to humanity, its progress, and the betterment of the laboring and suffering classes. "He broke a certain number of lives brutally . . . he used people but was not ambitious; his mission was truth."[16] He knew, according to Blanc, how to "penetrate the secrets of households, he engaged women in public confessions, and redoubtable confidences were made to him in an exaltation that approached delirium."[17]

It has recently been suggested that Enfantin may have been a student of the work of Mesmer, who, in turn, has been credited with the discovery of the technique of transference. Claire Demar, whose suicide was to be attributed to her Saint-Simonian experience by those eager to discredit the doctrine, makes the suggestion. There is talk of some of the faithful acting as if *"magnetisé"* during the most intense period of the crisis. But there is no evidence beyond these minor references to any particular or special interest in Mesmer.[18]

Enfantin seems to have discovered the possibilities of transference himself without discovering, ever, a means for resolving the relationships in which it played a part. This mixed success accounts for the many complicated reactions to him in the years following the crisis, the many unhappy lives that were indissolubly connected to his, the many "breaks" with the movement like that of Michel Chevalier. These "breaks" were later cited as evidence of the reaction of "sensible" men to the "madness" of Enfantin's sexual and social theories. When examined closely, as they will be, they can better be seen as products of an emotionally charged relationship that Enfantin did not know how to end without brutality and even danger. Often, consequently, the unhappy "son" or "daughter" never succeeded in coming to terms with the relationship at all.

The very insistence on the Saint-Simonian titles of "father," "son," "mother," and "daughter" and the final search for the "mother" of Saint-Simonianism are suggestive. Out of the investigations into the psyches of his followers, Enfantin appears to have come upon truths about human behavior without being able to construct an intellectual framework to account for them. Dreams were important to him. There is the record of one dream he felt it worthwhile to report to Aglaë Saint-Hilaire in 1828. He was in the country in a big room furnished with a bed almost touching the ceiling, to which one mounted by a ladder. One had then, in order to sleep, to wriggle with difficulty into a narrow green serge sack. There is no speculation as to the meaning of the dream. Perhaps it appeared too obvious for speculation.[19]

At a much later date, in Egypt, Enfantin suggested that his apostle Lambert's whole sexual being might be related to an early bed-wetting experience. He cited the importance for his dead brother Auguste of their father's breaking Auguste of bed-wetting by posting the news of it on the door of the local Mairie. All of this may not add up to a theory, but certainly Enfantin had an intuition of shame, sex, and the workings of an unconscious to which he could not give a name. Constructing a principle of explanation for what he discovered about human beings may have seemed of secondary importance. The real object was the "truth" about human relations, which must be revealed before it could be understood and which was to render men free to mold the future of family, sex, marriage, and property.

There is some evidence of the exact nature of Enfantin's inquiries, of how these matters came to the fore, of what his techniques were. It was his practice to engage all new converts in seemingly casual conversation when they first appeared at the rue Monsigny. Before or after the communal dinner, or even at dawn, there would be a walk in the Tuileries Gardens or in the streets around the common house. "The Father, wishing to know the morality of all those who surrounded him, had provoked in the bosom of the family confidences of an earlier life. Many lent themselves to it in the general interest. It was even said that many women had done so."[20]

One who had done so was Annette Flachat, wife of Stéphane, a *polytechnicien* early drawn to the group. Writing about yet another crisis, that of 1832, Enfantin asks:

My poor girl, do you recall the day when on your knees before me you so tenderly gave me the name of "Father"? When you said you found in me what had been missing for so long a time—a loving and respected guide? That day you received from me the kiss of adoption? I loved thee for the good I did thee and for that I expected from thee. And since then I have caused you much unhappiness. I have changed your life completely. I have touched all your thoughts to transform you, all your habits to give to Stéphane and to thee desires and a wider love than that with which you were satisfied. I wanted you both to feel the God you were ignorant of. I wanted to give you both GREATNESS and GOODNESS.

Remember this day when you wept so much with your father . . . ? You spoke to me of women and the way in which they love, of what you had been, of what you were for Stéphane, and of what you wished to be for your Father. You cried and your tears did you good, because you knew that your father also could cry. . . . You had seen him cry alone with you.[21]

Sometimes the communion between Enfantin and women was less than perfect. Suzanne Voilquin, who was an enthusiast but no fool, recounts her own somewhat crushing experience with Enfantinian feminism. "I need to be true" she told him, and wished to tell her husband all of her past, but in Enfantin's presence. One day he took her aside: "And, thee, daughter, have you nothing to say to me?"

"Yes, Father. I will come with Voilquin tomorrow."

When Suzanne had completed her confession, her husband, weeping at the horrors revealed, threw himself into the arms of Enfantin for consolation. Suzanne's reaction to him was, as she recounts, "You could have dried *my* tears with your caresses before throwing yourself into the arms of another man." But the "iniquitous partition of male justice" dried her tears.

"I looked at Voilquin harshly. 'Recall, I owe you my incomplete maternities.' The Father looked at me astonished . . . embraced me tenderly, *but it was too late.*"[22]

These were obviously not the only confessions Enfantin heard or the only lives in which he saw fit to intervene. The Flachat letter reveals in

part what he was after—an insight into women "and the way women love." The Voilquin experience revealed, not for the last time, the weakness of a feminism conceived by men. But there is no doubt that with both men and women Enfantin discovered much he found useful to his own concerns and his own purposes.

The cardinal facts in his biography, by his own reckoning, were his rejection as prospective army officer and as prospective husband because of his father's bankruptcy. He had early learned that the most immoral act in the eyes of his society was the declaration of bankruptcy. He hardly needed lessons from Saint-Simon on the connections between sex, economics, politics, and morality. He had lived these connections, suffered for them, and determined to be revenged for the assault on his personal worth. Marriage for cash—and this simple proposition was at the heart of the Saint-Simonian attack on bourgeois morality—was as brutally destructive of human beings as anything imaginable or imagined by the Saint-Simonians themselves.

IT WAS his own family tragedy that readied Enfantin for Saint-Simon as it had for so many others. When the first disciples had begun to take *Le Nouveau Christianisme* seriously, there were many questions left unanswered. What was the nature of God? Was there an eternal life? What would be the basic building block of the new society? the new social unit? Egoism was suspect, and individualism, although important, must develop through association. Buchez persuaded Enfantin that the irreducible social unit must be the couple—man and woman irresistibly attracted to each other and thus providing the paradigm for all association. If "God is all that is," then God must partake of the androgynous character of His-Her creation, must be male-female. And if all that were true, then He-She must have priestesses as well as priests. Men and women, while not the same, must be viewed as equal.

These conclusions had been arrived at as early as 1828. They had served as a basis for discussion on the place of women in the doctrine, although they did not yet enjoy the status of dogma. Enfantin had been hoping soon to speak *ex cathedra* on the subject of women but was not in fact able to do so until the crisis of November 1831. The source of these ideas on the androgynous God and on the place of women in society were quite frankly derived from Fourier's *Théorie des quatre movements* which saw in human relationships the gravitational pull that Saint-Simon, inspired by Newton, had taken as his model of the necessity of universal association. And Saint-Simon himself had spoken in somewhat sibylline fashion of "the social couple." The gravitational force in human relationships exhibited itself as love. In time it became important to understand how men and women loved and what woman's understanding could do to complete the imperfect universal design, which was man-made. Women had "revelations" to make.

That this love should be physical and that physical love should have a place in the extension of universal association was not a very great departure in the elaboration of Saint-Simonian doctrine; nor, as a matter of fact, was it a doctrine so remarkable in itself. That men and women should unite out of love rather than interest, out of personal choice and preference rather than in the interests of family strategy, were ideas whose time, evidently, was coming. That marriage might be a source of physical joy for men *and* women was more startling. In the Saint-Simonian leadership the Bazard ménage suffered from Claire's physical "aversion" for her husband. Euphrasie Rodrigues, wife of Olinde, at one point came to Enfantin to ask him to help in arranging a de facto "divorce." Claire, perhaps pushed into proximity with Margerin by their joint responsibility for educating women in the doctrine, had been seduced by him and confessed her shame to Enfantin.[23]

These last confessions gave a particular irony and bitterness to the discussions of the innermost circle. From the *Mémoires d'un industriel* Enfantin had hinted at the theories later developed on the natures of man, woman, and priesthood. His *industriel* had been frightened by his bride's "vivacity," as she had been frightened by his "passivity," but eventually "each gave and received as much pleasure as the other." Implicit here was a theory of sexuality of "mobile" and "passive" natures. The *Exposition* had suggested that the "rehabilitation of matter" would extend to the "most secret joys of private life." The sexual issue had become explicit when Eugène Rodrigues's love for a Mlle de Roissy and Charles Duveyrier's encouragement of the affair had brought from Enfantin a sharp and salty rebuke and a first essay on the nature of woman. Still later Claire Bazard had precipitated further discussion by her objections to Jules Lechevalier's passion for the actress Léontine Fay.

Claire herself had not been markedly successful in her apostolate to women. Enfantin insisted, however, that she be included, in the late spring of 1831, in a "privy council" to bring a woman's point of view to what were becoming fruitless discussions. A legislative proposal to reintroduce the possibility of divorce provided the occasion to bring some of the issues out of the privy council and into the college. By August of 1831 disagreement had become so passionate and intense that Bazard suffered a stroke during one of the debates and Edmond Talabot, during a promenade in the Tuileries, informed d'Eichthal that his views were "pure shit."[24]

The color of the arguments became all the more lurid after May of 1831, when Enfantin revealed to Bazard what he knew of Claire's affair with Margerin. At this point Margerin was causing scandal for the doctrine in Belgium and was about to be excommunicated. Enfantin had shortly before let Olinde Rodrigues know of *his* wife's sexual discontents. These breaches of the confessional were justified in Enfantin's mind by his colleagues' persistent refusal to accept his views on the ground that as a bachelor, if not a celibate, he knew nothing of the nature of marriage and marital relationships. His point was that Bazard and Rodrigues were as much in the dark, though married, as he. But what Fournel described as Enfantin's "inconceivable *démarche*" broke Bazard and wounded Rodrigues deeply.[25]

Again it is an index of their sincerity and conviction that despite these bitter revelations the three continued to argue for months on the highest possible level as to what the meaning of women in Saint-Simonianism should be. The facts of their lives as presented by Enfantin were treated as important and relevant data that had to be considered objectively like all others. The facts of Enfantin's life were, moreover, thought to be equally relevant. He asserted a certain authority because he was not bound up in the "old" world of marriage. His colleagues were quick to remind him that he had fathered a son and was bound to a highly questionable, in Saint-Simonian terms, relationship with Adèle Morlane, the child's mother.

Jules Lechevalier, whose love of an actress had excited the ire of Mme Bazard and brought her into the discussions on women, was himself severe on the subject of Enfantin's morals. Enfantin, in turn, wrote a vigorous defense of his constancy and fidelity to the four women he admitted knowing between 1820 and 1830.[26] All these matters soon became subjects of astonishment, dismay, and, above all, discussion for the college in October and November 1831. The first act of the drama ended with the abdication of Bazard. The second began with the enthronement of Enfantin as "supreme father" of the Saint-Simonian religion.

WHAT WERE the substantive issues? An androgynous God, a male-female equality, and male and female priesthood required some translation into existing Saint-Simonian thought, practice, and ritual. The issues had first arisen with the Buchez-Enfantin discussions in 1828 and 1829 on the nature of the social individual. Buchez may have been for a time the only person to whom Enfantin would bow his head. He apparently did not accept the idea of an equality or an identity of men and women. His notions on the subject were that in the past the fundamental element of society had been the family, whose responsible head was the father. The father's absolute power had diminished. Buchez could admit that in the future the direction of the family might be in the hands of man and woman, depending on which was higher in the Saint-Simonian social hierarchy. That place would be determined by the capacities and social value of the work of the respective individuals.

159

Enfantin had apparently suggested that there should be a "pope" heading society and that in conformity with the notion of an androgynous God, this "pope" should be male and female—there should also be a "popesse." Against this proposal Buchez argued that to think that two papal leaders could constitute a single social being, "male and female, united in a chaste marriage," was wrong. "When it is a question of social function, the social being is no longer sexual; one thinks only of aptitude; it doesn't matter whether the aptitude is enveloped in black or white, maleness or femaleness."[27] Enfantin felt that a woman should have a role in the Saint-Simonian priesthood because she had the capacity for it. Woman has, indeed, a special capacity. All humans wish to love and be loved, "but what dominates in women is that they love, in men that they wish to be loved. Saint-Simon's doctrine is empty of woman. It can be truly popular only when it possesses the grace that woman knows how to give all whom she loves. . . . Women must be called with love, must be summoned to unite their voices with ours."[28]

There was little support in 1828 and 1829 for Enfantin's idea of a pope and popesse of Saint-Simonianism or of a "chaste" marriage between them. The chastity envisaged seems to have been a compromise on his part to avoid irritating the susceptibilities of Buchez, Bazard, and Rodrigues, but it was an idea that persisted in his letters to Charles Duveyrier in August of 1829. These were occasioned by Eugène Rodrigues's affair with Mlle de Roissy. It seemed important to Enfantin, at this point at least, that there should be no mingling of the erotic and the religious, that Eugène should give up his worship of "the sacred tripod" and stick to missionary business. While reproving Duveyrier for encouraging Eugène's adventure, he continued to discuss his views on women. The thesis continued to be that the priest and priestess should be chaste, that to be involved in the "old" family and the "old" marriage would be to distract the priest from his universality. The priest and priestess would be separated from each other by "a cloud of incense" rising from humanity. Their satisfactions would derive from their community with all. To be bound to each other carnally would weaken their ability to receive and transmit the longings of humanity's love.

Later Enfantin commented that these were erroneous views, an exaggeration, and did not excite much discussion. But the letters to Duveyrier did include the idea that it was "the complete emancipation of women" that would signal "the Saint-Simonian era." And they also included the idea that "by the hands of women a new Adam, regenerated by Saint-Simon, will receive the fruit of the trees of all knowledge, because it is by her that he will be conducted to God as Christians believed she had distanced him from God."[29]

While feeding the discussion on women and entertaining the possibility of a priestly couple chastely presiding over the carnal destinies of the faithful, Enfantin seemed as anxious as his colleagues to avoid scandal and to maintain unity in the movement. But it was shortly after the Duveyrier letter that the first purge of the college took place, that Enfantin and Bazard were elevated to the position of fathers, Buchez was demoted to the college, and the announcement took place of a Saint-Simonian religion.

What emerged from the discussion was a feminism that in Enfantin's mind equated maleness with activity, femaleness with passivity, maleness with the search for love, and femaleness with the offering of love. The doctrine of universal association could be accomplished only by the proliferation of love, and that proliferation must be the contribution of women, women's experience and women's understanding. Until women had made their "revelations," the doctrine would be incomplete.

Creating a hierarchy, Michel Chevalier suggested, reflected Enfantin's ambition to represent, for the moment, the female principle — loving, understanding, accepting, *calming;* Bazard would represent thought, analysis, logic, force. It was an arrangement that worked while the doctrine was given its initial public exposure. Bazard lectured, and Enfantin listened and gathered ammunition for his next foray into feminism, his next effort to create the new Adam — and the new Eve. In all of these discussions the Buchez point of view was more rigorously, in twentieth-century terms, feminist. The place of any woman, as of any man, in the new society would be the by-product of individual and asexual capacity. Enfantin proposed a kind of "separate but equal" doctrine emphasizing the unique characteristics of women as complements of the unique characteristics of men. From a Saint-Simonian point of view the idea of complementary qualities underlined the idea of the need for a "spirit of association." From a contemporary feminist point of view, of course, the distinction is risible. But in the 1820s there were few men who had come as far as Enfantin and perhaps none who equaled Buchez.

So matters had continued until the end of 1830. In one of the *affiches* posted by the Saint-Simonians following the July Revolution of that year, two deputies had detected attacks on property and family and had accused the Saint-Simonians of advocating the community of property and the community of women. Bazard thought it important to reply to these accusations. Enfantin joined him in the document of October 1, 1830, which admitted the Saint-Simonian wish for emancipation but without "pretending to abolish the holy law of marriage proclaimed by Christianity." Enfantin, however, almost immediately declared that this affirmation must be viewed as provisional since a new moral law was imperative for the new world.[30]

Enfantin's opportunity came at the end of 1830. Claire Bazard was to direct the work on women, from the heights of the college itself. She became Mother Bazard in December and almost immediately precipitated controversy. She learned that Jules Lechevalier wished to marry Léontine Fay, a well-known actress. This time (unlike the similar case of Eugène Rodrigues a year earlier) Enfantin, playing the role of priest regulating the appetites of the faithful, had approved Lechevalier's intention.

Claire protested "in the name of God and Saint-Simon." Neither her "repugnance" nor her "affections" had been consulted when Enfantin permitted one of "her" sons to seek for himself a wife, "a daughter" for her, among those unfortunates she "pitied" and "loved," whom she did not believe capable of loving her as she would have them loved or separated with sufficient "purity" from a "corrupt milieu." A new religion, in Claire's view, ought to penetrate little by little "pure and devoted" beings. In time a corner might be found for the "repentant sinners."[31]

Enfantin's response suggested what was to come. There were fierce and furious discussions in the Bazards' rooms at the rue Monsigny, rumors of which could not fail to be heard. D'Eichthal and Laurent one day threw themselves into each other's arms crying "The pope is being made!" Enfantin's conclusion was revealing. Mme Bazard was the only female Saint-Simonian "mother." Soon, perhaps, a second woman must possess the same rank as Claire. "I have need of a woman who may be for me what you are for Bazard. You must aid me in finding her; you must open a sister's arms crying out when you see her, 'There is what my father Enfantin calls for.'"[32]

These events had to have taken place in the last days of December 1830. Enfantin already knew the facts of Bazard's and Rodrigues's conjugal life. He later wrote that he found these discussions a torture knowing what he did and unable, at that juncture, to speak out. But he also admits finding the discussion fascinating as evidence of a "divine conception presiding over the revelation of a new life." The discussion of course was not limited to the subject of Fay. It dealt with marriage, with divorce, with paternity, and with all possible expressions of sexual life. Margerin and Rodrigues were quickly brought into the privy council, and Claire joined it after the revelation by Enfantin to Bazard in May of Claire's and Margerin's adultery.[33]

Claire, although combative enough on occasion, had approached all these matters with a certain hesitation. Enfantin had wanted to raise her to the priesthood in the preceding October. She had replied, "Enough of these elevations . . . of these illusory distinctions that don't bring us together and distance us from our sisters."[34]

By March of 1831 she was writing that she had as yet done nothing, had realized none of the father's hopes: "The Mother doesn't know how to impose respect on the children, the children don't know how to submit

to the Mother. . . . Dignity and power we recognize only in the Master—
and the Master is man."[35] Claire's discouragement was well-founded.
Suzanne Voilquin, admitted to the salons of the rue Monsigny and manager of the kitchen at the rue Taitbout, felt that Mme Bazard knew how
to speak to workers but not to women. "She was too submissive to the
male hierarchy to control my independent spirit." Aglaë Saint-Hilaire was
a woman of "real merit" but "cold and grave," and Cécile Fournel was
benevolent, gracious, and good, but "I couldn't pronounce the word
'mother' in addressing these ladies."[36] Jealousies and susceptibilities that
were often evident in the relations of the male Saint-Simonians were
equally if not more evident among the women. It was all very well to declare the "classification according to capacities," to elevate some members
in the hierarchy and leave others behind, but the "others" often needed to
know what it was they lacked, what qualities the favored possessed. The
answers were not always convincing.

The question of "election" was in October and November of 1831 overwhelmingly important for Claire Bazard. Enfantin's declaration that he
needed a woman to be for him what Claire was for Bazard may have lit
the fuse of Claire's ambition to be that woman, to be the female pope.
And through all the debate on theory the personal relationships of all
those intimate friends was the leitmotif that appeared and reappeared in
startling ways. Some of the Saint-Simonians were convinced that Claire
had become Enfantin's mistress and that this fact alone explained Bazard's physical breakdown and eventual abdication from the movement.
D'Eichthal many years later maintained that this was not the case. But he
also noted marginally in his correspondence with Claire (to whose support he contributed for many years) that "*all* concerning Mme Bazard's
children and grandchildren must be suppressed."[37]

The record of the hectic days of early November was to be found in the
Archives of Saint-Simonianism. Some of the crucial materials have been
missing since the early 1930s. Henry René d'Allemagne was apparently
the last scholar to use them, and his account, with that of Thibert, who
had seen them earlier, has to provide the basis for understanding what
then took place.

If there were to be male and female Messiahs, only one of each was
necessary. If Claire wished to be female Messiah to Enfantin's male, then
Bazard was not needed and, apparently, for some time had not been
wanted. The discussion of priest and priestess, of male and female complements, had become known within the movement as an accompaniment
to the discussion of legislation on divorce. If one accepted divorce as a
possibility, then the understanding of marriage had to be modified, serial
polygamy accepted. And if one accepted this last, one had to accept the
psychology that underlay the desire for it.

In a letter to his mother of August 1831, while not quite laying all his cards on the table, Enfantin outlined the argument he would sustain in the months to come.[38] Earlier he had been arguing that in matters affecting family relationship one need not always speak the *whole* truth. It was an argument that Paulin Talabot would use in urging Enfantin to downplay the sexual themes of Saint-Simonianism and was itself a widely accepted truth among the Saint-Simonians. Truth was to be revealed as the observers were ready to see it.

One can imagine Mme Enfantin in her vast house high above Paris at Ménilmontant, a daughter of the eighteenth century and the anticlerical Revolution, tapping her fingers impatiently and wondering what exaggeration her Prosper was committing *now*. The tone of Enfantin's letter, while placatory, is firm:

One speaks of a law on divorce and we, dear mother, have busied ourselves with this great question, but more generally with the relations of man and woman in the future . . . at a time when woman will have duties and rights if not the SAME at least comparable to those of man. The thing is delicate, and one can say that there is the foundation of morality properly understood; Christian morality reposes on the celibacy of the Priest, expression of the repugnance of the flesh, as Muhammadan morality rests on polygamy, expression of the domestic slavery of woman and the grossness of the physical appetites of the still Warrior East. For us, you know, man and woman are equals and we treat the mind as equal to the body, work equal to knowledge; we LOVE both. Following these two ideas, what are the relations of the sexes?

Enfantin goes on to say that the difficulty is to "sense" a relationship that could be regular, correct, and useful only in a society raised from infancy in accordance with the new moral law. One needs guarantees against the vices existing "today" and against the resonances of Christian morality rejecting the flesh. One needs all the imprudence of the innovator, all the reserve of the conservative. "One needs to be Bazard and me."

The new idea must be "regularized," "limited," and "orderly." Eventually any exaggerations will disappear, but the future of man and woman is contained in it. One (male or female) has profound or passing affections; one is reserved, modest, moderate, and patient or enthusiastic, glory-loving, burning, ardent. Both of these forms of being are good; one wishes to conserve, the other to innovate. The dangers are stagnation, for one, and the risk of breaking the head against the wall, for the other. Both natures can diminish as they can grow by these two approaches, which are equally good and holy and "are besides the expression of human imperfection and perfectability; the one is immutable, the other is changing."

These predispositions of personality account for the marriages whose force grows or diminishes through time and enjoyment, boredom and disgust, constance and fidelity. These same predispositions account for marriages that are increasingly better as one has children, common habits, the same house, the same acquaintances, perpetual contact with each other. But also born of these predispositions are the need "for change of place, of things, of habits of society, and finally of husband and wife."

Up to the time of Enfantin's writing, coquetry, lightness, mobility, beauty, and grace have given birth only to vice, deception, hypocrisy, libertinage, and adultery. Society has not known how to regularize, satisfy, or use these human qualities, which have become sources of disorder instead of being, as they ought to be, the sources of joy and happiness. Changing, moving, light personalities, being demoted by Christian law (and these qualities belong more to women than to men), have often had to employ their far-from-mediocre power to demoralize rather than to moralize. "This explains very well the anathema against physical pleasure and against women, anathema that will be justified as long as labor and women are not associated the one with science, the second with men by the law of EQUALITY."

Enfantin moves closer to the central and sticking point of his new doctrine:

I ask myself how LIVELY, FLIRTATIOUS, SEDUCTIVE, ATTRACTIVE, CHANGING, ARDENT, PASSIONATE, EXALTED beings ought to be directed, considered, USED in the FUTURE so that their character may be for them and for humanity a source of joy, not of sadness, of fetes and not of mourning. . . . The education of children and the entirety of social morality will calm those out of bounds; some will need soporifics, others stimulants. What is the rule to which they ought to be submitted? Here it is, according to me.

Enfantin suggests, and he is careful in writing to his mother to suggest only, that the basis of a religion of love is the union of man and woman. One form of this religion is the union of the same man and the same woman throughout life. Divorce and a new union with a new spouse is another form. The new form is not a source of guilt or blame *as long as* the new marriage offers a "progress" for the two individuals and society. There is yet a third form of the religion: that of the priest and priestess. They see in each other the man and woman they love *most*. Time cements their love, but they do not tire of each other, since their function is to regularize the love of others. They find in this function, up to a certain limit, the means of achieving the variety that they need.

The wise and constant will love the priest and priestess for their constancy, but the priest and priestess will also be loved because of their "beauty, grace, amiability, flirtatiousness, their ardor, their burning and tender eyes." They will feel mounting toward them "the incense of the men and women who love the external, the dashing, glory, wealth, the body."

The priest and priestess will know all the joys of decency and abandon, of modesty and the most searing embraces. This most loving of couples, the most reserved and the most ardent, has lessons of tenderness to teach. From the priestly couple one will learn how one loves. "How far will the carnal expression, dear mother, go?" To answer correctly Enfantin has need of a woman who will join her views to his, but "I conceive CERTAIN CIRCUMSTANCES where I would judge that my wife alone would be capable of giving happiness, health, life to one of my sons in Saint-Simon; to recall him to social sympathies, to warm him when some profound sadness demands a diversion, when his broken heart would bleed with disgust for life."

Enfantin resumes the argument at the end of his letter. The couple with deep affections remains united; the couple with "lively" affections changes but under the direction of the priest, who consecrates or provokes divorces and new marriages. The sacerdotal couple guarantees the first couple in its immutable constancy, and it blesses the mobility of the other by its example of durable but not exclusive union reinforced by all the love that each member of the priestly couple inspires.

What does it all mean? To some of his contemporaries and many who came after, Enfantin's proposals seemed simply the expression of madness or the projection of his own unbridled sensuality. There may, indeed, have been a bit of both present in August of 1831. Enfantin's feminism was of the sort to invite the scorn of present-day feminists. Men were active, women passive; men sought love, women gave it. But to do him justice Enfantin was urging that, whatever the specific characteristics of male and female, each had as much to contribute to marriage as the other, and each contribution was as valid as the other.

Enfantin learned through his talks, confessions, and examinations that in women there was a whole range of anger, despair, and frustration, particularly in the sexual aspects of marriage, that men hardly suspected or, at best, discounted. This was certainly the case of Claire Bazard and Annette Flachat, and probably of Euphrasie Rodrigues. The increasing emphasis on "learning how one loves," on the physicality of love, on the importance of beauty and the body, point to the conviction on Enfantin's part that if the troubles of society were rooted in the slavery of the bourgeois marriage, the troubles of the bourgeois marriage were rooted in the slavery of the bourgeois bedroom.

Reduced to its bare essentials, the proposal Enfantin confided to his mother was to establish a kind of marriage and sex counseling service — including the use of surrogate partners — which a century and a half later might raise few eyebrows, but which in 1831 gave rise to horror and consternation. In the politics of the Saint-Simonian religion the idea at work was that Bazard and Rodrigues, totally involved in traditional marriage and guilty of its sins, could hardly perform the functions of priest, nor could their wives, as victims, the functions of priestess. Enfantin saw himself as the unencumbered father whose supremacy would be validated by the appearance of a mother who would "announce" herself. Until this happy event there could be no definitive moral law; until "woman" had been heard, what he proposed was only "provisional." Even in the delirium of the autumn of 1831 Enfantin was careful to hold on to this fundamental Saint-Simonian principal of progress, change, and continuing perfection. And in the letter to his mother he was careful to underline "*in the future*" when asking what the new moral law might be.[39] What Enfantin was also quite clearly challenging was the common notion that women could experience no joy in sex. He had evidence that they *did* not, but he was asserting that they *might* and *should*.

Enfantin's assertions were connected to a developing theory of personality. There were "constant" and "mobile" natures; there were male and female natures formed in the "Oriental" mode and in the Christian. There were archetypal symbols: "Othello" and "Don Juan," constant and fickle, respectively. In each human there might be elements of both traits in varying degrees. Finally, Enfantin was suggesting that what nature had created, the future should accommodate as the past had not. The thrust of the theory was certainly in favor of human liberation and against the repression of human sensibilities.

So once again in Saint-Simonian doctrine the irreconcilables are brought face to face. Enfantin's pushing for position, his elaboration of this most difficult-to-accept of all extensions of Saint-Simon, has two faces. On the one hand, the new doctrine was a doctrine of freedom, based on a recognition of the injustice toward women and the inadequacy of society's understanding of them. On the other hand, there was more than a hint that women were different from men: softer, more pliable, more emotional, less active, less strong. The burden of Enfantin's doctrine was that women in determining the nature of their marital lives and their sexual lives should be the equals of and enjoy the liberties of men. It was also an element of the doctrine that men would benefit thereby, as would society as a whole, that Christian "slavery" would come to an end with the emancipation of women.

There was more, which Enfantin had not discussed in his letter to his mother. During the passionate debates, Bazard came to accept the idea of divorce; he had more difficulty with the priest and priestess (and with a diminution of his own role); but he absolutely would not accept the unlimited independence of women. This independence was defined for Bazard by the question of "paternity." It was Enfantin's thesis that knowledge of the paternity of children in the "new" family must be the affair exclusively of the mother. There was no need for a child to know his or her father or for the father, whether constant or mobile spouse, to know a child to be his. In the new society children would be social beings, adopted at an early age by the society as a whole, not expecting to inherit property or to benefit from paternal social position. To be the son of "Mr. X" was no advantage, and indeed such knowledge might be an impediment to social regeneration. The opportunities for controversy and jealousy over a cuckoo in the nest of the "new" family could inhibit the freedom and equality of women.[40]

Bazard's intransigence on this point may have owed something to his own bastardy and his self-consciousness about it. Enfantin's may have had something to do with his own bastard and the crises and embarrassments the child's mother caused him over many years. Or it may have been the simple and understandable antagonism of the two men that accounts for the confrontation. It was becoming clear that Claire was moving toward the conviction that Bazard was of the "old" world and Enfantin of the "new" and that her future belonged with Enfantin's. But the paternity question rendered the two "fathers" of Saint-Simonianism irreconcilable. Bazard's stroke came in the wake of one of the debates on August 25, and the meetings between the two had to be adjourned.[41]

But by this time the entire school had become aware of the conflict, of some of its terms, and of the personal issues involved. "Two worlds at grips" was the way one of the school described the Enfantin-Bazard battle.[42] It was to be an apt description of the entire school in the weeks to come.

Charton, returning from missionary work in Brittany, found that the faces of the members of the college carried the signs of sleeplessness— sunken eyes, pale lips, disordered hair, trembling features, ecstatic looks. "What I heard made me dizzy."[43] Carnot described meetings lasting from two o'clock in the afternoon to ten or eleven o'clock in the evening.

Eighteen or twenty in Bazard's room heard the most burning, most delicate questions discussed. . . . This lasted many days. We didn't separate at meal time. . . . The meal over, we were enclosed anew. . . . The most scabrous points of the relations of the sexes were examined before a still young audience among whom were three women. I don't know, and none of us knows, if any word was pronounced that would in other circumstances have made them lower their eyes. The preoccupations were so austere that these women could hear all and say all without hesitation, without anybody's being surprised, without a smirk touching anybody's lips.[44]

Euryale Cazeaux, one of the first inhabitants of the rue Monsigny, urged a knife on Enfantin for his protection. At other times Cazeaux seemed to have fallen into a trance. More usefully, Cazeaux, Michel Chevalier, and Edmond Talabot joined forces to urge compromise and calm.

They accused Enfantin of exaggerating his own powers, and Bazard of being insufficiently appreciative of those powers. By early November it was hoped throughout the school that their efforts and those of Rodrigues had met with success.

Rodrigues in an effort to square the circle had composed a moral law, presented to the college on October 17. It included these points:

1. All social work in the Saint-Simonian family is the work of a couple, and marriage is their normal state.

2. In certain circumstances divorce represents the passage to another connection.

3. Marriage is the link of generations. The mother wishes always to offer the child the caresses of its father.

4. In the future the religious authority of Priest and Priestess will sanctify second marriages.

5. It is the first couple placed at the summit of the Saint-Simonian hierarchy that will be given the task of throwing light on the problems of individual life. The first woman to be seated on the Papal throne alone can reveal the law of proprieties beyond which immorality would commence.[45]

Certain safeguards were added that seemed designed to forestall Claire's ambitions. It had become clear by the time this document was read that Bazard had at most points bowed to Enfantin's preeminence, although recognition of paternity was retained in Rodrigues's proposal. Out of exhaustion, ill health, and the evidence that most of the doctrinaires were more attracted to Enfantin than to him, Bazard appeared ready for reconciliation.

Michel Chevalier sent out to the provincial churches on November 8, 1831, the announcement that Saint-Simonian power henceforth would be derived from the profound union of the *three* Saint-Simonian fathers. Bazard would devote himself to the perfection and the teaching of the doctrine, Rodrigues would manage the material interests of the school, and "Our Father Enfantin is placed between the two, giving special inspiration to artists of the word." It was vague, but it might serve as a rudder.[46]

Fournel tells us that it was on November 8 that the reconciliation of the moment took place and that Bazard accepted the idea of a presidency placed in Enfantin's hands. At 4 P.M. Claire brought the news. Pierre Leroux remembered that Mme Bazard had an air of triumph in her role of ambassadress, that she seemed to have "delivered Bazard wrists and ankles tied while her eyes proclaimed 'This is my work.'" It was during the immediately following scene of reconciliation that Claire said to Leroux, "Father Bazard is finished, he is old."[47]

But it was a brief reconciliation. According to Fournel, he entered the Bazards' room at eight the next morning. Bazard was abed, excessively fatigued; Claire was lying across an armchair, overcome. The previous evening Enfantin had disillusioned Claire. She had been rejected as priestess. Her intention of divorcing Bazard was rumored. It was also said that Enfantin had proposed to marry her and had sent by d'Eichthal a ring as the first jewel in her crown. This last was not true. D'Eichthal had simply offered a ring as a souvenir, although Claire may have thought he was offering himself as a substitute for Enfantin. Forty years later both would be embarrassed by their memories of the incident.[48]

On the morning of November 11 Claire left the rue Monsigny. Bazard and Enfantin had had a final interview in which Bazard rejected the work of the previous days. Claire wrote a letter of adieu to Enfantin—"Today you have broken me without pity,"[49]—and declared her intentions of breaking with Bazard. News of all these events had reached Enfantin's mother swiftly. "Is it thus that a chief shows his force? . . . Are you unfortunate enough to be the source of this disorder? You are going to be proclaimed sole chief of the Saint-Simonian doctrine, and to be complete you are perhaps also going to take the wife of the chief you despoil."[50]

So ended, in domestic disaster, the Saint-Simonian unity. Bazard and Claire, in fact, rejoined forces. Rodrigues retained, once again, a place in the hierarchy and, with some reservations, remained in Enfantin's camp.

The next weeks would bring no relief from the tensions in the school. The personal relationships of the leading Saint-Simonians were so complex that the torture of choosing Bazard or Enfantin was for some impossible and for all an obstacle not easily overcome. The Fournels would move back and forth in and out of Enfantin's orbit for years, simultaneously repelled and fascinated by him and pulled apart by family ties and intellectual conviction. Their choices and those of the others have often given rise to the assertion that with the departure of Bazard all respectable and serious people ceased to be Saint-Simonians.

The assertion, as we will see, was not true. But a more burning issue was left behind by the Bazard-Enfantin break. The equality of the sexes was announced, the claims of sexuality affirmed, and the coming of the new Eve anticipated. But where was she?

CHAPTER X

THE NEW ADAM

THE BREAK with Bazard left Enfantin in full possession of the Saint-Simonian battlefield at the rue Monsigny. But the field itself was strewn with those bloodied, wounded, and destroyed by the battle. A great deal had to be done, and in a short time, if the victory was to be more than pyrrhic. The provincial centers had to be informed, instructed, and rallied to Enfantin's leadership. At the center, opposition had to be met and overcome. Very serious attention had to be paid those who were disposed to follow Enfantin but who wished to do so only under very specific conditions. And there had to be some reconsideration of the sources of the troubles—the questions of priesthood and womanhood and their place in the total movement.

Questions of the "old world" of property would arise: for example, to whom did the publications of the school belong? Some of those who followed Bazard had given sizable fortunes to the movement and took what was left of them when they left. The Saint-Simonians kept good accounts, but they had spent lavishly. Where were more funds to come from, and how would they be managed?

The great debate over women had attracted great public attention. Saint-Simonian meetings drew even larger crowds than previously, and they were full of possible converts as well as of those who came to mock or to be scandalized or titillated by the notion of the "community of women." Public scandal confirmed governmental suspicions of the movement. Though the friends of the Saint-Simonians had persuaded Casimir Périer that they were not directly involved in the Lyons insurrection, the feeling remained that they were troublesome, potentially dangerous, and possibly criminal. In the wake of the schism the first steps were taken that would result in indictments against the Saint-Simonians for violating Article 291 of the Penal Code, on public assembly, and for offenses against public morality. They would also be accused of exerting undue influence and of embezzlement.[1]

In short it behooved Enfantin and his followers to cool their sexual fever and to take on as much of an aura of respectability as they could. The desire and the commitment to do so probably accounted for the fact that Olinde Rodrigues stayed with Enfantin and legitimized his supremacy.

Enfantin's failure to keep the bargain explains Rodrigues's withdrawal some months later.

During the days following Bazard's departure a regrouping of the school took place and with it a rapid rethinking by Enfantin. The combat had embittered and inflamed the faithful on both sides of the quarrel. November 19, 1831, saw the first of a series of meetings, recorded almost verbatim, which project not only the ideas but also the personalities of the Saint-Simonians on a stage alternately and simultaneously tragic and comic.

The rooms and corridors of the rue Monsigny were full as Enfantin rose to explain the new position. He had the capacity and the audacity to act the role he had written. The tone is that of command: "I called Bazard to share the supreme authority with me in December of 1830. He demanded TIME to think about it. There is the explanation of all our life with each other. Since then I have PROVOKED all that has been *thought,* all that has been *done.* I have PROVOKED it in the face of Bazard's negation."[2]

At this point Pierre Leroux interrupted Enfantin: "You outline a doctrine rejected by the College. I came here to say so and will now withdraw." Enfantin replied: "I said, myself, that these ideas were personal to me, that they would be disapproved by all men. But how can womankind speak if some man does not express himself as I have done." Carnot rose to reject the hierarchy, and Jules Lechevalier to announce his withdrawal, accepting neither Enfantin nor Bazard: "I am once more alone in the world."

Enfantin persisted in his argument over interruptions and objections. His ideas on women were "the opinion of a single man," not law; these would be neither law nor definitive moral doctrine until "a woman" had spoken. Any action rejected by custom and current morality "I would myself regard as an immoral act." But the men who had followed Enfantin still protested. "What do they fear—that woman speaks, expresses what she feels?" Do they think a woman degraded, soiled, infamous could have any effect on them? "A woman must come, must place herself at the head of humanity and say what she feels with the same courage I have had in calling out for her. You have only been able to deny and have nothing to affirm."[3]

Again discussion and accusations broke out, Lechevalier declaring that he had become once again a philosophe. Transon, the passionate preacher, accused Enfantin, justly, of having provoked private confessions and of having divulged them without the consent of the people involved. Michel Chevalier pleaded that minor errors should not be sufficient to divide the faithful. Charles Duveyrier admitted that personality had not been sufficiently respected but added that when the "woman" arrived, she would impose limits on behavior. Cécile and Henri Fournel expressed their repugnance for Enfantin's doctrine but declared that they would stay with the movement. Finally Jean Reynaud rose to proclaim that Enfantin's theory of women was only part of a theory of humanity. "I believe this theory abolishes all human liberty. He believes that woman will come to legitimize what he has first announced. I have faith that woman will crush him. I won't withdraw. I will be on his steps. I will reveal him SUCH AS HE IS."

Laurent concluded that this was a duel that ought not to take place. Enfantin declared that "if we continue to battle thus, the workers will die of hunger, the children we adopt will be abandoned."[4]

The discussion continued two days later, equally sharply but more decisively. Cazeaux, Dugied, Carnot, Leroux, Claire Bazard, and Cécile Fournel had now decided to withdraw, but they wished to explain their decisions. Enfantin rejoined that one could not continue with interminable discussions. "I am THE father of humanity. If someone here protests against the authority I assume in myself, let him go." To which Charton responded, "There is no doctrine here, only heresy." Barrault shouted, "All the doctrine is here," and Rodrigues promised to satisfy "all those who dare say that the Saint-Simonian religion is other than where I am."

When the protesters had departed, Enfantin and Rodrigues outlined the new directions in which the movement must proceed. Womankind was still in slavery. Before achieving equality with men, women must achieve liberty. All classification of women had been made by men, and badly made. There would be no more women in the degrees of the Saint-Simonian hierarchy. The empty chair beside Enfantin's would stand as a symbol of the woman, the "mother," awaited by the Saint-Simonians. Enfantin's declaration was followed by that of Rodrigues, who was to take in hand the financial and material interests of the movement and the "religious association" of the workers.

Rodrigues's opening words proclaimed that in the name of "THE LIVING GOD" his first act of faith must be to present Enfantin as "the most moral man of my time." He proceeded to announce once again that his mission was to declare "the moral power of money," and he promised that at the next meeting he would indicate how that mission should be carried out.[5]

This third postcrisis meeting, on November 27, posed a paradox, which was not unusual for the Saint-Simonians. It was decisive in bringing into the foreground the practical programs that had been discussed in Saint-Simon's last days and in the days of Le Producteur. It was also decisive in releasing a threat of religious hysteria directed at Enfantin himself.

It has often been remarked in these pages that whatever, at any given moment, the Saint-Simonians might be proclaiming to the public, there was always continuing a deeper and not yet fully exposed elaboration of doctrine. Up to November 1831 that agenda had usually been hidden because of the fear that its content would shock and drive away potential believers. In November the reverse process was taking place. The most shocking aspects of doctrine had been revealed and, indeed, had had the feared consequence. What was now being explored behind the scenes was the means whereby the worst harm might be undone.

The Pereires, Paulin Talabot, Michel Chevalier, Eugène Flachat, Henri Fournel, and Rodrigues were pushing for social and, particularly, economic programs that would give the movement both immediately practical and respectable objectives. But it should be noted that while pushing Enfantin in this direction for practical reasons and out of conviction, these Saint-Simonians were not, in fact, contesting the religious character of the movement or Enfantin's leadership of it. Nor did they ever.

The careers of the Pereires as protégés of Rothschild, railroad entrepreneurs, and bankers; of Talabot as engineer and developer of Algeria; of Chevalier as coauthor of the free-trade treaty of 1860; of Fournel, Flachat, and a host of others as architects of the French railroad system; and of General Lamoricière, who offered a formal profession of faith, were the careers of practical men. These practical men stayed with the doctrine and attempted to steer it through the narrow channels of economic reformation between the high cliffs of religiosity.

At the same time the crisis of November 1831 incited Enfantin and those most devoted to him to lay claim to an infallibility that would not brook restraints comfortably. As a strategy for keeping the movement whole, the assertion of supremacy had its strengths. To flounder was to fail. To maintain "calm" in the face of critics and to demand unwavering support from the faithful, to impose tests on them, was at one level good policy. But the young men and women around Enfantin were in a state of romantic susceptibility in which any limit, any doubt, any question might finally bring down the faith that was under attack. The response of the group to challenge was in effect to announce, "I believe; help me in my unbelief" and to invest the figure of Enfantin with almost supernatural attributes.

The schism had divided families and friends, had interrupted a euphoria of love and hope, and had denied apparent solutions to real individual problems. The meetings that had already taken place and those to come were not merely meetings of ideas but of persons—their angers, their disappointments, their tears, their embracings, their physical collapses. Transon and Cazeaux, the first residents of the rue Monsigny with Enfantin, were "as if mesmerized, hallucinatory." Rodrigues, failing to find adequate affirmative response to his declaration that he was the "living law," fainted and was removed from the room while discussion continued.[6] Unhappily, we can have no recordings or films of these events. But it is possible to envisage Enfantin using the beauty of his person, the caress of his voice, the much-discussed penetration of his eyes to encourage the outpouring of an emotion that, finally, did little that was good for him, the movement, or the apostles.

Obviously contributing to the excitement, the ardor, the fantasies of the disciples was the content of Enfantin's preaching: the liberation of the flesh and the freeing of women. Added to that excitement was the perverse pleasure of the martyr's role, the certainty that what was taking place in Saint-Simonianism would be misunderstood, mocked, and reviled. All Saint-Simonians at this juncture probably saw themselves as Sebastians penetrated by the multifarious arrows of an outraged and uncomprehending society. And all Saint-Simonians who stayed with Enfantin rejoiced in this martyrdom, exulted in their misery.

As usual with Enfantin, mingled with the man of high principle and high purpose was something of the trimmer and the seeker after petty revenge. The great doctrinal and organizational change—the removal of women from the hierarchy and the redefinition of their contemporary place in the historic cycle—was in part intended to minimize scandal. The Saint-Simonians would yet emit scandalous thoughts, but they were not—yet—practitioners of their ideas. The change was also a product of the stormy and bitter encounters with women that had marked the schism.

Enfantin accused some of his adversaries of being afraid of what women might say. He was not himself foreign to such fears. Women like Niboyet, Voilquin, and Pauline Roland sought a public theater for their voices. Roland was said to have been the first Saint-Simonian woman to perform the functions of "priestess" for Adolphe Guéroult. After Enfantin's release from prison and departure for Egypt, Aglaë Saint-Hilaire wrote him that one of his "sons" wished her to play the role of "priestess" and that she "might have something to do there." Enfantin's feminism was perfectly sincere but was flawed in twentieth-century terms by an assumption of masculine superiority justifying his acts. In his use of language he saw the problem and sought to overcome it. How to do so was a persistent problem.

The lofty language of the "appeal" to woman disguised an uncertainty over how she would appear, who she would be, and whether she could count on recognition. This infusion into the doctrine of the notion of a "woman," a "mother" who would match a "father," an Enfantin, would have its bizarre consequences. The burden of the message seemed to be that while prophesizing a new morality attendant on the arrival of the new Eve, the Saint-Simonians would concentrate on the acts that would offer material proof of the doctrine's validity. Rodrigues had given up his position at the Caisse Hypothécaire to devote himself to the material concerns of the movement. Talabot had argued that it was in the realms of banking, credit, communications, and commerce that the spirit of association might best be realized. It was on this basis that Saint-Simonianism proposed to build its future from November of 1831.[7]

BUT IT was not to be. Between November 28 and December 31 Enfantin delivered fourteen teachings: a New Testament of the doctrine. These constituted the breaking point for Rodrigues and for the public authorities as well. January 22, 1832, saw the descent on the rue Monsigny of justice, army, and police. By February 14 Rodrigues had publicly separated himself from the movement. Laurent and Transon, dissatisfied with the pacifism of *Le Globe* in the face of European repression of revolution, particularly in Poland, had first demanded editorship of the journal and, when refused, had threatened withdrawal from the school. Simultaneously Paulin Talabot had been criticizing the old-fashioned liberal tone of the journal and pressing for something new.[8]

In the first days of 1832 *Le Globe* did publish a new "industrial policy" and the announcement of a "Mediterranean system." But *Le Globe* ceased publication on April 20. Enfantin took an uncharacteristic (and unfulfilled) vow of silence. He withdrew with forty apostles to his mother's house on the heights of Ménilmontant overlooking Paris. There the apostles undertook to observe a vow of celibacy, adopted a Saint-Simonian costume, gave themselves up to domesticity, and added yet another colorful and much-jeered aspect to the tale of their common lives.

Before the "retreat" to Ménilmontant, however, the drama had to be played out. *Le Globe* reported that the "family," surrounded by a larger public, had witnessed a profoundly religious scene. Enfantin appeared, "a hundred times more moral and better, a hundred times greater and more profound, a hundred times more powerful and handsome, a hundred times more PRIEST than he had hitherto revealed himself."[9] The themes of Enfantin's teaching were those that had already been discussed. What was new was the outline of Rodrigues's projects. There was to be a workers' bank; there was to be a financial association of the Saint-Simonians; there were to be houses of education and industrial and agricultural associations. All these projects were to be financed by subscription. Subscribers were guaranteed no responsibility beyond the amount subscribed. Enfantin having spoken on women, and Rodrigues on money, Barrault was encouraged to make an appeal to artists, who had thus far been shy of submission to Saint-Simonian priestly authority.

When these three were done, Jean Reynaud rose, specter at the feast, to accuse Enfantin once again of immorality. There ensued a debate of an hour and a half involving Enfantin, Reynaud, Henri Baud, Laurent, and Edmond Talabot. The "profession of faith" of Baud "electrified" the assembly: "Father Enfantin, supreme father of the new religion, you are my chief, I salute you. Olinde Rodrigues, you will be my blood brother. I glory in it, you are my fathers, glory to you."[10]

Baud detailed the circumstances of his life. He was, he said, the son of a self-made man who had repudiated him because of his Saint-Simonianism and his lower-class wife. He declared that he had been fed with "the bread and the word" and clothed with the Saint-Simonian costume. "God would not permit a man to present himself to other men with this calm and serene presence, with this grandeur and beauty so that he might seduce and betray them. . . . Our father, Enfantin, is the genius of progress, the genius of peace, who comes to free the worker and the woman."

When Baud had finished, Enfantin rose, and all his "sons" threw themselves into his arms—including Reynaud, urged on by cries of "Embrace your father" from the audience. An observer, not part of the movement, commented that he felt as if he had been present at the Sermon on the Mount.[11]

It was, however, on December 7 and 9, when Enfantin lectured to large audiences on morality, that the new dispensation became most clear. These fifth and sixth teachings were the most disturbing and audacious of all. Enfantin begins with a discourse on arts and the artist. He seems always to have known that his was not the best intelligence to be found, nor was he the best technician, particularly skilled in his profession. What distinguished him, in his own eyes, was a sensibility superior to brain power, skill, or talent that he thought to be essentially artistic in nature.

The case of the artist was relevant to the "questions that had particularly upset the college and that had served as pretext or the motive for many deviations." Morality deals with human passions, and Enfantin wished to recall what had already been said about "those who experience them in a powerful fashion and express them in forms that penetrate the heart."

Artists are to be examined because in them the passions are made manifest by clear, sharp, general distinctions more than is the case with the priest, whose job is to harmonize rather than exemplify distinctions. Enfantin suggests that there are two forms of art: cult and dogma. What he meant by this is not immediately clear, but the two forms must correspond with spirit and matter, industry and science. The art of the cult, one supposes, is an art that accompanies and encourages the expression of religious feeling. The art of dogma is that which illustrates the truths that Saint-Simonianism teaches.

"The greatest art is no longer the harmonizing of ideas or things, sounds or forms, but the binding of men together." It is important to know characters, sentiments, passions in order to distinguish or synthesize, separate or bring men together, before one can "name" them according to their vocation and reward them according to their works. In art and in humans three different characteristics can be seen, the exaltation of the intellect, of the senses, and of the sentiment of love, which harmonizes thought and art, idea and form. These characteristics exist in the individuals who produce art but also in those who consume it.

The connection between aesthetics and the priesthood begins to reveal itself.

Some individuals produce and consume by intelligence, others through the senses, and others still live a life of love between the first and the second, uniting them, connecting them, and they consequently experience the sympathies of both, with the difference that they are HARMONIZED in them instead of being specialized, *abstract,* exclusive. The character of these last beings is especially known to you; it is that of the PRIEST, and what you know of the living law permits you to appreciate the truly religious morality that animates the man whose entire life is consecrated to facilitating the UNION of men of the flesh and men of the spirit, the ASSOCIATION of industry and of science, the HARMONY of practitioners and theoreticians, the combination of dogma and cult, the simultaneous progress of intelligence and human activity.[12]

Enfantin continues by noting that the mission of the priest consists of preventing too pronounced specialization while at the same time providing satisfaction, appropriate to the exigencies of time and place, to the needs of the society in which these specializations appear.

The diverse nuances in art (they are, as exposed here, so *nuancés* that one longs for the slow, steady logic of the now separated Bazard) correspond to the nuances in the character of the artist. Artists think and act differently, and their works reflect this diversity. Without the influence of the priest, for whom those differences are harmonic, social, and religious, they would become discordant, disordered, and irreligious. The priest poses, to each artist and to each difference, limits that contribute to the happiness and harmony of all. He traces the circle within which individuality can manifest itself in a legitimate manner. "The priest feels to a superior degree the demands of ORDER and those of LIBERTY."[13]

We are suddenly no longer hearing about the artist but about the priest, who is the regulator of the individualism of the artist and, it quickly appears, of other individualities as well. It takes a powerful life force to unite two individuals of different characters, Enfantin tells us. It takes a powerful life force to sense and understand them and to persuade them to draw close by the affection one feels and witnesses for them. It is not so much by the love that exists between two persons that their union is brought about as by their common love for him who brings them together. First, the priest brings both to him.

Such is the life of the priest; it is he who classifies each according to his vocation and assigns the milieu favorable to his progress. It is he who binds and looses, because he senses what each rejects and what attracts each. The priest by the power of attraction that he exercises groups around him individuals who seek or avoid one another and who without him would confound themselves in the most gross forms of idolatry or would fly to the most savage hate. Because, if there are some who ought to be closely linked, there are others whom the priest must hold at the two extremities of the moral world.[14]

These two poles often have been described by equally disaffirming terms, perhaps "fickleness" and "obstinacy." There ought to be equally approving terms for both states. The world is still so permeated with Christian morality that affections that are profound and durable; characters that are reflective, reasonable, and meditative; and virtues such as modesty, reserve, and abstinence are, if not in fact, at least nominally, viewed as more desirable than their opposites. Lively and burning passions; energy, ebullience, and enthusiasm; self-assurance, ambition, and glory; the love of luxury, of pleasure, of style, of brilliance—all the joys that the ancient church called profane are in the present world suspect.

Immobility and infidelity are two vices, and yet the desire to change and to conserve are two virtues indispensable to progress. The man of progress is he who knows what ought to be done and what *can* be done by both conservative and innovator—terms used by Saint-Simon himself.

The man of progress has up to now been a slave, since all societies are constituted for immobility or backwardness. The progressive has never been able to offer a hand to both those who wish to change and those who wish to conserve. In the battle between the two he has been compressed, flattened, ill-understood, and scorned.

At this point in his argument Enfantin admitted that he was still searching for the terms with which to present his ideas on the moral future. All that he had said up to this point was merely a prelude to his teaching on morality. His audience knew only at second hand what the issues dividing Saint-Simonians were and what his moral position might be. And having said this Enfantin proceeded to his central theme: women.

But this prelude of ten or a dozen printed pages requires closer examination. As so often with Saint-Simonian rhetoric, Enfantin's meanings are as fascinating as they are inchoate and obscure. Because he sees some parallelism between his conception of himself as priest and his conception of the artist essentially inspired rather than trained, intuitive rather than proficient, amateur but nonetheless respectable for that, Enfantin dwells on what he considers to be the nature of art. He sees it as an activity bridging the Saint-Simonian dualisms: mind and matter, spirit and flesh, science and industry. Art unites, exemplifies, instructs, and propagandizes through sensual and emotional means. So does the priest, whose raw materials are human personalities and whose art is creating human harmonies, emotional colors and designs, psychological pictures, poems, or symphonies from the congruent and incongruent personalities.

The argument is yet more involved. The artist is invincibly individualistic; the priest, it would seem, is invincibly authoritarian. The problem of order and liberty once again is raised in Saint-Simonian theory. It is the essential quality of the artist that must be limited, controlled, and defined. It is the priest's essentially artistic nature that qualifies him to undertake the job. It is without any doubt Enfantin's sincerest wish to liberate the qualities that Christian society has repressed; he liberates the classes, the sexes, the humanity of humans. But he once again runs up against the necessity of forcing people to be free. Enfantin is not alone in his century in meeting the problem, but he is perhaps bolder than many in facing its consequences. One of his disciples shortly after this session says, "Enfantin has revealed me to myself,"[15] and this, after all, was Enfantin's understanding of liberty.

Through the inchoate words the conviction comes that Enfantin sees himself possessed of a certain power to move and guide men, given a certain insight into human relationships; that he is "one of those lovable beings who is followed." He touches on the notion of the charismatic leader, of the leader who leads because of the love people have for him rather than that they have for one another.

Shortly after this meeting he would invite, indeed insist on, professions of faith in his powers. But the function of these professions was as much to inform him of the very nature of his appeal as to glorify him. In the whole realm of personality and human relationships Enfantin had stumbled on an area that frightened him as much as it fascinated him, on a set of personal powers he gloried in but did not fully understand.

The teachings of November and December 1831 constituted an effort to construct an edifice of meaning to house the intentions in which he had faith. The faith drove him to demand more of his followers, and the response of the followers encouraged him to demand even more. He fed on himself as served by them. Some of the followers were willing, finally, to see in him a reincarnation not merely of Saint-Simon but of Christ himself.

This élan pushed Enfantin to announce the most controversial of his dogmas as widely as possible. Despite warnings and reservations he continued the fifth teaching with a discussion of women and thereby doomed the Saint-Simonian religion (but not the school) to disintegration. At the same time he tried to bring the doctrine on women and the doctrine on industry together again in a synthesis that would be announced before the Saint-Simonians had to leave the rue Monsigny.

Taking up the theme of women, Enfantin says that the very women who ought to greet his revelation most warmly are those on whom Christian anathema lies most cruelly. The spiritual anarchy resulting from the war between church and enlightenment—the war of the sacred and profane, church and state, paradise and hell, God and devil, spirit and flesh, woman and man—has in effect sanctioned vice and crime.

Women in the moral order and industry in the political have sought freedom. They have wed gold and calculation to achieve it. Both woman and industry have revolted against a social order in which they were treated as minors. Industry dethroned the clergy after having bought and corrupted it; men have been dethroned by women when they consented to sell themselves for a dowry: "I would like to make this comparison so that you will remember constantly that our apostolic work consists principally in the Appeal to Women and in the Rehabilitation of the Flesh through the political organization of industry and the creation of a new cult."[16]

But neither women nor industry has, in fact, been freed. They are not yet associated: women with men, spirit with matter. Industry is without foresight, rule, or order; competition crushes workers; habits, modes, and tastes change with a destructive rapidity; quality is nothing, quantity is all.

On the other hand woman is no longer the complete slave of man, and if according to law, she is minor, according to custom, she is far from that. It is not difficult to see that all criticism of Christian moral law has depended for two centuries on the institution of marriage. "From Molière to the present it is with adultery that poetry and art have penetrated our hearts; in adultery is the secret of noble, bourgeois, and popular emotions."

But this is not all: "I have not talked of the entire life of woman, her brave life, her life of sadness, of her battle for freedom, independence, her life of revolt against the cloister, and her insurrection against MARY." Voltaire dared to soil Joan of Arc. "Well, I dare say to the world that I come to cleanse the daughter of the poorest and most numerous class, the daughter of the people, of the filth of *prostitution*."

We do not come, like Jesus, to drive the merchants from the Temple; industry is holy. We do not come like Saint Paul to tell woman to silence and veil herself in the Temple; her words and her flesh are agreeable to God. And if we expect of her, like the church, modesty, reserve, discretion, delicacy, propriety, constance, meditation, reflection, contemplation to the point of ecstasy, we know that God has given her the love of luxury, style, brilliance, display, ambition, glory; the joys of the Ball, the concert, of fetes and the dream of exaltation and enthusiasm to the point of delirium.[17]

The prodigious power of woman, Enfantin continues, has been tortured and strangled by a church that has in vain thundered for eighteen centuries against the daughters of Satan and crucified them in spirit. "I glorify God, Saint-Simon, and myself . . . in calling into the new temple all the men and all the women that the Christian church has tumbled into hell, because it was not vast and beautiful enough to contain them, because it was too sad, too somber, too monotonous to attract them."[18]

What future will give satisfaction to these "eternal gentiles?" What ministry will be loving enough to understand what Jesus and his ministers were not able to understand? Up to the present men alone—Moses, Adam, Paul—have delivered the law of man and woman. And even now, Enfantin underlines, he, a man alone, is speaking. But, he insists, he is not uttering a commandment but is making an appeal. Violence and dishonesty must disappear in the relations of men and women. Women will be embarrassed at first by the new state of affairs: veiled, obscure, lying, they have so long been slaves.

The new priest will be man and woman—a couple. The function of this couple politically is to encourage science and industry. They will use art to reach the masses. Artists awake intelligence and activity, they charm spirit and sense, and they exalt the workers.

Morally, the priest and priestess play a personal role with the faithful rather than a collective and public one. They bind and loose men and women, consecrate their union or divorce. The love of each is revealed to the priestly couple; all has been confided, avowed, confessed. The priest and priestess exercise their ministry with all their intelligence but also by means of their beauty and glamour. The priesthood of the future will not mortify the flesh, will not be veiled, and will not cover its face with ashes.

The priestly couple will be loved because they love, because they are enlightened, reasonable, wise, sensible, sweet, patient, and reflective, but also because in them are to be found, grace, elegance, taste, liveliness, ardor, and gaiety.

To those who fear seduction in this picture, Enfantin points out that spiritual seduction is quite as easy as physical, that the guidance of fleshly impulse can be as educational as spiritual guidance. Humanity has spent three centuries in seeking a new science; it has in that time reasoned, discussed, argued. But humanity, nonetheless, is ugly. It has a prodigious head; it is a monster that reasons terrifyingly. "It moves, it speaks, but it loves not."[19]

Mind and body will equally concern the priestly couple. The carnal attraction the couple excite will not degenerate into libertinism, delirium, or orgy and will not command idolatry or slavery. The priestly couple will calm the immoderate ardor of intelligence; they will moderate the demands of the senses. The couple will also rouse a sluggish satiety, because they know all the charm of decency and restraint but also all of the grace of abandon and voluptuousness.

And now, if one asks what limit I place on the influence of the priest and priestess, I answer "none." Woman will speak. . . . I call to her in the name of the poorest and most numerous class, whose daughters are sold and whose sons are delivered to war, in the name of all these men and all the women who throw the brilliant veil of lies or the dirty wrap of debauchery over their secret or public prostitution, in the name of Saint-Simon I conjure her to reply to me.[20]

"Voluptuousness" and "abandon," the glorification of the senses, the elevation of what the prostitute symbolized, resounded most widely in Paris and in the ears of the government. One can shake one's head with annoyance at the appeal to the mysterious woman. To whom is Enfantin calling? How will he know when she arrives? Clearly she must be beautiful, and presumably she must find Enfantin pleasing. She must be able to shut him up and lay down the law—to impose the limit on priestly activity that Enfantin will not or cannot. These were the sorts of perfectly reasonable queries and the bases of perfectly reasonable rejections that had greeted Enfantin's theories from their first appearance. It was not, on the whole, the "liberation of the flesh" that drove followers away but the peculiar role in that liberation that Enfantin saw for himself and his sister priestess. But to stop with the effort to understand these, as so many did in 1831 and so many have since, is not fair.

Insofar as Enfantinian novelty is concerned, the Saint-Simonians had long since made the link between proletarians and women. They had long since seen the bourgeois marriage as the root of social evil; they had for several years equated it with prostitution. And they had for several years linked prostitution, poverty, and economic disorganization. The doctrine of the liberation of women was a perfectly intelligible consequence of Saint-Simonian analysis.

What may have been novel was the meaning Enfantin gave to the term *liberty*. Marriage and other kinds of relationships might be entered into and dissolved. Personal predilection, not property, and taste, not reason, should determine how men and women might come together. An acceptance of sexuality and, in particular, of female sexuality; an appeal to woman to reveal herself, her needs, desires, likes, and dislikes—these were, if not original with Enfantin, at least products of his own observations and convictions. That such an invitation was liberating can hardly be denied, nor can its consistency with Saint-Simonian materialism.

The contrapuntal play of "industry" and "woman" in the fifth teaching is not simply a far-fetched rhetorical device. While reaching out to his most dangerous upper branches, Enfantin is also mindful of his roots. "Industry is holy" is meant quite literally. *Things* made are good; the making of things is good; life here and now is good; the sensual world is real and good. Humanity will know its heavenly city on earth when it knows itself and its desires; when it has rid itself of notions of guilt, damnation, future reward, and retribution; and when it has accepted and rejoiced in the material world, organized it, and ensured perennial progress. Saint-Simon did not discuss women, but Enfantin's view of their place in the Saint-Simonian world is perfectly congruent with that of his teacher.

The teaching is imbued with passion and with flashes of insight—for instance, the notion that feminine oppression is as degrading for men as for women—with courage as well as arrogance and a certain degree of confusion. But what one has as the teaching moves to its close is a celebration of womankind, of sex, of love in all its manifestations. With it there is a condemnation of a cruel, harsh, and unfeeling world that demands, although it does not accept, reform.

Stripped of exaggeration, comedy, pretension, and the assaults on the good taste and conventional wisdom of the 1830s, Enfantin's appeal is a call for male and female liberation whose echoes would return only a century and a half after its utterance. The achievement is not small, although his own age was incapable of recognizing it, and ours may be more struck by the problems he could not solve than by those that he posed with force and originality.

DRAMA of a different sort from that felt in the hall had surrounded the fifth teaching. On the day of its delivery Robinet, a judge and relation of Mme Petit, herself a heavy contributor to the school, died at the rue Monsigny. He had wished to be moved there as death approached so that he might be surrounded by his Saint-Simonian family. He had left his fortune to the movement and in so doing opened the Saint-Simonians to accusations of exerting undue influence on him. The Robinet family later broke the will, but the circumstances of his death contributed to the gossip and agitation of the moment. In the wake of the scandals of his fifth teaching Enfantin invited everybody to "confess" his or her personal life and Enfantin's role in it. He also announced that he saw no limit to the "medicinal" action of the "mother" who would come to guide his followers. The confessions and the subsequent regulation of the lives they revealed must be regarded as "moral medicine."[21] Fairly soon, however, Enfantin had to warn the disciples to avoid simple gossip, "listening to and especially retelling" all the "little" secrets of the relations of men and women.

At the same time the Father decreed that "your relations ought to be more frequent. You must all know one another." The professions of faith in Enfantin would get rid of dissension and hostilities. "Expressing your faith, you will feel the need to bare your hearts."[22]

These professions indeed mounted to delirium. Baud, already quoted and a much-favored confessor, announced that the greatest poverty was not that of bread. The world was especially poor in love and tenderness. "Father, you are for me the LIVING LAW. You are not God, but you are he who *knows* best the *thought* of God." Lesbazeilles: "Father, I believe in you, I love you."

Isaac Pereire's confession is of particular interest: "Father, I have loved you for a long time. I am indebted to you for revealing to me the power of love that is in me. I love you more than ever. I sense that industry will receive a powerful impulse from you — my shoulders will not fail." Pereire's intuition was correct, and his shoulders did not fail.[23]

Michel Chevalier, who as editor of *Le Globe* was rapidly becoming Enfantin's executive officer, declared: "I have never for a single instant doubted you. I accept completely what you have taught us about the relations of men and women." These declarations were often interrupted by sobs and embraces. D'Eichthal on December 16 had to interrupt his confession, shaken by emotion, and return to embrace Edmond Talabot before concluding, "It is the Father who has revealed me to myself." It was the conclusion to a discourse on his Jewish origins, Christian conversion, Comtian introduction to Saint-Simonianism, and veneration of Enfantin.

Raymond Bonheur's declaration was a good example of the lengths to which the disciples would go in their adoration of the supreme father of the Saint-Simonian religion: "Father, I believe in you as I believe in the sun. You are in my eyes the sun of humanity; you warm it with your love, which is the living image of the INFINITE love of God."[24]

The culmination of these venerations came not in December but in March. D'Eichthal late in February once again proclaimed, "I believe in God, I believe in Saint-Simon, and I believe that Saint-Simon is in you." Enfantin replied, "It is you who have said it, I ask no more." But there was to be more. At 6 A.M. on March 2, the day before the announcement that legal proceedings would be taken against Enfantin, Chevalier, and Duveyrier, d'Eichthal arrived in Enfantin's room announcing that he had been given the gift of prophecy. Enfantin rather grumpily told him to come back in an hour. On his return d'Eichthal announced that in Enfantin he saw the reincarnation of Christ and that Enfantin must announce himself as such. Enfantin replied, putting on a sock, that "in the absence of woman, I cannot name myself, *homo sum*." It was of course both a pragmatic and an ambiguous response. "I am *a* man?" "I am *the* man?" But it did serve in this chill dawn to quiet d'Eichthal's ardor.[25]

It was a scene soon recounted to all the faithful. The more enthusiastic took it up and professed their acceptance of d'Eichthal's illumination. They pushed Enfantin to a declaration that he must finally have found equally frightening and attractive.

Events by that time had outpaced theory. The Saint-Simonians were by now involved with Robinet's family, who during the summer would succeed in breaking his will. At noon on January 22, 1832, as Enfantin and Rodrigues were preparing to leave the rue Monsigny for the public teaching at the Salle Taitbout, a small army debouched into the short and narrow street: two detachments of municipal guards, a squad of national guards, a company of troops, and a squadron of hussars. To the accompaniment of light flashing on swords, the jingle of horse trappings, and the clatter of hooves, the house was placed under siege. Enfantin and

Rodrigues were forbidden to leave or communicate with the exterior.

Simultaneously the *procureur* Desmortiers and the *juge d'instruction* (examining magistrate) Zangiacomi closed the Salle Taitbout and dispersed the waiting audience. At 2:30 the crown officers arrived at the rue Monsigny, and three hours later they withdrew carrying the correspondence of the fathers, that of *Le Globe,* and account books.

The investigation was to last until June, which meant that much time had to be spent answering the inquiries of the police. The closing of the Saint-Simonian halls would bring propagation of the doctrine to a halt. In March the only avenue of publicity still open was that of the tract or broadsheet handed out by the thousands on Sunday mornings. *Le Globe* continued, but money was running out. In the face of police action and its possible economic consequences, Rodrigues withdrew from the movement on February 14.[26]

Bazard's account of that break was that, as in his own case, there had been a violent war between Enfantin and Rodrigues for two months because Enfantin wished to teach and *practice* his theories of priesthood. Enfantin's response to the break was that Bazard's and Rodrigues's mission had been accomplished, and "mine begins." Once again there were divisions, crises of conscience, and attempts at reconciliation. But the separation of Rodrigues and his declaration of himself as antipope of the Saint-Simonians were decisive for the continuity of the school.[27]

Rodrigues had been charged with the material interests of Saint-Simonianism. Now there was little management and less money. Distributing a free newspaper, maintaining support for the elaborate entertainments of the rue Monsigny, conducting a missionary effort, and meeting the inevitable costs of legal proceedings were clearly beyond Saint-Simonian means. "We have spent our substance as workmen spend theirs" was a proud cry, but like workmen the movement could not live without money.[28]

By June the government, with some difficulty, had made a case for the indictment of Enfantin, Chevalier, and Duveyrier for "outrages against public morality committed in writings printed and distributed." The public prosecutor appealed to a higher court and was successful in having added to the first charge the crimes of holding meetings of more than twenty people and embezzling. The court also ordered that the charge of embezzlement would be tried separately. The accused would have to face two trials: one might be fought on the basis of ideology, but the other would involve an accusation of a common criminal act.[29]

Decisions had to be made. Barrault told Enfantin on April 12, "You are the Messiah of God and the king of nations." The burden of his message was that a trial was beneath Enfantin's dignity and that Enfantin ought to leave for the Orient to look for the "mother" who had not yet shown herself in Paris. Enfantin's response was that the time was not ripe.[30] The solution at which Enfantin arrived ushered in a last and most notorious phase of the cult. *Le Globe* ceased publication on April 20. Enfantin withdrew to his mother's house at Ménilmontant with forty of his disciples. "A phase of my life is today accomplished. I have spoken; I wish to act. But I have need of repose and silence. A numerous family surrounds me. The apostolate is founded."[31]

The founding of the apostolate supposed, of course, the presence of a Christ. One can only dimly convey the degree of exaltation that had grown ever more intense among the faithful since the initial break in November 1831. Every word, every act, every relationship of the Enfantinians carried a mystic significance. Every thought was a revelation with a hidden meaning. And some of those involved, like d'Eichthal, whose family was in despair, or Alexis Petit, whose rich mother willingly underwrote the expenses of Ménilmontant, never fully recovered from or resolved in their own minds the meaning of the last common days at the rue Monsigny or in the Enfantin household.

Enfantin himself trembled on the razor's edge between rationality and madness during those days. On the very day of the cessation of *Le Globe* and the announcement of the retreat, Enfantin's mother, taken rapidly by cholera, died. During her agony, understandably enough, Enfantin succumbed to a fit of weeping that lasted for several hours. It was a recurrence of the crisis he had experienced at the death of his brother. He himself explained it as not merely sadness at the loss of a parent but also a kind of physiological crisis in which the being of his mother pushed into him.[32] This notion of the continuance beyond death of all life in other forms was an idea that Enfantin had proposed with relatively little success in the earlier religious discussions of the school. It was clearly Enfantinian and never Saint-Simonian. The occasion of his crisis and the death of his mother provided yet another opportunity to advance a debatable thesis. With that "curious lack of taste" so characteristic of him, Enfantin seized the opportunity.

Mme Enfantin's death offered, as well, a dramatic setting for the move from the rue Monsigny to Ménilmontant. There had to be a funeral, and it was a funeral in Saint-Simonian costume with Saint-Simonian ceremony, a procession of a thousand people witnessing the devotion of the Saint-Simonians to their father. It was also a funeral without funds for necessary expenses until Gustave d'Eichthal's father, the banker Louis d'Eichthal, sent a thousand francs to meet them.[33] He did this despite the fact that the d'Eichthals and their lost lamb had been at loggerheads for months and that the family apparently believed that Gustave was to disappear forever behind the monastic doors of Ménilmontant.

Three hundred people followed Enfantin and his chosen forty disciples to those doors at 145 rue Ménilmontant. There, Enfantin addressed the group on the nature of their retreat and concluded with an invitation to all those who in the last year had lost a woman dear to them to come forward and embrace him. In the midst of these general embracings the retreat to Ménilmontant began.

SINCE the schism of the previous November, Enfantin had placed the question of women at the center of Saint-Simonian ideology while, on the whole, relegating women themselves to a secondary or nonexistent role in the organization. Women had been removed from the hierarchy, and no woman had yet "revealed" herself as the priestess who would complete the priest. What morality, religion, and society would become awaited her advent. Men could only wait for the woman who was not there. Men had no right to classify, define, or elevate women; they had only to understand their own incapacity and incompleteness.

To Capella, an engineer in Switzerland disturbed by the retreat and urging industrial realization for the doctrine, Enfantin wrote that such realizations were expensive, that millions of francs did not abound and were difficult to convert. "I have constrained no husbands to quit their wives. But I feel the need to call woman to life, to a new union. It is better to be out of the old one, which doesn't mean to say one can't do good things married, only one can't be an apostle—that is, a caller of woman to a new destiny."

Enfantin continues:

You don't understand the apostolate. The apostles (laugh not) must be *bon coucheurs*, good children broken to a common life in the open. They must be characters who live everywhere, of all and with all. They must be men molded by the anguish of a life of *coterie* like that we have lived for the last two years—open to all the miseries and susceptibilities, molded by daily poverty. . . . What will be our acts? I don't know. They are prepared indirectly by our retreat; it has no other end.[34]

The creation of an apostolate and the withdrawal to Ménilmontant obviously drew on a Christian metaphor, but also on a Judaic one. Enfantin never minded mixing and confusing symbols. He would withdraw into the desert, which was simultaneously a garden of Eden until Eve was drawn from Adam's rib. In part these symbolic actions and stage sets were a product of necessity. The house, at Mme Enfantin's passing, became her son's. There is no indication of how the good lady had greeted the news that she was to be invaded by forty permanent guests. We do know that although she was loyal and loving, she was not unswervingly amiable.[35] The possibility of using the Enfantin house and vast gardens solved some financial problems. The forty apostles who would live there swore to do so as monks, and the house itself was to be a kind of monastery. Each resident took a vow of celibacy, wore a Saint-Simonian costume, grew a beard (the equivalent and the reverse of a tonsure?), and undertook some part of the domestic work of the community.

The emphasis on celibacy was clearly, at one level, an effort to refute the widespread notion, embodied in the criminal charges brought against it, that Saint-Simonianism was a doctrine of libertinism, a license for lust. Celibacy was to make the point that these were men who could master their passions, live without sex, devote themselves to industry, undertake domesticity. They would thus gain insight into women's lot without inviting scabrous comment.

On another, perhaps more serious, level it was undoubtedly Enfantin's intention to deepen his and his followers' understanding of their natures and the nature of sexuality. Living at close quarters, subject to constant introspection and examination, dependent in a number of ways on Enfantin, and not at all celibate by inclination, the apostles were in for a severe test of their personal resources and their religious faith.

Later, according to one of his followers, it would seem to Enfantin that Ménilmontant had represented "an exceptional education given by him to exceptional men like us. The extraordinary means employed would never be reproduced in the future. What is marvelous is that love affairs between men were not numerous. With some (Transon and Reynaud) it was a question of a mother calming and cradling her child."[36]

There must have been at the rue Monsigny intense discussion of the projected retreat, although in the recorded meetings there is no trace of it. Enfantin described his followers as a *"troupe des jeunes hommes tous aimant beaucoup les femmes."*[37] Among those who chose to join Enfantin were a number of married men whose choice was not well-understood by their wives. The monastic model seems to have been understood literally; the operative assumption was that celibacy and separation were permanent.

"Think of what affections surrounded this poor friend. Our love was certainly a love of the future, and yet you have separated us as if we were of those who suffer from being together. You have broken our union, the most complete, most tender union I have known. . . . Good-by, Father Enfantin, [I] am stricken by the hands of those in whom I put all my faith." So wrote Cécile Fournel to Enfantin. And to her husband, "From today I unite with women, I aid them, I sustain them, I call out to them."[38]

Enfantin's manifesto of April 20 had been a kind of abdication. The women of the movement were "free" to "name" their own destinies. Since they were not to come to Ménilmontant, they were "liberated" to carry on the Saint-Simonian work in the world. In other words, women and the rank and file must find their own way and separate themselves from the leader. Couched in high-flown terms, the message was still brutal. But

Enfantin could imagine no other way to cut the dependency that was becoming intolerable for him and that could not be happily resolved for the faithful.

Clever as the Ménilmontant strategy might have been in disarming suspicion of one kind of licentiousness and in solving a number of Enfantin's personal problems, it could boomerang. The Parisian populace, the press, and the police were to be as titillated by the spectacle of forty young men living together, abandoning women, and doing housework as they had previously been by the life of the rue Monsigny.

Broadsides bearing cartoons and satiric verse were widespread.[39] They depicted men washing dishes, scraping carrots, polishing kitchenware, emptying laundry tubs, and, best known of all, lacing each other's shirts up the back. This last was a reference to the costume adopted in June, which underlined the Saint-Simonian principle that the faithful must "associate" themselves even when they were dressing. The combination of celibacy and "domesticity" afforded possibilities for ridicule and scorn. To the French mind of that period the domesticity appeared as much against nature as the celibacy. It is an attitude not entirely foreign to the French mind of today.

Even among the faithful there was some not quite good-humored dissidence. The painter Paul Justus declared, "I have a pronounced antipathy for laundry and linen; my bed is made by chance once every two months; let my linen tear or wear, it is not I who will take up the needle."[40] Jean Terson, an enthusiast, nonetheless remarked in his memoirs that "most of us paid tribute to the new life with stiff backs, violent colds, fevers, and sore throats."[41] More grimly, cholera was still present in Paris during the early months of the retreat, and it took the life of Edmond Talabot as it had that of Enfantin's mother.

But at least at the beginning of the experiment, novelty and optimism reigned. Even today, under urban assault, the heights of Ménilmontant rising in the northeast of Paris seem to enjoy a sense of village intimacy, of clearer air and more open vistas, than the rest of Paris. The apartment towers have mounted the hill, but the passage des Saints-Simoniens, which bisects the former gardens of the Enfantin house, could be the subject of an early Utrillo. The house itself, at 145 rue de Ménilmontant, is separated by a wall from the street. Next to it there is a small, leafy public park, which underlines the village atmosphere of the crooked streets. In 1832 the house had a forecourt, a great garden behind it with an alley of lindens and chestnuts, a large lawn, and shrubbery. There was a separate pavilion housing a billiard room.

In these first days (April 23 to June 7) the gates were closed to outsiders. There was work to be done. The garden was cleared and redesigned, terraces and a temple were planned, and walls were rebuilt or leveled. All the parqueted floors were waxed. The routine of the household had to be organized, and the work parceled out.

The day began with Raymond Bonheur's trumpet call at 5 A.M. There was breakfast at 7:00, dinner at 1:00, supper at 7:00, and bed at 10:00. Léon Simon, a doctor, was, along with Rochette and Duveyrier, charged with cooking and the kitchen. Jean Terson peeled potatoes and set the table. Edmond Talabot, Gustave d'Eichthal, Charles Lambert, and Moïse Retouret washed dishes. Alexis Petit, one of the richest members of the group, cleaned stoves and dealt with garbage. Laundry used the military talents of Bruneau and the artistic talents of Justus. Barrault, Auguste Chevalier (eventually secretary to Napoleon III) and Duguet polished boots. Michel Chevalier waxed floors and waited on table. Henri Fournel, Beranger, and Enfantin had the pleasantest, but not easiest, task, gardening.

Others were assigned to jobs as needed. But once the initial effort had been made, ennui set in. What were they all to do? How were they to pass their time? How were they to survive? Simon's kitchen did not produce brilliant results. Breakfast was a *soupe au larde,* there was bread for lunch, and dinner was soup, meat, salad, vegetable, and cheese. The flesh turned brown, the hands hardened, the beards grew long. But the Saint-Simonians, good bourgeois or invincible males that they were, were as amazed as the onlookers that engineers, doctors, and artists should be washing dishes or polishing floors.[42]

"We must come out a nucleus, compact and unbreakable," Enfantin maintained. "I have better things to do than have myself adored by forty men around me, than amuse myself by annihilating their individuality or degrading them by personal services. I know how to make my bed."[43] He wrote to his father, "There are with us now some proletarians who are adventurers of great power. . . . They initiate us into the life of the people. We bourgeois are ignorant of the people . . . we are so habituated to the master's tone."[44]

But once the housecleaning had been done, the question remained: where would the Saint-Simonians go from here? At the beginning of June, Enfantin left Ménilmontant for three days, and when he returned he presented his son to the Saint-Simonians. Arthur was four years old at this time, and for the occasion he was tended by the family friend Aglaë Saint-Hilaire. Adèle Morlane, Arthur's mother, although known to many of the Saint-Simonians, never appeared in their activities. What the "presentation" of Arthur was supposed to signify is not quite clear. The meaning of a three-day disappearance and the presentation of a son is suggestive. Probably, however, the event had importance as evidence of Enfantin's honesty and of his ties with the "old" world, before taking the "habit" of the new.

The brotherhood was preparing for the "adoption of the habit," the most notable event of the summer. The ceremony took place on June 6 and was marked by a prodigious thunderstorm and the echoes of guns from Paris, where a minor Republican insurrection was in progress.

But the ceremony was itself colorful and emotionally charged. It attracted some thousands of Parisians. It brought forth another despairing letter from Cécile Fournel, and it added another turn of the screw for d'Eichthal, whose father was reported to be "suffering" at the news of the event. The assumption of a lifetime commitment to celibacy was widespread; the idea that the act was definitive was present in the minds of many of the participants.[45]

At 1:30 all the members of the Saint-Simonian family formed a circle before the house. At 2:00 Enfantin appeared to the strains of *Salut au Père,* written by Vinçard and Felicien David. Enfantin then talked about the significance of the costume. It was to wipe out the old hierarchy, it announced a new equality, and it reemphasized individuality. Its colors were seen in a red vest, a violet blue coat, and white trousers, representing love, labor, and faith. The name of each member (thus the individuality) was sewn on each shirt. These were the new—womanless—Adams.

The following Sunday there took place one of those prodigious public marches of which only the nineteenth century seemed capable: to the Père Lachaise Cemetery and the tomb of Enfantin's mother; then to Vincennes, to the site where Enfantin had guarded a piece of artillery during the siege of Paris; and then to Saint-Mandé, to visit the birthplace of the child whom Enfantin had "brought into the world with my own hands."[46] And then, as Pepys might say, so home and to bed.

In connection with the ceremonial adoption of the costume and the public march, the Saint-Simonians issued a new manifesto. It announced that they were pacific, religious, and loving and that violence was bad. They loved Republicans but were not themselves Republican. They loved legitimists, because of their love of order, but were not legitimist. They loved the members of the *juste-milieu* because they were economical, *soigné, rangé,* but they were not of the *juste-milieu.* They meant to reform the world by practical means: a railroad from Paris to Marseilles, a new avenue from the rue du Louvre to the Bastille, a new water system for Paris, an army to reclaim the *landes* of Brittany, and an army transformed from military to industrial purposes with every soldier made into a "good worker."[47]

Manifestoes and manifestations brought as many as 10,000 Parisians to gape and stare at the house and invade the gardens on Sunday afternoons. They were followed by the police with accusations of a new offense against Article 291. Michel Chevalier pointed out that the forty faithful were resident at Ménilmontant and thus did not fall under the provisions of the law. The offense, nonetheless, joined those already drawn up for the trial, scheduled to take place in August. In the meantime a temple built by Saint-Simonian hands began to rise in the garden, accompanied by Saint-Simonian song. Felicien David was at the piano, and 2,000 visitors watched the picks and shovels in action. By July 8 the military had posted guards around the house with orders to turn away the visitors.[48]

Two more of these happenings were of a different character. The most committed of the Talabot brothers, Edmond, died of cholera on July 17. His funeral provided an excuse for another public march and an opportunity for a meeting of the Pereire brothers and the engineers Lamé, Flachat, and Clapeyoron. Consequent to the meeting were the first concrete plans for the first Saint-Simonian industrial and technological achievement — the Paris–Saint-Germain railroad.

The second happening did not turn out so well. On July 29 Bazard, who had been ill for a month, died. Enfantin conceived the idea of bringing his troop in costume, singing Saint-Simonian "canticles," to pay tribute to the cofounder and one-time "father" of Saint-Simonianism. News of this project preceded the group on the day of the funeral. The distracted Mme Bazard sent friends to the mayor of Irvy begging him to send the cortege back. The display of solidarity ended at midnight in grief and, worse, in farce.

All this was not enough. During July and August there were concentrated night sessions at Ménilmontant to put together a "New Book" for the new life. There were fantasies of rebuilding Paris in the form of a woman; there were discussions of a "general formula of the human spirit and its corresponding graphic curve," an attempt to mathematize sentiment.

But as the August trial approached and passed with its verdict of guilty, the followers grew restive. Barrault thought only of the East and of founding the "companions of Woman" to search for their female Messiah. Others found the strain of celibacy too great, and as the date for Enfantin's and Chevalier's imprisonment drew near, there were defections. D'Eichthal wrote to Enfantin on October 22:

Finally after fifteen days of agitation and suffering I have had *my night*. Shaken with desire, in an irresistible transport, far from a woman, I made love to my bed, and then calm returned to me, my head cleared, my ideas became precise. . . . Don't hope to keep the group of men who are ranged around you today. The power of women will kidnap them one by one.[49]

On November 3, d'Eichthal and Duveyrier left Ménilmontant; others had preceded or would quickly follow them.

But the Ménilmontant experiment ended with as much bang as whimper. The trial in August, as will be seen, afforded the most effective and most affecting occasion for the diffusion of the doctrine. The second trial, for embezzlement, resulted in acquittal.

It was also true by September of 1832 that some of the "practical" proposals of the school had been taken up by the state. The pattern dictating that while one phase of Saint-Simonian doctrine was on public view, another phase was the subject of private debate had persisted. Through all the feverish and anguished months filled with open discussion of the most taboo aspects of Saint-Simonianism, the private debate, ironically, had been about respectability. Respectability would be obtained by returning the school to its material, industrial, and technological origins. How this was to be done had been the original work of the winter and spring of 1831 and 1832.

THE NEW EDEN

GRUMBLING ABOUT Enfantin's exaltation had risen from the provinces and abroad as early as the crisis of 1831: from Paulin Talabot, from Arlès-Dufour at Lyons, and from Capella in Geneva. In Paris the engineers Henri Fournel and Michel Chevalier had talked about devising a practical and convincing program of action. Enfantin responded by pointing out that it was all very well to talk of launching programs of industrial development but that one needed capital to accomplish anything. Neither capitalists nor governments displayed eagerness to implement the kind of appeal Enfantin persisted in making during the autumn, winter, and spring of 1831–32.[1]

Enfantin had agreed, nevertheless, to give at least lip service to the new industrial direction of the movement. The agreement, in fact, was a condition of the continued support of the "practical" Saint-Simonians. The compromise had been implicit in the appointment of Rodrigues to take over the business affairs of the school. *Le Globe* under Chevalier's direction predicted the inevitable conversion of society's "natural" leaders to the self-evidently rational Saint-Simonian proposals. But with the intervention of the police and Rodrigues's defection, conversion seemed less likely.

In the last days of *Le Globe*, however, a picture did emerge of where the Saint-Simonians would like to go. It was a picture that, although painted with a broad brush and highly colored, turned out to be simultaneously a startlingly accurate representation of the future and Saint-Simon's earlier vision of it.

Circumstances outside the Ménilmontant cloister had forcibly entered into Saint-Simonian thought during 1832. The death of Mme Enfantin and of Edmond Talabot during the cholera epidemic directed the school to think about public health in Paris. Chevalier had asked for governmental permission to open a kind of clinic where Saint-Simonian doctors would give free care to the sick. And indeed the Saint-Simonians did provide free care and earned much popularity among the masses in consequence. The somewhat less sensible suggestion that the fear and depression aroused by the epidemic be dispelled with public fetes and celebrations found no support. Instead it invited memories of a medieval dance of death.[2]

How much understanding there was of communicable disease is difficult to know. It was clear that cholera was related to a bad water supply, that it spread more easily in congested areas, and that sewers, the provision of pure water, and the creation of open spaces would better the chances of survival. One finds in these solutions the intuition that urban planning and development had become essential for the future of Paris. That same perception is found in Pierre Leroux's description of Lyons. It was, indeed, in the wake of similar circumstances twenty years later that Louis Napoléon's modernization of Paris began. The notions tossed in the air by the Saint-Simonians in response to the immediate crisis had, as usual, their absurd aspect: the new Jerusalem would take the form of a woman, breasts sprouting fountains, cathedrals in her crown. But the vision was quite specifically marked by the sort of project dear to the hearts of engineers: sewers, broad avenues, pipelines, quais—problem-solving structures of stone and metal.[3]

In time the Parisian sewers would be one of the wonders of Europe. The much-dreamed-of connection from the present place de la Concorde to the Bastille would be largely the work of the Pereire brothers. The broad avenues, open spaces, and network of quais would give Paris its special character and place among world capitals. Not least, Paris would become livable and available to its vast and "meritorious" population.[4]

That what Paris needed was self-evident can be argued. In the late 1820s and the 1830s, in fact, there was a building boom of considerable proportions. The rue Monsigny and some of the streets around it resulted from the carving up of the gardens of private mansions in the neighborhood of the rue de Richelieu. As with so much else, however, it was the Saint-Simonian engineers and businessmen who first pointed out specific needs. And it was the Saint-Simonian *Globe* that related those needs to the needs of the poorest and most numerous class.

In so doing the Saint-Simonians returned emphatically to the vision of their founder and to the economic theory that informed it. The takeoff point for the new Eden would be the creation of great public works in a state enlightened by the wisdom of businessmen and engineers. The employment created for the "pacific industrial army" would, in turn, provide the income to acquire and the demand for industrial production. Once launched, the system would feed on itself ad infinitum. For the Saint-Simonian engineers, almost necessarily, the significant challenge of their day lay in a particular work to be done. Saint-Simon's enthusiasm had been long-range transportation. He had proposed a canal to link Madrid to the sea; he had been fascinated by the idea of a Nicaraguan canal; and he had revived the idea of Suez. His followers were to be no less fascinated by such projects, but they assumed a new meaning with the new wonder of the age—the railroad. The railroad lay at the center of a Saint-Simonian synthesis that emerged in the pages of *Le Globe* during its last days, Chevalier's Mediterranean system.

Chevalier loyally avowed that his articles had been inspired by Father Enfantin, but it seems more likely that the inspiration came from Henri Fournel, Paulin Talabot, Lamé, Clapeyron, and Flachat. These men were precisely representative of the group on whom both Saint-Simon and Enfantin had pinned their hopes, graduates of the Ecole Polytechnique, "the canal through which our ideas will flow." It cannot be emphasized enough that these men, far from deserting the movement at its moment of crisis, as has so often been maintained, bent all their energies to giving Saint-Simonianism a renewed vigor. In this effort, joined by the Pereires, they largely succeeded.[5]

As early as 1828 Fournel, with the later discredited Margerin, had published proposals for a railway from Gray, on the Saône, to Verdun, on the Meuse. It was a plan that a later railroad historian and distinguished railroad administrator viewed as eminently sensible. The plan envisaged a "natural" crossing of French rail routes in Champagne rather than the actual "unnatural" diversion to the Parisian center. Fournel's concern had mainly been the connection of the metallurgy of the upper Marne with the coal of the Rhone Valley. Earlier still, J.-J. Dubochet had written for *Le Producteur* on the relative utility of rails and canals. In 1832 there were in France only three rail lines; Saint-Etienne–Andrézieux, Saint-Etienne–Lyons, and Andrézieux–Roanne. These had been built to serve a local and limited purpose without particular thought of their possible relationship to a national need or a national network. The Ponts-et-chaussées, the state corps of engineers, had during the 1820s and 1830s invested its ambitions in canals. It was to the junior members of the corps, among them Chevalier, that the image of the future would become clear.[6]

That image was projected in the articles that appeared in *Le Globe*. The design for a national railway system advanced by Chevalier was, in its broad outlines, that which France eventually adopted. The Mediterranean system additionally offered a synthesis of the diverse and divergent elements of the thought of Saint-Simon and the Saint-Simonians. It explored, and to a considerable degree resolved, the ambiguities, ambivalences, and conflicts inherent in the doctrine. Not at all incidentally the system provided a blueprint for the activity of Saint-Simonians over the following thirty to forty years. It can be argued that in consequence French consciousness would bear the indelible imprint of Saint-Simonian thought for the next century and a half.

The system did not spring full blown from the head of Zeus, Enfantin, or Chevalier. One can hear its tentative strains from the beginning of 1832. And one can sense behind each of a number of articles the passionate debate that resulted in synthesis. Among Paulin Talabot's sharpest displeasures had been the degree to which *Le Globe* during the autumn of 1831 had followed a liberal line in foreign policy. Saint-Simonians, moved in particular by the plight of Poland, had favored intervention on behalf of liberation movements across Europe. Intervention meant war, and Saint-Simonianism had from its origins and in its most essential meaning been pacifist. Cooperation, not competition, had been Saint-Simon's goal, peace, not war, its mode, and the worker, not the soldier, its hero.[7]

There had been a battle over the direction of *Le Globe;* the intervention-ists lost and withdrew from the movement. So the first stimulus to the new politics of the movement was an authentic Saint-Simonian pacifism. The first sketch to bear the title "Système de la Méditerranée" appeared on January 20, 1832, and began with the assertion that "peace is today the condition of the emancipation of the peoples." On the 31st the *Globe* said it was an impossibility to establish a European balance by warfare, and on February 5, "Definitive peace ought to be built on the association of East and West." On the 12th there appeared the full outline of the Medi-terranean system, which, with the preceding articles and some few follow-ing, was published as *Politique industrielle, système de la Méditerranée.*

The final formulation included in the *Politique industrielle* is a return to the most fundamental of Saint-Simon's own concerns. "The . . . govern-ment is imbued with the prejudice inseparable from its feudal origins." There is a minister of war to whom one gives 300 million francs. There is no minister of industry. One does not discuss military expenses. "With-out consultation the ministry sends expeditions to Lisbon, another to Ancona. . . . But let industrial crisis ruin the workers of Lyons or Mul-house, let a hurricane of bankruptcies menace a whole locality, and the powers-that-be cross their arms."

The liberals maintained that it was the government's duty to let industry drown without offering a hand. "Yet industry is the nursery of empires. Yet all parties agree war is a terrible calamity. The present government's motto is 'conserve material interests'; its most important aspect is the presence of Laffitte and Casimir Périer."

There is, then, a contradiction between the practice and the intimate thought of the government. Mulhouse tells the king that the workshops are deserted and the workers without bread. His response: "I can only sympathize." Suppose someone had broken France's boundaries, that the troops were restless, the colonels in disagreement, and 80,000 Austrians at Montmélimar. "Suppose the king were to say the same thing—what would people think, what would *he* think?"[8]

If industrial interests are recognized as superior to the warrior's, why is there so much zeal for war, such meager solicitude for labor? To stop a ter-rible uprising the government surrounded Lyons with 40,000 men at a cost of four to five million francs. An equal sum for schools, model workshops, and banks would have done ten times as much for public tranquillity. If workshops were busy, there would be no insurrections. Maintaining peace by developing the forces of war is bad. The Havre-Marseille railroad could be done for one hundred million francs. The French government was regimenting 400,000 of the most robust, most alert part of the population. "Suppose instead of harrassing the flower of its youth, teaching it maneuvers that produce nothing for society, we profited from the situation by giving it a professional education, by making of regiments schools of art and crafts. Then measure the perfection of French industry."[9]

In the past the army had unsuccessfully undertaken public works. Its failures were due to the imposition of unattractive work. Drying up swamps and digging canals ought to be done by machines. The principal occupation of military service ought to be industrial; the principal attraction, the learning of a profession. Bring this about, and what has been fled from would be sought after. The product would pay for the cost. When the army is transformed into an industrial corps, the reign of peace will be assured.

But, the article proceeds, independent of an organizaton of workers one needs a plan of work. Such a plan is found in the Mediterranean system, and its first requirement is the creation of a railway from Le Havre to Marseilles. The initial sketch of the Mediterranean system (January 20, 1832) bore the subtitle "Peace considered from the viewpoint of self-interest." After the July Revolution, the article pointed out, everyone had revived memories of 1789. The idea of war was everywhere. Frenchmen felt that the principles of freedom could spread over Europe only in the train of French armies. "Progress had to have its passport inscribed on a bullet." But times have changed. French blood ought to flow only for France. France has changed its character. Manufacturing towns have doubled in population since 1790. Lyons and Rouen are unrecognizable. In the last half-century civilization has given birth to hundreds of industrial establishments, the life of which is *credit*. War would bring this development to a stop.[10]

"Industry is eminently pacific. Instinctively it repulses war. What creates cannot conciliate itself with what kills." War suspends credit and thus industry. The immense power of industry is sufficient to impose an insurmountable barrier against war; banks, in particular, have a vast social importance. "The House of Rothschild enjoys the most cordial relations with the House of Hapsburg." It may seem good to make war, but who "today would win the laurels of a revolution?"[11]

The real object of politics ought to be the founding of a definitive peace through the "association" of East and West. The principles of hierarchy, unity, and order are immune to revolution; they are the principles of Saint-Simonianism and the principles that pervade the Orient. Why should France fight more?

Is it not enough that generous France has alone undergone the cataclysm of a terrible revolution? Is it not enough that she has received a baptism of fire, has audaciously plunged into the blood bath? Why, Great God, should not France's merits and labors benefit all of humanity? France has drunk the revolutionary chalice, swallowed it at a gulp; France has mounted the cross; France has been the Christ of the nations. She has bought the progress and the peace of the world by her treasures, her anguish, and the life of her sons.[12]

Pacifists will unite the entire world, not just Europe. The church would have done it if it had been able. But now it must be done by the association in a common and creative work of the two great belligerent powers, France and England.

"Look at the Mediterranean: it ought to be a vast forum on all points of which people previously divided will be in communication. The Mediterranean is destined to be the nuptial bed of East and West. There must be a system to regenerate the countries bordering it."

The themes explored in other articles were brought together in *Le Globe*'s February 12 issue. Chevalier maintains that history's greatest warfare has been the war of East and West. It has reflected the war of mind and matter, which in the Saint-Simonian future must be at peace with each other. The Mediterranean has been a continuous battlefield where East and West tear themselves apart. From the Greeks at Troy to the battle of Navarino, the Mediterranean has been the main road used by Easterners and Westerners to attain mutual extermination. But, Chevalier repeats, the Mediterranean must be the marriage bed of East and West.[13]

Europe's old policy had been that of making "barbarians, and in particular Easterners," submit to its rule. Christianity had sought to repel infidels, to deliver the holy places from them. This Christian crusade had lost its intensity since the Reformation. The East had been allowed to sleep as Europe devoted its energies to the destruction of the Holy Roman Empire. Europe's future policy ought to be one of association with the East, and the constitution of a Mediterranean system will be the first step to universal association.

Politics is essentially the regulation of the interests of peoples and individuals. What would be the impact of the Mediterranean system from an industrial point of view?

Industry, if one leaves aside those who work in and for it, is composed of centers of production united by a relatively material link—transport—and a relatively spiritual link—banking. There is such a close relationship between the network of banks and the network of transport that one of the two having been blocked out for the best exploitation of the globe, the other is similarly determined in its essential elements.

The easiest means of transport—aside from the sea—are rivers, canals, and railroads. Railroads up to the present have been viewed in the abstract. Those who study them, the engineers, have understandably neglected political and moral questions in favor of technique. They measure the costs of establishment, the cost of transport itself. The question of rapidity is viewed as secondary.

For men who have faith in the march of humanity toward universal association, the railroad is something quite different.[14]

Chevalier goes on to say that by railroads passengers and products move at a fabulous speed; railroads multiply the contacts between people and places. In the material order the railroad is the most perfect symbol of universal association. It will change the condition of human experience at ten leagues an hour. It will transform Rouen and Le Havre into suburbs of Paris. There will be caravans between Paris and Saint Petersburg. The traveler from Le Havre will lunch at Paris, dine at Lyons, and join his boat to Algiers the same night. Vienna and Berlin will be closer than Paris and Bordeaux. Constantinople will be the distance of Brest. What is now a vast nation will be a medium-sized province.

The introduction of the railroad will make a political revolution as much as an industrial one. It will become easy to govern the major ports of the continents bordering on the Mediterranean with the same unity and instantaneity as prevails now in France. Among all the nations, England excepted, France is best situated to communicate from a center to an extreme circumference. There are still more marvels of steam to come from railroads and shipping. Steam engines (it is the old *polytechnicien* speaking) use only 4 to 5 percent of the caloric force of combustibles. What will it be like when new scientific inspirations bring unity to theory and order out of chaos? England and America already prefer railroads to rivers and canals. France must follow.[15]

What will be the principal features of the system? The Mediterranean consists of great gulfs, entries to the sea for large land areas. In each gulf there is a principal port at the axis of the valleys reaching the gulf. The port is the pivot for the most important operations of the railroad seeking other valleys. These connected systems will add up to the general plan. Railroads will carry men and lightweight production. The rivers will carry what is heavy and cumbersome.[16]

In Spain the main lines to follow are from Barcelona on the Ebro to Saragossa and the basin of the Tagus, and from Madrid to Lisbon by Castille, Estremadura, and Portugal. The result will be the unification of Spain and Portugal. Barcelona and Tortosa will be linked to Bordeaux by means of the Garonne, offering passage between the Mediterranean and the Atlantic. Branches will go to Porto, the coal and iron of the Asturias, and the lead mines of Andalusia. They will invigorate Spain and free her from Catholic bondage. "They will sanctify an industry redolent of oranges and aloes."

As for France, nobody looking at a map had not dreamed of some great communications system between Marseilles and Le Havre by the valleys of the Rhone, Saône, and Loire. From Rhone to Loire will be a difficult road, but the result will be the opening of the shores of the Mediterranean to England. Industry has a great role to play in the region, and "the queen of industry," England, cannot fail to take its part in the peaceful crusades rising in the West to raise the East from its ruins. "A railroad from Le Havre to Marseilles will be as a bridge thrown across France for the passage of powerful Albion, its engineers, and its treasures."[17]

The other principal lines in France will be from Toulouse and Bordeaux to Paris by Orléans and then to Metz, Saarbrücken, and the coal of Mainz and Frankfurt with branches to Mons, Brussels, and Antwerp. The Lyons line will join with the Meuse and Rhine to Amsterdam. Another line will join Nantes and Brest.

"Italy . . . is the messenger of Europe to Africa and Asia." Italy is artistic, voluptuous, and laughing as a daughter of the East. Italy without unity is impotent. The emblem of her unity will be a railroad from Venice to Taranto, Florence, Rome, and Naples. "The last days of Venice have not yet come. The Adriatic will penetrate the heart of Germany. It is the shore to which Germany will pour forth her and Scandinavia's goods. Lines will reach Genoa, Turin, and Hamburg from the Danube, the Moldau, and the Elbe. Prague, Dresden, Venice, and Trieste will be the most beautiful bazaars of the world.

Germany must be understood as the Turkey of Europe. Everywhere in Germany "there is the perfume of mystic contemplative poetry." The universities have a sense of German unity, but as yet there is no commercial unity. Railroads will link people speaking the same language and practicing the same customs but who as yet are strangers to one another. The rail lines of Mainz and Frankfurt will join Cadiz to Paris, Regensburg, Linz, Vienna, Bratislava, Belgrade, Split, Sophia, Salonika, Constantinople, Bucharest, and Odessa. A second route from Mainz will go north all the way to Kamchatka by way of Breslau, Warsaw, and Saint Petersburg. Dresden will join these to Venice and Hamburg.

Russia's place in the Mediterranean system poses special problems, but it stands to gain the most from it. Some Mediterranean populations are docile and passive. For the Frenchman, vivacity equals progress; for the Italian, mobility; for the Briton, dexterity. But the Slavic populations and the peasants of Austria and Hungary "die without having lived." Russia would be the easiest land in which to build railroads, being flat and wooded. Railroads would be most useful there, since the great river system is often frozen.

Beyond Russia, the East: Constantinople, Baghdad, Cairo, Teheran, Ceuta, and Alexandria will all be joined. Finally, Suez and Panama will

202

be pierced. The world will be one network, "one ravishing picture" of transportation systems complementing and reinforcing one another.[18]

Steamboats will ply all navigable waterways, irrigation systems will flourish, and mineral wealth will be easily exploited. The transport network will inevitably be accompanied by a network of banks extending credit to make the earth fruitful. Fifteen thousand leagues of railroad could be accomplished with four and a half billion francs. The project could put three million men "under arms for industry." This is a small price to pay if one considers that France since the Revolution has borrowed eighteen billions to make war.

There is place in this work for the scholars who will enlighten the plan and whose thought will prepare its realization, place for technicians of all countries, for engineers who in England and on the continent have gathered and multiplied the heritage of Watt. There is place for the industrialist, into the hands of whom Nature pours its products and who changes them in a hundred ways for the embellishment of humanity and the globe. There is place for the indefatigable merchant, who from one pole to another will seek products; there is a greater and greater place and one more and more sufficient for the poor of the workshops and the countryside.[19]

The bankers are not forgotten, nor are the poets and artists surrounded with "purple and gold" and "garlands of flowers." They will give up the themes of war and sing the epithalamion of East and West. "Such is our political plan. . . . It must assure the triumph of our faith."

The political plan was characteristic of Saint-Simonianism. Its grandiose dimensions were certain to frighten the cautious French bourgeoisie, its rhetoric to invite mockery, and its content to project an accurate vision of the future. It was, indeed, a most practical plan. The plan was so practical that it would require ten years to sink into the consciousness of French businessmen and the French government. It would require a generation to carry the plan beyond its first requisites.

The plan, as usual, requires translation. Reliance on Saint-Simonian code words like "association" seems to obscure rather than reveal meaning. The lofty and vague references to the innate characteristics of East and West need to be explored. The assumed national characters did not simply repeat existing stereotypes but had their places in the Saint-Simonian hierarchies of the sentiments. They were seen as complementary pieces in a great kaleidoscopic unity. Those eminently practical and equally romantic engineers, Henri Fournel and Paulin Talabot, had imposed the emphasis on railroads and canals. The resurgence of the role of bankers owed something to the Pereires. The brothers were already planning an assault on Gustave d'Eichthal's brother and on the financial Zeus of the age, Baron James de Rothschild.

Imbedded in the plan was a theory of economic growth and an understanding of the relationship of credit to it that had its clear origins in Saint-Simon himself. The theory revealed a greater understanding of the economic forces already in motion than that of any other contemporary theorist. There was, as one might expect, a clear grasp of the potential consequences of economic growth for the poorest and most numerous class. But beyond that was an understanding of the worldwide consequences of European Industrial Revolution. Underlying the entire theory was a faith that this revolution would be beneficial for all humankind.

In a curious way the Saint-Simonians were saying to everyone within the boundaries of the Mediterranean system what their liberal opponents were saying to Frenchmen of the July Monarchy: *"Enrichissez-vous."* But the Saint-Simonians were saying more. They were, without quite realizing it, perhaps, elaborating a theory of economic and cultural imperialism based on the endemic French assumption of a *mission civilisatrice*. For this many will deride or dismiss the doctrine, but one cannot have it both ways. The function of this "pacific and industrial" conquest was to resolve the painful dilemma of using force to make people free. The liberal and human sympathies that had pushed some members to advocacy of militarism had been rejected. Reason, logic, experience, and self-interest would do more to make a better world.

And a better world, a more human and bearable existence for more and more people, was never out of the minds of the Saint-Simonians. The excursions into city planning during the spring of 1832 were not merely opportunistic efforts to use current events to make the doctrine more palatable. They reflected genuine aesthetic and moral concerns as well. A well-organized world would provide a sufficiency for all. Sufficiency included planning for human delight as well as individual need. Saint-Simon had talked of turning France into a *"jardin à l'anglais"*; his followers foresaw a Paris and a whole world of delights. Although they preached the exploitation of the globe in the interests of the poorest and most numerous class, they were also, perhaps, among the earliest ecologists.

But there were other and more important paradoxes to be found in Chevalier's plan. Saint-Simonians had previously sought earnestly to explain its special understanding of individualism and freedom within the framework of hierarchy and authority. Now they had to resolve the dichotomies between pacifism and nationalism and between nationalism and universal freedom. They were indeed among the earliest to recognize these dichotomies.

Simultaneously, Saint-Simonianism was declaring the moral supremacy of France and its earned right to lead the nations of the West in a peaceful "Eastern" crusade. The logical walls between peace and a crusade had somehow to be stormed. And finally, although Chevalier could proclaim the moral supremacy of France with certainty, there was the galling fact of British material supremacy, which somehow had to be taken account of in the plan.

All of these pieces were made to fit into the puzzle, and the picture that emerged had a design and unity. These had always been present, dimly sensed, but they were now made explicit in what constituted an economics of romanticism. Romanticism might appear to be a red herring dragged across the path of Saint-Simonianism, but nothing could be further from the truth. The connections of the Saint-Simonians with the recognized standard-bearers of French romanticism had always been strained. At the moment when the French literary romantics were moving from political reaction to liberalism, the Saint-Simonians were, like Saint-Simon before them, vigorously attacking economic and political liberalism. The two camps had seemed to draw together in their fury and despair at the repression of Poland and Italy after 1830. That coalition had seriously shaken the faith of one faction among the Saint-Simonians and driven them away from the movement into the arms of the liberals.

One cannot, however, deny the Saint-Simonians a romanticism that they so vigorously promulgated. Its components were the glorification of the passions and sentiments, the veneration of the *idea* of woman, the fascination with the faraway, and the imagined mystical, revelatory character of the "East." The Saint-Simonian notion of history as predetermined, organic, and moving according to law progressively revealed through the infinite exploration of the possibilities of the material universe linked the school both to Hegel and the young Marx.

The capacity of the Saint-Simonians to "feel" the truth, as well as to understand it rationally, placed them firmly among the romantics. Enfantin's glorification of the senses, of beauty, of physical love, of the variety and infinitude of possible human relationships, and of the search for the unattainable "mother" added up to his own version of the cult of the "blue flower." Certainly he saw himself as Prometheus bringing fire and light to a joyless humanity, as a world historical figure, and certainly, at one stage of the school's development in 1832, his followers saw themselves as damned heroes, Fausts all. These aspects of the doctrine were those that interested complex, but on the whole romantic, figures like Thomas Carlyle and John Stuart Mill.

How do all these apparently extraneous matters add up to an economics of romanticism? The focal point is the fascination with the East. As early as 1827 Enfantin had complained that the movement had no insights about the Orient, no way to deal with it intellectually, and no way to fit it into the doctrine.[20]

The complaint was an important and perfectly just criticism of Saint-Simon's philosophy of history. It was a philosophy based on the Western record with an occasional glance over the shoulder at Islam. The problem was that the alternately critical and organic epochs of the West did not appear to be characteristic of the East. The progress of the West seemed to be twinned to organic but stagnant epochs in the East. In the *Mémoires d'un industriel* Enfantin arrives at the governorship of Russian Georgia through a peaceful conquest, but it is not at all clear how that conquest has taken place. A number of the Saint-Simonians had been invited to aid Russian engineering projects. Enfantin himself had worked for a French bank in Russia. Dimly, perhaps, the Saint-Simonians saw a kind of technical aid program as the instrument of the pacific conquest of new ideas. Certainly, if one rejected the idea of military domination, it was by some such means that "conquest" would take place.

How were the energies of the East to be aroused? How was the stagnation to be terminated? The answer seemed to be that the self-evident attractiveness of what the West had to offer in the way of technique, power, and wealth would in itself be sufficient to open Eastern arms to the West. Given this opportunity, the East would "rouse itself from its centuries-old slumber."

It was to the credit of Enfantin that he believed with total sincerity that the West had as much to learn (as well as to gain) from this encounter as the East. In his discourses on the passions he had posited Don Juan and Othello as the archetypes of West and East, respectively. Neither was despicable, and both natures were essential. Don Juan was, of course, fickle, mobile, energetic, restless, and tireless. Othello was, of course, constant, immobile, and passive. Both were tragic figures; each needed qualities of the other. The East, in Enfantin's thought, equaled the female, the mother: mysterious, thus far impenetrable, passive, silent. She was at the same time wise and powerful and awaited only an awakening from the West to reveal herself in majesty, love, and wisdom. The insistent sexual imagery in discussions of East and West was not at all unconscious. The perplexing question was whether one was dealing with rape or seduction.

The question had particular point for Frenchmen after the conquest of Algiers in 1830. It had even more point for Saint-Simonians, because the conquest presented a new opportunity, a new testing ground, for Saint-Simonian theory and practice. Here was a fresh field that demanded (even the government recognized this) pacification, planning, and organization. Ultimately the Saint-Simonian role in Algeria would be a major one. Talabot, the Barraults, and Lamoricière would all help to make its history. Enfantin himself would serve in the 1840s on a scientific commission for Algeria. The immediacy of Algerian questions drew Saint-Simonian attention to the Mediterranean. But there were other attractions in the area. Mehemet Ali, the Egyptian khedive, appeared to be breaking the pattern of Eastern passivity; British and French interests in Egypt were lively; and among the territories controlled by the khedive were the lands of ancient Israel.

Their Jewishness was an important issue for many of the most important Saint-Simonians; Rodrigues, the Pereires, but most of all d'Eichthal had, each in his own way, to come to terms with the past and present of European Jews. D'Eichthal had passed from Judaism to Catholic assimilationism to Saint-Simonianism. He often, and most notably in his correspondence with Metternich and Baron James de Rothschild, proclaimed that the future of the Jews and of "Judaea" had always been one of his major concerns in his conversion to Saint-Simonianism. In the doctrine there was an openness to Jews, he said, and in Palestine there was perhaps a solution to Jewish problems.[21]

D'Eichthal was not alone. The Saint-Simonians thought Palestine might provide a logical place and opportunity for Saint-Simonian ventures and for European Jews. A little later, when Enfantin was in Egypt, he urged Palestinian undertakings as a logical starting point for Saint-Simonian efforts. They could be made attractive on historic and religious grounds to the greatest of the European Jewish banking houses — in particular, to the house of Rothschild.[22] And there was the bizarre twist that Enfantin's call to woman had persuaded some of the faithful that the mother of Saint-Simonianism, the female Messiah, would be found in the sleeping East. She would be, must be, like Christ, a Jew.

Finally there was the very solid attraction for engineers and businessmen of a Suez Canal. If Chevalier supposed that nobody could look at a map of France without discussing a great railway from Le Havre to Marseilles, it was doubly true that no engineer (save Stephenson, who could only dream railways) could look at a map of Egypt without dreaming of a canal at Suez. So, from the epithalamion of East and West, their marriage bed the Mediterranean, one comes finally to the transportation system as the concrete goal of the economics of romanticism.

Building the network of rails, canals, and steamship lines was the practical task toward which the followers of Saint-Simon should now direct themselves. The economic theory underlying the project is clear enough and was Saint-Simon's own. The resources of the universe are practically limitless; they will provide a sufficiency for all. The main problem for humanity is getting to those resources. The solution is to create an industry whose manifest profits will invite credit and banking. The very building of the system will create markets for the products it carries; it will fill purses to buy ever yet more goods. The railroads and steamboats will bring goods and people together. In so doing they will create further demand. The demand created will multiply the uses of transportation and the flow of credit. It is by interest and by need that the East will be brought into "association" with the West.

A century and a half after *Le Globe*'s manifesto we may have some questions about the theory. It is less clear to us than to the Saint-Simonians that the world's resources are limitless. They did not foresee the growth in the world's population. One can say with some certainty, however, that faced with the problem, they would have sought to place limitations on that growth. We may cynically assume that the Saint-Simonians are merely economic imperialists and the Mediterranean system merely an elaborate rationalization for the European domination of the rest of the world. If that is true, one must at least give the Saint-Simonians credit for conceiving a planned and peaceful imperialism rather than the bumbling, brutal, and military imperialism that left so much hatred and moral confusion behind it. It is not the case, however, that Saint-Simonianism was simply a rationalization of greed.

The Saint-Simonians did, after all, like Saint-Simon, believe in the infinite capacities of science and technology to solve problems. They also believed that it was better to eat than to go hungry, better to live than to die. They thought health better than disease, cleanliness better than dirt. They thought foresight better than fortuity, and they may be forgiven for believing that all these values had universal import. Again, one hundred and fifty years after them, we may have less faith in science and technology than they. But the real tragedy is that although science and technology have everywhere prevailed, some of the most important of the Saint-Simonian values have failed to prevail with them.

If nothing else the Saint-Simonians, like their Master and in much the same way, saw the world as it was and as it very shortly was going to be. They also had devised an ingenious and prophetic means of arriving at a takeoff point for economic revolution. They had perhaps better than anyone up to their time understood the relationship between banking, credit, transportation, and industrial growth. Their criticism of classical liberalism, laissez-faire, and the permanent economic crisis arising from it was incisive and just.

The Saint-Simonians differentiated themselves from those others whom Marx and Engels would label utopian. Their projections for the future were, unlike the phalansteries of Fourier, the workshops of Louis Blanc, or the harmonies of Robert Owen, firmly rooted in the existent world, not set apart from it. They did not, like Rousseau, venerate an irrelevant Geneva or Corsica. Utopian and mad as their global scheme might have appeared in 1832, it was only by thinking on a global scale that one could approach the underlying realities of the nineteenth century.

The Saint-Simonian intuition of contemporary reality derived much from the experience of England. Part of its originality lay in devising a means whereby English experience could be translated into French — largely at English expense. Saint-Simonian understanding of England and of England's place in the Mediterranean system was central to its understanding of nationhood, of French nationhood, and of the relationship of nationalism to peace and freedom. The ambivalence toward England, for which there was an obvious historical context, begins with Saint-Simon.

Saint-Simon's ideas on the Franco-British relationship, on nationalism, and on the respective national roles of France and Britain (explored in Chapter 2) are replicated exactly by his followers in the Mediterranean system. The difference is that in the railway the followers have found the tie that binds the two nations.

The interests of all being so clearly involved, how could egotistical, separatist, divisive, regional interest prevail? Given such unity of purpose in creative industry, how could France fail to equal the rival from whom it had learned so much? How could the rival fail to adopt measures so inevitably leading to success? How could the two, France and England, fail to impose their civilizing mission on the rest of the world?

Nowhere is the continuity of thought between Saint-Simon and the Saint-Simonians more apparent than in their discussions of Anglo-French relationships, the national idea, and the transportation revolution.

The Mediterranean system required a state that, rather than mediating between local and special interests, would think and act nationally, most necessarily in the matter of railroad planning. Indeed, when the Saint-Simonians themselves a decade later embarked on large-scale railroad building, they met innumerable problems thrown up by the "other France," which was resistant to the centralizing tendencies of the nation-state. The Saint-Simonians certainly did not invent French nationalism, but they experienced it. They contributed to the extension of French national consciousness both in word and in deed. That consciousness was linked to an understanding of England very much like Saint-Simon's.

Enfantin in 1837 wrote to his cousin:

Which of all the nations has been most victorious? Precisely that which was most industrial. You see, it would not be a bad calculation to push the [French] government to be *re* other governments what England was vis-à-vis Europe. Only our position is more favorable. If we do not have as much of the sea to ourselves, the land makes up for this. . . . From the moment when France, instead of warring with England, moved to equal her, the peace between the two nations has been felt not only as a necessary repose but also as a mutual advantage. If this is true of France in relation to England, it is a thousand times more evident in France's relations with her continental neighbors.[23]

Five years after his ostensible break with Saint-Simonianism Chevalier would footnote Enfantin's observations by declaring that by means of the Le Havre-Marseille railway England would find itself "in a kind of dependent relationship to France."

The Saint-Simonians needed a French nation to make a French railway network. They also needed England as its ultimate best client and as its financier. Emile and Isaac Pereire maintained that French resources were adequate to the task of railway building, but they admitted that mobilizing those resources was a problem yet to be solved. The French Rothschild was open to the initiatives of the Pereires regarding a Paris–Saint-Germain railway precisely because his English brother had avoided involvement in the building, and consequently in the profits, of British railways. In a short time it would become gospel that no French railway company could be successful without English participation in its financing.

Creating a French railway network as a model for the rest of Europe and as "royal road" to Suez was the central proposal of the Mediterranean system. Radiating out from that network would be the lines of other nations, each having its functions and embodying the characteristics of its nation. Each of these national characters was essential to the moral and material welfare of humanity. They were to be complementary rather than competitive.

The Saint-Simonian idea of nationalism was not unlike the Mazzinian, except that the Mazzinian rested on spirit alone. The Saint-Simonian idea rested on spirit and on interest. The notion of a universe whose parts are so inextricably interconnected that war between them becomes unthinkable may be utopian. Or it may be that it has never been fully realized.

The notion of specific national characters reflected the Saint-Simonians' ideas of hierarchy and order as well as their efforts to resolve some of the political embarrassments of the 1830s. The movement generously identified with the causes of Belgium and Poland, and the desire to fight for them was rejected only with difficulty. The movement recognized the tyranny of the czars, predicted the decadence of the Austro-Hungarian Empire (and consequently saw in Prussia the hope of Germany), found the church's domination of Spain repellent, and was sympathetic to the unification of Italy.

All these liberal national causes offered what seemed an insoluble dilemma. It was insoluble until one recognized that the legitimate aims of liberty could be achieved through the nation and that the nation might be the product of the logic of economics. Railroads and banks would achieve what rebellions could not.

The opponents of such achievement might also be persuaded to give way before the onslaught of economic interest. Russia might cease persecution of the Poles, if it could be directed to the exploitation of its own vast and passive territories. German poetry and philosophy might accept a transfusion of material reality as it knit itself into a fabric of iron, coal, and rail. And so the examples continued across Europe, informed by that key idea of Saint-Simon that the fundamental law of nature was cooperation, not competition, that the parts exist to support and give life to the whole. Romantic and utopian, perhaps; consistent with the origins of the doctrine, certainly.

The Saint-Simonians were not totally reasonable men or women; had they been, nobody would have paid them any attention. They were, however, rooted in everyday existence, in the material conditions of reality. Their grandiloquent vision of the world was held together by the "relatively material" network of rails and the "relatively spiritual" network of banks. The vision was a relatively accurate projection of the economic structure of the industrial age to come. That the age that did come rejected Saint-Simonian vision was hardly the fault of the Saint-Simonians. Their Eden of foresight, planning, intelligence, industry, association, sexual equality, productive work, and international and intercontinental interpenetration was as much a possibility, an opportunity, a hope as what indeed did happen in the course of the nineteenth century.

Chevalier's *Système de la Méditerranée* offered, to use the famous and misleading description of the revolutions of 1848, a turning point in history when history failed to turn.[24] But like the revolutionaries of 1848 the Saint-Simonians would have their day. Ironically that Saint-Simonian day would dawn after the long penumbra of 1848 itself. Many of the hopes of the Saint-Simonians would have been dashed by 1848's permanent legacy of class suspicion, hatred, and distrust. Under the Second Empire, nonetheless, the Saint-Simonians would have their opportunity to lay the foundations of their new Eden. Among the most expert masons would be Emile and Isaac Pereire.

Throughout the crises of 1831–32 the Pereires had continued among the faithful. A recent study based on the personal papers of the family confirms what one could guess from more public sources. Emile thoroughly disapproved of Enfantin's "appeal to woman." Isaac for a time wished to join the apostolate at Ménilmontant. Emile passionately placed obstacles in Isaac's way and was, in the end, successful. But both brothers continued to act for the movement outside the constraints of Ménilmontant, pushed the "practical" doctrine, and fortified it by speculating and writing on the subjects which they knew best: finance and credit.[25]

The originality of the eventual creators of the Crédit Mobilier is not certain. Belgium had experimented with joint-stock banks designed to stimulate industry. The notions of Jacques Laffitte during the Restoration are cited as precedents for the Pereires' ideas about credit. This last suggestion is particularly interesting. It merely confirms the continuity of thought between Saint-Simon and the disciples. Laffitte had been one of those who supported Saint-Simon financially and who found him not without interest intellectually. Whether he saw Saint-Simon as one of a troop whose pens and good will might be useful in support of his political ambitions or whether Saint-Simon's ideas were of genuine interest to him is not clear. What is clear is that Saint-Simon had certainly intuited that the mobilization of capital was the essential condition for industrial take-off and that prevalent patterns of investment and credit were obstacles to that takeoff.

Laffitte, himself, had touted a *société commanditaire de l'industrie* commented on by Michel Rouen in *Le Producteur.* The Pereires were, consequently, familiar with that project. Bertrand Gille has suggested that among the earliest efforts to loosen credit were those of the Caisse Hypothécaire. The Rodrigueses, Enfantin, and Duveyrier had all been tied to that institution in important ways. Isaac Pereire was head accountant and Holstein was an employee of the Vital-Roux Bank, which had close associations with Laffitte. In short, the problems of credit constituted a persistent theme in the works of Saint-Simon, in the thought of his circle, and in the publications of the Saint-Simonians.[26]

During the last days on the rue Monsigny and at Ménilmontant a doctrine of credit to launch the Mediterranean system was increasingly a preoccupation of the Pereires. They had addressed themselves to three questions: taxation, finance, and credit. The three were obviously interrelated and were further related to the governing ideas of Saint-Simonianism: productivity and the amelioration of the lot of the poorest and most numerous class. It made sense, then, that the Pereires were opposed to indirect taxation, which weighed most heavily on those least able to bear it, and that they advocated an increase in inheritance tax proportionately greater on indirect successions than on direct. They argued, and were not alone, that an indirect tax consumed money that could be used as a stimulus for production.

From Saint-Simon on, the capital of the *oisif* had been targeted as the necessary source for investment in new industry, and, of course, the Saint-Simonians had argued for a revision of the institution of property. Increased inheritance tax and a levy on individual property to the benefit of "social" property were consistent stages on the way to that revision. Social property thus acquired would provide means for the projects of the most essential and creative enterprises. The need for freeing capital and finding ways in which it might be multiplied was the driving motive of Saint-Simonian financial thought. Taxes of the right kind administered correctly by the state would help the process; taxes of the wrong kind surrendered by the state would remove barriers to economic development.

The Pereires supported the suppression of the *octroi,* the local tax on goods entering cities. They advocated the issuance of bearer bonds in small denominations as a means of conscripting small amounts of capital from many investors and, incidentally, breaking the strangle hold of major banking houses on the bond market. They advocated the suppression of the Caisse d'Amortissement, which accumulated a sinking fund to redeem state bonds. It was a fund that paralyzed capital and was in itself useless. The Pereires, above all, advocated the use of the loan rather than the tax as the chief means of financing large-scale projects. The language was different, the sophistication greater, but the point of view was essentially that of Saint-Simon inviting savants, industrialists, and artists to gather at the tomb of Newton to open a subscription for the great works to be accomplished.[27]

At about the time the Ménilmontant experiment was, in its turn, crumbling, the Pereires were elaborating a scheme for a European Omnium, a company that would issue bonds to investors, the proceeds, in turn, to be invested in European bonds. The Omnium by its purchases and its balancing of occasional losses against regular gains would subsidize the European bond market. Investors would accept a lesser interest against a greater security. The difference would represent administrative cost and profit. There was in the proposition the germ of the idea of the mutual fund and in structure and scope the germ of the idea of the Crédit Mobilier.

When Enfantin had been pushed to take up the "practical" themes of the movement once again, he had complained that it was all very well to talk of greater enterprise but that no one was beating on the Saint-Simonian door to finance such projects. Where was the money to come from? The Pereires during 1831 and 1832 were working their way toward an answer to that question. They were the most obvious, but not the only, Saint-Simonians to be involved with it. Chevalier by 1833 would have broken with Enfantin but, as one of the most skeptical assessors of the Saint-Simonian myth admits, he would work closely with the Pereires well into the 1840s. Indeed, Chevalier was shortly to assume a position as the almost official academic economist of the July Monarchy and the Second Empire.[28]

So, while the night session in the gardens at Ménilmontant had been deteriorating intellectually and the anticipated martyrdom of the public trial loomed, the bankers, financial journalists, and engineers were reinvigorating the economic theory of Saint-Simonian doctrine. They were in the same gardens, while attending Saint-Simonian religious rituals, laying the groundwork for the industrial and financial revolutions that were to come. In their views on banking and taxation, as in their views on transportation, they were magnetized by the hope of an ever-richer world benefiting more and more people. It is in this sense that the Saint-Simonian capitalists can be understood, in their own peculiar way, as socialists. That their brand of socialism was utopian is far from clear; that their new Eden might one day be entered appeared in 1832 far from unlikely.

CHAPTER XII

THE FIRST JUDGMENT

"**B**ROËT MUST HAVE told you about our life of the past four months—a veritable life of the barracks or the convent. Reveilles, reviews, inspections, communal work in silence, absolute equality under the despotism of one, complete celibacy, more or less complete abstinence."[1] This was Gustave d'Eichthal's summation in October 1832 of the months preceding the trial that was to bring to an end the communal life of the Saint-Simonians. There were, in fact, to be two trials. The first was essentially political. The second, in some ways more worrisome because it questioned the personal honesty and integrity of members of the school, was to be a trial on charges of embezzlement.

The first trial, in a sense, presented no problem. Those charged would admit that they were teaching what they had been accused of teaching, that they were writing and printing what they thought, and that they were doing so to a band of followers of more than twenty people. They would argue, as they already had, that they were not an "association" but a religion and thus were entitled to meet and practice their faith freely. They would argue that the public morality they were said to have "outraged" was itself outrageous. They would point out that *Le Globe* itself had criticized an article by Charles Duveyrier for the same reasons for which the law had indicted him.

The strategy for the trial was to be one of obstruction and instruction. At the worst the members of the school saw it as a necessary and desirable descent into hell so that they might rise redeemed. The Christian analogies were very much present in their minds. When Emile Barrault urged Enfantin to leave France, Enfantin replied that the government "owed" him prison. After the trial, in August, Isaac Pereire wrote: "Finally the immortal judgment comes. Like Jesus you have been condemned and will be crucified."[2]

One senses a certain shakiness in the group as the members realized that they might very well be judged guilty of crimes and punished for them. When Michel Chevalier argued in June with the local police commissioner (who bore the name of a more famous later inspector of police— Maigret) that the Saint-Simonians were a body of residents at Ménilmontant enjoying the right to receive their friends, he was also careful to list the occupations and professions of those residents. Duveyrier and d'Eichthal would make it clear at the trial that they were the sons of *rich* men. As the trial came closer, however, the spirits of the group picked up. They readied themselves for battle, and in the fray they acquitted themselves well.[3]

The trial became, in effect, the last of the Saint-Simonian sermons. The judge, whose impartiality does not shine from the pages of the transcript, later commented that although the group was dangerous to society, this did not diminish, in his eyes, the vigor of its ideas or the ardor with which they were presented and defended.

The subject of the second trial was inevitably present at the first. In theory it was not to be discussed, although allusions to the finances of the group and assumptions as to its motives were frequent. The danger was that if a jury concluded that Saint-Simonianism was as crooked as it was said to be crazy, the trial's outcome might be very harsh indeed. It was characteristic of the Saint-Simonians that they might have spent their money as "the poor spend theirs," but they were also capable of accounting for every penny of it. The group had received some support from the Court of Versailles when the judge who overturned Robinet's will (of which Enfantin had been beneficiary for the Saint-Simonians) specifically rejected the charge of undue influence raised by Robinet's family.[4]

The ways in which the defendants would deal with the accusations made against them had been worked out well before the trial began. As early as April, Enfantin had, on the first page of *Le Globe,* instructed Chevalier to find out all he could about those who would judge him. "I want to know their *life,*" he proclaimed in something like a threat.[5]

At 7:30 A.M. on August 27, "a very fine day," the Ménilmontant household, garbed in the variously prescribed shades of red, white, and blue, breakfasted. At 7:45 Chevalier gave the order to march. To the strains of *Salut* (words by Rousseau, music by Felicien David)—"Hail Father, / Jesus told his disciples to watch and they slept / You told us to work and we will"—the group set forth.

Three members led, followed by two rows of twelve flanking Enfantin who was in turn followed by Aglaë Saint-Hilaire, Cécile Fournel, and the others accused: Duveyrier, Chevalier, and Barrault. Behind them came the 140 other members of the group, led by Henri Fournel, who had been called as witnesses. Enfantin wore a specially designed light blue suit that was open across the chest so that "Le Père" embroidered on his shirt could be seen. His long hair flowed behind and his full beard before. He had changed much from the rather soft dandy of the earlier portraits. With due consideration given to the romanticizing of his visage, he now had the look of a mature prophet.

The procession made its way down the rue Ménilmontant to the rue Saint-Maur, the rue du Temple, and, by streets now gone, to the place des

215

Grêves, the quai aux Fleurs, and the Palais de Justice on the Ile de la Cité. It arrived at nine o'clock, followed and surrounded by an "immense crowd." Eleven o'clock had sounded in the *salle des pas perdus* before the case was called. The courtroom was filled with fashionable women and a number of political figures. The liberals, although often attacked by the Saint-Simonians, had to see in the case an infringement of freedom of the press and of religion. Casimir Périer himself had attacked Article 291 as outworn and irrelevant. In addition, the touch of scandal, the promise of salacious revelations, had made the Saint-Simonian trial the event at which one wished to be seen, quite literally the cause célèbre of the day.[6]

Drama was quick to develop. One cannot escape seeing the scene in terms of Daumier: a judge, fussy, irritable, apparently ill disposed; a prosecutor, superb, accusing, insinuating, and sarcastic, appealing to the prejudices of the jury and assuming an agreement of all reasonable men on the moral or immoral issues raised by the Saint-Simonians. The Saint-Simonians themselves displayed more than a little fright but also—young, handsome, brilliantly costumed—more than a little determination.

Formalities over, the judge asked Enfantin to name his advocate. Enfantin replied that he had none. His counsel? "These two ladies" (Aglaë and Cécile). "It is impossible. It is singular. You cannot have counsel of the feminine sex." "The questions we deal with concern women." "Impossible. The ladies must be removed." "Let it be noted that the court refuses women as counsel."[7]

From the first moments the tone was set. The court was on trial; the court was an oppressor of women. The issues of women, of morality, of male-female relations were the focus of the accusations against the Saint-Simonians. Their tactic was to demonstrate that the criminality was not theirs, but that of their accusers. When the time came to swear in witnesses, Moïse Retouret affirmed that the taking of an oath was a religious act and that he would take the oath only with the permission of the father. Turning to Enfantin he asked permission to take the oath. Enfantin refused it. Thirty others followed suit. The court ruled that they must take the oath in the prescribed form if they were to testify. Among the lawyers present there was a "sensation." Apparently the law did permit the taking of the oath "before God and man," as the Saint-Simonians wished.[8]

At long last came the presentation of the case by De la Palme, the prosecutor. He outlined the ideas of Saint-Simon. He described the Saint-Simonians as outside society and outside the law. He asserted that apart from the ridiculous there was also the dangerous in their ideas. Saint-Simonians attacked property and inheritance, incited to rebellion, and preached the equality of sexes, the community of goods and persons.

"The Saint-Simonians say, 'We profess a faith, the law protects religion, it should protect us.' But religion is the adoration of God, faith in the

216

future, rituals, ceremonies. The distinctive character of religion, gentle-men, is that it exercises no action on the material world. Can you call that a religion which acts against the social order? We who are the great society come to demand the dissolution of [this] small society."[9]

It was a revealing argument and made the Saint-Simonians' point better than they could have done it themselves. De la Palme further found him-self embarrassed when he read a letter of Cécile Fournel's declaring that she had freed herself from Saint-Simonian illusions. She rose protesting that the letter no longer reflected her views. She was silenced by the judge.[10] But once again the impression of a determination to get through a nasty business quickly was inescapable.

De la Palme's most telling shot was the reading of Duveyrier's article on women. "One will see men and women whose love would be as a divine banquet increasing in magnificence with the number and choice of their guests." When he had finished it was after 2 P.M. The trial was adjourned, and it reassembled at 3:00.[11]

Then came the turn of Olinde Rodrigues and his brother-in-law Baud, who had converted Robinet to Saint-Simonianism. Once again the specter of embezzlement appeared. Rodrigues was careful to separate himself from the other accused and to draw the line of his responsibilities at the point when he had refused to follow Enfantin. He read from Saint-Simon's *Le Nouveau Christianisme* to establish the religious character of the movement. He pointed out that the group had met for four years with-out exciting official interest. *Le Globe* had been printed in issues of three to four thousand copies, distributed free, and read by perhaps four times as many readers. Why were they *now* accused? It did not seem rational.[12]

Rodrigues was followed by Léon Simon, who was, in fact, to act as counsel for the defense. He argued that the moral susceptibility of the century was, at best, murky. There was no correspondence between theory and practice. Nothing equaled the indecency and the cynicism of the critics of Saint-Simonianism. If one looked about in society, amorous intrigue was the vital force in salon life. Society trafficked in the beauty and money of young girls. The theater educated young people in the duperies of love: "We are accused because we are feared. You are incom-petent to judge us."[13]

The Saint-Simonians were accused of begging for money. Didn't every-body else? The Saint-Simonians had been suspected of having a hand in the riots at Lyons during 1831. But Simon could point out with perfect justice that *Le Globe* and its correspondence editor, Isaac Pereire, had in-structed the Saint-Simonians at Lyons to discourage such outbreaks. They were to explain to the workers that their masters were forced by the grind-ing laws of competition to exploit them; they could not help themselves. The workers should express compassion and not resort to social violence.

The Saint-Simonians preached peace, not war, and could prove it. Their fundamental view was of a God who was the connectedness of things. Competition and egoism had their necessary consequences; masters and workers were equally victims of a vicious system.

By six o'clock Simon was exhausted and requested a recess. The president of the court commented, "There will be little to say after you." Simon replied, "I have merely touched on the major questions; others will deepen them."[14]

In the evening at 8:00 it was the turn of Chevalier, accused of outrages against public morality. Like Simon he argued that public morality was itself outrageous. In response to De la Palme he asserted that all religions were political, economic, and social. "The kingdom of France is a kingdom made by bishops." A government that licensed prostitution was ill-placed to argue the immorality of its citizens. The article by Duveyrier on women might well seem outrageous, but the fathers of the Saint-Simonian school had publicly corrected its import. The words "banquet of love" were perhaps ill chosen, but they did not constitute an injunction; they were, rather, a speculation.[15]

Chevalier went on to review the history of the movement from its beginnings in the salon of the marquis de Lafayette, the untouchable hero of the two worlds and of the July Monarchy in particular.[16] He outlined his work at *Le Globe* and the respectability of the retreat to Ménilmontant. He read long extracts from his writings, including passages from the *Système de la Méditerranée*. Finally the president interrupted: "You are giving a course in Political Economy. You've been talking for two hours." Enfantin broke in, accusing the court of cowardice: "Let him speak. We have been here eight hours, we have known as many months of defamation."[17]

Chevalier continued with a discussion on the necessity of the suppression of indirect taxation. When the court once again manifested its impatience, Enfantin instructed Chevalier to finish. He was followed, briefly, by Lambert, Rogé Auguste Chevalier, and the reading of a deposition, confirming the probity and sincerity of the Saint-Simonians, offered by Baron d'Eichthal, Gustave's father.

Duveyrier then rose in his own defense. It was the most brilliant and most forceful argument to be heard and, even more than the others, was an indictment of contemporary society. Simon in his remarks had defined God as "the connectedness of things." Duveyrier most dramatically and explicitly made clear the connections between sex, society, money, and property between the exploitation of women and that of workers. He admitted that "banquet" had been a poor word to describe future sexual relationships, but he pointed out that the French had already abandoned the church for the theater. "The government gives more to the Opera than to the Bishops." This was true: the last budget had allotted a million francs to the opera and 800,000 francs to the bishops. The matter had been much discussed in the press.

"What is the Opera" but a vast reservoir of powerful sensual excitement? Duveyrier asserted that a third of the children born in France were illegitimate and that there were 35,000 prostitutes in Paris. "Not long ago under the same roof where there slept public women, there also slept the queen and her young family." The reference was to the Palais Royal, home and real-estate speculation of the Orléans family, whose gardens and galleries were centers of Parisian vice.

Duveyrier accused official moralists of admitting that treason and discord troubled half of France's households; that half the daughters of the people "are seduced, prostituted, poisoned"; and that the race "bastardizes and destroys itself with shameful maladies." But, the moralists say, "We do have a respect for principles."[18]

Duveyrier continued:

I tell you in the sincerity of my heart, no matter how far from your superb and mystic principle our morality seems to you, if, by it, we destroy the vices of your colleges, diminish by a quarter your adulteries, eliminate illegitimacy and the orphans of living fathers, lift the weight of debauchery and sickness that weighs on public women . . . I would declare a victory more glorious than any of those of the Empire.[19]

"Your defense aggravates your cause," the judge interrupted. "Please don't interrupt" was the quick response.

"We are told that God condemns us. No, God has not condemned the earth and the race of men to return to chaos, but he has made of their alliance a creation of infinite and inexhaustible wealth. . . . I have judged the case."

Barrault followed: "Everybody in this great Babylon drinks the wine of a furious prostitution."

It was too much for the judge: "The defense degenerates into scandal." The session was ended at 11:30. A hundred people accompanied the accused on the long journey, this time uphill, back to Ménilmontant and to bed. The next day's departure was set for 6:45 to meet a 9:30 session.[20]

On the trial's second day—foggy, rainy, and in every way less electric than the first—Enfantin opened the proceedings. The enthusiasm, sincerity, and vigor of the young disciples who had spoken on the first day and the logic and even the justice of their attacks had been telling and embarrassing for the court. Enfantin's own approach to the proceedings, while consistent with that of the others, had elements of the comic in it. One can appreciate the evident irritation of the president.

Enfantin rose slowly to his feet when called and gazed wordlessly about him for a very long time. The president asked if he needed time to collect himself. Enfantin replied, "I don't defend or justify. I teach by means of my regard." There were rustlings in the courtroom.

"You don't comprehend," he said, with more gazing about the courtroom. "The court displays flagrant incompetence." The president again suggested that Enfantin take time to pull himself together. "No, I need to see and be seen. I require that [the audience] feel the importance of the flesh, that their senses feel my looks. I reveal all my thought in my face. I want specially to call beautiful bodies to a better life, to save them from anathema."[21]

"We are not here to await the result of your contemplations," the judge said, suspending the session. When it resumed, Enfantin took up the theme of the connection between workers' misery, unproductive wealth, prostitution, and adultery. "We hope for the coming of a female Messiah. I am her precursor. I am what Saint John was for Christ."

Enfantin's earlier and not markedly successful performance had been an effort to introduce the notion of the priest manifestly, by his appearance, chosen for the role. He had great faith in his "calm" and had never doubted his *"beauté."* The rehabilitation of the flesh was a doctrine that celebrated the senses and made much of beauty. For Enfantin, at least, truth was beauty and beauty, truth. How to square this view with the accusations of his disciples about the bourgeois glorification of the ball, the opera, prostitution, and adultery? The whole point of the Saint-Simonian teaching was that the life of the senses should first be recognized and admitted, then organized and directed to avoid the evident social evils that had hitherto attended it.

D'Eichthal followed Enfantin with an exegesis on the family and the ways in which the "old" family tyrannized over its young. Chevalier returned to the theme of bourgeois hypocrisy in sexual matters: "How many men out of a hundred having arrived at the thirtieth year and having had good luck sexually do not boast of it?"[22]

The proceedings closed with Enfantin's declaration that he had neither toyed with people nor speculated on religion, and at 3:30 the jury retired. By six o'clock the verdict was in. All the accused were found guilty on all counts. The justice of the Saint-Simonians' accusations of incompetence was at once evident in the verdict. Duveyrier somewhat plaintively pointed out that he had just been found guilty of crimes of which he had not been accused. Again there was a "sensation" in the courtroom. The magistrates retired for yet another hour and returned to deliver sentence.[23]

Enfantin, Duveyrier, and Chevalier were sentenced to a year in prison and fines of one hundred francs each. Rodrigues and Barrault were fined fifty francs. The Saint-Simonian society was declared dissolved. The condemned, once again accompanied by a crowd, returned to Ménilmontant, where present and future problems would have to be faced quickly.

This first judgment had been a curious one. The sentences were not heavy, the fines a token; it would not be difficult to substitute the more agreeable *maison de santé* (clinic) for prison by pleading ill health. Duveyrier and, later, Chevalier would elect to do so. What had been the point of it all?

The July Monarchy, newly established and dubiously legitimate, had been as suspicious of plots as had the Restoration. Social and economic disorder frightened it perhaps more than it had frightened the preceding regime. The Saint-Simonian mission to Lyons in the spring of 1831, led by Jean Reynaud and Pierre Leroux, had known a great success. Simon could assert that the official line of the school had been the maintenance of social order, but the fact was that Reynaud and Leroux had raised passions with their analysis of contemporary society.[24] It was an analysis all too easily confirmed by the experience of the silk workers.

Saint-Simonian notions and influence would persist in France's "Birmingham" until at least 1848. The attacks on property did not endear the school to the bourgeois monarchy. A series of commentaries on the evils of property as evidenced in the lawsuits over the inheritance of a royal prince may have offended royalty itself. But these were not, in theory, issues at the trial. Holding meetings of more than twenty people might conceivably be dangerous. It is hard to believe that *le pouvoir* was seriously shocked by Saint-Simonian advocacy of free love. That advocacy did, however, permit power to adopt a high moral tone in prosecuting a troublesome sect that was attracting large and potentially troublesome working-class audiences.[25]

The Saint-Simonians were certainly subversive of the existing social order, but they were not yet dangerous. Prosecution had first been thought of before the occasion for scandal cited in the indictment. The first descent on the rue Monsigny took place a little over a week after the appearance in print of the article on women. On that occasion the accounts and the correspondence were seized. It was obviously a fishing expedition in which no fish were caught.[26] But the indictment remained.

The matter was delicate. An end to Saint-Simonian activities was desired, but the Saint-Simonians had to be treated gently. They were allied to persons who were natural supporters of the regime. Lafayette and Bazard had been close. Enfantin's cousin was a general, Duveyrier's father a peer and a banker, the Talabots' father a judge, and d'Eichthal's father and brother bankers. Laffitte, a founder of the new order, had been benevolently disposed toward Saint-Simon and had been a subscriber to Saint-Simonian projects. The Pereires were beginning their all-important relationship with that all-important personage, Baron James de Rothschild.

Henri Fournel had administered what was probably the most important industrial complex in France. The Saint-Simonians must be put in their place, but that place must be sufficiently large for maneuver. Once chastised they might return to public favor. Chevalier, indeed, went from the *maison de santé* to a governmental mission in the United States and thereafter to a chair of political economy at the Collège de France. His only training for such a post had been in the school of Saint-Simon.

From the government's point of view Saint-Simonianism had been dealt with as a potential source of trouble, and the Saint-Simonians had been rather lightly slapped on the wrist. Their characters were not permanently stained, and no impediments to their careers were envisaged. Enfantin's friend Arlès-Dufour was, for example, reasonably certain of obtaining a subprefecture for him on his return from Egypt. Not glorious, but certainly respectable.

The second trial, in October, confirmed these consequences of the first. Unlike the first, it was a matter of twenty minutes. The government had maintained that the "Saint-Simonian loan" was a fraudulent means of obtaining money for the movement. At the point when Bazard withdrew but Rodrigues had not yet done so, the school proposed a sort of bond issue on which it would pay interest guaranteeing the capital with the funds and property of a Saint-Simonian association. The government maintained that there were obligations of 450,000 francs and no resources.

It was a weak case. There were too many Saint-Simonian financiers to permit this particular trap to snap. They were able to show that they had paid interest, that they did hold property in excess of obligations, although it was property whose worth could not immediately be realized. Enfantin, for example, could not dispose of his own property until after the death of his mother. It was shown that the Petits, mother and son, had contributed 94,000 francs, Fournel 80,000, d'Eichthal 50,000, and Enfantin 75,000—clearly these were not thieves robbing themselves.[27]

The judges this time were competent, at least in matters of finance, and acquitted the Saint-Simonians of the charges of fraud and embezzlement without any fines or expenses. Again, the stick was followed by the carrot. The verdict was greeted enthusiastically by crowds at the place du Châtelet. The assembled school had dinner at the Veau Qui Tette. Later they went to the Opéra. This triumph of October 19 did something to palliate the August verdict. It left the Saint-Simonians with reputations as honest men and trustworthy businessmen. It did nothing, however, to change the circumstances of Enfantin and Chevalier, who could expect to be in prison by Christmas. Nor did it erase the problems that the dissolution of the school inevitably presented for the group as a whole and for the individuals who were its constituents.[28]

DURING the six weeks between the first and second trials life continued at Ménilmontant, but there is not much in the *Archives* about this period of depression and dissolution. D'Eichthal's letter about the life of barracks and convent summed up the prevailing mood. The group held firm until late October and went out into Paris on October 22 in costume expressing a kind of defiance of its enemies. After that, the members began to doff the habit of Saint-Simonians and go away. D'Eichthal had his famous "night," found himself "clear in his ideas," and announced his determination to leave. Enfantin had not yet seen his own course clearly and warned d'Eichthal that in "fleeing" his "paternity and our fraternity you must suffer and weep."[29] But it was Enfantin himself who was to suffer and weep. Duveyrier followed d'Eichthal, along with Auguste Chevalier, Simon, and Lambert. In early December Enfantin was undergoing a *"crise,"* as he wrote later to Aglaë Saint-Hilaire, like that of 1827. "But the coffer is strong despite the nails pounded in and wrenched from it. I am a little tired of being both hammer and claw."[30] As in 1827 one has only hints of tears, tremblings, a worsened handwriting (it was surely one of the very worst hands of the nineteenth century), and the testimony of Michel Chevalier, who stayed on. "I have seen the pain of the Father and felt it myself."[31]

There can be no doubt that at this period Enfantin was experiencing an agony for which there could be no cure. There was, indeed, no vocabulary to describe it adequately. He had trembled on the brink of realizations that would not be commonplaces for another hundred years. The role of sexuality in human affairs, the possibility of a "talking cure" for those afflicted by its complications, the role he as "priest" might play in such a cure, and the extraordinary magnetism he exercised over the faithful added up to a burden whose weight he had not fully realized until this moment of dissolution. He had known an extraordinary power over others, he had enjoyed using it, and he had used it without fully understanding it. Enfantin had also fallen victim to his own power, and, faced now with its erosion and certain disappearance, he felt himself alone and afraid. The death of his brother had afflicted him in much the same way. In the present case, as in that, the affliction was deepened by a sense of guilt.

If his own situation was terrifying, Enfantin had soon to recognize that the situation of those who had followed him was even more so. The followers found themselves suddenly without direction, purpose, and, worst, without leadership. They had invested so heavily in Enfantin that they could not believe the return on the investment would ever cease. Many of the inner group were hardly capable by 1832 of organizing their lives without him. Michel Chevalier could still write to Arlés-Dufour in October, before his imprisonment, that "the retreat is finished, we are going to flood the world," and to his friend Brisbane:

During the theoretical period we descended from high places step by step, and at each step we lost some of ours. We left them, despite ourselves, having exhausted and uprooted them. . . . During the practical epoch we will scale a mountain step by step; at each step we will lose some, but gain more.[32]

But Chevalier alone was still sheltered under the wing of the father whose interlocutor and defender he was against the onslaughts of all the rest. The resolution, or lack of it, in the Enfantin-Chevalier relationship during the coming months was a paradigm for all the other Saint-Simonian relationships.

It was not only those of the inner group who were left spiritually destitute. There were the scores, hundreds, even thousands who had listened with fascination and understanding to the Saint-Simonian preachings, including the workers who had founded communal houses and the women in whom an urgent feminism had been wakened by the Saint-Simonian message. Many of these, to be sure, would seek and find other prophets, but two years later Aglaë Saint-Hilaire spoke of trying to do something for and with the *"prolétaires"* of Paris. In Lyons, Avignon, Rouen, Toulon, and scores of other towns and villages across France a few of the faithful would keep alive the meaning of Saint-Simonian ideals and Saint-Simonian brotherhood. Dr. Guépin at Nantes, for example, emerges as a formative influence in the life of René Waldeck-Rousseau, the prime minister whose task it would be to close the Dreyfus case some seventy years later.[33]

Some awareness of this side of the coin, the immense responsibility he had assumed, must have been borne in on Enfantin during his crisis of November and December 1832. His instincts and intuitions were probably both selfish and sound. He had resisted the first departures, viewing them almost as betrayals. But quite soon his persistent theme was that the autocratic period was over. No order would be given. Each must find his or her own way. He refused after his entry into the Sainte-Pélagie prison to read most letters or to receive visits. He had arrived at a clear understanding that the dependence of others on him was unhealthy and destructive and that it must end. The tragedy was that he did not have a technique for ending these relationships in a way that would be comforting or constructive for those involved. The followers' reward for their love, their submission, their conviction, and their desire to serve was, they had to feel, simple rejection.[34]

Often in later years, as at the time of the Bazard schism, people would speak of Enfantin as one who had "broken" men (and women) "brutally." He did not know how to accomplish the act otherwise. Gustave d'Eichthal would spend the rest of an otherwise interesting and productive life, as his papers testify, in turning round the Enfantinian relationship in his mind and in assuming Saint-Simonian obligations expensive in terms of time and money. The Fournels before, during, and after Ménilmontant were tortured by the relationship. Enfantin said of Cécile:

Cécile had only one thing to do, to say how she loves, to recount her life. If she doesn't understand, I'm sorry, but I don't know what to do about it. I believe that the manner in which Cécile loves and wishes to be loved is one of the most important chapters of the female human heart. I have never known Cecile entirely. One night I thought I did, but it was a dream of which I have only a memory.[35]

Of Henri, Enfantin said, "Fournel is dishonest. I think unfortunately all this takes its source in an affection to which he wishes to give a character that it *cannot have,* and the anguish he feels as a result." The comments are ambiguous, but they underline the character of all the Saint-Simonian relationships. Enfantin's followers had given, told, revealed everything. They were particularly vulnerable. They had put their most intense emotions at his disposal and had offered him the last vestiges of their privacy. What would happen now?

Fournel, who claimed to have been the first source for the idea of the Mediterranean system, would play a key role both in the first efforts to accomplish a Suez Canal and in the Egyptian expedition that was to be Enfantin's escape route from prison back to respectability. The two men would be embroiled there. In later years Fournel would believe his career as a state engineer had been short-circuited because of his Saint-Simonian past. The brilliant, wealthy, successful, loving Henri Fournel of the 1820s became the embittered middle-level civil servant of the 1850s and tended to blame Enfantin for the result.[36]

There were other cases equally complicated, some even more pathetic. Claire Demar and her lover, Dessessarts, who had both been part of the movement, committed suicide shortly after the trial. Saint-Simonianism was blamed. Alexis Petit, who still had an important part in the movement, flirted with madness. The son of the minister of finance, Humann, had to be removed from Ménilmontant to a hospital for the insane.

Some of the stories were happier. Enfantin wrote that he had no worries about Duveyrier, "although the poor Hoart must suffer terribly."[37] Those who had kept one foot in the world like the Pereires and the surviving Talabots could absorb the Saint-Simonian experience and use it to great advantage. The euphoric Barrault would conceive the maddest and most endearing of Saint-Simonian schemes. He would lead the "Compagnons de la femme" across seas, deserts, and mountains in search of the female Messiah, scandalizing a sultan, attempting to convert the young Garibaldi, and awakening the sympathy of Lamartine, who found "the debris" of the Saint-Simonians at Smyrna—complete with piano![38]

As the prison gate closed on him, Enfantin confessed that his major concern was to eclipse himself completely. He and Michel Chevalier had been seized by a delicious *farniente,* troubled in Enfantin's case only by a rheumatic knee acquired while gardening at Ménilmontant.[39] On the night before the entry into prison there was a gathering at Ménilmontant, during which Enfantin was particularly moved by the presence of women "speaking the language of our faith." It was "the most extraordinary communion we have had."[40]

Prison itself was not, for the privileged, a very terrible place. Sainte-Pélagie was on or near the site of the present Paris Mosque. The place du Puits de l'Ermite, adjoining it, retains something of the air it must have had in the 1830s; with severe walls, irregular roof lines, and a rather pleasant, leafy square sequestered from busy streets around it, it is still strangely quiet for modern-day Paris. The Saint-Simonians would undoubtedly have seen some great symbol of the wedding of West and East in the transformation of the site from liberal bourgeois penitentiary to Islamic mosque.

With money one could arrange to live quite comfortably. Enfantin amused himself by executing an engineer's drawing of his cell. On the corridor side were two chairs, an elegant bureau, a mirror, and a shelf with a cigar box and carafe on it. On the wall was a map of Paris. Opposite was a sort of service wall with a pail, broom, woodpile, and wood stove. Along the third wall was Enfantin's cot, mounted very high, a water container with spigot, a wash stand, and table and chairs. A shelf ran the length of the wall, holding at one end the Saint-Simonian *Archives* and at the other, dishes. The fourth side was a kind of parlor with two large double windows, chairs, and a secretary topped by a lamp.

The details of the drawing make it clear that the furniture was of high quality; the lines are Empire, the bureau and secretary are decorated with brasswork sphinxes, and the chairs are upholstered. Food came from a nearby *estaminet* and was not, apparently, very good. Prisoners were expected to care for their rooms and to exercise in the courtyard. Chevalier and Enfantin apparently had free access to each other's rooms and to a common room, which was arranged like a café. There they preached Saint-Simonian ideas to their fellow prisoners and treated them to cognac and tobacco.[41]

Imprisonment began pleasantly enough. Chevalier's resolution of his own dilemma had been to become the chief servant and sole aide of Enfantin. It was he who would write explaining that "for the moment the Father is a chief without a people [and] . . . the family a family without a head. The Father gives no new orders." It was he who was interpreter to the outside world and most involved with it. For Chevalier it must have been an agreeable sensation to be in sole possession of the Father. The life of the brotherhood had not been without its rivalries and jealousies. Chevalier and d'Eichthal had on the whole disliked, distrusted, and envied each other. The notions of hierarchy and the elevations in rank, while publicly a subject of rejoicing, produced bitterness and hurt feelings. Chevalier now appeared to have triumphed in his relationship with Enfantin and was, initially, happy with the situation.[42]

Enfantin himself did write letters to those who asked nothing of him and to those of whom he asked something. Saint-Hilaire, as family friend and keeper, more or less, of Enfantin's father, was the most favored correspondent. What to do with Ménilmontant was a preoccupation, and Enfantin shared his worries about a number of the disciples as she fed information to him.

On one subject Enfantin was intransigent. At various points in his life, from 1827 on, friends and family would try to persuade him to marry Adèle Morlane. If there was any general criticism of the father by his "children" it was that he had treated her badly. Their son had been legitimized, but this respectable lady suffered much from her status. Saint-Hilaire suggested that now might be the time to start a new and more regular life. Enfantin would have none of it; this was not the new direction he must take.[43]

What the new direction would be was puzzling, but there would presumably be time to think about it in prison. As the sense of relief that Chevalier and Enfantin felt on entering prison wore off, it was Michel himself who became Enfantin's major preoccupation. It was not at all surprising that prison could take on the allure of a rest cure. Given the activity, the variety of experiences, the intensity of emotion, the friendships made and broken, the revelation absorbed and rejected, and the public acclaim and scorn of the last five years, it is not surprising that in the uneventful world of prison Enfantin quickly reestablished himself. His insatiable curiosity, his need to penetrate the minds of others, his talent for manipulation, and the demands of his not inconsiderable ego were soon awake.

Sometime in February of 1833 Enfantin launched his attack. Why was Chevalier there? Did he want to be, or did he think he *ought* to be? Michel "is as strong as he is weak. I don't know what he has in his soul," an intolerable state of affairs for Enfantin. By mid-March, "We communicate only at meals and there speak as much of the beans and lentils as of anything. We sleep at 10, are up at 7, clean the room, dress—all this takes time. At 10 we lunch, stroll, smoke, see people, read the papers. We make dinner, dine, walk in the court, receive the *prolétaires*. If it has its ennuis, it also has its charms." This was the state of affairs on March 13. On March 17 Enfantin again wrote to Saint-Hilaire: "I have been looking for a long time for a solution for Michel. I don't yet find it."[44]

Later on that day the solution arrived. Enfantin never put down in writing what exactly transpired, nor apparently did Chevalier. There was a confrontation of some sort. Chevalier refused to dine with Enfantin and his companions. He apparently announced his separation from the Father and paced back and forth between his cell and Enfantin's. "Would Enfantin write him?" "No." All that Enfantin said was that "the thunderclap of the 17th was most remarkable."[45]

A week later, decisions having been made, relations had calmed somewhat. "Michel is much better, and I, too; the terrible habit of looking at each other was killing; we ended by emptying ourselves of our feelings with ever-significant looks or of submerging them with ever-fearful ones. Now each is at home, each has his rights—to get there we've had a hard month. I made poor Michel suffer. All terminated with the storm of the 17th."[46]

The separation took place in stages over the next six weeks; each stage was marked by a significant symbol. On March 17 Chevalier decided to request a transfer to a clinic, abandoning his sacrifice of prison for Enfantin's sake. On April 7 he shaved the beard that the apostles had adopted as an additional sign of brotherhood. On the 8th he appeared in correct bourgeois clothing. On May 5 Chevalier changed rooms, and shortly thereafter he left prison.[47]

News of the break spread quickly among those outside the prison walls. It had for them much the same significance as for other, later faithful a break between Marx and Engels might have had. To one letter of protest Enfantin explained that it was almost in "brutalizing" the religious faith of Chevalier that "I have made him understand." The Œuvres note simply that Chevalier understood the need for his "liberation" only after "long and painful" efforts and that Enfantin had undertaken a "conscious cutting of the cord linking himself and his disciples."[48]

And what did Chevalier have to say? There is a brouillon,[49] not signed but almost certainly Chevalier's, in the d'Eichthal manuscripts. In the "old" world, he tells us, "I found benevolence everywhere, intimacy nowhere. Out of Saint-Simonianism I never got more than a sweet and cordial benevolence." In the "middle of the conscientious, but deceiving, limits of the rue Monsigny, at the breast of the religious comradeship of Ménilmontant, among all these supposed brotherhoods," he was never fully at ease. "Sainte-Pélagie revealed my isolation." The Eygptian project, already in the works, made no sense to Chevalier; he felt himself cut off from the general movement. He not only was not ready to practice his Saint-Simonianism, he no longer knew what it was.

In June, Chevalier summed up the entire incident by saying:

We love each other sincerely, despite all. We are full of gratitude for the past whatever may be the imperfections that have marked it. It is he [Enfantin] who developed us and made us men; but it is completely useless to see him again. We would give each other a sad handshake in separating ourselves till a date that no one knows.[50]

In fact, although their paths were to cross frequently in the years to come and their worlds of friendship and professional activity overlapped at many points, there was always from this time on a certain discomfort in the relations of the two men. Chevalier in the end would appear to be the more important figure of his time; to have collected the fruits of the seeds sown by Enfantin. Enfantin could not preserve himself from a certain bitterness on this score.

This "brutalizing" of Michel Chevalier is the case of which we know most, although we do not know nearly enough. Something like it touched the relationships of all the Saint-Simonians with their father. The point is not, however, that Enfantin was cruel or that others suffered from his cruelty. He was, and they did. The point is that Enfantin drove from his side those who depended on him. His was a conscious program directed to a necessary end: the liberation of those whom he had perhaps less consciously enslaved.

Chevalier's story has considerable importance for an understanding of Saint-Simonianism. After many of the actors in the Saint-Simonian drama had become figures of the first importance in French national life, their earlier notoriety required explanation. The usual explanation for those embarrassed by it (and many were not) was that they had been for a moment attracted by Saint-Simonian idealism but, in the face of Enfantin's follies, the sound and practical men had left the movement. The thrust of the argument was that, in consequence, the great achievements of these sound and practical men had no connection with their Saint-Simonian past. The corollary was that Saint-Simonianism had no real importance in the social and economic development of nineteenth-century France.

The facts, as the cases of Chevalier and several others illustrate, were quite different. It was not the practical men who left Enfantin. It was Enfantin who, in the interests of their psychic safety, drove them from him. Indeed it was the practical men who stayed closest to him for the longest time: Chevalier, the Pereires, Fournel, Paulin Talabot, Arlès-Dufour, and Lambert, to name only the most prominent. One has to conclude that through all the complexities of Enfantin's personality there ran a thread of good sense and decency, sometimes tangled with threads of another kind, which held the fabric together. If Enfantin sometimes looked crazy, he was most often crazy like a fox.

ENFANTIN'S capacity to come out at the right place by whatever tortuous means became clear in the spring of 1833. Some time before the break with Chevalier news had reached France that the khedive of Egypt was looking for engineers to assist him in the creation of considerable public works. Among these projects was a dam at Aswan, the stone for which he proposed to obtain by demolition of the pyramids. It was a project for which Saint-Simonians could feel sympathy. In his great days as a *brasseur d'affaires* during the Directory, Saint-Simon had flirted with the idea of stripping the roof of Notre Dame de Paris for its lead. Later on the Pereires thought it would be nice to turn the Church of the Madeleine into a railway station in the heart of Paris for their Paris–Saint-Germain line. The pyramids were saved by, among others, the nearly apoplectic protest of Mimaut, the French consul at Alexandria.[51] But the pasha's projects remained.

Enfantin urged Alexis Petit to find out if Fournel could be attracted to an Egyptian expedition; Chevalier's Mediterranean system seemed trivial to him now. "We could offer Mehemet Ali five hundred workers led by fifty men, half of them from the Ecole Polytechnique."[52] For the moment Enfantin should not be directly involved in the project. Fournel accepted the idea. It was clear in his mind and in Enfantin's that the real object was to gain the confidence of Mehemet Ali and to persuade him to authorize the building of a Suez Canal.

Suez, or the hope of it, was the perfect "out" for Enfantin and the perfect solution for all those who had urged the rebirth of the economic themes of Saint-Simonianism. Here was a project of practical engineering to be sponsored by political authority. Its objects coincided with Saint-Simonian theory and offered a place for the erstwhile Saint-Simonian leader. The place itself was consonant with his own estimate of his dignity; it had the advantage of removing him from a France that would not quite know what to do with him once he was released from prison.

Fournel in a letter to Arlès-Dufour published in a brochure in August made much of this scheme clear. He foresaw an international cooperative effort. England would have to aid in the making of Suez "in her own interest, of course"; Asia and Europe would be put in communion with each other.[53] What had only a year before seemed a chimera now could be thought of as an imminent reality. The last great achievement envisaged by the Mediterranean system might now be the first.

Before the project could be brought to full life, however, something had to be done about Sainte-Pélagie. In April a law had been passed recognizing the religious character of the Saint-Simonian movement. After the fact it removed one of the accusations that had been responsible for the convictions of Enfantin and his fellows. Cécile Fournel (who, leaving their child in France, would accompany Henri to Egypt) announced that the king on his birthday would declare an amnesty and that he had himself placed the name of "Le Père Enfantin" on the list of those to be liberated.[54]

The official order of liberation arrived at Sainte-Pélagie on Thursday, August 1, 1833, at 6 P.M. By nine o'clock Enfantin had left the prison. A week later he was writing Barrault about his plans for Suez and Panama and was busily engaged in organizing the Egyptian expedition.

Enfantin concluded that he had needed the seven months in prison to "change his skin." Whether he had really done so remained to be seen. Trial and prison had not been without their small results. Only a week after the August trial *Le Moniteur* announced that a 500,000-franc credit had been authorized to examine the possibilities for railroad construction in France. Not long after that the journals announced that a cleanup campaign had begun in the precincts of the palais Royal, whose kingly owner had apparently been piqued by references during the trial to debauchery there. The Saint-Simonians had legally established their religious identity.[55]

Enfantin had acted to free his followers from their dependency, whether successfully also remained to be seen. Some disciples might spend nights in the sultan's prisons, and others might be stoned in the remoter regions of France. But in August 1833 Saint-Simonian ideas were not dead, and Saint-Simonian energies had been offered an opportunity on a scale that they alone could have imagined.

The descent into the slough of despond had come to an end. The difficult and trying months seemed to have been crowned with hope. Enfantin left prison on August 1; he set sail for Egypt on August 29. The superabundant energy of the man and the fateful magnetism flowed as they never had before. The followers were once again caught up in the flood.

Fournel's letter to Arlès-Dufour announced that he was setting sail to complete the studies made during Napoleon's Egyptian campaign, to adopt the best method of transit from the Gulf of Suez to the Mediterranean, and to put India in touch with Europe. Such was the plan to be accomplished on African soil, in Egypt "old of memory, young in hope, land where for the ancients the known world stopped; land that the new wishes to touch" to bring life to it, "to conquer its wealth, by giving it wealth and not by exchanging blood over a scene of devastation."[56]

Enfantin, even more maniloquently, in an effort to tie past, present, and future together, proclaimed:

I march to the East, toward my work. . . . By this work . . . I wish that France, Europe, and the World be initiated into the practice of my industrial theories. I wish that our army of workers may be the seed of the pacification and the glory of God, through us, promised humanity. . . .

We will not decipher the hieroglyphics of Egypt's past grandeur, but we will engrave on the soil the signs of its future prosperity. . . .

231

Our political and religious ideas are everywhere; the moral and religious awakening that we sounded is felt.

Hostility against us is extinguished. A first justice will soon be rendered unto us.

Recall that if God has given us the mission to fertilize the seeds of the future, it is because life has put in us His strength. . . .

There is strength in all the classes, all the parties, all the peoples. . . .

God converts, He dethrones no one. . . . He makes the master love the emancipation of the slave, man that of woman, kings that of peoples; and it is thus that all will march peacefully and in order towards equality, liberty, and association.[57]

The leopard seemed not to have changed his spots, the snake not to have cast off the old skin. The tone is as magnificent, as priestly, as ever. Enfantin perhaps, at this moment, might be forgiven. The Egyptian expedition had all the marks of his fantasy of the *Mémoires d'un industriel* of 1828. He would lead a great work of pacification and construction and would enjoy the esteem of all. After the recent humiliations and agonies, Egypt was the Saint-Simonian promised land.

So began with great hope, after great despair, the first effort to translate Saint-Simonian thought into Saint-Simonian action.

CHAPTER XIII

CONCLUSION: THE PROFFERED
CROWN OF HOPE

THE PURPOSES of this book were set forth in its introduction: to tell a story and to establish the content of the thought of men and women called Saint-Simonians. If the dictum that one is what one studies holds true, then the writer is to some extent (and with some reservations) a Saint-Simonian. And if this narrative appears to be an apologia for Saint-Simonian life and thought, it is meant to. The time has certainly come to redress the balance of those scales on which admitted Saint-Simonian silliness is invariably held to outweigh Saint-Simonian good sense, largely because the commentator's mental thumb is firmly pressed down on the side of silliness.

One hopes certain questions will have been answered and certain dubious propositions refuted. It should be clear that there is a continuity of thought between Saint-Simon and his disciples. This link can be established not only in the realms of historicism, organicism, technocracy, and economic possibility but also and without any question in the realms of religion, priesthood, the "rehabilitation of matter," and even the "rehabilitation of the flesh." These last were not Enfantinian inventions and were not even, at the beginning of the movement, Enfantinian enthusiasms. They belonged more properly to Saint-Simon's last secretary, Olinde Rodrigues, who spoke with authority on Saint-Simon's last days and last thoughts.

The myth of Enfantin's "aberrations" from Saint-Simonian purity is shown to be just that. The argument is important because it undercuts the thesis of the existence of "real" and "false" Saint-Simonianism and of "serious" and "mad" Saint-Simonians. The received dogma has been that serious people separated themselves from the doctrine and that these *former* Saint-Simonians were responsible for the major material achievements of the July Monarchy and the Second Empire. It should be clear from the story told here that the serious Saint-Simonians, rather than separating from the doctrine, were busy shoring it up and rebuilding it at its moment of greatest crisis. They were Saint-Simonians to the end. Breaks with Enfantin were usually, as in the case of Michel Chevalier, at the behest of Enfantin himself and in the best interest of the followers.

The argument assumes added importance because these "breaks" were usually assumed to have taken place in reaction to the Enfantinian emphasis on the condition of women. That emphasis was absolutely central to the Saint-Simonian concern for the amelioration of the poorest and most numerous class. Remove the concern for women and you remove the foundations of the Saint-Simonian attack on property, marriage, and the politics of "liberal," bourgeois society, which were chief obstacles to the "new world" of Henri Saint-Simon and to the hope that was the characteristic Saint-Simonian gift to the time.

It should also be clear that the Saint-Simonians were strikingly devoted to individual freedom and personal fulfillment. They have been condemned for political authoritarianism, but they were among the first to see that political rights do not in and of themselves provide sufficient guarantees of freedom. The Saint-Simonians were also, as has been shown, rigorously democratic and egalitarian in their understanding of talent and productivity and of the rewards that society should assign them.

Pacifism was a consistent Saint-Simonian theme. "That which creates cannot reconcile itself to that which kills." The attacks on Saint-Simonianism accusing it of militarism, totalitarianism, and imperialism are based on writings *not* approved by the leadership of the Saint-Simonian school. These writings were the real aberrations, from the pens of precisely those who would accuse Enfantin of aberration; those who before becoming Saint-Simonian had been romantic liberals. By and large the aberrationists would return to that fold.

The Saint-Simonian impact during the Second Empire and subsequently poses questions that, along with the question of "influence" itself, are better treated elsewhere. But it should be clear that most of the arguments, particularly those based on some vague principles of arithmetic calculation against a continuing Saint-Simonian tradition, are without much merit. Humans grow, change, and modify or expand their views. There is little reason to believe, however, that there is no correspondence between the Saint-Simonian dreams of the 1830s and the Saint-Simonian realities of the 1850s.

So the Saint-Simonian story is somewhat other than a variety of legends would have it. Furthermore, many Saint-Simonian concerns continue to be the concerns of contemporary—and not exclusively Western—men and women. What the Saint-Simonians have to say may be intrinsically useful to us. What is this hope they offered their time and ours?

Saint-Simon had adjured his followers to greet the stars of the nineteenth century at their rising. These followers between 1825 and 1832 obeyed Saint-Simon's call. They found a world in which there were rich and poor; they envisioned a world in which, if its resources were adequately organized, there would be a sufficiency for all. They found a world divided by interest and sentiment; they envisioned a world unified in its search for and its creation of that sufficiency. They found a world in which power was manipulated by a class in the interests of its own perpetuation; they envisioned a world in which competence would breed plenty. They found a world in which material plenty was everybody's object and nobody's sure possession; they envisioned a world in which the assurance of plenty would modify the quality of life for individuals, sexes, races, classes, and nations.

The Saint-Simonians grasped what the technical competence of the engineer, the scholar, and the "priest" might do in bringing about a new world. They grasped that that new world would inevitably be conditioned by technical revolution. They grasped equally the threat to humanity that such a revolution would pose. But they insisted always on the capacity for correction inherent in that revolution.

What underlay the Saint-Simonian doctrine is "possibilism." Whatever conditions existed at a given time could, indeed must, undergo change. Change could always be made for the better. "Better" applied to everyone. The Saint-Simonians did not invent a doctrine of progress any more than they invented a creed of nationalism, but they particularized the idea of progress, and they projected a route for it.

Progress meant progress for everybody. What strikingly differentiates Saint-Simonian doctrine from that of other "utopians" is its inclusiveness. A moral and interior revolution is required of all people, but *not* a confrontation and elimination of classes. The *oisifs* disappear, by definition, when they and their money go to work.

A great work, a transformation of consciousness, is required, but it is not impossible. Distasteful as Saint-Simonian aesthetic theory may be to the individual artist, the Saint-Simonian notions of the social role of art and the power it can have on the mind seems to have been substantiated rather than denied over the last century. What religions have already done religions may continue to do: move men from idea to action. Nothing is more revelatory of the society Saint-Simonianism was fighting than the comment of the prosecuting attorney during the first trial of 1832 that one did not expect religion to affect the conduct of people's lives. It is in their understanding of religion that another of the Saint-Simonians' identifying characteristics emerges, illustrating both their desire and capacity to square circles. Religion is understood by Saint-Simonianism as the embodiment of the scientific knowledge of a given epoch. It is what we truly believe to be true. Religion that does not embody that knowledge demands renewal. Knowledge is continuously growing and cumulative; consequently, religion must also grow and change. God, the Saint-Simonians tell us, reveals Himself successively as we are able to see Him. In these propositions one can perhaps see the glimmer of an answer to the question of whether truth makes consent redundant in the Saint-Simonian scheme of things. We must want what is true. How not? Believing, we have in fact consented.

What is most important here is the intuition of the importance of science in the century to come, of the grasp it will have on human minds, the imperatives it will impose on human action. Given that importance, science offers an unequaled opportunity to make all people brothers and sisters. Organized, applied to the exploitation of the material universe, it can provide for humanity's material needs. Having done that, it will remove the impetus to exploitation. Science, technology, and organization will, or can, create conditions in which it is possible for people to love, rather than to war with, one another. What reasonable person would not wish this result?

Anyone might wish for the result, but was it not hopelessly naïve to assume it possible? Again it was a strength of the Saint-Simonians that they proposed techniques and devices for success that were not in the least naïve or utopian. The proof is that their techniques and devices became the current coin of nineteenth-century industrialism. The mobilization of capital in support of transportation networks that would trigger demand for goods and stimulate productivity, the search for markets, and the interdependence of economies and cultures was not a wild and woolly chimera; it was a projection of what actually happened and what the Saint-Simonians, both in thought and deed, helped to make happen.

Their notions of planning, or the allocation of resources to large social ends executed by experts, seem in twentieth-century terms neither unrealistic nor reprehensible. These notions in the 1820s and 1830s offered hope: hope for escape from a heartless laissez-faire liberal economic system in which there were inevitably more losers than winners; hope for escape from ruthless exploitation of workers by helpless masters; hope for escape from the vagaries of boom and bust; and hope for escape by women and children from the necessities of prostitution and early death. An industrialism untempered by Saint-Simonian humanism may not have achieved the hoped-for results, but that was hardly the fault of the Saint-Simonians or a consequence of their errors. Ironically it has been at the moments of most intense economic crisis in Western capitalist systems that Saint-Simonian ideas have reemerged as inspiration for reform and reconstruction.

The analysis of the political and economic system of their time and their France had necessarily led the Saint-Simonians to an understanding of the social system and to the central role of property and inheritance in it. Undoubtedly the attack on property was to the bourgeoisie of the Restoration and July Monarchy the most frightening aspect of the theory.

What is most interesting in it, however, is the broadcasting of the implications of the connection between the institutions of marriage, family, and property. The cash nexus of bourgeois marriage; the enslavement of wives; the misery of husbands; the necessity of prostitution; the prevalence of disease; and the guilt, shame, hatred, and fear that characterized such marriage aroused the pity of the Saint-Simonians for the "respectable" society of their time. But these also opened up Saint-Simonian compassion for those outside "respectable" society, its helpless victims enjoying no respect.

The poor, the miserable, and the exploited of whatever class could hope for an end to their material miseries. They could also hope for an end to their moral miseries. Saint-Simon had said that his new Christianity would take for its slogan "We must love one another." The Saint-Simonians regenerated the conception of love and preached it as the key to all economic, political, and personal transformation. Prosper Enfantin might well be described in contemporary terms and by cynical feminists as a male chauvinist pig. He believed that men and women were equal but different; he believed that there were feminine and masculine characteristics that should complement each other, and he was himself patronizing to and a fairly ruthless user of women. But his efforts to understand woman's pain, frustration, and desires; his insistence on the legitimacy of a wide spectrum of sexuality; and his "rehabilitation of the flesh" offered hope to women and to men.

The invitation to self-understanding and self-acceptance offered a liberation that bourgeois society might pretend to think scandalous but that in its heart it found hard to refuse. Again, as with Saint-Simon's intuition of the significance of the industrial age to come, so Enfantin's intuition of what our understanding of personality would become offered hope to an age that was beginning to sense itself as spiritually imprisoned despite all the great freedoms achieved after 1789.

Enfantin's sensitivity to individuality, first his own and then that of others, undoubtedly informed his understanding not only of women but also of work and workers. It was central to the Saint-Simonian outlook that efficient planning and use of resources depended on the rigorous recognition of ability. The techniques to determine a meritocracy may have been lacking, but the commitment to individual excellence and the rejection of privilege and authority was total. Anyone might hope to become what he or she was capable of being.

What was possible in Saint-Simonianism for individuals and sexes was equally possible for nations and races. The West's accomplishments would be translated to the East. Another chimera? Hardly. Separating high-flown rhetoric from the reality may be necessary to understand Saint-Simonianism, but there *is* a reality being described. Algeria was to be shaped by Saint-Simonian patterns. Israel was to take a form not unlike that dreamed of by Enfantin and d'Eichthal. The "relatively spiritual" link of banking and the "relatively material" link of transportation dreamed of by Chevalier rather quickly became a worldwide reality.

In short, the Saint-Simonians looked at their world quite realistically. They had some profound intuitions about where it was going and how it might get there. They preached that there was hope for humanity if people used their heads and listened to their hearts. One can argue that the world is more cruel and more stupid than the Saint-Simonians were willing to believe. But it can also be argued that the European world before the revolutions of 1848, which opened chasms between masses and classes, was perhaps more ready and more able to pursue hope than it has been since.

The central question "Does truth make consent redundant?" has, in part, been answered. But commentators like Hayek, Iggers, Arendt, and most followers of the classical liberal tradition see in the assertions of scientific certainty and omniscience only pretension, arrogance, the justification of the totalitarian state, and the enslavement of the masses by the imperatives of a dehumanized technocratic elite. Further, they see in the vision of the Saint-Simonian religion the glorification of the charismatic leader, the surrender of the will and the mind of the faithful to unchecked and uncheckable impulses, and the perversion of reason to irrational ends. Others would suggest that, although technocracy pretends to neutrality and is apolitical, in fact the Saint-Simonian appeal to hierarchy, order, and efficient administration has often been heard by those who have most to lose, whatever their political affiliation. Saint-Simonianism is an appeal to maintain things as they are, in the hands of irresponsible oligarchs whether commissars or the running dogs of capitalism.

It is held that the emotional appeal and the rational appeal of Saint-Simonianism contrive to build the roads to serfdom: communist, fascist, socialist, nationalist. No room is left for variety, individuality, accident, the richness of human experience, and historic continuity. The system is not only evil but also unworkable. In the light of this sort of criticism Saint-Simonianism has had terrible historic consequences; it is to be regretted, feared, uprooted.

Another brand of criticism would have it that whatever importance Saint-Simonianism has had is greater than it deserves. It is a fundamentally foolish doctrine. Saint-Simon's inspiration in Newton's laws of gravity is simply bad science. His philosophy of history, the organic and critical epochs, crumbles under close historical analysis and at best would be applicable only to the exceptional Western example. The idea that humans are capable of philanthropy is utopian and manifestly silly. We are permitted to suppose that the state may wither away, but in Saint-

Simonianism, finance capitalism remains always supreme. It is simply an apology for bourgeois exploitation of the masses. Or, alternately, its attacks on family, property, and the place of women are violations of natural law, subversive of an orderly society.

Saint-Simonianism has something to displease everybody. There is no simple political group that finds itself glorified and gratified by the doctrine. What better index could there be of the intensely radical character of the doctrine than the Saint-Simonian capacity to uproot conventional political categories as it searches for answers to problems unsatisfactorily resolved?

All the sins of which the Saint-Simonians are accused are sins in which their accusers share. The accusers have been no more successful than the Saint-Simonians in eliminating the occasion for sin. Yet they maintain that Saint-Simonianism offers even more unsatisfactory results than the unsatisfactory results of other doctrines by which we purport to live. Saint-Simonianism would enslave us more or feed us less.

We come back to the question that occasioned the writing of this book. Why do some find it important to disprove the merits of Saint-Simonianism? What is the answer to the question of truth versus consent? What difference does it make?

The answers to the above questions have been implicit, and in some cases explicit, throughout this book. The notion that ideas and the individual thinkers of ideas may have some bearing on the direction taken by human history makes many historians uncomfortable. If the Saint-Simonians had the historic importance sometimes attributed to them (and equally often denied), then other principles of explanation would have to be modified. Changing one's ideas in the light of evidence is painful, so the myth of the Saint-Simonian myth continues. This book constitutes an effort to "demythify" the school.

The greatest common concern of the critics is the Saint-Simonian assault on freedom—the assertion of Saint-Simonian truth against the need for consultation and consent. But the Saint-Simonians never made that assault on freedom, asserting always, everywhere, and with the utmost consistency the provisional character of truth, leadership, and priesthood and the inevitability of constant change. This was true at their most exalted moments. So Saint-Simonian totalitarianism is a straw man of whose possibilities they were fully aware and against which they guarded themselves fiercely.

Finally, what difference did the Saint-Simonian doctrine make? It offered to every class of man and woman in the France of the Restoration and the July Monarchy a hope, based on a keen perception of social and economic reality, that the world could offer more material and moral satisfaction than it had. It offered a hope of liberation from economic, political, social, and personal bondage. It offered techniques whereby liberation might be accomplished. It offered examples of individuals who with great pain and hard work had achieved such liberation. And in doing these things Saint-Simonianism laid the foundations for a tradition that, if it did not dominate, has never entirely disappeared. The comment of Theodore Zeldin that Saint-Simonian ideas became everybody's ideas is perhaps the most unwitting admission of the difference made by the Saint-Simonians' doctrine of hope. The tragedy may be that everybody did not act upon their ideas.

NOTES

INTRODUCTION

1. Theodore Zeldin, *France,* I, 509–10. Zeldin would disagree—but more of Zeldin's understanding of Saint-Simonianism later.

2. Jean Walch's *Bibliographie* gives some indication of the range of Saint-Simonian controversy. The bibliographical flood continues; see, for example, the April, June, and October 1970 and July 1971 issues of *Economies et sociétés,* devoted in their entirety to Saint-Simonian questions.

3. Sébastien Charléty, *L'Histoire.*

4. Sadi Carnot, son of Hippolyte, assassinated in 1894.

5. Frank Manuel, *New World,* 6.

6. Ibid., 342–43.

7. Karl Marx and Frederick Engels, *Collected Works,* III, 214, 294, 394–96, 398 ("Economic and Philosophic Manuscripts of 1844," "Progress of Social Reform on the Continent"); V, 226, 232, 464, 468–69, 475, 481, 493–510, 535 ("Critique of German Socialism"), XVII, 88–89, 341 ("Techow's Letter," "The New Treaty between France and England").

8. Friedrich von Hayek, *Counter Revolution.* Georg Iggers, *Cult of Authority.*

9. Contrasting but complementary discussions are in Léon Halévy, "Souvenirs de Saint-Simon" and Hippolyte-Lazare Carnot, *Sur le Saint-Simonianisme.*

10. In this category might fall the *Œuvres de Saint-Simon et d'Enfantin,* published by the council created by Enfantin's will and with his funds and those of other Saint-Simonians.

11. Rondo Cameron, *Economic Development,* 60.

12. Louis Girard, *La Politique des travaux publiques.*

13. Barrie M. Ratcliffe, "Les Pereires."

14. Barrie M. Ratcliffe, "Economic Influence."

15. Charles Morazé, *La France bourgeoise au XIXème siècle.* David S. Landes, "French Business and the Businessman."

16. Zeldin, *France,* II, 430–38.

17. George Weill, *L'Ecole Saint-Simonienne,* 306. Weill published rather hastily in 1896 (probably with the hope of anticipating Charléty's well-researched work—the consequence of the opening of the Saint-Simonian archives at the Bibliothèque de l'Arsenal), asserting that those archives might be interesting for business history but had nothing in them of interest for the history of the Saint-Simonians!

18. Zeldin, *France,* II, 436.

19. Ibid.

20. Ibid., 437.

21. Ibid., 82, 438.

22. The rhetorical method persists through generation after generation of those who must mention the Saint-Simonians while preferring to ignore the questions they raise. See, for example, John Hubbel Weiss, *Technological Man:* "In the first place the role of Saint-Simonians in French economic growth has been shown to have been considerably exaggerated." Has it indeed? What is being shown is never quite clear in these "showings," and it is never recognized that what is not quantified may be important.

23. Zeldin, *France,* II, 88.

24. Ibid., 438.

25. The work of S. Joan Moon, Claire Goldberg Moses, and Laura Strumingher has largely created that audience. See Moon, "Saint-Simonian Association"; Moses, *French Feminism;* Strumingher, "The Artisan Family" and "À bas les prêtres."

26. Charles P. Kindleberger, *Economic Growth,* 157–59, 186–88.

27. William H. Sewell, Jr., *Work and Revolution,* 8–9.

CHAPTER I. PARIS, FRANCE, 1825

1. Widener Library at Harvard University possesses a rich collection of nineteenth-century Paris guidebooks, the most useful of which are F. M. Marchant de Beaumont, *Le Nouveau Conducteur* and Galignani, *New Paris Guide.* The guides stole from each other, were revised periodically though not annually, and drew on official statistics of population, trade, commerce, and consumption. The 1846 Galignani, in particular, offers retrospective statistics.

2. Manuel, *New World,* 43.

3. Louis Blanc, *Dix ans* (1841), III, 97. Bibliothèque de l'Arsenal, *Fonds Enfantin,* 7861/13, "Souvenirs de Saint-Simon" (Halévy). The library will hereafter be cited as "Arsenal."

4. Bibliothèque Nationale, *N.A. Fr. 24609,* Gustave d'Eichthal to Resseguier, February 26, 1830.

5. Maurice Dreyfous, *Les Trois Carnot,* 184.

6. Alfred Pereire, *Autour de Saint-Simon,* 91.

7. Manuel's *New World* is the best and most trustworthy biography. The legends, as Manuel points out, were transmitted by Saint-Simon in his old age to Rodrigues, who in turn passed them to the English biographers Hubbard and Booth.

8. Ibid., 58.

9. Ibid., 347. The account of the Saint-Simonian schism is not entirely accurate.

10. Cf. Alfred de Musset, *La Confession,* 4ff.

11. Henri de Saint-Simon and Prosper Enfantin, *Œuvres,* XVIII, 100ff. Hereafter cited as "*Œuvres.*"

12. N. G. A. Hubbard, *Henri Saint-Simon,* 109.

13. Manuel, *New World,* 365. *Œuvres,* I, 118–22. Hubbard, *Henri Saint-Simon,* 106.

14. A. Jardin and A. J. Tudesq, *La France des Notables,* II, 216–17.

15. Others might argue (and have argued) the opposite, but the persistent Paris is to be seen in the "views" of the seventeenth, eighteenth, and nineteenth centuries and in the photographs of the nineteenth and twentieth. Cf. F. Ventouillac, *Paris et ses environs,* and Yvan Christ, *Les Metamorphoses de Paris.*

16. Marchant de Beaumont, *Le Nouveau Conducteur,* title page.

17. Galignani, *New Paris Guide,* 15; G. Bertier de Sauvigny, *La Restauration,* 324.

18. Marchant de Beaumont, *Le Nouveau Conducteur,* 11–12.

19. Ibid., 13.

20. *Guide des étrangers* preface.

21. Galignani, *New Paris Guide, 1829,* 2–3.

22. *Guide des étrangers,* 12.

23. Jardin and Tudesq, *La France des Notables,* II. David H. Pinkney, *Paris in the Nineteenth Century.* L. Chevalier, *La Formation de la population parisienne.* Galignani, *New Paris Guide, 1846.* No two accounts will agree in precise numbers, but the total picture is clear.

24. Charles Pouthas, *La Population française,* 157ff.

25. Louis Chevalier, *Leçon inaugurale.*
26. Marchant de Beaumont, *Le Nouveau Conducteur,* 42–43.
27. Pinkney, *Paris in the Nineteenth Century,* 166.
28. Ibid., 162.
29. Ibid., 311.
30. Ibid., 327–29.
31. Ibid., 386ff., 24–30.
32. Marchant de Beaumont, *Le Nouveau Conducteur,* 108, 197.
33. Pinkney, *Paris in the Nineteenth Century,* 47.
34. A. J. B. Parent-Duchatelet, *De la prostitution,* I, 27–33. Parent reports these figures to be exaggerated, but his reliance on official police registers gives for 1825 a constant figure of 2,600, undoubtedly too low.
35. Pinkney, *Paris in the Nineteenth Century,* 19.
36. Marchant de Beaumont, *Le Nouveau Conducteur,* 46–48.
37. Emile Barrault, *L'Occident et l'Orient,* 247.
38. Quoted in Henri Louvancour, *De Henri Saint-Simon,* 11.
39. Bertier de Sauvigny, *La Restauration,* 445, 459. Jardin, and Tudesq, *La France des Notables,* 87–113.
40. Bertier de Sauvigny, *La Restauration,* 466.
41. Ibid., 319.
42. Ibid., 322.
43. Pereire, *Autour de Saint-Simon,* 105.
44. Barrie M. Ratcliffe "Saint-Simonianism and Messianism."
45. Arsenal, *Fonds Enfantin,* 7804/2, "Notes" of Lambert.
46. Bibliothèque National, *N.A. Fr. 24608,* Enfantin to Cappella, April 30, 1832.
47. Bertier de Sauvigny, *La Restauration,* 486.

CHAPTER II. "IF . . ."

1. Henri de Saint-Simon, *Du Système industriel* (Paris, 1821), Preface. Manuel, *New World,* 254.
2. Jardin and Tudesq, *La France des Notables* I, 1; VIII, 1.
3. *Œuvres,* XXII, 91.
4. Ibid., XXXII, 6; I, 156.
5. Ibid., XXXIX, 175ff.; I, 156, 159.
6. Hannah Arendt, *Origins.* Hayek, *Counter Revolution.* Iggers, *Cult of Authority.* Karl Popper, *The Open Society.*
7. Saint-Simon himself commented to Gustave d'Eichthal that the "Savants" would cause the doctrine more trouble than the theologians.
8. *Œuvres,* XXXIX, 176–97. The essay appeared in a collaborative work, *Travaux Philosophiques,* at the end of Saint-Simon's life. Rodrigues maintained that it summarized the whole doctrine and separated it from what had gone before: ibid., I, 101.
9. Ibid., XL, 11.
10. Ibid., 305, "Mémoire sur la science de l'homme."
11. Ibid., XXXIX, 176–77.
12. Ibid., 188.
13. Ibid., 194.
14. Manuel, *New World,* 117–21, 139–147.
15. *Œuvres,* XXXIX, 193–96 passim.
16. Quoted in Henri Gouhier, *La Jeunesse,* II, 185.

17. *Œuvres,* XXXIX, 197.
18. Ibid.
19. Ibid., XXXVII, 4ff., "Catéchisme des industriels."
20. Ibid., XXXIX, 148.
21. For one example among many, ibid., 165–66, "De l'organisation sociale."
22. Ibid., 6.
23. Ibid., XXXII, 249.
24. Ibid., XX, 17.
25. Ibid.
26. Ibid.
27. M. Leroy, *Le Socialisme des producteurs,* 59.
28. *Le Producteur* IV (1826): 382.
29. *Œuvres,* XIX, 73; XXXVII, 178ff.
30. Ibid., XX, 62.
31. Ibid., XXIII, 108.
32. Ibid., 116.
33. Quoted in Manuel, *New World,* 355.
34. Repeating the warning in *Œuvres,* XXII, 139ff.
35. Ibid., XL, 56–57.
36. Ibid., 128.
37. Ibid., XXXIX, 97ff.
38. Ibid., XXIX, 148–49.
39. Ibid., XXIX, 97.
40. Ibid., XX, 52.
41. Manuel, *New World,* 174–75.
42. Michel Chevalier, *Politique industriel* (Paris, 1833), 121. Charles Duveyrier, *Lettres politiques,* 123.
43. *Œuvres,* II, 117.

CHAPTER III. THE YOUNG TECHNOCRATS

1. *Œuvres,* XXIV, 79.
2. Ibid., I, 157–58, Enfantin to Pichard, August 23, 1825.
3. Ibid., XX, 62.
4. Ibid., XXIV, 47–48, Enfantin to Thérèse Nugues, August 18, 1825.
5. Ibid., I, 165.
6. Quoted in Maurice Wallon, *Les Saint-Simoniens,* 28.
7. *Œuvres,* II, 108, 143. Bibliothèque Thiers (hereafter, "Thiers"), *Fonds d'Eichthal,* IV N. *Arsenal, Fonds Enfantin,* 7861/13.
8. Arsenal, *Fonds Enfantin,* 7804/2, "Notes" of Lambert.
9. Blanc, *Dix ans* (1845), I, 66.
10. Thiers, *Fonds d'Eichthal,* IV R1. Blanc, *Dix ans* (1841), III, 97. *Histoire du Saint-Simonisme.*
11. Blanc, *Dix ans* (1841), III, 121.
12. Thiers, *Fonds d'Eichthal,* IV R1.
13. Aresenal, *Fonds Enfantin,* 7804/2, "Notes" of Lambert. *Œuvres,* I, 136.
14. Hayek, *Counter Revolution,* 117.
15. Ibid., 94.
16. Ibid.
17. Ibid.

18. Ibid., 110.
19. Ibid.
20. Gouhier, *La Jeunesse,* I, 96. *Bibliothèque Nationale, N.A. Fr. 24608,* Enfantin·to Capella, April 30, 1832. *Œuvres,* I, 149.
21. See Cameron, *Economic Development,* 50ff. for a discussion of French engineers and engineering.
22. Arsenal, *Fonds Enfantin,* 7804/2, "Notes" of Lambert. *Œuvres,* I, 136.
23. Arsenal, *Fonds Enfantin,* 7804/2, "Notes" of Lambert.
24. Ibid.
25. Ibid.
26. Ibid.
27. The source is Léon Halévy, not an admirer of Enfantin, who was described by Heine as being "as dull as an opera composed by his brother Fromental."
28. Bibliothèque National, *N.A. Fr. 24608,* Enfantin to Capella, April 30, 1832.
29. Edward Blount, *Memoirs,* 246.
30. Arsenal, *Fonds Enfantin,* 7861 Br. 16, on the Pereires and Rodrigues; 7645/132. Thiers, *Fonds d'Eichthal,* IV R5. Henry-René d'Allemagne, *Les Saint-Simoniens,* 31–32. *Œuvres,* I, 181; II, 186.
31. *Le Producteur* I (1825): Introduction.
32. Ibid., 9.
33. Leo Tolstoy, *War and Peace* (New York: New American Library, 1968), 1438.
34. *Œuvres,* XXIV, 54, Enfantin to Thérèse Nugues, August 18, 1825.
35. *Le Producteur,* I (1825): *Introduction.*
36. Ibid., IV (1826): 382.
37. Ibid., I (1825): 412.
38. Hippolyte-Lazare Carnot, *Sur le Saint-Simonisme,* 18.
39. *Le Producteur,* I and II (1825–26): passim.
40. Ibid., II (1825): 289ff.
41. Ibid., 290.
42. H. Beyle, *D'un nouveau complot.* D'Allemagne, *Les Saint-Simoniens,* 33. *Le Producteur* I (1825): 437ff.
43. Arsenal, *Fonds Enfantin,* 7744, "Journal" de Lambert.
44. Ibid., 7676/175, "Notes"; 7643, "Archives" I, 39. Frank Manuel, *Prophets of Paris,* 260.
45. Manuel, *New World,* 2–3.
46. Carnot, *Sur le Saint-Simonisme,* 36.
47. Arsenal, *Fonds Enfantin,* 7651/40.
48. *Œuvres,* II, 171ff. The typography follows the style used by the Saint-Simonians to emphasize points.
49. Ibid., 84.
50. Ibid., 186.

CHAPTER IV. "THE OLD FAMILY"

1. *Œuvres,* II, 186.
2. Ibid., 5. Arsenal, *Fonds Enfantin,* 7804/2, "Notes" of Lambert.
3. Ibid.
4. Blanc, *Dix ans* (1841), I, 96.
5. D'Allemagne, *Les Saint-Simoniens,* 214. Arsenal, *Fonds Enfantin,* 7643/507.
6. Arsenal, *Fonds Enfantin,* 7804/2, "Notes" of Lambert. Olinde's younger brother

Eugène was to take up the religious theme even more enthusiastically: *Œuvres*, II, 11.

7. D'Allemagne, *Les Saint-Simoniens*, 58. *Œuvres*, XXIV, 80.

8. Arsenal, *Fonds Enfantin*, 760–61 contain Adèle's letters to Enfantin.

9. Thiers, *Fonds d'Eichthal*, IV P.

10. D'Allemagne, *Les Saint-Simoniens*, 57, Enfantin to Aglaë St. Hilaire, January 21, 1833.

11. Thiers, *Fonds d'Eichthal*, IV P.

12. Arsenal, *Fonds Enfantin*, 7804/2.

13. *Œuvres*, II, 211.

14. Arsenal, *Fonds Enfantin*, 7663/2, Enfantin to Arlès-Dufour, February 1828.

15. *Œuvres*, II, 95–96. *Le Globe*, July 29, 1830. Blanc, *Dix ans* (1841), III, 90ff. Charléty, *L'Histoire*, 319. J. S. Mill, *Correspondance inédite*. Arsenal, *Fonds d'Eichthal*, 14385/40, Thomas Carlyle to Gustave d'Eichthal, August 9, 1830. (There are *Fonds d'Eichthal* in both Thiers and Arsenal.)

16. Blanc, *Dix ans* (1841), 97ff.

17. *Œuvres*, III, 133–35. Jean Vidalenc, "Les techniques."

18. Thiers, *Fonds d'Eichthal*, IV R5. Blanc, *Dix ans* (1841), I, 89.

19. Arsenal, *Fonds Enfantin*, 7804/2, "Notes of Lambert."

20. Cited in Charléty, *L'Histoire*, 72.

21. The marriage of uncle and niece, under Jewish law, constituted a "virtuous act," but in the case of Isaac it required a dispensation from the emperor. Jean Autin, *Les frères Pereire*, 214.

22. Pereire, *Autour de Saint-Simon*. Arsenal, *Fonds Enfantin*, 7861 Br. 16.

23. Arsenal, *Fonds d'Eichthal*, 14390.

24. Thiers, *Fonds d'Eichthal*, IV N. Arsenal, *Fonds Enfantin*, 7861/13.

25. Thiers, *Fonds d'Eichthal*, IV N, O, "Mon rôle" and "Sur la part."

26. Bibliothèque national, *N.A. Fr./24609*, Gustave d'Eichthal to Resseguier, February 26, 1830.

27. *Œuvres*, VI, 231.

28. Ibid., II, 14–15, Isaac Rodrigues to Enfantin, November 5, 1828.

29. Arsenal, *Fonds Enfantin*, 7804/1.

30. Ibid., 7645/132, Margerin to Fournel, May 15, 1826.

31. E. M. Butler, *Saint-Simonian Religion*, 27ff.

32. Blanc, *Dix ans* (1841), III, 121.

33. *Œuvres*, VI, 133–35.

34. Ibid., XIII, 255.

35. To be found in the Arsenal papers in many categories, but the railroad correspondence and that having to do with Lyonnais business affairs (7841–43 and 7852) are particularly revealing and useful.

36. *Le Petit Journal*, September 1864; 1.

37. Arsenal, *Fonds Enfantin*, 7682/39, Arlès-Dufour to Enfantin, January 30, 1842.

CHAPTER V. THE REIGN OF REASON
IN THE GARDEN OF LOVE

1. *Œuvres*, XVII, 143ff.

2. Ibid., II, 14–15.

3. Ibid., 24.

4. Arsenal, *Fonds Enfantin*, 7861 Br. 16, *Arlès-Dufour* by "C. L.," 52 ff.

5. Walch, *Bibliographie*, 104.

6. *Œuvres,* XVII, 147–52.

7. Ibid., 154.

8. Ibid., 155.

9. Ibid., 169.

10. Ibid., 214.

11. Arendt, *Origins,* 337.

12. Iggers, *Cult of Authority,* 87.

13. Ironically the Iggers account of Saint-Simonian "totalitarianism" is based largely on a reading of contributors to *Le Globe* who in the wake of the 1830 revolution wished to intervene militarily in Poland, Belgium, and elsewhere and whose militarism occasioned their expulsion from *Le Globe* and from Saint-Simonianism. The Saint-Simonian "totalitarians" were, in fact, liberals like Laurent and Carnot judged insufficiently orthodox by the Saint-Simonian leaders.

14. Emile Pereire and Isaac Pereire, *Œuvres,* I, 4. *Œuvres,* XLIII, 122; XXXIX, 25; XX, 150.

15. *Œuvres,* II, 115–16.

16. Ibid., 117.

17. Ibid., 115 in a footnote to the above passage added to the original manuscript while Enfantin was in prison at Sainte-Pélagie.

18. Ibid., XXIV, 152–53, Enfantin to Bailly, July 6, 1827.

19. Ibid., II, 202.

20. Ibid., XVII, 226.

21. The point is explored at length in "Note d'Enfantin sur le Prêtre de l'Avenir," *Œuvres,* XVII, 230–40.

22. Ibid., XXIV, 152 ff. "Notes" of Enfantin.

23. Ibid., 160.

24. Ibid., XVIII, 229–30.

25. Eugène Rodrigues, *Lettre sur la religion.* The *Lettre* was essentially the fruit of the correspondence with Resseguier, who was to head the Church of the Midi. Enfantin recounts in Lambert's "Notes" how he and Eugène "worked" the pages of Saint-Simon's *Le Nouveau Christianisme.* The *Lettre* appears with the Lessing translation because Lessing appeared to confirm Saint-Simon's notion of religion as the state of knowledge of a given epoch.

26. *Œuvres,* XXV, 32, Enfantin to Thérèse Nugues, August 17, 1828.

27. Ibid., 33.

28. Ibid., 34.

29. Ibid., 38.

30. Ibid., 40.

31. Ibid., I, 224.

32. Ibid., XXV, 95, 103, Enfantin to Thérèse Nugues, November 15, 1828.

33. Arsenal, *Fonds Enfantin,* 7620, Enfantin to Thérèse Nugues, December 1828.

34. *Œuvres,* II, 28.

35. Ibid., 24.

36. Ibid., 28.

37. Ibid.

38. Ibid.

CHAPTER VI. THE GOOD NEWS

1. Quoted in D'Allemagne, *Les Saint-Simoniens,* 64.

2. Charton, *Mémoires.*

3. *Œuvres,* IV, 109, P. Talabot to Enfantin, October 30, 1831.

4. *Doctrine de Saint-Simon, Exposition première année 1829,* 2d ed. (Paris, 1830), 76, 95, 164–65. This account includes materials from the 1829–30 *Expositions.*

5. Ibid., 102–4.

6. Ibid., 82–83, 87.

7. Ibid., 104, 189.

8. Ibid., 93–98 passim.

9. Ibid., 76.

10. Ibid., 81–82.

11. Ibid., 87.

12. Ibid., 89.

13. Ibid., 89–93.

14. Ibid., 92.

15. Ibid., 98.

16. Ibid., 91.

17. Ibid., 105.

18. Ibid., 108–9.

19. Ibid., 112–15; 123–39 (all the 3d *séance*).

20. Charles Darwin, *Origin of Species* (New York: Modern Library, 1936), 373.

21. *Exposition première année,* 119.

22. Ibid., 117.

23. Ibid., 110–15.

24. Ibid., 118–19.

25. Ibid., 120–21.

26. Ibid., 146.

27. Ibid., 148.

28. Arsenal, *Fonds d'Eichthal,* 14408.

29. David McLellan, *Marx before Marxism,* 39.

30. *Exposition première année,* 164, 177.

31. Ibid., 171.

32. Ibid., 178–82.

33. Ibid., 186–89.

34. Ibid., 203–8.

35. Ibid., 194.

36. Ibid., 208.

37. Hayek, *Counter Revolution,* 110.

38. D'Allemagne, *Prosper Enfantin,* 165–69.

39. *Exposition première année,* 211.

40. Ibid., 251.

41. Ibid., 253ff.

42. Ibid., 268.

43. Ibid., 269–70.

44. Ibid., 272–74.

45. Ibid., 272.

46. Ibid., 282.

47. Ibid., 329.

48. *Œuvres,* XIII, "Exposition première année," 13th *séance,* 5.

49. Ibid., 10.

50. Ibid., 87.

51. Ibid., 94.

52. Ibid., 147–48.

53. *Œuvres*, XLII, "Exposition deuxième année," 172–75; 187, 265.

54. Ibid., 265–77 passim.

CHAPTER VII. "FROM ON HIGH"

1. Blanc, *Dix ans* (1841), I, 95ff. Thiers, *Fonds d'Eichthal,* IV R1.

2. Carnot, *Sur le Saint-Simonisme,* 36.

3. *Revue Historique* 82 (1903): 1, quoted in d'Allemagne, *Les Saint-Simoniens,* 155.

4. *Œuvres*, XXIII, 116.

5. Ibid., 179.

6. Thiers, *Fonds d'Eichthal,* IV P.

7. *Œuvres*, XXVI, 158, Enfantin to Thérèse Nugues, October 1829.

8. Ibid., XXVII, 85, Enfantin to Bailly, April 1830.

9. Ibid., XXV, 44–45, Enfantin to Thérèse Nugues, August 17, 1828. Original in Bibliothèque National, *"N.A. Fr. 24608/313."*

10. Bibliothéque Nationale, *N.A. Fr. 24608/313/2.*

11. Bibliothèque Nationale, *N.A. Fr. 24611.* St.-Cyr Nugues to Enfantin, April 26, 1829.

12. Bibliothèque Arsenal, *Fonds Enfantin,* 7804/2. *Œuvres,* II, 50–60.

13. *Œuvres,* II, 61ff.

14. Ibid., 70.

15. Ibid., 74.

16. D'Allemagne, *Les Saint-Simoniens,* 114. Arsenal, *Fonds Enfantin,* 7644/56–59.

17. Blanc, *Dix ans* (1841), III, 89ff.

18. D'Allemagne, *Les Saint-Simoniens,* 116.

19. *Œuvres,* XVIII, 227–30.

20. Ibid., II, 110.

21. Ibid., 117–26.

22. Arsenal, *Fonds Enfantin,* 7644/50.

23. Vidalenc, "Les Techniques."

24. Butler, *Saint-Simonian Religion,* 12.

25. Arsenal, *Fonds d'Eichthal,* 15031/231/933. *Le Temps,* September 10, 1864.

26. Arsenal, *Fonds d'Eichthal,* 14387/7.

27. Ibid., *Fonds Enfantin,* 7804/2.

28. *Œuvres,* II, 102ff.

29. Ibid., 201–2, "Manifesto," August 1, 1830.

30. Ibid., III, 25.

31. Ibid., 52–64.

32. Arsenal, *Fonds Enfantin,* 7861/28, "Rapports aux pères suprèmes de G. d'Eichthal"; 7822/20.

33. Archives Nationales, *Series F14*, 2205² (P. T. de Charme); *F14*, 2185² (J. C. Capella).

34. R. B. Carlisle, "Birth of Technocracy," 459.

35. *Œuvres,* VI, 208.

36. D'Allemagne, *Les Saint-Simoniens,* 94–110, 114–18.

37. Ibid., 116–20.

38. *Œuvres,* XLIII, 162ff., 8th *prédication.*

39. *Œuvres,* XLV, 190ff., 41st *prédication.*

40. H. J. Hunt, *Le socialisme,* 272.

41. Arsenal, *Fonds Enfantin,* 7780 includes 220 letters from Aglaë Saint-Hilaire to Enfantin.

42. Blanc, *Dix ans* (1841), III, 90ff.

43. Ibid., 92–93.
44. Ibid., 93.
45. *Œuvres,* II, 193.
46. Ibid., 197.
47. Ibid., 201–2, 213–14.
48. Ibid., III, 12.

CHAPTER VIII. THE MEN OF THE FUTURE

1. Blanc, *Dix ans* (1845), III, 79–80.
2. Ibid., 79.
3. *Œuvres,* V, 2; III, 49. Arsenal, *Fonds Enfantin,* 7822/20.
4. Arsenal, *Fonds Enfantin,* 7804/2, "Notes" of Lambert. *Œuvres,* III, 56. Enfantin to Michel Chevalier, October 30, 1830. Bibliothèque National, *N.A. Fr/24609,* Chevalier to Duveyrier, May 9, 1831.
5. *Le Globe,* November 11, 1830. *Œuvres,* III, 238.
6. *Œuvres,* III, 52.
7. Bibliothèque National, *N.A. Fr. 24609,* Claire Bazard to Cécile Fournel, no date.
8. Marcel Emérit, *Les Saint-Simoniens,* 59.
9. For Mill: J. S. Mill, *Correspondance inédite,* 25. For Mendelssohn, Liszt: *Œuvres,* III, 49. It was long believed that whole sections of George Sand's *Spiridion* had been written by Pierre Leroux.
10. For Marx: McLellan, *Marx before Marxism.* For Disraeli: most notably but not exclusively in *Sibyl.* Heine dedicated *De l'Allemagne* to Enfantin.
11. Bibliothèque National, *N.A. Fr. 24613,* Louvot de Martincourt to Alexis Petit, July 19, 1832.
12. Arsenal, *Fonds Enfantin,* 7861/23.
13. P. Sorlin, *Waldeck-Rousseau* (Paris, 1966), 31.
14. Maurice Agulhon, *Une ville ouvrière.*
15. *Œuvres,* III, 3.
16. Vidalenc, "Les Techniques." D'Allemagne, *Les Saint-Simoniens,* 142.
17. *Œuvres,* II, 157–62.
18. Carnot, *Sur le Saint-Simonisme.* Baron Ernouf, *Paulin Talabot.* Arsenal, *Fonds Enfantin,* 7681/Br. 18. Suzanne Voilquin, *Journal d'une Saint-Simonienne.* Thiers, *Fonds d'Eichthal,* IVN. Arsenal, *Fonds Enfantin,* 7676, Aglaë Saint-Hilaire to Enfantin, Oct. 10, 1835.
19. Elie Halévy, "La Doctrine économique de Saint-Simon" and "La Doctrine économique des Saint-Simoniens." Emérit, *Les Saint-Simoniens,* 174. P. Rude, "Les Saint-Simoniens," 345.
20. *Œuvres,* XVII, 11.
21. Archives Nationales, *Series F14,* 2724[7]. *Œuvres,* II, 170, 190.
22. *Œuvres,* III, 117ff.
23. D'Allemagne, *Les Saint-Simoniens,* 140.
24. *Œuvres,* IV, 81.
25. Arsenal, *Fonds Enfantin,* 7815/66, "Reports 4th and 5th Arrondissements," July–December 1831.
26. Ibid., "Reports 3d Arrondissement," August and September 1831.
27. Ibid., "Reports 1st and 2d Arrondissements," no date.
28. Ibid., 7816, "Reports 10th Arrondissement."
29. Ibid., "Reports 11th Arrondissement." Parent to *Pères,* November 27, 1831.

30. Ibid., 7815/66, E. Niboyet to *pères, "et je vous en supplie, laissez-moi dans mon élément."*

31. Ibid., 7822/44. *Œuvres,* IV, 81.

32. Jehan d'Ivray, *L'Aventure,* 49.

33. Arsenal, *Fonds Enfantin,* 7816, "Reports 12th Arrondissement," October 27, 1831; 7815/66, "Reports 4th and 5th Arrondissements."

34. Ibid., 7816.

35. D'Allemagne, *Les Saint-Simoniens,* 134–36.

36. Ibid., 142.

37. Bibliothèque National, *N.A. Fr. 24610.* Pierre Leroux to "mes Pères," May 18, 1831.

38. D'Allemagne, *Les Saint-Simoniens,* 139–40.

39. *Le Globe,* December 12, 16, and 18, 1831.

40. D'Allemagne, *Les Saint-Simoniens,* 139–40.

41. *Œuvres,* III, 87.

42. Ibid., 148.

43. Ibid., 87ff.

44. Ibid., VI, 106–7.

45. Ibid., IV, 52–60.

46. Ibid., III, 229.

47. Iggers, *Cult of Authority.* Although I have been critical of Iggers throughout, it should be said that his is an honest interpretation based on real but incomplete and incompletely understood sources. For example, Talabot wrote in October 1831 to Enfantin of *Le Globe,* "The journal gives you an ultra-liberal varnish unworthy of you," *Œuvres,* V, 80.

48. *Œuvres,* V, 76; *Le Globe,* February 1, 1832.

49. *Le Globe,* March 14, April 28–29, August 21, 1831.

50. *Œuvres,* IV, 107, Paulin Talabot to Enfantin, October 30, 1831.

CHAPTER IX. THE NEW EVE

1. *Œuvres,* XV, 50.

2. Ibid., XX, 52.

3. Arsenal, *Fonds Enfantin,* 7804/2; 7644/46. *Œuvres,* II, 115–16.

4. Blanc, *Dix ans* (1845), III, 64.

5. Parent-Duchatelet, *De la prostitution,* I, 194ff. Blanc, *Dix ans* (1845), I, 195.

6. Arsenal, *Fonds Enfantin,* 7804/2.

7. Parent-Duchatelet, *De la prostitution,* II, 522.

8. Arsenal, *Fonds Enfantin,* 7824/6, "Conversations with L. Simon, July–August 1832."

9. Ibid., 7804/2.

10. Arsenal, *Fonds d'Eichthal,* 14387/27.

11. Ratcliffe, "Saint Simonism and Messianism," 496–98.

12. Linda Kelly, *The Young Romantics,* 61.

13. Arsenal, *Fonds Enfantin,* 7804/2.

14. Thiers, *Fonds d'Eichthal,* IV P.

15. Arsenal, *Fonds d'Eichthal,* 15031/893, Petit to Enfantin, February 4, 1833; *Fonds Enfantin,* 7777, "Je me sens sa mère, sa mère en amour."

16. M. Thibert, *Le Féminisme* 70. Arsenal, *Fonds Enfantin,* 7687, "Mémoires" of Jean Terson. C. L., *Arlès-Dufour,* 45.

17. Blanc, *Dix ans* (1845), III, 121ff.

18. Arsenal, *Fonds Enfantin,* 7804/2, "Notes on Cazeaux." "Cazeaux gave the general

impression of being magnetized by Père [Enfantin] and of becoming the expresser of his intentions." See Moses, *French Feminism*, 58.

19. Describing one such break, Enfantin wrote, "J'ai pris un forceps pour l'accoucher," Arsenal, *Fonds d'Eichthal*, 15031/893. Ibid., *Fonds Enfantin*, 7828, "Journal de Lambert."

20. Arsenal, *Fonds Enfantin*, 7861 Br. 18, Suzanne Voilquin, "Souveniers d'une fille du peuple ou la Sainte-Simonienne en Egypte," 83; ibid., 7828, "Journal de Lambert."

21. Ibid., 7621, Enfantin to Mme Flachat (1832); also duplicate 7646/84.

22. Ibid., 7861 Br. 18, 83–85.

23. Ibid., 7645/138, Claire Bazard to Enfantin (also quoted in Thibert, *Le Féminism*); *Archives*, III, 138.

24. Ibid., 7647, 155, Henri Fournel to Enfantin, February 4, 1833.

25. Ibid., notes of Enfantin to the above letter written at Sainte-Pélagie in January 1833.

26. *Œuvres*, XII, 51.

27. Arsenal, *Fonds Enfantin*, 7643/507. For a discussion of the issues, *Œuvres*, II, 63, 87. D'Allemagne, *Les Saint-Simoniens*, 66.

28. Arsenal, *Fonds Enfantin*, 7643/512.

29. Ibid.

30. d'Allemagne, *Les Saint-Simoniens*, 215.

31. *Œuvres*, III, 72; Arsenal, *Fonds Enfantin*, 7645/40.

32. *Œuvres*, III, 74; Arsenal, *Fonds Enfantin*, 7645/42.

33. Arsenal, *Fonds Enfantin*, 7645/138.

34. Ibid., 7644, Claire Bazard to Enfantin and Bazard, October 6, 1830.

35. Charléty, *Les Saint-Simoniens*, 125.

36. Arsenal, *Fonds Enfantin*, 7861 Br. 18, Voilquin, "Souvenirs," 81.

37. Thiers, 14387/129.

38. There are several copies of this letter, which is the single most important delineation of Enfantin's thought on women. What follows is drawn from it. Arsenal, *Fonds Enfantin*, 7645/258; Bibliotheque Nationale, *N.A. Fr.* 24608, 12–18; printed in *Œuvres*, XXVII, 193ff.

39. Ibid.

40. D'Allemagne, *Les Saint-Simoniens*, 221. *Œuvres*, V, 241.

41. D'Allemagne, *Les Saint-Simoniens*, 219.

42. *Œuvres*, VI, 54.

43. Charton, *Mémoires*. Arsenal, *Fonds Enfantin*, 7861.

44. Carnot, *Sur le Saint-Simonisme*. Arsenal, *Fonds Enfantin*, 7861.

45. D'Allemagne, *Les Saint-Simoniens*, 221.

46. Arsenal, *Fonds Enfantin*, 7645/327.

47. Ibid., 7647/152.

48. Ibid., *Fonds d'Eichthal*, 14387.

49. Arsenal, *Fonds Enfantin*, 7645 (*Archive*, III), Claire to Enfantin, November 11, 1831.

50. Ibid., *Fonds Enfantin*, 7656. Mme Enfantin to Enfantin, November 10, 1831.

CHAPTER X. THE NEW ADAM

1. Robert B. Carlisle, "The Saint-Simonian Threat."

2. *Œuvres*, IV, 156–60.

3. Ibid., 161.

4. Ibid., 163–83.

5. Ibid., 196–97, 201.

6. Arsenal, *Fonds Enfantin*, 7804/2, "Notes" of Lambert on Cazeaux. Autin in *Les Frères Pereire*, pp. 32–33, has been able to document for the first time, I think, the precise point

of view of the two brothers. Emile, while working with the Saint-Simonians on finances and legal matters, distanced himself from the religious retreat to Ménilmontant. Isaac wished to join it but was prevented from so doing by his elder.

7. *Œuvres*, IV, 107ff., Paulin Talabot to Enfantin, October 30, 1831.

8. *Œuvres*, V, 78.

9. *Le Globe*, November 28, 1831.

10. *Œuvres*, IV, 239.

11. Ibid., 240.

12. Ibid., XIV, 136–65, 5th teaching.

13. Ibid., 157–60.

14. Ibid., 168, 6th teaching.

15. Ibid., VI, 185.

16. Ibid., XIV, 163.

17. Ibid., 164.

18. Ibid., 164–65.

19. Ibid., 160.

20. Ibid., 172, 6th teaching.

21. Ibid., XIV, 214.

22. Ibid., XVI, 42.

23. Ibid., 50.

24. Ibid., VI, 5ff.; XLV, 268; XVI, 170ff.

25. Ibid., VI, 184–97.

26. Ibid., V, 224.

27. Ibid., VI, 231.

28. Ibid., V, 196.

29. Charléty, *Le Saint-Simonisme*, 200. *Œuvres*, V, 190ff.

30. *Œuvres*, VI, 201–3.

31. Ibid., 224.

32. Ibid., 240.

33. Ibid., 239.

34. Arsenal, *Fonds Enfantin*, 7620, Enfantin to Capella, April 30, 1832.

35. According to Lambert's biographical sketch in Arsenal, *Fonds Enfantin*, 7804/2, Mme Enfantin greeted her son on his return from the defense of Paris in 1814 with a thrown book and three days of silence.

36. Ibid.

37. Ibid., 7620, Enfantin to Capella.

38. Ibid., Cécile Fournel to Enfantin, May 22, 1832; Cécile Fournel to Henri Fournel, June 4, 1832.

39. The colored illustrations in d'Allemagne's *Les Saint-Simoniens* offer a good sample. The "Collection Vinck" of the Cabinet des Etampes of the Bibliothèque Nationale has perhaps a dozen examples.

40. Arsenal, *Fonds Enfantin*, 7604/99.

41. Ibid., 7787–88, "Mémoires" of Jean Terson.

42. Charlèty, *L'Histoire*, 164ff. D'Allemagne, *Les Saint-Simoniens*, 270–79.

43. *Œuvres*, VII, 24–25, letter to Capella, May 1832.

44. Ibid., 31–32.

45. Blanc, *Dix ans* (1841), III, 288–89. Arsenal, *Fonds Enfantin*, 7620, Cécile Fournel to Henri Fournel, June 4, 1832. Arsenal, *Fonds d'Eichthal*, 14390/21, Rodrigues père to Gustave d'Eichthal, July 1832.

46. *Œuvres*, VII, 104–16.

47. Ibid., 116–23.

48. Ibid., 157.

49. Arsenal, *Fonds d'Eichthal,* 14390.

CHAPTER XI. THE NEW EDEN

1. *Œuvres,* XV, 22; IV, 109.

2. Ibid., VI, 110ff.

3. D'Allemagne, *Les Saint-Simoniens,* 309–12. Arsenal, *Fonds Enfantin,* 7641, 7646. The original plan was for a city in male form, because woman had not yet emerged from man's rib, but d'Eichthal conceived of a female palace and a male palace.

4. Louis Napoleon and Haussmann wanted this improvement, but they required that the streets be lined with suitable edifices. The financing of the clearing away of the old quarter and the construction of the Hôtel and Grands Magasins du Louvre, which gave the street its character in the neighborhood of the Palais Royal and the Louvre itself, was the work of the Crédit Mobilier and of the Pereires, holders of 148,000 shares out of 240,000 in the company formed to undertake the project. Autin, *Les Frères Pereire,* 179–81.

5. See Robert B. Carlisle, *Paris-Lyon Railway* and "Les Chemins de fer."

6. L.-M. Jouffroy, *Une étape.* A. L. Dunham, "French Railways."

7. *Œuvres,* V, 76–80.

8. For the texts of the *Politique industrielle* and the *Système de la Méditerranée* I have used the 1832 edition, to be found in the *Collection of Saint-Simonian Tracts* from the library of Comte Alfred Boulay de la Meurthe, which is in the Widener Library at Harvard University. These are extracts from *Le Globe* of the spring of 1832 published in book form. Chevalier, *Politique,* 7–9.

9. Ibid., 12.

10. Ibid., 13.

11. Chevalier, *Système,* 103–8 (*Le Globe,* initial sketch, January 20, 1832).

12. Ibid., 121.

13. Ibid., 127–29.

14. Ibid., 131.

15. Ibid., 134.

16. Ibid., 134–35.

17. Ibid., 137.

18. Ibid., 138–45.

19. Ibid., 150.

20. *Œuvres,* V, 71, Lamoriciere to Enfantin, December 27, 1831, explores some of these themes: "*chez les peuples peu avancés, la guerre est un œuvre d'apostolat.*" Also *Œuvres,* XIV, 58ff.; XXIV, 161.

21. Arsenal, *Fonds d'Eichthal,* 13758/10/16, letters to Archduke Ludwig and to Baron James de Rothschild; 14890/4, "Méditation sur la juive."

22. *Œuvres,* IX, 183.

23. Ibid., XXI, 118–19.

24. A. J. P. Taylor, *German History,* 68. First in G. M. Trevelyan, *British History in the Nineteenth Century* (New York and London, 1927), 292.

25. Autin, *Les Frères Pereire,* 32. The early journalistic writings are contained in Emile Pereire and Isaac Pereire, *Œuvres,* I.

26. Autin, *Les Frères Pereire,* 27–46. Bertrand Gille, "Les Saint-Simoniens et le Crédit," *Economies et sociétés* IV (June 1970): 1176.

27. *Saint-Simonian Tracts,* "Leçons sur l'industrie et les finances." Barrie M. Ratcliffe, "Some Ideas on Public Finance in France in the 1830's: The writings of Emile and Isaac

Pereire, 1830–35," *Revue internationale d'histoire de la banque* X (1975), 170–91.

28. Ratcliffe, "Les Pereires." Ratcliffe has written extensively on d'Eichthal and the Pereires and is preparing a biography of the brothers.

CHAPTER XII. THE FIRST JUDGMENT

I have been criticized in another place for using Volume 47 of the *Œuvres* of Saint-Simon and Enfantin, "Le Procès," as the basis of my account of the August 1832 trial of the leading Saint-Simonians. This account is drawn from that published in 1832 accompanied by a number of *"pièces justificatives,"* which are clearly official documents, Arsenal, *Fonds Enfantin,* 7861. I see no reason to suppose that the trial account is less reliable. As my critics admit (and as Walch confirms in his bibliography) *sotto voce* and parenthetically, the official court record is not where it should be in the Series BB of the Ministry of Justice. I myself long ago examined the police records before they were moved from the quai des Orfèvres and found nothing illuminating there.

1. Arsenal, *Fonds Enfantin,* 7646/"Archives" IV, Gustave d'Eichthal to Laurent, October 16, 1832.
2. Ibid., Isaac Pereire to Enfantin, August 31, 1832.
3. *Œuvres,* XLVII, 34.
4. D'Allemagne, *Les Saint-Simoniens,* 257.
5. *Le Globe,* March 29, 1832.
6. *Œuvres,* XLVII, 49ff.
7. Ibid., 51.
8. Ibid., 77.
9. Ibid., 100–115.
10. Ibid., 106.
11. Ibid., 108.
12. Ibid., 173.
13. Ibid., 195.
14. Ibid., 228.
15. Ibid., 241.
16. Ibid., 244.
17. Ibid., 266–78.
18. Ibid., 312–19.
19. Ibid., 320.
20. Ibid., 339.
21. Ibid., 362–71.
22. Ibid., 424ff.
23. Ibid., 507.
24. *Le Globe,* May 28, 1831.
25. Ibid., November 18, 1831. Vidalenc, "Les Techniques."
26. *Œuvres,* XLVII, 1ff. Arsenal, *Fonds Enfantin,* 7861, first edition of "Le Procès," first "pièce justificative," November 28, 1831.
27. Arsenal, *Fonds Enfantin,* 7861, 540ff.
28. D'Allemagne, *Les Saint-Simoniens,* 302.
29. Arsenal, *Fonds Enfantin,* 7646/IV, Enfantin to d'Eichthal, November 9, 1832.
30. *Œuvres,* VIII, 126ff.
31. Arsenal, *Fonds Enfantin,* 7646/IV, Chevalier to Arlès-Dufour, December 1, 1832.
32. *Œuvres,* VIII, Chevalier to Brisbane, December 9, 1832.
33. Sorlin, *Waldeck-Rousseau,* 31.

34. *Œuvres,* XXVIII, 134, Enfantin to Aglaë Saint-Hilaire, January 16, 1833. Arsenal, *Fonds d'Eichthal,* 15031, Chevalier to Fournel, December 24, 1832.

35. Ibid., *Fonds Enfantin,* 7676/96, Enfantin to Saint-Hilaire, January 6, 1833.

36. Ibid., 7804/2, "Notes" of Lambert. *Œuvres,* XLVII, 557. Arsenal, *Fonds d'Eichthal,* 15031, Chevalier to Fournel, December 24, 1832.

37. *Œuvres,* IX, 93.

38. Charléty, *L'Histoire,* 212. There is an extract from Lamartine's *Voyage en Orient* in Arsenal, *Fonds d'Eichthal,* 14697/1, describing the event; see also *Fonds Enfantin,* 7861 Br. 11, "La Femme nouvelle."

39. *Œuvres,* XXVIII, 50–51, Enfantin to Saint-Hilaire, December 2, 1832.

40. Arsenal, *Fonds Enfantin,* 7676/95. Enfantin to Saint-Hilaire, January 6, 1833.

41. One drawing is reproduced in d'Allemagne, *Les Saint-Simoniens,* 334.

42. Arsenal, *Fonds d'Eichthal,* 15031(I), Michel Chevalier to Henri Fournel, December 24, 1832; Chevalier to Petit, January 1833; et al.

43. Ibid., *Fonds Enfantin,* 7676/96, Enfantin to Saint-Hilaire, January 1833.

44. *Œuvres,* XXVIII, 197, Enfantin to Saint-Hilaire, March 13, March 17, 1833.

45. Ibid., 206.

46. Ibid., 201.

47. Arsenal, *Fonds Enfantin,* 7655/41.

48. *Œuvres,* XXIX, 33, Enfantin to Holstein, April 19, 1833.

49. Arsenal, *Fonds d'Eichthal,* 15031/875–76.

50. Quoted in Samuel Nichard des Rieux, *Michel Chevalier,* Chevalier to Olivier June 11, 1833.

51. Arsenal, *Fonds Enfantin,* 7676/126. *Œuvres,* X, 152.

52. *Œuvres,* IX, 38–40.

53. Henri Fournel, "Communication des deux mers, Lettre à M. A———" (Marseilles, 1833), printed in *Œuvres,* IX, 88ff.

54. *Œuvres,* IX, 42, Cécile Fournel to Enfantin, July 23, 1833.

55. *Le Moniteur,* September 11, 1832.

56. Fournel, "Lettre à M. A———," 88.

57. *Œuvres,* IX, 99–105.

BIBLIOGRAPHY

I. SAINT-SIMONIAN SOURCES

THE MAIN POINT of bibliographies, aside from verification, is to help interested readers explore a subject. In the case of Saint-Simonianism this goal is best served by indicating the relationship between manuscript and printed sources rather than simply listing these separately and sequentially. The pillars on which Saint-Simonian investigations have long rested are *L'Histoire du Saint-Simonisme,* by Sébastien Charléty (Paris, 1896, 1931, 1950), and the two handsomely produced and illustrated volumes of Henry-René d'Allemagne, *Les Saint-Simoniens, 1827–1837* (Paris, 1930), and *Prosper Enfantin et les grandes entreprises du XIXième siècle* (Paris, 1935).

Charléty was the first scholar to make real use of the Saint-Simonian archives at the Bibliothèque de l'Arsenal in Paris, which were opened to perusal thirty years after the death of Prosper Enfantin. The book remains a trustworthy and informative guide. One's respect for the d'Allemagne volumes grows with time. They constitute a catalogue raisonné of the Arsenal manuscripts and are a helpful guide to them. To these standard works must be added the *Bibliographie du Saint-Simonisme* of Jean Walch (Paris, 1967), which is not complete but which does list over a thousand items of Saint-Simonian bibliography. There is also the not entirely trustworthy, but nonetheless essential, *Catalogue général des manuscrits des bibliothèques publiques en France,* XLIII, Supplément IV (Paris, 1904) 1–115.

Before going directly to the *Fonds Enfantin* of the Arsenal, however, the scholar would be best advised to deal with the *Œuvres de Saint-Simon et d'Enfantin, précédées de deux Notices Historiques, et publiée par les membres du Conseil institué par Enfantin pour l'exécution de ses dernières volontés* (Paris, 1865–78). These forty-seven volumes, with the Arsenal manuscripts, constitute the principal sources for the present work. They contain no indices, they are repetitive in their selection of materials, they are printed with no particularly logical sequence, and they are numbered in such a fashion as to guarantee that no library runner will produce the right volume at first request.

Approximately half of Volume I offers a biography of Saint-Simon himself; the second half and the subsequent twelve volumes are devoted to the "biography" of Enfantin. This biography includes letters, extracts of letters, extracts of writings, teachings, and preachings, which may appear in their entirety in the other division of the work. Volumes XIV, XVI, XVII, and XXIV–XXXV contain the "Works" of Enfantin, largely his correspondence, arranged more or less chronologically. Volumes XV, XVIII, XIX, XX–XXIII, and XXXVII–XL contain the "Works" of Saint-Simon. Volumes XLI and XLII contain the *Expositions* of Saint-Simonian doctrine (in reverse chronological order). Volumes XLIII, XLIV, and XLV contain the *Prédications,* or sermons, of the Saint-Simonian preachers. Volume XLVI has some late writings of Enfantin, and LXVII, "Religion Saint-Simonienne: Procès en la Cour d'assises de la Seine, Les 27 et 28 août, 1832."

The *Œuvres* are derived largely from the *Fonds Enfantin,* the collections of Enfantin and other Saint-Simonians, which enjoy their own *fantaisiste* organization. Again much material is duplicated; the *Archives* and some of the correspondence are copied in a clear, round hand; most of the material is not. The collection comprises, depending on how one counts, more than 40,000 pieces and is divided into four main sections and an appendix.

The first section includes the corrrespondence of *Le Globe* in nine volumes (7601–09); the Paris correspondence (7616–17) in two volumes; letters of Enfantin and copies of letters of Enfantin (7620–21); the book of *Enseignements,* the *grand-livre de la doctrine* (7622–23); further correspondence in seven cartons (7624–31); and the *Archives* of Saint-Simonianism in five volumes (7643–47), portions of which are missing.

The second section of the *Fonds Enfantin* is devoted to Enfantin family papers, Enfantin's biography (7648–55), and letters of Enfantin's son and of his son's mother, Adèle Morlane (7656–78).

The third section includes the very important correspondence of Thérèse Nugues (7765–66) and Aglaë Saint-Hilaire (7780), as well as the manuscript "Mémoires" of Jean Terson (7787–88).

The fourth section of the Enfantin manuscripts is largely devoted to the later business enterprises and projects of the Saint-Simonians, but cartons 7793–7826 are devoted to the religious life of the Saint-Simonians. A considerable number of Arlès-Dufour letters, which often illuminate the earlier religious experience, are to be found in the business correspondence.

The appendix includes a variety of rare Saint-Simonian tracts, publications, newspapers, photographs, and prints left to the Arsenal by d'Allemagne and by Mme Lemonnier.

To the *Fonds Enfantin* at the Arsenal must be added the *Fonds d'Eichthal,* which are listed in *Cataloge général des manuscrits des bibliothèques publiques en France,* 50 (Paris: Bibliothèque de l'Arsenal, 1954), pages 95–106, manuscript numbers 13728–59. There is an *inventaire* at the Arsenal for manuscript numbers from 14126. This collection duplicates much that is in the *Fonds Enfantin* and more that is in the d'Eichthal papers at the Bibliothèque Thiers, but it includes ample materials for the period involved in this book. Additional and interesting papers continue to filter in to the Arsenal collection. Walch's bibliography specifies some of these. One feature of the d'Eichthal collection is an album of photographs of Saint-Simonians. As indicated above, the Bibliothèque Thiers has another *Fonds d'Eichthal,* which again duplicates some materials found elsewhere; but in the series of carton IV to IVu7 there is much that has been useful here.

The Bibliothèque Nationale possesses the papers left by Alfred Pereire and catalogued as "Nouvelles acquisitions françaises," 24605–14. These include some manuscripts of Saint-Simon himself but, most notably, letters of Enfantin, Saint-Simonian correspondence (24608–11), and provincial Saint-Simonian correspondence (24612–13).

The Pereire family papers have been used by Jean Autin and by Barrie Ratcliffe, who have reported on them in works cited below. The Chevalier papers belonging to J. B. Duroselle have been used by Walch in his Chevalier biography.

Of other manuscript collections, Walch (page 26 of the *Bibliographie*) notes that the records of the Saint-Simonian *procès* are not to be found in the Archives Nationales, *Series BB, 20*. What is useful in the Archives is the *Series F14*, 2000ff., which includes dossiers on engineers of the Ponts-et-chaussées, many of them Saint-Simonian.

Finally, in the effort to link printed and manuscript resources one should mention the massive and apparently incomplete project of the *Oeuvres* of Emile and Isaac Pereire (Paris, 1920). The four volumes cited are available at the Bibliothèque Nationale. I have seen another, unbound, and there may be others available. The first volume includes the early writings of the Pereires on railways and finance.

Saint-Simon himself seems to have been somewhat neglected. Here, as with the Saint-Simonians, there is a basic authoritative book, that of Frank Manuel, *The New World of Henri Saint-Simon* (Cambridge, Mass., 1956). Since the publication of the *Oeuvres* a number of Saint-Simon *inédits* have come to light, and those are described and discussed by Manuel. Walch lists the various available, or unavailable, editions of Saint-Simon's works. Availability and uniformity have led me to use the *Oeuvres* described above for accounts of Saint-Simon's writings. I have generally used the *Oeuvres* for Saint-Simonian writings where possible, with the exception of Michel Chevalier's *Politique industrielle,* and *Système de la Méditerranée.* There are Paris editions of 1832 and 1833, which turn up in university libraries, but for this book I have used the version found in the *Collection of Saint-Simonian Tracts* from the library of comte Boulay de la Meurthe, which is in Widener Library at Harvard University.

Works cited in *The Proffered Crown* are listed hereafter. It should be noted that in recent years there has been something of a Saint-Simonian renaissance, to which the work of Claire Goldberg Moses, T. Joan Moon, Laura Strumingher, Barrie Ratcliffe, James Briscoe, Ralph Locke, and Maurice Agulhon has contributed. The four volumes of *Economies et sociétés* (April, June, and October 1970 and July 1971) under the direction of François Perroux, containing nearly forty articles on Saint-Simonian topics, have also enriched our understanding of Saint-Simonianism.

II. WORKS CITED

NEWSPAPERS (All in the Bibliothèque Nationale)

Le Producteur. 5 vols. Paris, 1825–26.
L'Organisateur. Paris, 1829–31.
Le Globe IX–XII. Paris, November 11, 1830 to April 20, 1832.

BOOKS AND ARTICLES

Agulhon, Maurice. *Une ville ouvrière au temps du socialisme utopique: Toulon de 1815 à 1851.* Paris, 1970.
Alem, Jean Pierre. *Enfantin, le prophète aux sept visages.* (Pauvert, *éditeur*), 1963.
Allemagne, Henry-René d'. *Les Saint-Simoniens, 1827–1837.* Paris, 1930.

——. *Prosper Enfantin et les grandes entreprises du XIXième siècle.* Paris, 1935.

Arendt, Hannah. *Origins of Totalitarianism.* New York, 1951.

Autin, Jean. *Les Fréres Pereire: Le Bonheur d'entreprendre.* Paris, 1984.

Barrault, Emile. *L'Occident et l'Orient.* Paris, 1835.

Bertier de Sauvigny, G. de. *La Restauration.* Paris, 1963.

Beyle, H. (Stendhal). *D'un nouveau complot centre les industriels.* Paris, 1825.

Blanc, Louis. *Histoire de dix ans.* 4 vols. Paris, 1841; 5 vols. Brussels, 1845.

Blount, Edward. *Memoirs.* London, 1902.

Booth, A. J. *Saint-Simon and Saint-Simonism.* London, 1871.

Briscoe, James B. "Enfantinism, Feminism and the Crisis of Saint-Simonism," Paper delivered to Society for French Historical Studies, University of Virginia, April 6, 1984.

——. "The Unfinished Revolution: The Saint-Simonians and the Social Question. Origins of Socialist Debate in France." *Proceedings of the Fourteenth Consortium on Revolutionary Europe,* 1986.

——. "From Industrialism to Socialism: The Saint-Simonian Movement and the Origins of Socialist Discourse in France." Unpublished manuscript.

Butler, E. M. *The Saint-Simonian Religion in Germany.* Cambridge, 1926.

C. L. *Arlès-Dufour.* N.p., n.d.

Cameron, Rondo. *France and the Economic Development of Europe.* Princeton, N.J., 1961.

Carlisle, Robert B. *The Saint-Simonians and the Foundation of the Paris-Lyon Railroad.* Ann Arbor: University Microfilms, 1957.

——. "Les Chemins de fer, les Rothschilds, et les Saint-Simoniens," *Economies et sociétés* V, no. 7 (1971): 647–76.

——. "The Birth of Technocracy," *Journal of the History of Ideas* XXV (July–September 1974): 445–64.

——. "The Saint-Simonian Threat." Paper delivered at American Historical Association, Session 19, December 28, 1985.

Carnot, Hippolyte-Lazare. *Sur le Saint-Simonisme, lecture faite a l'académie des sciences morales et politiques.* Paris, 1887.

Charléty, Sébastien. *L'Histoire du Saint-Simonisme.* Paris, 1896.

Charton, Edouard. *Memoires d'un prédicateur Saint-Simonien.* Paris, 1832.

Chevalier, L. *La formation de la population parisienne au XIXième siècle.* Paris, 1950.

Chevalier, Louis. *Leçon inaugurale faite le lundi 28 Avril, 1952. Chaire d'histoire et structures sociales de Paris et de la région parisienne.* Collège de France.

Christ, Yvan. *Les Metamorphoses de Paris.* Paris, 1967.

Clark, M. A. *Heine et la monarchie de juillet.* Paris, 1927.

Dreyfous, Maurice. *Les Trois Carnot.* Paris, 1888.

Dunham, "How the First French Railways Were Planned," *Journal of Economic History* I (1941): 12–25.

Durkheim, Emile. *Le socialisme, sa definition, ses débuts, la doctrine saint-simonienne.* Paris, 1928.

Duveyrier, Charles. *Lettres politiques.* Paris, 1843.

Emérit, Marcel. *Les Saint-Simoniens en Algérie.* Paris, 1941.

Ernouf, Baron. *Paulin Talabot, sa vie et son œuvre.* Paris, 1886.

Galignani. *New Paris Guide*. Paris, 1826 et seq.

Girard, Louis. *La Politique des travaux publiques du Second Empire*. Paris, 1952.

Gouhier, Henri. *La Jeunesse d'Auguste Comte et la formation du positivisme*. 3 vols. Paris, 1941.

Guide des étrangers à Paris, precédés d'un avertissement aux étrangers. Paris, n.d. (before 1830).

Hagan, Dorothy Veinas. *Felicien David, 1810–76, a Composer and a Cause*. Syracuse, N.Y., 1986.

Halévy, Elie. "La doctrine economique de Saint-Simon," *Revue du mois* IV (December 1907): 641–76.

———. "La doctrine economique des Saint-Simoniens." *Revue du mois* VI (July 1908), 39–76.

Halévy, Léon. "Souvenirs de Saint-Simon," *Revue d'histoire economique* XII (1925): 1966–76.

Hayek, Friedrich von. *The Counter Revolution of Science*. New York, 1952.

Histoire du Saint-Simonisme et de la famille Rothschild ou biographie de Saint-Simon et Bazard. N.p., n.d. Goldsmith's Collection, University of London.

Hubbard, N. G. A. *Saint-Simon, sa vie et son œuvre*. Paris, 1857.

Hunt, H. J. *Le Socialisme et le romantisme en France: Etude de la presse socialiste, 1830 à 1848*. Oxford, 1935.

Iggers, Georg. *The Cult of Authority: The Political Philosophy of the Saint-Simonians, a Chapter in the Intellectual History of Totalitarianism*. The Hague, 1958.

Ivray, Jehan d'. *L'Aventure saint-simonienne et les femmes*. Paris, 1928.

Jardin, A., and Tudesq, A. J. *La France des notables, 1815–1848*. 2 vols. Paris, 1973.

Jouffroy, L.-M. *Une etàpe de la construction des grandes lignes de chemin-de-fer en France*. 3 vols. Paris, 1932.

Kindleberger, Charles P. *Economic growth in France and Britain, 1851–1950*. Cambridge, Mass., 1964.

Landes, David S. "French Business and the Businessman: A Social and Cultural Analysis." In *Modern France*, edited by Edward Meade Earle, 334–53. Princeton, N.J., 1951.

Leroy, M. *Le Socialisme des producteurs*. Paris, 1924.

Locke, Ralph. *Music, Musicians and the Saint-Simonians*. Chicago, 1986.

Louvancour, Henri. *De Henri Saint-Simon à Charles Fourier*. Chartres, 1913.

Manuel, Frank. *The New World of Henri Saint-Simon*. Cambridge, Mass., 1956.

———. *The Prophets of Paris*. Cambridge, Mass., 1962.

Marchant de Beaumont, F. M. *Le Nouveau Conducteur de l'étranger à Paris*. Paris, 1826 et. seq.

Marx, Karl, and Engels, Frederick. *Collected Works*. New York, 1975–.

McLellan, David. *Marx before Marxism*. New York, 1970.

Merriman, John M. *1830 in France*. New York, 1975.

Mill, John Stuart. *Correspondence inédite avec Gustave d'Eichthal, 1828–1842; 1864–1871*. Paris, 1898.

Moon, S. Joan. "The Saint-Simonian Association of Workingclass Women, 1830–1850." In *Proceedings of the 5th Annual Meeting of the Western Society for*

French History, edited by Joyce Duncan Falk, 274–79. Santa Barbara, Calif., 1978.

Morazé, Charles. *La France bourgeoise du XIXième siècla.* Paris, 1946.

Moses, Claire Goldberg. *French Feminism in the 19th Century.* Albany, N.Y., 1984.

Musset, Alfred de. *La Confession d'un enfant du siècle.* Paris, 1857.

Nicard de Rieux, Samuel. *Michel Chevalier, Saint-Simonien.* Limoges, 1912.

Parent-Duchatelet, A. J. B. *De la prostitution dans la ville de Paris.* 2 vols. Paris, 1836.

Pereire, Alfred. *Autour de Saint-Simon.* Paris, 1912.

Pereire, Emile, and Pereire, Isaac. *Œuvres,* ed. Laurent de Villedeuil and G. Pereire, Series G, 4 vols. Paris, 1912–20.

Pinkney, David H. *Paris in the Nineteenth Century: A Study in Urban Growth.* Ph.D. diss., Harvard University, 1941.

——. *The French Revolution of 1830.* Princeton, N.J., 1972.

Popper, Karl. *The Open Society and Its Enemies.* 5th ed. Princeton, N.J., 1966.

Pouthas, Charles. *La Population française pendant la premiére moitié du XIXe siècle.* Institut national d'études demographiques, travaux et documents, Cahier 25. Paris, 1956.

Ratcliffe, Barrie M. "Les Pereires et le Saint-Simonisme," *Economies et sociétés* V (July 1971): 1215–56.

——. "Saint-Simonism and Messianism: The Case of Gustave d'Eichthal," *French Historical Studies* IX (Spring 1976): 484–502.

——. "The Economic Influence of the Saint-Simonians: Myth or Reality?" In *Proceedings of the Fifth Annual Meeting of the Western Society for French History,* edited by Joyce Duncan Falk, 252–62. Santa Barbara, Calif., 1978.

Rodrigues, Eugène. *Lettre sur la religion et la politique.* Paris, 1831.

Rude, P. "Les Saint-Simoniens à Lyon." *Actes du 89e Congrés des sociétés sávantes* II, no. 1 (1964): 345.

Saint-Simon, Henri de, and Enfantin, Prosper-Barthélémy. *Œuvres.* 47 vols. Paris, 1865–78.

Sewell, William H., Jr. *Work and Revolution in France: The Language of Labor from the Old Regime to 1848.* Cambridge, 1980.

Simon, Jules, *Notices et portraits.* Paris, 1892.

Simon, Walter. "History for Utopia, Saint-Simon and the Idea of Progress," *Journal of the History of Ideas* XVIII (June 1956): 311–31.

Struminger, Laura S. "The Artisan Family: Tradition and Transition in 19th-Century Lyon." *Journal of Family History* II (1977): 211–22.

——. "A bas les prêtres, à bas les couvents," *Journal of Social History* V (March 1978): 546–63.

——. *Women and the Making of the Working Class: Lyons, 1830–70.* Saint Albans, Vt., 1979.

Szajkowski, Zoza. *The Jewish Saint-Simonians and Socialist Anti-Semites in France.* New York, 1947.

Taylor, A. J. P. *The Course of German History.* New York, 1946.

Terson, Jean. "*Mémoires.*" Unpublished manuscript. Arsenal, *Fonds Enfantin,* 7787–88.

Thibert, M. *Le Feminisme dans le socialisme français.* Paris, 1926.

Ventouillac, F. *Paris et ses environs.* 2 vols. Paris, 1829.

Vidalenc, Jean. "Les Techniques de la propagande saint-simonienne à la fin de 1831." *Archives de la sociologie des religions* X (July–December 1960): 3–21.

Voilquin, Suzanne. *Journal d'une Sainte-Simonienne en Egypte.* N.p., 1866.

Walch, Jean. *Bibliographie du Saint-Simonisme.* Paris, 1967.

———. *Michel Chevalier, economiste saint-simonien, 1806–1879.* Paris, 1975.

Wallon, Maurice. *Les Saint-Simoniens et les chemins-de-fer.* Paris, 1908.

Weill, Georges. *L'Ecole saint-simonienne.* Paris, 1896.

Weiss, John Hubbel. *The Making of Technological Man.* Cambridge, Mass., 1982.

Zeldin, Theodore. *France, 1848–1945.* 2 vols. Oxford, 1973–77.

Robert B. Carlisle is John Stebbins Lee Professor
of History at St. Lawrence University.

The Proffered Crown

Designed by Susan Bishop
Composed by A. W. Bennett, Inc. in Sabon text and display
Printed by BookCrafters on S. D. Warren's 50-lb. Eggshell Cream Offset paper
and bound in GSB #22 (sherbet) and stamped in gold